MIRACLE DISCOURSE IN THE NEW TESTAMENT

Society of Biblical Literature

MIRACLE DISCOURSE IN THE NEW TESTAMENT

MIRACLE DISCOURSE IN
THE NEW TESTAMENT

Edited by
Duane F. Watson

Society of Biblical Literature
Atlanta

MIRACLE DISCOURSE IN THE NEW TESTAMENT

Copyright © 2012 by the Society of Biblical Literature

All rights reserved. No part of this work may be reproduced or transmitted in any form or by any means, electronic or mechanical, including photocopying and recording, or by means of any information storage or retrieval system, except as may be expressly permitted by the 1976 Copyright Act or in writing from the publisher. Requests for permission should be addressed in writing to the Rights and Permissions Office, Society of Biblical Literature, 825 Houston Mill Road, Atlanta, GA 30329 USA.

Library of Congress Cataloging-in-Publication Data

Miracle discourse in the New Testament / edited by Duane F. Watson
    p. cm.
    Includes bibliographical references and index.
    ISBN 978-1-58983-118-6 (paper binding : alk. paper) — ISBN 978-1-58983-698-3 (electronic format)
    1. Miracles—Biblical teaching. 2. Bible. N.T.—Criticism, interpretation, etc. I. Watson, Duane Frederick.
    BS2545.M5M57 2012b
    225.6—dc23
                                                                                                2012037193

Printed on acid-free, recycled paper conforming to
ANSI/NISO Z39.48-1992 (R1997) and ISO 9706:1994
standards for paper permanence.

Contents

Abbreviations vii

Introduction 1
    Duane F. Watson

Sociorhetorical Interpretation of Miracle Discourse in the
    Synoptic Gospels 17
    Vernon K. Robbins

The Role of Argumentation in the Miracle Stories of Luke-Acts:
    Toward a Fuller Identification of Miracle Discourse for Use in
    Sociorhetorical Interpretation 85
    L. Gregory Bloomquist

Res Gestae Divi Christi: Miracles, Early Christian Heroes, and
    the Discourse of Power in Acts 125
    Todd Penner

Miracle Discourse and the Gospel of John 175
    Gail R. O'Day

Miracle Discourse in the Pauline Epistles: The Role of Resurrection
    and Rhetoric 189
    Duane F. Watson

Toward a Sociorhetorical Taxonomy of Divine Intervention:
    Miracle Discourse in the Revelation to John 197
    David A. deSilva

Miracle Discourse in the New Testament: A Response 211
    Wendy J. Cotter

Miraculous Methodologies: Critical Reflections on "Ancient
    Miracle Discourse" Discourse 225
    Davina C. Lopez

Bibliography 249
Contributors 267
Index of Primary Sources 269
Index of Modern Authors 277

Abbreviations

Primary Sources

Adv. Math.	Sextus Empiricus, *Adversus Mathematicos*
Alex.	Lucian, *Alexander (Pseudomantis)*
Amph.	Plautus, *Amphitruo*
Ann.	Tacitus, *Annales*
Ant.	Josephus, *Jewish Antiquities*
Hel.	Euripides, *Helena*
Hist.	Tacitus, *Historiae*
Inst.	Quintilian, *Institutio Oratoria*
Nat. d.	Cicero, *De natura deorum*
Od.	Homer, *Odessea*
Part. or.	Cicero, *Partitiones oratoriae*
Poet.	Aristotle, *Poetica*
Resp.	Plato, *Respublica*
Rhet.	Aristotle, *Rhetorica*
[*Rhet. Alex.*]	Aristotle, *Rhetorica ad Alexandrum*
Thes.	Plutarch, *Theseus*
Top.	Aristotle, *Topica*
Vesp.	Suetonius, *Vespasianus*

Secondary Sources

AB	Anchor Bible
AGJU	Arbeiten zur Geschichte des antiken Judentums und des Urchristentums
ANRW	*Aufstieg und Niedergang der römischen Welt: Geschichte und Kultur Roms im Spiegel der neueren Forschung.* Part 2, *Principat.* Edited by Hildegard Temporini and Wolfgang Haase. Berlin: de Gruyter, 1972–.

BETL	Bibliotheca ephemeridum theologicarum lovaniensium
BibInt	*Biblical Interpretation*
BIS	Biblical Interpretation Series
BR	*Biblical Research*
BTB	*Biblical Theology Bulletin*
BZNW	Beihefte zur Zeitschrift für die neutestamentliche Wissenschaft
CurBS	*Currents in Research: Biblical Studies*
EPRO	Etudes préliminaires aux religions orientales dans l'empire romain
ESEC	Emory Studies in Early Christianity
EstBib	*Estudios biblicos*
ETL	*Ephemerides theologicae lovanienses*
FCNTECW	Feminist Companion to the New Testament and other Early Christian Writings
FRLANT	Forschungen zur Religion und Literatur des Alten und Neuen Testaments
GRBS	*Greek, Roman, and Byzantine Studies*
GRRS	Graeco-Roman Religion Series
HDR	Harvard Dissertations in Religion
HTR	*Harvard Theological Review*
JBL	*Journal of Biblical Literature*
JCPS	Jewish and Christian Perspectives Series
JHS	*Journal of Hellenic Studies*
JSJSup	Supplements to the Journal of the Journal for the Study of Judaism in the Persian, Hellenistic, and Roman Periods
JSNT	*Journal for the Study of the New Testament*
JSNTSup	Journal for the Study of the New Testament Supplement Series
JSOT	*Journal for the Study of the Old Testament*
JSOTSup	Journal for the Study of the Old Testament Supplement Series
JTS	*Journal of Theological Studies*
LNTS	Library of New Testament Studies
MAA	*Marcus Aurelius Antonnius* in the *Historia Augusta*
NovTSup	Supplements to Novum Testamentum
NTOA	Novum Testamentum et Orbis Antiquus
NTS	*New Testament Studies*

PGM	*Papyri graecae magicae: Die griechischen Zauberpapyri.* Edited by K. Preisendanz. Berlin: Teubner, 1928.
PRStSSS	Perspectives in Religious Studies, Special Studies Series
RGRW	Religions in the Graeco-Roman World
SA	*Sociological Analysis*
SBLDS	Society of Biblical Literature Dissertation Series
SBLMS	Society of Biblical Literature Monograph Series
SBLSBS	Society of Biblical Literature Sources for Biblical Study
SBLSP	Society of Biblical Literature Seminar Papers
SBLSymS	Society of Biblical Literature Symposium Series
SBLWGRW	Society of Biblical Literature Writings from the Greco-Roman World
SBT	Studies in Biblical Theology
SEÅ	*Svensk exegetisk årsbok*
SNTS	Society of New Testament Studies
SNTSMS	Society of New Testament Studies Monograph Series
SP	Sacra pagina
SR	*Studies in Religion*
TUGAL	Texte und Untersuchungen zur Geschichte der altchristlichen Literatur
UTB	Uni-Taschenbücher
VC	*Vigiliae christianae*
VCSup	Supplements to Vigiliae christianae
WMANT	Wissenschaftliche Monographien zum Alten und Neuen Testament
WUNT	Wissenschaftliche Untersuchungen zum Neuen Testament
ZNW	Zeitschrift für die neutestamentliche Wissenschaft und die Kinde der älteren Kirche

Introduction

Duane F. Watson

The following essays were presented at the Society of Biblical Literature Annual Meeting in 2001 in Denver, Colorado. They were presented in the Rhetoric and the New Testament section in a session titled "The Rhetorical Function of Miracles in the New Testament." These essays all interact with Wendy J. Cotter's volume *The Miracles of Greco-Roman Antiquity*,[1] to which Professor Cotter formally responded. These essays and the response have all been recently updated, and an essay on the Pauline Epistles along with an additional, invited response have also been included. Several essays also interact with Cotter's newest book, *The Christ of the Miracle Stories: Portrait through Encounter*.[2]

Clearly miracle discourse has been at the center of the debate between faith and reason since the Enlightenment. Higher-critical scholars have been uneasy in analyzing miracle accounts as they walk the tightrope between faith and scholarship. Form, source, tradition, and redaction criticisms allow analysis of miracle discourse to take place without the necessity of making a definitive claim about the historicity of miracles and make the tightrope walk a lot easier. At the beginning of the last century, form-critical analysis of miracle discourse focused in the work of Martin Dibelius and Rudolf Bultmann. Dibelius classified miracle accounts as "tales,"[3] while Bultmann classified these accounts as narratives intended to dem-

---

1. Wendy J. Cotter, *The Miracles of Greco-Roman Antiquity* (London: Routledge, 1999).

2. Wendy J. Cotter, *The Christ of the Miracle Stories: Portrait through Encounter* (Grand Rapids: Baker Academic, 2010).

3. Martin Dibelius, *From Tradition to Gospel* (trans. Bertram Lee Woolf; New York: Scribner's), 70, but see 70–103.

onstrate Jesus' divine power and authority.[4] Gerd Theissen's work greatly elaborated this form-critical work, further refining and reclassifying the miracle accounts. He examined them "synchronically as structured forms, diachronically as reproduced narratives, and from a functional point of view as symbolic actions."[5] Source criticism and tradition criticism enable the interpreter to trace the origins of miracle accounts in early Christian streams of tradition; Jewish traditions like the miracles of Moses, Elijah, and Elisha; and Greco-Roman traditions like those surrounding Asklepois and Isis. Redaction criticism emphasizes how the Gospel writers modified miracle accounts to further their theological agendas, and has long played a major role in the exegesis of the four Gospels. These criticisms compare the miracle accounts to similar forms, sources, traditions, and redaction in miracle accounts in the Mediterranean world.

Through the study of ancient miracle traditions, Howard Clark Kee gave us a better reading of miracle discourse in its original social and cultural contexts—that is, how the audience and author understood these accounts.[6] Recently Wendy Cotter's two volumes have accelerated that effort. She defines miracle accounts as "those narratives in which a wonderful rescue or salvation of someone takes place by the overturning of the 'canons of the ordinary' through the intervention of a deity or hero."[7] They are narratives describing the intervention of the divine in the affairs of humans to alleviate distress, once conditions are met by humans (such as prayer or faith), with the divine power coming through a human intermediary. Cotter's work helps us more fully understand what would be considered miraculous in the first century and to better understand its functions. Her work provides the context for the miracle discourse of the Gospels so that its significance, meaning, and message can be more fully comprehended.

---

4. Rudolf Bultmann, *History of the Synoptic Tradition* (trans. John Marsh; rev. ed.; New York: Harper & Row, 1963), 209–44.

5. Gerd Theissen, *The Miracle Stories of the Early Christian Tradition* (ed. John Riches; trans. Francis McDonagh; Philadelphia: Fortress, 1983), 2.

6. Howard Clark Kee, *Miracle in the Early Christian World: A Study in Sociohistorical Method* (New Haven: Yale University Press, 1983); Kee, *Medicine, Miracle and Magic in New Testament Times* (Cambridge: Cambridge University Press, 1986).

7. Cotter, *Miracles of Greco-Roman Antiquity*, 2, in part citing a phrase by Harold Remus, *Pagan-Christian Conflict over Miracle in the Second Century* (Patristic Monograph Series 10; Cambridge: The Philadelphia Patristic Foundation, 1983), 7–26.

The rhetorical approach of this volume investigates form, source, tradition, redaction, history, and theology, not as individual elements, but as interactive elements in miracle discourse. Rhetorical criticism recognizes that topics and arguments are embedded in miracle discourse in the New Testament to create a new Christian paideia, thus creating new functions for the discourse. From this perspective analysis moves beyond traditional criticisms that treat miracle discourse as primarily revealing manifestations of divine power to demonstrate that miracle discourse has multiple functions within the narrative in which it is embedded and in the social and cultural contexts in which that narrative itself is embedded.

The rhetoric of the miracle discourse is discussed in several essays in this volume from the perspective of sociorhetorical analysis as created by Vernon Robbins. In this analytic, Christian discourse in general is understood to be a blend of modes of discourse called "rhetorolects."[8] Robbins defines *rhetorolects* as forms of "language variety or discourse identifiable on the basis of distinctive configuration of themes, topics, reasonings, and argumentations."[9] There are six rhetorolects: wisdom, miracle, apocalyptic, prophetic, priestly, and precreation. The miracle rhetorolect in the New Testament "presupposes that God responds to humans in contexts of danger or disease and that Jesus is the mediator of these benefits to humans," and its common topoi include fear, cowardice, and the response of belief.[10] Miracle discourse and its argumentation is typically composed of a blend of the miracle rhetorolect and one or more of the other rhetorolects. Miracle discourse tells of a

> rehearsal of unusual and dramatic displays of God's power to restore life and health, furnish food, or remove personal crisis. In this discourse, Jesus and holy spirit function as agents of God's power in various contexts in God's created world. The goal of the discourse is to increase the intensity of adherence to belief in God's power as so great that it can,

---

8. For further discussion of rhetorolects, see Robbins's essay, "Argumentative Texture in Socio-Rhetorical Interpretation," in *Rhetorical Argumentation in Biblical Texts* (ed. Anders Eriksson, Thomas H. Olbricht, and Walter Überlacker; ESEC 8; Harrisburg, Pa.: Trinity Press International, 2002), 27–65; Robbins, "The Dialectical Nature of Early Christians Discourse," *Scriptura* 59 (1996): 353–62.

9. Robbins, "Dialectical Nature," 356.

10. Ibid., 358.

under the right conditions, function unusually and dramatically in the human realm.[11]

In his essay "Sociorhetorical Interpretation of Miracle Discourse in the Synoptic Gospels," Vernon Robbins examines miracle discourse using sociorhetorical analysis. Miracle discourse is one of the six blended discourses or rhetorolects in first-century discourse. These rhetorolects emerged from and functioned in social and cultural spaces, and can be blended to create rhetorical amplification and argumentation. Miracle discourse in the Synoptic Gospels focuses almost exclusively on God's enactment of power in relation to individuals. A considerable amount of miracle rhetorolect in the New Testament is inductive narrative that describes how Jesus and his followers encounter people and heal them, but it also develops into inferential argumentative discourse, often blending with the other rhetorolects to create a dynamic and multidimensional way of thinking.

A large portion of miracle discourse in the Synoptic Gospels is inductive narrative, in which the narrative moves from cases to results without any rationales introducing deductive reasoning and argumentation: Jesus meets a person in need (case) and heals that person (result). With its display of actions, attitudes, and values, miracle rhetorolect is epideictic—it affirms or reaffirms a point of view. Inductive-narrative miracle discourse in the Synoptic Gospels usually amplifies topoi and creates mental pictures without elaborating those topoi into logical argumentation. Ancient rhetorical discourse elaborates topoi in two ways, as amplificatory-descriptive and argumentative-enthymematic. In other words, discourse creates pictures (rhetography) and reasoning (rhetology). Miracle discourse elaborates the topoi of healing an afflicted body pictorially in a way that remains inductive. The case and result of the narrative are not accompanied by a rule, inference, or premise that explains Jesus' miracle. There is no inference of the source of Jesus' power, his identity, or even the need to have faith—just the inference that Jesus is worthy of praise for his ability to heal others. However, sometimes introducing well-known topoi in the narration of a miracle can evoke a particular cultural and conceptual network that helps people make inferences about a miracle. For example, in Matt 15:29–31 the result of Jesus' healing is that the crowd glorifies the God of

---

11. Vernon K. Robbins, "The Invention of Early Christian Paideia: Sociorhetorical Interpretation of the New Testament," paper presented at the Annual Meeting of the Society of Biblical Literature, Nashville, Tennessee, November 17, 2000.

Israel, which allows the reader to infer that the source of Jesus' healing power is God and to speculate about Jesus' identity.

When prophetic rhetorolect blends with miracle rhetorolect, it focuses the discourse on the identity of Jesus as a prophet who transmits God's will and power in the human realm. This blending can be accomplished by Jesus' use of prophetic phrasing, or by the narrator's recontextualizing and reciting prophetic texts. Prophetic and priestly rhetorolects blend in miracle discourse when Jesus' compassion motivates him to pray and utter prophetic reasoning about why he miraculously intercedes for those in need. Priestly rhetorolect is particularly obvious in the healing of a leper, which involves verification by the priests in the temple (Mark 1:44 || Matt 8:4 || Luke 5:14).

Apocalyptic rhetorolect blends with miracle rhetorolect when demons and evil spirits are presented in challenge-riposte with Jesus, who eventually casts them out and heals the afflicted person. This narration evokes a conceptual domain of the broader battle of the God of Israel with demonic powers in which disease is attributed to unclean spirits. This is especially true when the apocalyptic topos of the demons who know the identity of Jesus is blended with the miracle topos of the healing of the body. Inductive reasoning leaves the reader seeking Jesus' identity and the source of his power, a reasoning sometimes negotiated by attributed speech in the narration (e.g., of the demons) or a revelation about Jesus from the narrator. Prophetic rhetorolect blends with apocalyptic and miracle rhetorolects when Jesus is identified, not by the demons in the narrative, but by a quotation of an Old Testament prophet that replaces or overrides demonic identification, or by the narrator, who identifies Jesus using the prophetic expectation of a coming Messiah.

Wisdom rhetorolect blends with miracle, apocalyptic, prophetic, and priestly rhetorolects in the Synoptic Gospels to widen the reasoning about Jesus as a miracle worker. Argumentation can be inductive by narrating of a series of pictures (rhetography) as Jesus is portrayed as teacher, healer, exorcist, prophet, and forgiver of sins without discursive argumentation explaining just who he is (rhetology). However, introducing speech, question and answer, and debate with Jesus into a blend with miracle rhetorolect introduces enthymematic form and inner reasoning. The narrational base of the miracle rhetorolect moves into reasoning characteristic of wisdom rhetorolect—that is, into early Christian wisdom that reasons about the nature of Jesus as a miracle worker. For example, in miracle narratives that feature controversy, like healing on the sabbath, this wisdom rhetorolect negotiates important life issues like "what is lawful." In these narratives Jesus does not respond with Torah, but wise sayings that dishonor his opponents. Often Jesus' prophetic miracle wisdom is pitted against the priestly wisdom of the authorities. Wisdom rhetorolect blends with the prophetic rhetorolect to show that Jesus' death by his opponents for breaking the law is a judgment against them, not him.

For another example, in controversies about Jesus' healing ability, those healed blend prophetic rhetorolect with wisdom and miracle rhetorolects to identify the source of Jesus' healing power in the God of Israel, while the opposition blends apocalyptic rhetorolect with wisdom and miracle rhetorolects to root the source of Jesus' healing power in the demonic. Wisdom rhetorolect and its use of deductive argumentation is employed to address this controversy because miracle rhetorolect with its inductive narrational argumentation is unable by itself to negotiate the nature of the personages of the realms of good and evil (Matt 12:22–37).

Twelve miracle stories in the Synoptic Gospels include the topos of faith and lack of faith, great faith and little faith. On the one hand, miracles elicit faith from the heart, mind, and body of an onlooker, the places where wisdom typically resides. On the other hand, faith can also motivate Jesus to respond with a miracle. The faith topos blends the wisdom and miracle rhetorolects into Christian wisdom rhetorolect. This blend also nurtures a special kind of priestly rhetorolect, for now those with faith can praise and worship God in both secular and sacred spaces.

In "The Role of Argumentation in the Miracle Stories of Luke-Acts: Toward a Fuller Identification of Miracle Discourse for Use in Sociorhetorical Interpretation," L. Gregory Bloomquist identifies two types of miracle discourse and how they function in the argumentation of Luke-Acts. In identifying miracle discourse, he moves beyond form-critical matters to use sociorhetorical analysis, particularly its concern to place miracle discourse in the broad context of Greco-Roman miracle discourse. As noted above, Robbins identifies six rhetorolects or discourses of the first-century Mediterranean world that are identifiable by their distinctive configuration of topics and argumentation. Miracle rhetorolect is characterized by topoi of fear, cowardice, and faith used in argumentation. In early Christianity, miracle discourse is based on the ideology taken from Judaism that all things are possible for God the creator, sustainer, and redeemer as humans fulfill the prerequisites of faith, prayer, and fasting. In early Christian miracle discourse Jesus is the one through whom God addresses human petitioners and their fears and needs, using Jesus' mouth and hands.

What Robbins has identified as miracle discourse or rhetorolect, Bloomquist considers to be too general. He proposes that two types of miracle discourse need to be differentiated on the basis of the use of different topoi and argumentation. These are "thaumaturgical" and magic or "gnostic-manipulationist" miracle discourse. The former involves petition to the gods to act to meet human need, while the latter involves formulas, pronouncements, and rituals performed in a precise way to coerce the gods to act. These two types of miracle discourse are also distinguished by the topics and argumentation they use and the goals of that argumentation. Thaumaturgical miracle discourse uses inductive or qualitative (paradigmatic) argumentation or rhetography that relies on images, descriptions, analogies, examples, and citations of ancient testimony to persuade. The audience is left with confusion and wonder, and the rationale for the miracle is not always obvious. Gnostic-manipulationist miracle discourse uses deductive or logical (enthymematic) argumentation or rhetology, which relies on tight reasoning from assertions, rationales, clarifications, and counterarguments to be convincing. The audience is clear about why the miracle happened. These two types of miracle discourse can be woven together (e.g., the healing of the woman with the flow of blood in Mark 5) according to the ideology of the author and the local culture in which the discourse is embedded (e.g., Jewish thaumaturgical versus Isis gnostic-manipulationist miracle discourse).

Bloomquist explores the interweaving of thaumaturgical and gnostic-manipulationist miracle discourse in Luke-Acts. In Luke 5:1–11, the miracle of the great catch of fish, gnostic-manipulationist miracle discourse is subordinate to thaumaturgical miracle discourse. There is no rationale given for the miracle and no conclusion offered for why the miracle occurred. The rhetography is primary, as Jesus overturns Peter's rationale for why sinners and holy men should not associate with one another. Acts 3:1–10, Peter's healing of the lame man at the temple gate, is solely thaumaturgical miracle discourse. The miracle is unexpected, and no rationale is given for the healing. Instead Peter preaches on the meaning of the miracle in the broader plan of redemption (3:11–26). The account of the Gerasene demoniac in Luke 8:22–39 contains rhetology in the form of three examples of logical argumentation with rationales typical of gnostic-manipulationist, yet remains predominantly thaumaturgical.

These three miracle narratives leave unanswered questions. Why do many of those involved react with fear? What does Jesus mean for them and they for him? The relationships between action and result could be answered with the logical argumentation of gnostic-manipulationist miracle discourse. Rather, these questions are being answered by the qualitative argumentation characteristic of thaumaturgical miracle discourse that relies heavily on cultural knowledge and seeks to move people to new understandings without reliance on rationales and logical argumentation. Thaumaturgical miracle narratives "do not so much contain argumentation as they *are* argumentation"[12] and thus bear a strong resemblance to parables. In Luke-Acts Jesus' and the apostle's normative response is thaumaturgical, not formulaic; it moves the audience from a more formulaic and ritualistic approach to the divine, which gnostic-manipulationist miracle discourse creates, to the less-nuanced and divine silence, which thaumaturgical miracle discourse creates. In other words, miracle discourse in Luke-Acts works to facilitate an ideological shift that brings the audience to less rationally assured conclusions that are beyond existing cultural logic.

In his chapter, titled "Res Gestae Divi Christi: Miracles, Early Christian Heroes, and the Discourse of Power in Acts," Todd Penner examines the sociocultural world of narrative texts to see what the miracles performed in them meant to ancient readers and how the language of power and miracle supports, modifies, or overturns their value systems. A central role of miracle in narrative is the creation of character and the manifestation of that character in the narrative. Miracles performed by a narrative character develop patterns of persuasion and amplify key themes. For example, in Roman narratives the Roman emperor is characterized as having political and religious power expressed in word and deed, which makes claims on the loyalty of the reader. Similarly, in Acts the apostles also make claims to power and loyalty through word and deed. These characterizations are part of the sociocultural world encoded in the narrative that is being worked out in the rhetoric.

Partly due to the discomfort of addressing the question of the authenticity of miracles, much scholarship neglects the unfolding of power and miracle in the presentation and performance of the narrative of Acts. Instead, scholarship tends to treat miraculous material in Acts as an element of tradition and focuses on redactional issues of how Luke utilized the miracle tradition. This approach removes the miraculous features of the Lukan narrative from cultural and religious features of its environment,

---

12. See page 123 below.

and distances them from the magical and supernatural world of antiquity. One contributing factor to this distancing is the desire to separate Acts from similar apocryphal texts, even though the role of miracle in both is similar in form and function. Another factor is the use of comparison from the history of religions approach, which is useful in highlighting patterns of characterization and topics but ignores the function of miracles in the narrative and rhetoric of Acts. As a result miracles in Acts are sanitized and subordinated to other aspects of the narrative, such as the mission to spread of the gospel, rather than explored as manifestations of power that shape the meaning of the text. Luke is understood to emphasize ethics and morality in Acts to keep the reader from being captured by the magical worldview of its Greco-Roman context.

These emphases of current scholarship neglect the central role of miracles in Acts—manifestation of power in narrative form. Power in the ancient world is a complex of relationships that includes the miraculous. Narratives help negotiate these webs of power, and miracles within the narrative help identify where true political and cultural power lies. The politics of miracles in Acts are further obscured by the false dichotomy of magic/pagan versus miracle/Christian. Rather, magic and miracles should be understood as manifestations of the numinous in the ancient world, the former viewed as a negative, deceptive, and illegitimate use of numinous power, and the latter as a positive, true, and legitimate use of such power. In the vying for power and constructing rhetorical strategies, magic is associated with negative characterization involving deception and treachery, and miracles are used in positive characterization involving mercy, faith, and purity.

Luke is writing Hellenistic history, which aims to be plausible for the readers. Thus the manifestations of the numinous in his narrative must correlate with the values of the political, social, and cultural power structures. For example, readers anticipated reading about divine men, that is, the wonder-working philosophers, prophets, and kings who functioned at the intersection of heaven and earth, combining religious and political power. This is especially expected in the presentation of the emperor as a wonder-worker and source of power and beneficence in establishing a political and civic *oikoumene*. Luke's narrative is co-opting Roman imperial rhetoric in order to present Christ as the founder of a new *oikoumene*. Miracles are not in conflict with Luke's narrative, but integral in showing the messengers of the gospel and their deity to be more powerful and beneficent than the emperor and his conquering force. "Analyzing miracle/power discourse in Acts in conjunction with Luke's emergent political interests reveals a resultant ideology that lays claim to the polis of the Greeks and Romans for Christ and underscores the apostles as heroes for both emulation and adulation."[13] Miracles in Acts are manifestations of power integrated with culturally coded power language, and are a part of the negotiation of power relationships in Acts, making Acts itself a medium of that power.

Miracles in Acts characterize the heroes, the divine men or "wonderworkers" as the loci of divine power in the world. This is especially true for Peter and Paul, whose words and deeds are both manifestations of their power and garner power at the expense of others in the text. Christian heroes demonstrate power over all facets of their culture, that their power is true, and that they are the "ideal founders of the expanding Christian *politeia*."[14]

Miracles in Acts also play a role in the relationship of power and space. The hero of Acts uses word and miraculous deeds to claim the public space of the *polis* for Christ as part of a concerted effort to usurp the Roman *imperium*. The power in the empire resides in the Christian community and its heroes. The representatives of the emperor's divine and political power are bested by the heroes of Christ in Roman space, who prove where real power resides. Miracles in Acts, especially those of healing, also illustrate where the true power to control and claim bodies lies, and facilitate the transfer of allegiance of these bodies from the emperor of the *polis* to the living God of the *kosmos*. Luke appropriates and reconfigures the language of the *polis* and *imperium*, with its blend of the religious and political, to his own ends as he describes Christian heroes laying claim to the empire and its citizens through the name and power of Christ.

In her essay, "Miracle Discourse and the Gospel of John," Gail O'Day moves well beyond the agenda of redaction criticism to look at miracle accounts rhetorically. Redaction criticism tries to isolate sources, like miracle accounts, that predate the Gospels and trace their modification and placement in the Gospels as a way to grapple with the theology of the Gospel writers. Rhetorical analysis looks at history, form, and theology of miracle accounts, often studied separately, as interrelated constitutive elements. Topics and arguments are embedded in miracle stories and create a new Christian *paideia*.

---

13. See page 149 below.
14. See page 156 below.

Ancient authors felt free to mold miracle accounts to better serve their rhetorical goals. This understanding moves the discussion beyond the identification of the forms of miracle accounts to what these accounts are trying to communicate beyond the obvious manifestation of divine presence and power. This move is anticipated by ancient authors who embedded topics and argumentation in their miracle accounts and gave interpretive comments about the significance of these miracles. This practice suggests that the formal classification of miracle accounts and their rhetorical functions cannot and should not be neatly separated. The miracle account and the narrative in which it is embedded interpret one another. This is the situation in the Gospel of John—the miracle accounts and their interpretive elaboration are blended.

The miracle account of the wedding of Cana (2:1–11) is illustrative of this blend. While it possesses all the key elements of a miracle story in antiquity—setting, need, miracle, and corroboration of the miracle by witnesses—the focus is not on the miracle itself but on the meaning of the miracle within its narrative. Key Johannine topics are embedded in the miracle account to create this meaning. For example, the topic of Jesus' hour ties this miracle account to the story of the entire Gospel, linking the beginning of Jesus' ministry with his death and showing that the miraculous in Jesus' ministry is intrinsic to key christological issues. The narrator's commentary on the miracle in verse 11 embeds three key topics recurring throughout the Gospel: signs, glory, and coming to believe. The miracle and the interpretation are a composite. "The narration of the Cana wine miracle communicates more than the power and presence of the divine at work in Jesus. It also guides the reader in the appropriate response to such a manifestation—belief—and gives this miracle a distinct content by grounding it in the death of Jesus, and provides the reader with a lens for reading the rest of the Jesus story."[15]

While topics may be embedded in miracle accounts, miracle accounts are also embedded in other topics and arguments in the Gospel of John. There is cross-referencing and self-reference about miracles. Jesus and his miracles are a topic of conversation for Jesus and others in which the Gospel characters enact the process of discernment and learning that the readers of the Gospel are invited to imitate. The vocabulary of miracles—such as sign,

---

15. See page 184 below.

work, works, and working—pervades the speeches of Jesus in the Gospel, providing the rhetorical frame for the theology of the Gospel.

Exorcisms are absent in John because the struggle between good and evil is resolved when people encounter the light and accept it, and evil is decisively conquered at the single point of Jesus' hour of death, resurrection, and ascension. Individual exorcisms are not needed rhetorically to demonstrate Jesus' power over evil when that power is so localized in his hour.

In his essay, "Miracle Discourse in the Pauline Epistles: The Role of Resurrection and Rhetoric," Duane Watson notes that miracle discourse plays a minor role in the undisputed Pauline Epistles and none at all in the disputed Pauline Epistles. Paul refers to his performance of miracles only five times, three directly and two indirectly. He directly refers to them to defend himself as a genuine apostle (2 Cor 12:11–12), defend his gospel (Gal 1:1–5), and legitimize his Gentile mission (Rom 15:17–19); he also refers to them indirectly when he assumes the recipients of his letters know that miracles accompanied his preaching (1 Cor 2:4–5; 1 Thess 1:4–5).

It may seem that Paul is an incompetent rhetor when he uses his ability to perform miracles to defend himself and his gospel, because he concedes that other apostles and those with certain spiritual gifts also perform miracles. How effective for defense is the argument that he performs miracles when others can do the same thing? Paul's forceful proclamation of the gospel as an apostle is the overlooked key to the effectiveness of his argumentation (Rom 15:17–19; 1 Cor 2:4–5; Gal 3:1–5; 1 Thess 1:4–5). Whenever Paul preached he exhibited a combination of forceful proclamation and working of miracles that distinguished him as an apostle from others that proclaimed the gospel and performed miracles.

While Paul refers to his performance of miracles in defense of his apostolic status and his gospel, he does not utilize miracle discourse in his argumentation. Miracles accounts did not help him address the theological and ethical issues his churches raised, nor were they part of a Greco-Roman rhetor's training and public rhetoric. While supernatural oracles were included in rhetorical instruction, their practical use was limited. And while supernatural oracles and miracles were used as *chreiai* in the Gospels for proclamation, Paul could not use them as effectively to address contextual issues, other than as prophetic oracles from the Old Testament. Paul's neglect of miracle discourse is to be expected from a rhetor of his day who was trying to be rhetorically effective in specific rhetorical contexts.

In "Toward a Sociorhetorical Taxonomy of Divine Intervention: Miracle Discourse in the Revelation to John," David deSilva examines Revelation to see if the themes, topics, rationales, and argumentation of miracle discourse are employed. He relies on the definition of the miracle rhetorolect proposed by Vernon Robbins that God comes to the aid of those in danger and suffering from disease, through the mediation of Jesus Christ and the Holy Spirit, and with preconditions met like prayer, trust, and confession of sins. No specific social conflict underlies miracle rhetorolect. DeSilva points out that this definition and understanding of miracle rhetorolect is supported by Wendy Cotter's collection of miracle accounts. These accounts demonstrate a similar pattern of intrusion of the divine in personal affairs, the work of an intermediary in directing divine power to address human need, and preliminary conditions being met on the part of the human recipient.

Revelation is filled with divine intervention in the world and would seem to be a natural source for finding miracle discourse. However, unlike miracle discourse, Revelation is written to address a specific social conflict that will escalate if the audience acts faithfully, as the book advises. It also does not address individual human need seeking God's intervention through intermediaries. Rather, it describes God's judgment against a world that has been unfaithful to God's values. These features explain Revelation's heavy use of themes, topics, rationales, and argumentation of apocalyptic and prophetic discourse rather than miracle discourse. For example, the narratives of God's interventions in delivering his people from Egypt are miracle discourse in their context in Exodus. In their distress the Hebrews pray to God, who acts through the human intermediaries of Moses and Aaron to deliver them from plagues, part the Red Sea, and provide manna and water in the desert. In the recontextualization of these Exodus narratives in Revelation, the plagues are used in judgment upon those who turn from God and persecute God's people, as is common in apocalyptic and prophetic discourse. Also, the two witnesses of chapter 11 perform miracles, but their intent is not to free people from their distress. Rather, it is to move them to repentance, as is common to prophetic discourse. DeSilva concludes that there is no significant miracle discourse in Revelation.

In "Miracle Discourse in the New Testament: A Response," Wendy Cotter responds to all the essays in the volume. In summary, she argues that Vernon Robbins's prophetic, priestly, and apocalyptic rhetorolects are too narrowly defined and predicated on Jewish literature and understandings to the exclusion of the broader Greco-Roman milieu. She suggests that his categories need to be expanded to include social challenge and restoration and power for this life, which were part of the wider culture's understanding of the prophetic, priestly, apocalyptic, and miraculous. She also finds Robbins's need to trace the power of Jesus' miracles to God and to expect faith to play a role in the miracles accounts to be drawn more from later theological reflection and the redaction of the Evangelists than from the original form of the miracle accounts. Cotter likes Bloomquist's subdivision of miracle discourse into thaumaturgical and gnostic-manipulationist, but suggests that while his analysis accounts for the respective redaction of the Evangelists, he needs to pay more attention to the miracle accounts in their immediate and full Gospel contexts to fully understand their message. She strongly agrees with Penner that miracle accounts in Acts are intended to demonstrate that Jesus' power is superior to Roman imperial power. She adds that because the recipients of miracles come from all walks of life, the miracle accounts also function to break down social categories and create a new social vision of equality and unity of all people as children of God. Cotter affirms O'Day's observation that the miracle accounts in John's Gospel both anticipate the message of the Gospel to follow and are themselves necessary to undergird that message, even though ironically this Gospel promotes faith that is not reliant on miracles. Cotter agrees with Watson that the resurrection of Jesus should be viewed as part of Paul's use of miracle discourse to support his authority and the authority of his message, as well as a way for communities he addresses to confirm the reliability of their faith. She concurs with deSilva that miracle accounts are not present in Revelation because they are not helpful in a context of such cosmic grandeur, but would hope that this book's analysis, using rhetorolects, would work to incorporate more of how a Greco-Roman audience would perceive Revelation's unique mixture of literary elements.

Davina Lopez provides a fitting conclusion to the volume with her response, "Miraculous Methodologies: Critical Reflections on 'Ancient Miracle Discourse' Discourse." She reviews the many versions of Marcus Aurelius's "rain miracle" to make the point that analysis of miracle accounts is as much about the rhetorical aims of their interpreters and their audiences' perceptions of miracle accounts as it is about "what really happened." Studying ancient miracle accounts involves our present ideologies and commitments as we decide what accounts to use or not use, and how to use them and to what ends—more than it involves the ideologies and commitments of those of the ancient past. She underscores this point with the second-century Column of Marcus Aurelius, which depicts the "rain miracle," noting that the basic instability of miracle discourse lies in the lack of control of the associations that the viewer makes when viewing the column. This reality undermines a major assumption of interpreters of miracle discourse: that the authorial intent and the effects the representation of the miracle in written or artistic form has on an audience are closely aligned. Thus "what really happened" is in the eye of the beholder.

Rhetorical-critical analysis of miracle discourse has three advantages over previous scholarship, which can conflate the supposed reality of miracles with their representations. First, such analysis takes the burden of verifying miracles as historical events and the personal belief in miracles out of the hermeneutical equation. Second, it recognizes the role of ideology and power dynamics in narrative discourse, so that the question is not "what happened" but how the discourse works to strengthen or weaken allegiances, social arrangements and hierarchy, and articulations of knowing and doing. Third, it recognizes that miracle discourse provided an abundance of tropes that New Testament writers could creatively incorporate into many new representations as they negotiated their message in a world saturated with miracles.

Lopez also has three concern about the methodological and discursive assumptions involved in the rhetorical-critical analysis of miracle discourse in this volume. First is the desire to create a false dichotomy between magic and miracle, in part to make claims for the uniqueness of early Christian miracle discourse, and partly to isolate this component of the narrative of the life of Jesus as a pretext for methodological reflection. Second is a lack of the analysis of power in the study of miracles, for such study tends to configure early Christian discourse in differentiation from the "other," perhaps motivated by the desire to maintain Christian texts as unique or superior to those of other religions of the classical world. Third, the term *miracle discourse* may be really more about our discursive constructions of miracle discourse and our interaction with these constructions in isolation from the world around the New Testament. She suggests that this problem can be addressed through comparison with other religions using categories that do not privilege one tradition over another and are more genuinely attuned to the commonality of human experience. Lopez concludes that as interpreters we need to ask what we are seeking to gain and to be or become through our constructs and classifications; to be aware of the frameworks that we create through power configurations and to be responsible for them.

Sociorhetorical Interpretation of Miracle Discourse in the Synoptic Gospels

Vernon K. Robbins

This paper presupposes a view, which has resulted from sociorhetorical analysis of the New Testament, that six major kinds of cultural discourse blend with each other in first-century Christian discourse: wisdom, prophetic, apocalyptic, precreation, priestly, and miracle.[1] Sociorhetorical interpreters refer to each different mode of discourse as a rhetorolect, which is a contraction of the phrase *rhetorical dialect*.[2] The presupposition is that each early Christian rhetorolect emerged in relation to multiple social and cultural spaces, functioned in dynamic ways in multiple public settings, and responded in appealing ways, both then and now, to multiple kinds of evil in the world. Early Christians blended the six rhetorolects in multiple ways.[3] The potential for each rhetorolect to function in multiple

---

1. Vernon K. Robbins, "Socio-rhetorical Interpretation," in *The Blackwell Companion to the New Testament* (ed. David E. Aune; West Sussex, U.K.: Blackwell, 2010), 192–219; idem, *The Invention of Christian Discourse* (vol. 1; Blandford Forum, U.K.: Deo, 2009); idem, "Argumentative Textures in Socio-Rhetorical Interpretation," in *Rhetorical Argumentation in Biblical Texts* (ed. Anders Eriksson, Thomas H. Olbricht, and Walter Übelacker; ESEC 8; Harrisburg, Pa.: Trinity Press International, 2002), 27–65; see idem, "The Dialectical Nature of Early Christian Discourse," *Scriptura* 59 (1996): 353–62, http://www.religion.emory.edu/faculty/robbins/SRS/vkr/dialect.cfm.

2. See Robbins, "Dialectical Nature," 356: "A rhetorolect is a form of language variety or discourse identifiable on the basis of a distinctive configuration of themes, topics, reasonings, and argumentations." See also Vernon K. Robbins and Gordon D. Newby, "A Prolegomenon to the Relation of the Qur'ān and the Bible," in *Bible and Qur'ān: Essays in Scriptural Intertextuality* (ed. John C. Reeves; SBLSymS 24; Atlanta: Society of Biblical Literature, 2003), 31–32 (23–42).

3. For conceptual blending, see Gilles Fauconnier and Mark Turner, *The Way We Think: Conceptual Blending and the Mind's Hidden Complexities* (New York: Basic,

ways equipped early Christians with a wide range of speech and argumentation that focused on Jesus as God's Messiah and on the Holy Spirit as an active agent in the world.

The books in the New Testament exhibit many skills and strategies of speaking and arguing that early Christians achieved during the first century. There may have been additional skills that the present-day interpreter is unable to hear as a result of both the absence of evidence and challenges in the data that have survived. However, interpreting the discourse in the New Testament in relation to discourse prior to and during the first century, and in relation to discourse that emerged during the second through the seventh centuries,[4] can present a vantage point for analyzing and interpreting assertions and arguments that were valued in Christian discourse alongside assertions and arguments of other people in the Mediterranean world.

Miracle rhetorolect features unusual enactment of the power of God in the created realm of the universe. This essay will demonstrate that God's enactment of unusual power in the Synoptic Gospels focuses almost exclusively on personal bodies of individual people. There are at least four exceptions to this: (1) Jesus' cursing of the fig tree (Mark 11:12–14, 20–25 ||

2003); Todd V. Oakley, "Conceptual Blending, Narrative Discourse, and Rhetoric," *Cognitive Linguistics* 9.4 (1988): 321–60; idem, "The Human Rhetorical Potential," *Written Communication* 16.1 (1999): 93–128; Vernon K. Robbins, "Conceptual Blending and Early Christian Imagination," in *Explaining Christian Origins and Early Judaism: Contributions from Cognitive and Social Science* (ed. Petri Luomanen, Ilkka Pyysiäinen, and Risto Uro; BIS 89; Leiden: Brill, 2007), 161–95; Robert von Thaden, *Sex, Christ, and Embodied Cognition: Paul's Wisdom for Corinth* (ESEC 16; Blandford Forum, U.K.: Deo, 2012).

4. I am interested in taking the analysis and discussion of the six rhetorolects down through the seventh century, which includes the emergence of Islam in the context of seventh-century Jewish and Christian traditions. From a sociorhetorical perspective, multiple modes of discourse powerfully blend in the Qur'an as it speaks as the authoritative agent of the actions and attributes of God, Holy Spirit, and prophetic revelation in the world. See Vernon K. Robbins, "Lukan and Johannine Tradition in the Qur'an: A Story of *Auslegungsgeschichte* and *Wirkungsgeschichte*," in *Moving Beyond New Testament Theology? Essays in Conversation with Heikki Räisänen* (ed. Todd Penner and Caroline Vander Stichele; Publications of the Finnish Exegetical Society 88; Helsinki: Finnish Exegetical Society; Göttingen: Vandenhoeck & Ruprecht, 2005), 336–68; Gordon D. Newby, "Quranic Texture: A Review of Vernon Robbins' *The Tapestry of Early Christian Discourse* and *Exploring the Texture of Texts*," *JSNT* 70 (1998), 93–100; Robbins and Newby, "A Prolegomenon," 23–42.

Matt 21:18–22); (2) the appearance of a star at Jesus' birth (Matt 2:10); (3) the three-hour period when God either causes or allows darkness to cover the earth before Jesus' death (Mark 15:33 || Matt 27:45 || Luke 23:44–45a); and (4) the splitting of the curtain of the temple at the time of Jesus' death (Mark 15:38 || Matt 27:51 || Luke 23:45). This essay contains a discussion of these exceptions after analysis of the manifestations of God's power that focus on the bodies of individual people.

Wendy Cotter's excellent collection helps us to see the widespread presence of miracle discourse in Mediterranean antiquity.[5] Moving from her collection to the New Testament, it is remarkable how much focus on the miraculous there is in early Christian discourse. A substantive amount of miracle rhetorolect in the New Testament is inductive narration—description of circumstances in which Jesus, and subsequently his followers, miraculously heal people through direct encounter, or through the power of their word, clothing, or an object from them (like a handkerchief or a shadow). These are, however, confined to five books in the New Testament—the four Gospels and the Acts of the Apostles.[6] One of the major tasks of rhetorical investigation must be to analyze and interpret the manner in which inductive narration of miraculous healing is nurtured into argumentative discourse that serves many different purposes within Christianity.[7] As miracle rhetorolect moves beyond description into a

---

5. Wendy J. Cotter, *Miracles in Greco-Roman Antiquity: A Sourcebook for the Study of New Testament Miracle Stories* (London: Routledge, 1999).

6. Wendy Cotter has delimited her approach in a subsequent book, *The Christ of the Miracle Stories: Portrait through Encounter* (Grand Rapids: Baker Academic, 2010). This book presents a very interesting analysis and interpretation of eight miracle stories in the Synoptic Gospels as anecdotes that feature one or more petitioners who, in her view, rudely and brusquely confront Jesus with their wishes. From her perspective, Jesus' compassionate response to the petitioners, rather than abrupt dismissal of them, exhibits, in Plutarch's words, the "soul" of Jesus in the form of various philosophical, biographical virtues. Cotter's approach, in line with other current studies that show the relation of New Testament literature to Mediterranean moral philosophy, is in essence an extension of nineteenth-century interests in presenting Christianity as a philosophical movement rather than as a multiply nuanced religious movement in the context of a wide variety of religious activities and perceptions in the Mediterranean world during the first century C.E.

7. For an alternative, but very important, rhetorical approach to miracle discourse, see Klaus Berger, "Hellenistische Gattungen im Neuen Testament," *ANRW* 25.2:1212–18; idem, *Einführung in die Formgeschichte* (UTB 1444; Tübingen: Taschenbuch, 1987), 76–84; idem, *Formgeschichte des Neuen Testaments* (Heidelberg: Quelle

mode of early Christian argumentative discourse, a major question will be how miracle rhetorolect blends with prophetic, apocalyptic, priestly, and wisdom rhetorolect in the Synoptic tradition.[8] This essay, therefore, moves from analysis of inductive narration of miracle events to inferential, argumentative miracle discourse in the Synoptic Gospels. As early Christian miracle discourse becomes explicitly argumentative, a guiding question will be the manner in which inferences from prophetic, apocalyptic, priestly, and wisdom rhetorolect blend with miracle rhetorolect to produce a dynamic, multidimensional mode of thinking that plays an important role in the formulation of the full-bodied discourse that emerged among Christians during the first centuries of their existence in the Mediterranean world.

1. Epideictic Narration of Jesus' Healings

A significant amount of miracle discourse in the Synoptic Gospels builds on the rhetorical dynamics of inductive narration.[9] This means that narration proceeds from Cases (Jesus encountering a person whose body somehow needs restoration) to Results (the restoration of the body of the person), without containing argumentative rationales that introduce substantive deductive reasoning or argumentation. The most obvious

---

& Meyer, 1984), 305–10. For exceptional social analysis of early Christian miracle discourse, see Gerd Theissen, *Miracle Stories of the Early Christian Tradition* (ed. John Riches; trans. Francis McDonagh; Philadelphia: Fortress, 1983); idem, "Jesus as Healer: The Miracles of Jesus," in *The Historical Jesus: A Comprehensive Guide* (ed. Gerd Theissen and Annette Merz; London: SCM, 1998), 281–315. For a specifically social-scientific interpretation of the healing stories, see John J. Pilch, *Healing in the New Testament: Insights from Medical and Mediterranean Anthropology* (Minneapolis: Fortress, 2000). Also see the sociorhetorical approach in Elaine M. Wainwright, *Women Healing/Healing Women: The Genderization of Healing in Early Christianity* (Oakville, Conn.: Equinox, 2006).

8. No precreation rhetorolect blends with miracle rhetorolect in the Synoptic Gospels.

9. For a discussion of inductive, deductive, and abductive argumentation in the Gospels, see Vernon K. Robbins, "Enthymemic Texture in the Gospel of Thomas," in *1998 Society of Biblical Literature Seminar Papers* (SBLSP 37; Atlanta: Scholars Press, 1998), 343–66, http://www.religion.emory.edu/faculty/robbins/SRS/vkr/enthymeme. cfm; idem, "From Enthymeme to Theology in Luke 11:1-13," in *Sea Voyages and Beyond: Emerging Strategies in Socio-Rhetorical Interpretation* (ESEC 15; Blandford Forum, U.K.: Deo, 2010), 349–71.

public function of this kind of miracle rhetorolect is epideictic: a display of actions, values, and attitudes that affirm or reaffirm some point of view in the present.

The account of Jesus' healing of Peter's mother-in-law in Mark 1:29–31 || Matt 8:14–15 || Luke 4:38–39 is strictly epideictic in nature. In a direct and simple manner, Jesus enters the house of Simon[10] and heals Simon's mother-in-law, who is afflicted with a fever. In Mark 1:29–31, the disciples tell Jesus about the woman, and he simply goes to her, takes her hand, and lifts her up. At this point, the fever leaves her, and she serves the five men. In Matt 8:14–15, Jesus comes to the house of Peter alone, sees the woman, touches her hand, and the fever leaves her. At this point, she gets up and serves Jesus. In Luke 4:38–39, when Jesus comes to the house of Simon, "they"[11] make a request to him concerning the woman. Standing above her, Jesus rebukes the fever,[12] it leaves her, and immediately she arises and serves them. None of the accounts presents the direct speech of anyone. In other words, the narration presents every instance of speech simply as an action, rather than a moment when the narratee attributes particular words to someone.

Wilhelm Wuellner taught us, basing his insights on ancient rhetorical treatises and Curtius's interpretation of them, that rhetorical discourse elaborates topoi in two ways: (1) amplificatory-descriptive and (2) argumentative-enthymematic.[13] From a rhetorical perspective, this means that discourse contains both rhetography (narration that creates pictures) and rhetology (assertions that create reasoning).[14] The story of Jesus' heal-

---

10. Matt 8:14 refers to Simon as Peter; Mark 1:29 adds "and Andrew, with James and John."

11. Presumably, members of the household or the crowd from Capernaum.

12. In Luke 4:39 Jesus treats the fever like a demon, rebuking it: see John G. Cook, "In Defense of Ambiguity: Is There a Hidden Demon in Mark 1.29–31?" *NTS* 43 (1997): 184–208; Wainwright, *Women Healing/Healing Women*, 172–75.

13. Wilhelm H. Wuellner, "Toposforschung und Torahinterpretation bei Paulus und Jesus," *NTS* 24 (1977/1978): 467: "eine zweifache Funktion: eine argumentativ-enthymematische und eine amplifikatorisch-darstellerische Funktion." See also Walter J. Ong, *Orality and Literacy: The Technologizing of the Word* (New York: Routledge, 1982), 110–11. See the less explicitly rhetorical approach to "motifs" in F. Gerald Downing, "Words as Deeds and Deeds as Words," *BibInt* 3 (1995): 129–43.

14. Vernon K. Robbins, "Rhetography: A New Way of Seeing the Familiar Text," in *Words Well Spoken: George Kennedy's Rhetoric of the New Testament* (ed. C. Clifton Black and Duane F. Watson; Studies in Rhetoric and Religion 8; Waco, Tex.: Baylor

ing of Peter's mother-in-law presents pictorial narration (rhetography) of the topos of "healing an afflicted body." This topos is central to miracle discourse in the Synoptic Gospels. The account of the healing does not elaborate the topos with rhetology (argumentative enthymeme). Rather, it presents elaborated pictorial narration of the topos of healing an afflicted body in a manner that is argumentatively inductive. The story presents a Case (Jesus takes the woman's hand and lifts her up, touches her hand, or rebukes the fever) and a Result (the woman is healed and serves someone). The story itself presents no Rule (premise) that explains the empowerment of Jesus to heal like this.[15] The narration is straightforwardly epideictic, implying a positive view (praise) of Jesus and his actions. Stories regularly evoke one or more Rule for a listener through inference, since this is the nature of inductive narration. Rather than presenting inferential reasoning, however, the final comments in the story simply encourage the listener to focus on the Result of the healing, including the woman's action, which is made possible by the healing.

As Perelman and Olbrechts-Tyteca have made clear, epideictic discourse naturally evokes deliberative effects (decisions to act in ways that benefit society).[16] The woman's serving of the people in the house may be understood to infer a social principle (a Rule) that people who receive healing traditionally reciprocate with appropriate benefits.[17] By itself, however, this story does not emphasize the woman's action as a deliberative

---

University Press, 2008), 81–106; idem, "Enthymeme and Picture in the *Gospel of Thomas*," in *Thomasine Traditions in Antiquity: The Social and Cultural World of the Gospel of Thomas* (ed. Jon Ma Asgeirsson, April D. DeConick, and Risto Uro; Leiden: Brill, 2005), 175–207, http://www.religion.emory.edu/faculty/robbins/Pdfs/Thomas PicEnth.pdf.

15. Each of the Gospels contains narrational comments, narrational depiction of events and actions, and attributed speech (either direct or indirect) that either evoke or state one or more Rules (premises) for Jesus' ability to heal in this manner. For inductive reasoning in early Christian texts, see Vernon K. Robbins, "Enthymemic Texture in the Gospel of Thomas"; idem, "From Enthymeme to Theology in Luke 11:1–13"; idem, "Enthymeme and Picture in the Gospel of Thomas."

16. Chaim Perelman and L. Olbrechts-Tyteca, *The New Rhetoric: A Treatise on Argumentation* (trans. J. Wilkinson and P. Weaver; Notre Dame, Ind.: University of Notre Dame Press, 1969), 47–51.

17. Bruce J. Malina, *The New Testament World* (Louisville: Westminster John Knox, 1993), 100–101.

moment.[18] Rather, the story encourages a positive response to the Result of the action of Jesus, which is displayed in the ability of the healed woman to rise and honorably perform activities of hospitality in her household.[19] It is also important to notice that there is no mention of faith in the story. The story proceeds simply through a process in which disciples take Jesus to a sick woman, Jesus heals her, and the healing of the woman allows her to resume her usual activities in her household.

Sometimes a miracle story contains attributed speech, yet this speech simply carries the story forward narrationally without introducing argumentative speech that creates a logical argument. Jesus' healing of the blind man in Mark 8:22–26 (cf. John 9:1–7) contains attributed dialogue that moves the narration forward in an inductive manner from Cases to Results:

> **Case:** People brought a blind man to Jesus asking Jesus to touch him (v. 22).
> **Result/Case:** Jesus led the blind man by the hand out of the village, spit on his eyelids, laid his hands on him, and asked him what he saw (v. 23).
> **Result/Case:** Opening his eyes, the blind man said he saw men like trees walking (v. 24).
> **Result/Case:** Again Jesus laid his hands on the man's eyes, and the blind man looked intently (v. 25ab).
> **Result/Case:** The blind man's sight was restored, and he saw everything clearly (v. 25cd).
> **Result:** Jesus sent the healed man to his home saying, "Do not even enter the village" (v. 26).

While this story contains an important double healing that must not prolong us here, it proceeds in a straightforward, inductive manner from Cases to Results. The final Result includes an unexpected phenomenon.

---

18. In the context of specific arguments about the value of "serving," however, this story will naturally function in a supportive manner; Wainwright, *Women Healing/Healing Women*, 106–12, 143–46, 172–75.

19. See Bruce J. Malina and Richard Rohrbaugh, *Social-Science Commentary on the Synoptic Gospels* (Minneapolis: Fortress, 1992), 70: "Serving those in the house after being healed indicates that the mother-in-law's place in the family has been restored"; see also pp. 181, 311.

Why does Jesus tell the man not to enter the village? This is an enthymematic moment that, along with other commands by Jesus to demons or healed people, has given rise to theories concerning "messianic secrecy" or "healing secrecy" in the Gospels.[20] In the context of the other miracle stories in the Synoptic Gospels, most interpreters have thought this command concerns the identity of Jesus. When early Christian miracle summaries and stories contain attributed speech, the primary focus of that speech is regularly on the identity of Jesus. In this instance, the statement at the end is not clearly a statement about the identity of Jesus, though it may be understood and interpreted in this way. Rather, it is an enigmatic statement that the healed man should go directly to his home without entering the village. In addition to having no focused narration on the identity of Jesus, there is also no presence of the topos of "faith" in the story.

Jesus' healing of a deaf and dumb man in Mark 7:31–37 (no parallels) contains a charge to people similar to the charge in Mark 8:26 to the blind man whom Jesus healed. When Jesus returns from the region of Tyre to the Sea of Galilee, through Sidon and the Decapolis, people bring a man to Jesus who is deaf and has an impediment of speech, and they ask Jesus to lay his hand on the man (vv. 31–32). Jesus takes him aside privately, puts his fingers in the man's ears, spits and touches the man's tongue, looks up into heaven, sighs, and says, "Eph'phatha," which means "Be opened" (vv. 33–34). The Result of these actions is that the man's ears are opened, his tongue is released, and he speaks plainly (v. 35). At this point:

Case: Jesus told "them" to tell no one.
Contrary Result: but the more he charged them, the more zealously they proclaimed it.
Result/Case: And they were astonished beyond measure,
Result/Rule: saying, "He has done all things well; he even makes the deaf hear and the dumb speak" (vv. 36–37).

---

20. William Wrede, *The Messianic Secret* (trans. J. C. G. Greig; Cambridge: Clarke, 1971); H. J. Ebeling, *Das Messiasgeheimnis und die Botschaft des Marcus-Evangelisten* (Berlin: A. Töpelmann, 1939); G. Minette de Tillesse, *Le secret messianique dans l'Évangile de Marc* (Paris: Cerf, 1968); Heikki Räisänen, *The "Messianic Secret" in Mark* (trans. C. Tuckett; Edinburgh: T&T Clark, 1990); Theodore J. Weeden, *Mark—Traditions in Conflict* (Philadelphia: Fortress, 1971).

The narration leaves unstated that Jesus and the healed man go back to the people who have brought the man, but it is clear that they do so. In addition, the narration does not explain why Jesus takes the man to a private place to heal him, and why Jesus tells the people not to tell anyone once they come back. The narration presents a Result that the people are astonished beyond measure (*hyperperissōs exeplēssonto*: v. 37). This Result functions as a Case that produces a Result of speaking. The speaking then presents a Rule that explains why the people cannot refrain from speaking: The focus of their speech is not on the healed man. The focus is on Jesus, who has done all things well. He even makes the deaf hear and the dumb speak! In all of this, there is no question concerning who Jesus is, no one draws an inference about powers within Jesus or about Jesus' relation to God, and there is no mention of faith. Rather, there is a direct epideictic focus on Jesus, whom they praise as a person who is able to do these things so well. There is, however, a very interesting sequence of action by Jesus: "Looking up to heaven, he sighed, and said to him, 'Eph'phatha,' that is, 'Be opened.'" This sequence calls attention to a relationship between Jesus and "heaven" as he heals. What is this relationship? How does this relationship work in the context of Jesus' miraculous healings? The story does not say. Rather, the story emphasizes the manner in which people are amazed at what Jesus is able to do, and the people speak openly to one another about it.

Sometimes in the Synoptic Gospels, summaries of Jesus' healings that do not contain attributed speech show movement toward argumentation about how Jesus is able to perform his miraculous deeds. Mark 6:53–56 || Matt 14:34–36 presents a summary of Jesus' healing that contains only narration. The action in the summary begins with a Rule that "the people recognized" Jesus (Mark 6:54 || Matt 14:35). This Rule explains why people bring sick people on pallets to Jesus (Mark 6:55 || Matt 14:35), lay the sick in market places, and ask Jesus if they might touch even the fringe of his garment (Mark 6:56 || Matt 14:36). The Result of the action of the people (the Case based on the Rule) is that "as many as touched it were made well" (Mark 6:56 || Matt 14:36). For purposes of rhetorical analysis and interpretation, it is necessary to observe three aspects of the narration. First, "people" are the agents who recognize Jesus' identity as a healer. Second, the people's recognition (*epignontes*: Mark 6:54 || Matt 14:35) of Jesus simply evokes a premise that Jesus was a person who could heal afflicted bodies, rather than necessarily evoking any deeper "knowing" (*oida*: cf. Mark 1:34) of who Jesus is and why he can heal. Third, the action of asking

Jesus if they can simply touch the fringe of his garment evokes a premise that healing power is so present in Jesus' body that simply touching the outer edge of his garment can effect healing. Overall, the topos of the identity of Jesus may evoke a question: How could healing power be so present within Jesus' body? The narration, however, does not enter this conceptual arena. Rather, the narration focuses simply on presenting Jesus as a person within whom healing power is so present that simply touching the fringe of his garment can bring healing to an afflicted body. In some ways, this is early Christian miracle rhetorolect "at its highest point." The focus is strictly on Jesus as a healer, on people's recognition of Jesus' healing power, and on people's access to this power simply by touching the outer border of his garment. Again, there is no statement about faith in the narration. Rather, people come to Jesus, touch the hem of his garment, and are healed simply on the basis of people's recognition that it is possible to be healed in this way.

In contrast to Mark 6:53–56 || Matt 14:34–36, the miracle summary in Matt 15:29–31 exhibits an initial step in "narrational inference" concerning the means by which Jesus is able to heal. When Jesus goes up on the mountain and sits down, great crowds come to him, "bringing with them the lame, the maimed, the blind, the dumb, and many others; and they put them at his feet" (vv. 29–30). In this instance the description of the action of the crowds implies a Rule evoked by Jesus' previous actions of healing in the story. The implied Rule is something like: "because they knew Jesus could and would heal them." The Case produces the expected Result: Jesus heals them (v. 29). This Result becomes a Case that produces yet another Result. The crowd marvels when they see the dumb speaking, the maimed healthy, the lame walking, and the blind seeing. This produces the Result that "they glorified the God of Israel" (v. 31):

> **Case:** People brought sick people to Jesus.
> **[Implied Rule:** Because they knew he could and would heal them.]
> **Result/Case:** Jesus healed them.
> **Result/Case:** The crowd marveled when they saw the sick people healed.
> **Result:** The crowd glorified the God of Israel.

Again, the sequence does not express a Rule (premise) for the initial Cases and Results. In this instance, however, the action of the people at the beginning implies a Rule that the people know Jesus can heal, and the final Result introduces the hearer to an inference that the God of Israel is somehow involved in Jesus' ability to heal. Perhaps the people conventionally express gratitude to God for special blessings that come to their lives, perhaps they think God is actually the one who has healed people in the context of Jesus' activity (a Rule), or perhaps they think the God of Israel has endowed Jesus with special powers to heal people (a slightly alternative Rule). The narration clearly moves beyond Jesus as a primary focus to the God of Israel, but the manner in which the people blend the conceptual network of the God of Israel and the conceptual domain of Jesus as healer is undefined.

The shift from Jesus to God in Matt 15:29–31 (which perhaps also hovers over Jesus' look to heaven in Mark 7:34) is an important moment in early Christian narration of miracle stories, since it introduces the conceptual network of the God of Israel in addition to a domain of reasoning about Jesus as a healer. Following direct principles of inductive reasoning, the people should glorify Jesus in verse 31. From the perspective of conceptual-blending (or "conceptual-integration") theory, the move in the narration beyond Jesus the healer to the God of Israel introduces a "double-scope network" of reasoning.[21] One network is the relation of people to Jesus as a healer. The other network is the relation of Jesus and the people to the God of Israel. The issue now is the manner in which a hearer may blend the two networks. Will a hearer simply be grateful to God that there is a person on earth like Jesus who is able to heal? Do the people presuppose that Jesus is using God's power, rather than his own powers, to heal? Do the people think healing occurs by means of God's healing powers traveling through Jesus' body, something like the powers of the Lord God of Israel that were present in and around the tabernacle or the ark of the covenant? Or do people think Jesus is more of a prophetic agent than a personal embodiment of the powers of God, in the mode of the prophet Elijah, Elisha, or Moses? In other words, perhaps the people think God's power directly heals people, but Jesus is an "agent of God" who provides the occasions for God to heal. In any case, the people's praising of God rather than Jesus is "an enthymematic moment."[22] An enthymematic

---

21. Fauconnier and Turner, *The Way We Think*, 131–35, 179–83, 274–75, 340–45, 353–60, 389–92.

22. The understanding of enthymeme that guides this essay can be found in Richard L. Lanigan, "From Enthymeme to Abduction: The Classical Law of Logic and the Postmodern Rule of Rhetoric," in *Recovering Pragmatism's Voice: The Classical Tradi-*

moment regularly invites multiple possibilities of reasoning available in the culture. Inviting hearers to draw their own conclusion can be a powerful way of leading people into one's own point of view. In cultural situations where well-known topoi are near at hand, a narrator's presentation of Rules that evoke a particular conceptual network without giving specific answers may evoke a cultural frame of reasoning that a majority of people recognize and happily select as the means to understand and interpret the event. In this instance, the narration introduces the conceptual network of the God of Israel. Again, however, there is no mention of faith in the narration of the story.

2. Prophetic Rhetorolect Energizes Early Christian Miracle Narration

In early Christian discourse, prophetic rhetorolect energizes miracle rhetorolect in various ways. When Luke 7:11–17 narrates the account of Jesus' raising of the son of the widow of Nain, it moves beyond a pictorial narration of the topos of raising the dead to a recontextualization of Elijah's raising of the son of the widow of Zarephath (see Luke 4:26).[23] There is no focus on "faith" in the account of Elijah's raising of the widow's son; nor is there such a focus in the Lukan account of Jesus' deed. Rather, there is a focus on the identity of the agent of healing in both stories. Prior to Elijah's raising of the widow's son, the woman refers to him as "man of God" (1 Kgs 17:18). Twice in the account, Elijah prays to "O Lord, my God" (1 Kgs 17:20–21).[24] After the son is revived, the woman says, "Now I know that you are a man of God, and that the word of the Lord in your mouth is truth" (1 Kgs 17:24). The account does not focus on the faith of the widow, then, but on the identity of Elijah in relation to God.

In a similar manner, Luke's account of Jesus' raising of the son of the widow of Nain in 7:11–17 also does not focus on the widow's faith. Rather, it focuses on the identity of Jesus in relation to God. In contrast to the story concerning Elijah, the story concerning Jesus contains no speech by the widow. There is an assertion that the revived son spoke (v. 15), but there is no narration of the content of his speech. The content of Jesus'

---

tion, Rorty, and the Philosophy of Communication (ed. Lenore Langsdorf and Andrew R. Smith; Albany: State University of New York Press, 1995), 49–70.

23. Robbins, *Exploring the Texture of Texts*, 48–50.

24. Cf. the presence of prayer in Jas 5:14–18.

speech addresses the woman's weeping (v. 13) and effects the restoration of the young man in tandem with Jesus' touching of the bier (v. 14). The narrator asserts that Jesus' speech to the widow was motivated by "compassion" on her (v. 13: *esplangchnisthē ep' autēi*). After the revival of the young man, the narrator asserts:

> **Result/Case:** Fear seized them all.
> **Result/Case:** They glorified God, saying, "A great prophet has arisen among us!" and "God has visited his people!"
> **Result:** This report concerning him spread through the whole of Judea and all the surrounding country.

The Elijah account raises the topic of "fear" in the exchange about the jar of meal prior to Elijah's reviving of the widow's son. Elijah tells her not to be afraid, but to act as she herself had intended with the wood and the meal, but also to make him some cake to eat (1 Kgs 17:13). When she does not allow fear to stop her actions, the oil and meal remain sufficient "according to the word of the Lord that he spoke by Elijah" (1 Kgs 17:16). The effect of Elijah's raising of her son from death, then, is "knowledge" of his identity as "a man of God," and certainty that "the word of the Lord in his mouth is truth" (1 Kgs 17:24).

Fear and certainty work somewhat differently in the Lukan account of 7:11–17. There is no statement about the widow's fear, but only her weeping. Also, there is no focus on the woman's response to Jesus' raising of her son. Rather, all the focus is on the people who see the deed. Fear seizes all of them and they glorify God (v. 16). Interpreters can dispute the exact function of the fear. Perhaps the people overcame fear and glorified God; perhaps fear was a stimulus that moved people toward glorification of God; or perhaps fear refers to awe that is simply the beginning process of glorifying God. However an interpreter might think fear functions in the account, the final Result is the people's glorification of God with speech that identifies Jesus as "a great prophet" and associates Jesus' deed with God's visitation of his people (v. 16). The "reasoning" in this discourse is clearly embedded in Septuagint discourse about prophets as agents of God who transmit God's will and engage in actions that bring God's powers into the realm of human life and activity. But there is still another Result. The content of the people's speech becomes a message that people carry throughout all of Judea and the surrounding region (v. 17). In this instance, the discourse functions as "gospel story" that spreads throughout all of Judea and the surrounding country. Even in this story featuring fear, the identity of Jesus, and the relation of Jesus to God, however, there is no reference to anyone's faith in the context.

Matthew 12:15-19 exhibits yet another way in which prophetic rhetorolect energizes early Christian miracle discourse. Instead of putting "prophetic" phrasing on the lips of Jesus or recontextualizing a story from the biblical tradition of Elijah or Elisha, Matt 12:15-19 presents an explicit recitation of verses from prophetic biblical text. The opening and middle of the verses present a sequence of Cases and Results common to a narrational summary. In the final verses, however, the narrator attributes speech to Isaiah that presents a syllogistic argument about Jesus' relation to God:

Opening:
   Case: Jesus knew that the Pharisees had met in council to destroy him.
   Result/Case: Jesus withdrew from their synagogue (vv. 14-15a; cf. v. 9).

Middle:
   Result/Case: Many followed him,
   Result: and he healed them all, and ordered them not to make him known (vv. 15b-16).

Closing:
   Rule: This was to fulfill what was spoken by the prophet Isaiah (v. 17):
   Rule: "Behold, my servant whom I have chosen, my beloved with whom my soul is well pleased.
   Case: I will put my Spirit upon him,
   Result/Case: and he shall proclaim justice to the Gentiles (v. 18).
   Contrary Result/Case: He will not wrangle or cry aloud, nor will any one hear his voice in the streets; he will not break a bruised reed or quench a smoldering wick, till he brings justice to victory (vv. 19-20).
   Result: And in his name will the Gentiles hope" (v. 21).

The Matthean narration here does not, like the Lukan narration above, simply make its own assertions about the relation of Jesus to God. Rather, Matthean narration attributes extended speech to Isaiah, who interprets

God's selection of Jesus in the mode of prophetic discourse.[25] Jesus has been selected by God to bring justice to the nations in the context of injustice in the world. A central part of this action of justice is Jesus' healing of people.

3. Prophetic and Priestly Rhetorolect Blend in Early Christian Miracle Stories

Prophetic rhetorolect naturally blends with priestly rhetorolect when the healed person is a leper. On the one hand, the prophet Elisha oversees the cleansing of the leper Naaman in biblical tradition (2 Kgs 5:1–14), and there are no noticeable priestly dynamics in the story. The Gospel of Luke perpetuates the tradition of this cleansing in the mode of prophetic rhetorolect in Luke 4:27. In Mark 1:40–45 || Matt 8:1–4 || Luke 5:12–16, however, the priestly domain of leprosy blends with Jesus' healing of a leper in the mode of a prophetic healing.[26] Priestly dynamics appear at the opening of the story, when the leper kneels before Jesus (Mark 1:40), worships him (Matt 8:2), or falls on his face (Luke 5:12) as he petitions (Luke 5:12) Jesus as *kyrie* (Matt 8:2 || Luke 5:12) to cleanse him. Being "moved with compassion" (*esphlangchnistheis*: Mark 1:41), Jesus heals the leper with his prophetic word, which uses passive voice to refer to God's cleansing of the man (Mark 1:41 || Matt 8:3 || Luke 5:13).[27] Blending the prophetic mode with miracle rhetorolect, however, they also feature Jesus' touching the leper as he speaks to the man to heal him. When the man is immediately healed, Jesus charges him to go and show himself to a priest and make the offering Moses commanded for the completion of the priestly cleansing ritual (Mark 1:43 || Matt 8:4 || Luke 5:14).

In a related manner, Jesus' feeding of five thousand and four thousand people in the wilderness blend prophetic with priestly rhetorolect as they recount Jesus' miraculous feeding of people with small amounts of food. Precedents for Jesus' action exist both in the tradition of Moses' feeding of the Israelites with manna and quail in the wilderness, and in

---

25. See Robbins, "Argumentative Textures," 44–50.
26. Cf. Cotter, *Christ of the Miracle Stories*, 19–41. In her view (p. 41), this story possibly exhibits *syngnōmē* (the willingness to overlook a provocation) and certainly exhibits *praos* (meekness), compassion, and *ēpios* (gentleness).
27. Cf. LXX 2 Kgs 5:10 (*katharisthēsēi*), 13 (*katharisthēti*), and 14 (*ekatharisthē*).

the tradition of Elisha's feeding of one hundred men in 2 Kgs 4:42–44.[28] Mark 6:34 || Matt 14:14 emphasizes that Jesus "was moved with compassion" (*esplangchnisthē*) for the huge crowd. Mark 6:34 adds from prophetic tradition that they were like sheep without a shepherd (Num 27:17; 1 Kgs 22:17; Ezek 34:8; Zech 10:2). Luke 9:11 features prophetic rhetorolect with Jesus' speaking about the kingdom of God. The stories contain no reasoning about the identity of Jesus,[29] and they contain no statements about amazement, fear, or glorifying God at the end of the accounts. Wisdom rhetorolect stands in the background of the Markan account when Jesus begins to teach them (Mark 6:34). In contrast, the Matthean and Lukan versions emphasize miracle rhetorolect as they feature Jesus' healing people who are sick (Matt 14:14 || Luke 9:11).

On the one hand, the stories of Jesus' feeding of large groups of people function nicely alongside other miracle stories that focus on bodies in special need. On the other hand, these bodies are only in "daily" need, rather than in a state of permanent need as a result of an affliction.[30] A special feature of the stories is the achievement of the miracle of feeding through an action of prayer. When Jesus receives the five loaves and two fish:

> **Case:** Taking the five loaves and the two fish, Jesus looked up to heaven, blessed and broke the loaves, and gave them to his disciples to set before the people; and he divided the two fish among them all (Mark 6:41 || cf. Matt 14:19 || Luke 9:16).[31]
> **Result:** All ate and were filled; and they took up twelve baskets full of broken pieces and of the fish. Those who had eaten the loaves numbered five thousand men (Mark 6:42–44 || cf. Matt 14:20–21 || Luke 9:17).

---

28. See 2 Kgs 4:43–44: "But his servant said, 'How can I set this before a hundred people?' So he repeated, 'Give it to the people and let them eat, for thus says the Lord, "They shall eat and have some left."' He set it before them, they ate, and had some left, according to the word of the Lord."

29. In contrast to the Synoptic accounts, cf. John 6:14: "When the people saw the sign that he had done, they began to say, 'This is indeed the prophet who is to come into the world.'"

30. Cf. Robert M. Grant, "The Problem of Miraculous Feedings in the Graeco-Roman World," *Protocol of the Forty-Second Colloquy: 14 March 1982* (Berkeley, Calif.: Center for Hermeneutical Studies, 1982).

31. Cf. John 6:11, where the narrator uses the verb *eucharisteō* rather than *eulogeō*.

One notices here an action of prayer without an explicit reference to prayer. It is especially interesting that elsewhere in the Synoptic Gospels Jesus teaches the disciples to pray for daily bread or bread for tomorrow (Matt 6:11 || Luke 11:3). Early Christian tradition also features prayer action in relation to bread in the stories and tradition of the Last Supper (Mark 14:22 || Matt 26:26 || Luke 22:19).[32] This means that prayer is regularly present with daily food, with commemorative food, and with miraculous food.[33]

The accounts of the feeding of the four thousand in Mark 8:1–10 || Matt 15:32–39 (no parallel in Luke) attribute speech to Jesus that elaborates Jesus' prophetic reasoning about his compassion for the people. The Markan version proceeds as follows:

> **Case:** He called his disciples and said to them, "I have compassion for the crowd,
> **Rule:** because they have been with me now for three days and have nothing to eat.
> **Result:** If I send them away hungry to their homes, they will faint on the way—and some of them have come from a great distance."[34]

This Case/Rule/Result sequence in speech attributed to Jesus sets the stage for dialogue between Jesus and his disciples concerning how to get food for the people. When Jesus tells his disciples to get food for this large group of people, they respond with incredulity at his statement. This leads to the presentation of seven loaves and a few small fish (Mark 8:5, 7 || Matt 15:36), Jesus' action of prayer with the food, and the miraculous multiplication of the food, signified by the baskets filled with pieces after everyone has eaten.

Again, there is no reference to amazement, the identity of Jesus, or praise to the God of Israel at the conclusion of the Synoptic accounts of Jesus' miraculous feeding of five thousand and four thousand people with small amounts of food in the wilderness. As attributed speech in the accounts moves the story forward, it presents prophetic reasoning about Jesus' compassion on the people. The accounts feature prayer action by Jesus, without

---

32. Cf. 1 Cor 11:24.
33. Cf. John 6:11.
34. Cf. Matt 15:32.

any attribution of words of prayer to Jesus, and there is no mention of faith in the accounts either in the narration or on the lips of Jesus.

Many additional miracle stories feature the presence of priestly rhetorolect. These stories, however, feature unclean spirits or demons as the cause of the illness that Jesus encounters. It is necessary, therefore, to turn now to summaries and stories that feature unclean spirits and demons.

4. Apocalyptic Rhetorolect Energizes Early Christian Miracle Narration

Early Christian miracle discourse moves decisively beyond biblical prophetic rhetorolect when it features unclean spirits and demons in challenge-riposte with Jesus. Demons, both positive and negative, were a widespread phenomenon in Mediterranean society and culture. Jesus' miraculous exorcism of a negative demon, therefore, could simply be internal to Mediterranean miracle rhetorolect. In early Christianity, however, there are only negative demons, although there are positive and negative spirits. The perception in early Christian tradition that all demons are negative appears to be the result of the conceptual domain of Jewish apocalyptic literature and discourse. New Testament literature always refers to demons as evil and regularly blends demons conceptually with "unclean spirits."[35] This early Christian perception of demons as equivalent to unclean spirits has a close relation to the reasoning in passages in apocalyptic literature like 1 Enoch 8:2; 15:6–12; and Jubilees 5:2–3, 10; 7:20–21; 10:5, 8; 11:4; 50:5. It appears that most stories in the Synoptic Gospels that refer to demons and unclean spirits do so as a result of the conceptual domain of apocalyptic rhetorolect in the background.

The narrational summary of Jesus' miracles in Luke 6:17–19, in contrast to the summaries discussed in the previous sections, exhibits the presence of unclean spirits. When Jesus comes down from the mountain with his twelve "apostles" (v. 13), he stands on a level place (v. 17). The pictorial narration describes Jesus as surrounded by a crowd of his disciples and a huge throng of people who have come both to hear him and to be healed of their diseases (v. 17). This Case immediately evokes a Result that "those who were troubled [*enochloumenoi*] with unclean spirits were

---

35. Vernon K. Robbins, "The Intertexture of Apocalyptic Discourse in the Gospel of Mark," in *The Intertexture of Apocalyptic Discourse in the New Testament* (ed. Duane F. Watson; SBLSymS 14; Atlanta: Society of Biblical Literature, 2002), 22–28.

cured" (v. 18). There is no sure way to know that the reference to unclean spirits is the result of the conceptual domain of apocalyptic literature and reasoning, but it probably is. The verb "to be troubled" (*enochleō*) was commonly used to mean simply that someone was sick (Gen 48:1; 1 Sam 19:14; 30:13). The perception that "unclean spirits" caused the sickness is probably to be attributed to the presence of apocalyptic reasoning like one sees in 1 Enoch 15:8–12 and Jubilees 10:6, 10–12. In the summary, in Luke the Result becomes a Case that evokes another Result, namely, that "all the crowd sought to touch him" (6:19). At this point the narration blends argumentation with pictorial description. Instead of the crowd's seeking to touch Jesus simply evoking a Result that "those who touched him were healed," it evokes a Rule/Result: "For power [*dynamis*] came forth from him and healed them all" (6:19). The sequence is as follows:

Case: Jesus was surrounded by disciples and other people who came to hear him and be healed.
Result/Case: Those troubled with unclean spirits were healed.
Result/Case: Therefore, all the crowd sought to touch him.
Rule/Result: For power came forth from him and healed them all.

A display of the sequence of reasoning reveals a Result that is presupposed in the Rule at the end of the pictorial narration. The natural movement of inductive reasoning is from Cases to Results to Rules. In this instance, the reasoning moves to the Rule that "power in Jesus" heals by coming forth from Jesus' body. This can be either an additional or an alternative assertion to a statement about Jesus' identity. The shift to a discussion of "power" in Jesus' body encourages a search to understand the source of the power. Since the discourse in Luke 6:17–19 does not focus the search, multiple answers (candidate inferences)[36] could emerge as possibilities: from God ("heaven," to which Jesus looks in Mark 7:34); from prophetic authority like Elijah's and Elisha's (which appears to be very close to "from God" in early Christian tradition); from wisdom (perhaps like Solomon's); from Beelzebul (who rules over unclean spirits in apocalyptic rhetorolect);

---

36. See Dedre Gentner, Keith J. Holyoak, and Boicho N. Kokinov, eds., *The Analogical Mind: Perspectives from Cognitive Science* (Cambridge: MIT Press, 2001), 24–25, 38–40, 50–51, 128, 219, 237–38, 289, 307, 337, 372. Cf. "inference schemas" in Seana Coulson, *Semantic Leaps: Frame-Shifting and Conceptual Blending in Meaning Construction* (Cambridge: Cambridge University Press, 2001), 177–78.

or from being John the Baptist raised from the dead. Early Christian narration containing attributed speech raises these possibilities and negotiates them in various ways. The narrational summaries without attributed speech in them do not raise these various possibilities and negotiate them.

A miracle summary featuring demons who are able to speak occurs in Mark 1:32–34, immediately after the healing of Simon's mother-in-law in the Markan account. That evening, at sundown (thus at the beginning of a new day), people bring sick and demonized people to the house; and "the whole city" gathers around the door (vv. 32–33). In response to these actions, Jesus heals those who are sick and casts out many demons (v. 34). The description of the actions of the people is so dominant that it implies the Rule "because they (the people) knew he could and would heal them." The people's action becomes the Case, and Jesus' healing of the afflicted people is the Result of the people's actions. In this instance, however, the narration becomes argumentative, presenting a Case that Jesus "would not permit the demons to speak" supported by a Rule (rationale) that "they knew him" (v. 34). The end of this narrational account, therefore, introduces a conceptual domain featuring "demons," rather than the conceptual network of "the God of Israel," like that present in Matt 15:31, discussed in the previous section.

Mark 1:34, like Matt 15:31, is enthymematic rather than explicitly argumentative, because it evokes social and cultural reasoning without specifically focusing on it. Who do the demons think Jesus is? How do the demons know who Jesus is? Why are demons able to know who Jesus is when people seem not to know? How did Jesus know that the demons knew who he was? Why doesn't Jesus want the people to hear what the demons say about Jesus? If the demons know who Jesus is, Jesus should want people to hear their "testimony" to him, shouldn't he? Like the story of Jesus' healing of people on the mountain in Matt 15:29–31, this story embeds enthymematic discourse in pictorial narration. In this instance, however, the argumentation focuses on challenge-riposte between Jesus and demons rather than some kind of relationship between Jesus and the God of Israel.[37] But who are demons, that they can speak to Jesus and Jesus can speak to them?

---

37. Malina, *New Testament World*, 34–44; Robbins, *Exploring the Texture of Texts*, 80–82.

The portrayal of the demons in this summary surely introduces the conceptual domain of apocalyptic reasoning when it introduces the topos of "knowing" the identity of Jesus. This "knowledge" of Jesus is likely to be part of a conceptual system in which Jesus is aligned with divine powers on the side of the God of Israel versus demonic powers like those described in 1 Enoch and Jubilees. The narration does not state who the demons "know" Jesus to be. A still more advanced step of argumentation would be for the (reliable) narrator to "reveal" to the narratee who Jesus is. This additional argumentative step will appear in summaries discussed below. When we come to them, it will be obvious that they move beyond the basic enthymematic reasoning present in Mark 1:32–34, which simply points to a conceptual domain of apocalyptic reasoning in the background as it portrays demons in challenge-riposte with Jesus without asserting who the demons "know" Jesus to be.

From a rhetorical perspective, then, Mark 1:32–34 embeds an enthymematic moment concerning the identity of Jesus in pictorial narration that blends apocalyptic conceptuality with the topos of healing an afflicted body. This moment points to the conceptual domain of early Christian apocalyptic rhetorolect without asserting who the demons "know" Jesus to be. There is only narration in Mark 1:32–34, with no attributed speech. Like other passages discussed above, people recognize that Jesus is a healer. In contrast to Matt 15:31, which introduces a double-scope network of reasoning about "the God of Israel" in the context of Jesus' healings, Mark 1:32–34 presents a double-scope network that features "agents of affliction" in the personage of "demons" from the domain of apocalyptic reasoning over against Jesus as an "agent of healing." The narration in Mark 1:32–34 does not mention God nor does it mention faith. Instead, it presents demons who "know" the identity of Jesus and are able to speak so that people can hear them. One can readily anticipate that the two double-scope networks of (1) Jesus and the God of Israel and (2) Jesus and demons could blend together in various ways to form multiple-scope networks of reasoning.[38] The presence of the conceptual network of the God of Israel, on the one hand, could invite various ways of reasoning about the relation of both Jesus and God to the people in the setting of the miraculous healings. The presence of the conceptual domain

---

38. For multiple-scope networks, see Fauconnier and Turner, *The Way We Think*, 279–98.

of apocalyptic, on the other hand, may not only introduce demons as personal agents of affliction, but it may also introduce different relationships between God and Jesus, between God and the people, and among God, Jesus, and yet other agents of evil (like Satan or Beelzebul) in the context of miraculous deeds that occur in the context of Jesus' activities.

Sometimes in the Synoptic Gospels, attributed speech in miracle discourse focuses on Jesus' identity in a context where unclean spirits/demons assert that they know who Jesus is. In other words, in certain instances Synoptic Gospel discourse moves beyond pictorial narration which simply asserts that demons knew who Jesus was to a presentation of what the demons asserted. Mark 3:7–12 intertwines attributed speech (v. 11) that evokes a Rule that the unclean spirits knew who Jesus was (cf. 1:34) with a series of intermingled Case/Result sequences and a Rule about the possibility that the crowd might crush him (v. 9):

1. **Case:** Jesus withdrew with his disciples to the sea,
Result: and a great multitude from Galilee followed (v. 7).

2. **Case:** People from Judea and Jerusalem and Idumea and from beyond the Jordan and from about Tyre and Sidon a great multitude heard all that he did,
Result: and they came to him (vv. 7–8).

3. **Case:** Jesus healed many,
Result/Case: so that all who had diseases pressed upon him to touch him (v. 10).
Result: He told his disciples to have a boat ready for him,
Rule: because of the crowd, lest they should crush him (v. 9).

4. **Case:** Whenever the unclean spirits beheld him, they fell down before him and cried out, "You are the Son of God" (v. 11).
Result: And he strictly ordered them not to make him known (v. 12).

The attributed speech in this narrational summary focuses directly on the identity of Jesus. The narrator does not interpret the speech of the demons in any way. Rather, the narration leaves the narratee to decide exactly what the title "Son of God" implies. The answer clearly lies in the conceptual network of "the God of Israel." Somehow Jesus is aligned with the God of Israel against unclean spirits. The unclean spirits even fall down before Jesus in a posture that may imply the presence of priestly rhetorolect. Unclean spirits are not simply obedient to his command, as wisdom and prophetic rhetorolect assert. Rather, the unclean spirits adopt a position of honoring Jesus in a manner characteristic of worship.

The most fully developed story focusing on the identity of Jesus and containing no reference to faith is the account of the Gerasene Demoniac in Mark 5:1–20 and its parallels in Matt 8:28–34 || Luke 8:26–39. The account in Mark and Luke contains three reasons or explanations that support assertions in the story. The Matthean account multiplies the demoniac person to two people and presents the story without the three reasons or explanations. The approach here will focus on the Markan and Lukan accounts, which contain the supporting reasons or explanations.

The opening-middle-closing texture of the Markan and Lukan accounts of the Gerasene demoniac features Jesus and the demoniac in the opening and closing (Mark 5:1–13, 18–20; Luke 8:26–33, 38–39) and swineherds in the middle (Mark 5:14–17; Luke 8:34–37). In this context, the narrational texture of the accounts alternates between picturesque action (Mark 5:1–6, 13–18; Luke 8:26–27, 29, 32–38) and challenge-riposte dialogue (Mark 5:7–12; Luke 8:28, 30) as it progresses toward speech by Jesus at the end that produces a good form of speech in the healed man (Mark 5:19–20; Luke 8:39).[39]

The Markan account presents three explanations or reasons in the first half of the story (5:1–9) that explain the man's dwelling among the tombs (vv. 4–5), the demoniac's challenging of Jesus by crying out his name as "Jesus, Son of the Most High God" (v. 8), and the name "Legion" for the demon in the man (v. 9). In the last half (5:10–20), the Markan account presents a chain of Cases and Results:

1. **Case:** Jesus gave permission to the unclean spirits to enter the swine;
2. **Result/Case:** the unclean spirits entered the swine and the herd rushed down the hill and drowned in the sea (v. 13).
3. **Result/Case:** The swineherders ran off and told the people in the surrounding city and country;

---

39. For progressive and narrational texture, see Robbins, *Exploring the Texture of Texts*, 9–19.

4. **Result/Case:** the people came to see what had happened (v. 14).
5. **Result/Case:** the people saw the healed demoniac;
6. **Result/Case:** the people became afraid (v. 15).
7. **Result/Case:** The people who had seen the event reported it to the people who came (v. 16).
8. **Result/Case:** everyone began to ask Jesus to leave their neighborhood (v. 17).
9. **Result/Case:** As Jesus began to leave, the healed man begged to go along with Jesus (v. 18).
10. **Result/Case:** Jesus refused the man and told him to go home and tell them what the Lord has done for him (v. 19).
11. **Result/Case:** The man went throughout the Decapolis and proclaimed what Jesus did for him;
12. **Result:** all the people were amazed (v. 20).

The Lukan account presents the same features with slight variations.[40]

The overall rhetorical effect of this story, of course, is a depiction of Jesus with tremendous power to confront violent unclean spirits directly and to enact a means to destroy them. As in the narrational summary above, the man with the unclean spirit adopts a position of worshiping Jesus (Mark 5:6; Luke 8:28). The three explanations or reasons give argumentative support to the dramatic pictorial narration of the violence and help to create a sharp contrast between the presence of violence from the beginning through the healing process (Mark 5:1–14; Luke 8:26–34) and the portrayal of the man "sitting, clothed and in his right mind" after the healing (Mark 5:15; Luke 8:35). The first part of the story features the identity of Jesus as "Son of the Most High God" and the identity of the man as "Legion," since he had many demons in him. Throughout all of this, we remind ourselves again, there is no mention of faith or belief. Perhaps the most noticeable rhetorical shift occurs at the end of the story: (a) Jesus tells the man to proclaim how much God has done for him; (b) the man goes forth and tells people how much Jesus did for him. The inductive rhetorical force of the story lies in the possessed man's identification of Jesus' relation to God prior to his healing (Mark 5:7; Luke 8:28) and his

---

40. Perhaps most important, the Lukan account groups the three explanations or reasons together in the dialogue between Jesus and the demoniac (8:29–30).

redirection of Jesus' command at the end of the story so the credit for the healing focuses on Jesus rather than God (Mark 5:19–20; Luke 8:39).

5. Apocalyptic Rhetorolect Blends with Prophetic Rhetorolect in Synoptic Miracle Stories

In certain instances, early Christian discourse blends prophetic rhetorolect with apocalyptically energized miracle rhetorolect. This occurs in Matt 8:16–17:

> **Case:** That evening they brought to him many who were possessed with demons;
> **Result:** and he cast out the spirits with a word, and healed all who were sick (v. 16).
> **Rule:** This was to fulfill what was spoken by the prophet Isaiah, "He took our infirmities and bore our diseases" (v. 17).

In this instance, the narration in verse 17 attributes authoritative testimony about Jesus' identity to the prophet Isaiah. In Matthew's account, Isaiah, rather than demons or people who observe the miraculous events, explains the identity of Jesus. This is a direct alternative to Mark 1:34, where the narrative asserts that the demons knew who Jesus was. Matthew, in contrast to Mark, authoritatively grounds Jesus' healing activity in prophetic rhetorolect through the voice of "Isaiah the prophet." In other words, rather than bringing into the foreground the apocalyptic conceptual domain where agents of affliction confront Jesus as the agent of healing, this Matthean discourse pushes apocalyptically energized miracle rhetorolect into the background to feature prophetic rhetorolect. The result is to move the discourse toward the conceptual arena of the God of Israel and away from a conceptual arena that focuses on unclean spirits, demons, and possibly other agents of evil in the world.

Luke 4:40–41 presents yet another alternative to Mark 1:32–34 and Matt 8:16–17. The Lukan summary allows the demons to identify Jesus, but then the narrator interprets what the demons' identification means:

> **Case:** Now when the sun was setting, all those who had any that were sick with various diseases brought them to him;
> **Result/Case:** and he laid his hands on every one of them and healed them (v. 40).

> **Result/Case:** And demons also came out of many, crying, "You are the Son of God!"
> **Contrary Result:** But he rebuked them, and would not allow them to speak,
> **Rule:** because they knew that he was the Messiah (v. 41).

In this Lukan summary, speech attributed to the demons identifies Jesus as the Son of God. The narrator then interprets the speech of the demons as evidence that they knew Jesus was the Messiah. This Lukan discourse, then, directs the demons' identification of Jesus as the Son of God toward prophetic rhetorolect that features the coming of an anointed one who will oversee God's kingdom on earth. In this instance, the narrator allows the demons to speak but then "speaks over" the demons with a statement that brings prophetic rhetorolect into the foreground as the summary closes.

The two miracle summaries discussed above show how early Christian discourse could blend apocalyptically energized miracle rhetorolect with the conceptual domain of the kingdom, to whom the God of Israel sent the prophets to confront people and give promises for renewal. As early Christians blended apocalyptically energized miracle rhetorolect with prophetic rhetorolect, they introduced a specially honed form of wisdom rhetorolect as a "debate arena."[41] This "wisdom" arena replaced confrontation between Jesus and unclean spirits or demons with debate between Jesus and scribes, Pharisees, and chief priests about the nature, propriety, and authority to heal. It is important, then, to turn to miracle summaries and stories that blend early Christian wisdom rhetorolect with prophetically and apocalyptically energized miracle rhetorolect.

6. Wisdom Rhetorolect Blends with Apocalyptic, Prophetic, and Priestly Rhetorolect in Synoptic Miracle Stories

We have seen above how early Christian discourse blends prophetic, priestly, and apocalyptic rhetorolect with miracle rhetorolect. In early Christian discourse, "multiply blended" miracle discourse functions as an "emergent blend structure"[42] in which early Christian wisdom rhetorolect

---

41. I am grateful to L. Gregory Bloomquist for insight into debate arenas in the rhetorolects.
42. Fauconnier and Turner, *The Way We Think*, 42–50.

creates ever-widening networks of reasoning about Jesus as a miracle worker. In some instances, wisdom rhetorolect only stands implicitly in the background. The miracle summary in Matt 4:23–25 presents Jesus as going throughout Galilee teaching in the synagogues, proclaiming the good news of the kingdom, and curing every disease and sickness among the people (a Case: v. 23). This sentence blends wisdom, prophetic, and miracle discourse as it opens a summary of Jesus' activity. When the narration describes Jesus as teaching, it evokes wisdom rhetorolect. When it describes Jesus as proclaiming the kingdom, it evokes prophetic rhetorolect. This passage, then, blends wisdom, prophetic, and miracle rhetorolect as it presents Jesus as a teacher, a prophet, and a healer. When Jesus teaches, speaks prophetically, and heals, his fame spreads throughout all Syria (the Result: v. 24a). This Result (Jesus' fame spreading) in turn becomes a Case that evokes a Result: they bring to him all the sick, those who were afflicted by various diseases and pains, demoniacs, epileptics, and paralytics (v. 24b). Again this Result becomes a Case that evokes yet another Result: Jesus cures them (v. 24c). Still once again, this Result becomes a Case that evokes a Result. In this instance, however, the result is that great crowds follow Jesus from Galilee, the Decapolis, Jerusalem, Judea, and from beyond the Jordan (v. 25).

The shift in the final Result suggests a sequence of persuasion that moves from being attracted to Jesus because he can heal to being persuaded that Jesus is a person worth following so that one may see all he does and says. The "following" in the closing of the sequence calls special attention to the opening, where Jesus is not only a healer but also a teacher and a prophet.[43] When Jesus teaches in synagogues, preaches about the kingdom, and heals people of every kind of affliction, "the God of Israel" is implicitly in the background of Jesus' speech and actions. But the blending and the background occur implicitly, rather than explicitly, in this narration, and it occurs without the aid of attributed speech. Every reason or rationale in the narration is a Case rather than a Rule, as is characteristic of inductive miracle rhetorolect. In other words, it presents no Rule like, "because God's power was in Jesus to heal" or "because Jesus was God's Son." Argumentation lies in a linear progression of narrational picturing (rhetography) that contains no discursive argumentation (rhetology).

---

43. For opening-middle-closing texture, see Robbins, *Exploring the Texture of Texts*, 19–21; idem, *Tapestry of Early Christian Discourse*, 50–53.

Jesus' fame spreads because of his teaching, preaching, and healing (a Case); people bring sick people to Jesus because his fame spreads (a Case), and large crowds of people follow Jesus because he teaches, preaches, and heals sick people. Conceptually, the people's following of Jesus in the closing is likely to be as highly influenced by Jesus' teaching and prophetic speaking as by his miraculous cure of afflicted people. The narration, however, emphasizes actions by Jesus, and this produces inductive, rather than deductive, argumentation. All of the activities blend together and produce a result of large crowds following Jesus.

In the narrational presentation of Jesus as teacher, prophet, and healer in Matt 4:23–25, there is no specific reference to God, no portrayal of demons in challenge-riposte with Jesus, and no reference to faith. The conceptual network of "the God of Israel" clearly seems to stand in the background both of Jesus' "teaching in their synagogues" and of Jesus' "preaching the gospel of the kingdom." Apocalyptic rhetorolect probably stands implicitly in the background with the reference to "demonized people" in verse 24. Thus the pictorial narration presents a blend of wisdom, prophetic, miracle, and perhaps apocalyptic domains of meaning in early Christian discourse. In all of this, however, the "argumentation" occurs strictly through rhetography, picturing of the people bringing sick people to Jesus and following him. The narration does not move beyond "picturing" the people (rhetography) into "inner reasoning" by the people, by Jesus, or by the narrator (rhetology). The narration simply shows a picture of the people bringing sick people to Jesus and then following him, rather than presenting one or more argumentative reasons, like "because they had faith," for their following of Jesus.

Matt 20:29–34, which features two blind men who are healed by Jesus, ends with a Result that the men follow Jesus. The story has a close relation to Mark 10:46–52 || Luke 18:35–43, which feature only one blind man, except that the topos of "faith" is not present in the Matthean story. Jesus speaks only once in the story, asking the men, "What do you want me to do for you?" (v. 32). In contrast, the men speak three times. The first two times, the men cry out, "Have mercy on us, Lord, Son of David!" (vv. 30–31).[44] The third time they speak, they say, "Lord, let our eyes be opened" (v. 33). The rest of the story is narration:

---

44. Some manuscripts either put "Lord" first or omit "Lord" from the first cry in v. 30.

Result/Case: Moved with compassion, Jesus touched their eyes.
Result/Case: Immediately they regained their sight.
Result: And they followed him (v. 34).

This story ends without any statement about the identity of Jesus, about the means by which the miracle occurred, about God, or about faith. The final Result is that the two men follow Jesus. The story does not, however, feature only narration. The blind men introduce the topoi of "mercy" and "Son of David" through their repetitive speech, and the narration afterward introduces the topos of Jesus' "compassion." The healing of blindness, which is a repeated emphasis in Isa 29:18; 35:5; 42:7, 18, points to a background of prophetic rhetorolect for Jesus' miracle activity in this story. The constellation of "mercy," "Son of David," and Jesus' "being moved with compassion" may also point in this same direction, though there is not space here to test this presupposition. The successful exchange of information in Jesus' question and the answer of the blind men points implicitly, but not profoundly, to wisdom rhetorolect. The end result of this blend of miracle, prophetic, and possibly wisdom rhetorolect is that the two men follow Jesus, which is likely to imply some level of discipleship.

The discipleship that may be implied at the end of the two stories above becomes explicit in Luke 5:1–11. In this story, Simon, James, and John become disciples of Jesus after experiencing a miraculous catch of fish as a result of Jesus' intervention into their daily activity. There is no direct focus on the transformation of an afflicted body in this story. An overall focus on "redeeming" a body so it functions dynamically in God's world, however, is clearly present in the story. An important feature of the story is the sequence involving Peter's response to the miracle of the large catch of fish:

Result/Case: But when Simon Peter saw it, he fell down at Jesus' knees, saying,
Result: "Go away from me, Lord,
Case: for I am a sinful man" (v. 8).
Rule: For he and all who were with him were amazed at the catch of fish that they had taken; and so also were James and John, sons of Zebedee, who were partners with Simon (vv. 9–10a).
Result/Case: Then Jesus said to Simon,
  Contrary Result: "Do not be afraid;
  Contrary Case: from now on you will be catching people" (v. 10b).

Result: When they had brought their boats to shore, they left everything and followed him (v. 11).

This story, like the others above, contains no reference to faith. Rather, it features "immediate confession" of unworthiness by Simon. Jesus responds to Simon's action, which emerges out of laudable attributes of character, with an appeal to Simon not to be afraid and a pronouncement that from now on he will be catching people. Jesus' pronouncement to Peter functions like a healing statement. Peter is changed from a person whose body is dominated with sin and fear into a person who "leaves everything and follows Jesus." In this story, then, discipleship is the result of a miraculous transformation of a person with laudable attributes of character in a context of miracle and open confessional statement. Simon's confession of sin introduces a dimension of priestly rhetorolect into a miracle story in which the final result of discipleship points to wisdom rhetorolect. This blending of miracle, priestly, and wisdom rhetorolect ends with a focus on people who move into a special relationship to Jesus, rather than a focus on Jesus' identity, on the God of Israel, or on "faith" as something that made the events in the story occur.

Luke 7:18-23 || Matt 11:2-6 (Q), in contrast to Matt 4:23-25, contains a sequence of attributed statements that refer to Jesus' performance of miraculous healings. In this instance, wisdom rhetorolect moves into the foreground of the presentation as a result of people bringing an inquiry to Jesus and Jesus' response to the inquiry. In other instances we will see below, wisdom rhetorolect features people entering into debate with Jesus rather than simply asking him a question. Luke 7:18-23 blends wisdom and prophetic rhetorolect as disciples of John come to Jesus asking about his identity. Jesus' answer dynamically blends miracle and prophetic rhetorolect as it presents a series of Cases without stating any clearly defined inference on the basis of them.

Case: John the Baptist heard[45] that Jesus was performing miraculous deeds.
Result/Case: John told his disciples to go to Jesus and say,
[Rule] "Are you he who is to come, or shall we look for another?" (Luke 7:19 || Matt 11:3).

---

45. From his disciples: Luke 7:18 (Matthew leaves the source unspecified); while he was in prison: Matt 11:2 (Luke leaves the place unspecified).

Result/Case: John's disciples went to Jesus and asked him this question, in a context where Jesus was curing many people of diseases, plagues, evil spirits, and blindness (Luke 7:21).
Result/Case: Jesus said, "Go and tell John what you have seen and heard: the blind receive their sight, the lame walk, lepers are cleansed, the deaf hear, the dead are raised up, and the poor have good news preached to them. And blessed is the one who takes no offense at me" (Luke 7:22-23 || Matt 11:4-6).

The opening features miracle rhetorolect in narrational form. Having received information about Jesus' miracle activity, John tells his disciples to ask Jesus about a topic concerning prophetic rhetorolect. Thus the opening seeks an answer about Jesus' miraculous deeds in a rhetorolect that features God as one who selects, calls, and sends people to perform functions related to God's kingdom on earth. Jesus answers the question of John's disciples with a series of Cases of miraculous deeds that ends with "preaching good news to the poor," which is a prophetic activity. The discourse has the rhetorical effect of having Jesus agree, through the medium of a rehearsal of Cases, with the Rule (premise) that "he is the one to come." The moment is, however, enthymematic. The narration does not explicitly state the Rule. Rather, it places the "potential" Rule in the form of a question on the lips of John's disciples.

The Hebrew Bible attributes to Isaiah most of the speech that Luke 7:22-23 || Matt 11:4-6 attributes to Jesus in this passage: the blind receive their sight (Isa 29:18; 35:5; 42:7, 18); the lame walk (35:6); the deaf hear (29:18; 35:5; 42:18); the dead are raised (26:19); and the poor have good news brought to them (61:1). Matthew and Luke (Q) do not attribute this speech to Isaiah, however, but to Jesus. In other words, Jesus answers a question concerning his identity with a series of Cases that thoroughly blends miracle rhetorolect with prophetic speech from Isaiah. About the only Case Jesus' speech could include from Isaiah, which it does not, is "making the dumb speak" (Isa 35:6). Jesus' speech adds an item that the Hebrew Bible attributes to Elisha rather than to Isaiah: "the lepers are cleansed" (2 Kgs 5:1–14). It is also important that "the dead are raised" is supported by a Case attributed to Elijah in 1 Kgs 17:17–24 in addition to the statement in Isa 26:19. Thus this early Christian prophetic-miracle rhetorolect is related both to tradition about Isaiah and tradition about Elijah and Elisha.

As Matthean and Lukan discourse blend miracle and prophetic rhetorolect enthymematically, they produce early Christian wisdom rhetorolect. The topic of Jesus' identity becomes a matter of early Christian wisdom as disciples of John ask Jesus a question that he answers with reference to actions that blend the conceptual domains of miracle and prophetic rhetorolect together. Jesus' blessing at the end of his statement further evokes the discourse of a prophet as it encourages the hearer not to reject either the message that is heard or the person to whom the message is attributed.

The presence of wisdom rhetorolect in Luke 7:18–23 is clear from the questions toward which the passage points but leaves unanswered. Is Jesus saying he is "the prophet" who is to come? Is Jesus saying he is someone greater than the prophets? Is there a better term than "prophet" for him? In this passage, Jesus is an authoritative witness "to himself" through his rehearsal and enactment of Cases. He noticeably leaves the Rule (the premise concerning who he is) unstated, however, and thus he leaves his answer in a rhetorically enthymematic form. The hearer must "infer" who Jesus is on the basis of Cases (inductive speech). But the topic of Jesus' identity has been "nurtured" with inner reasoning by a series of questions and answers. In contrast to other passages discussed above, the scene is set up as a question-and-answer sequence, which introduces the topic of Jesus' identity as an issue in early Christian wisdom rhetorolect. Once again, in a context where Jesus' identity is at issue, there is no explicit discussion of "faith." There is, however, an explicit issue of who one "thinks" or perhaps "believes" Jesus to be. This implicit "conviction" or "belief" is not focused primarily on receiving the benefits of Jesus' actions, as miracle rhetorolect tends to be, but on a question-and-answer sequence that explores the identity of Jesus. Thus it moves beyond the narrational base of miracle rhetorolect into the sphere of "inner reasoning" characteristic of wisdom rhetorolect.

Matthew 11:20–24 and Luke 10:11b–16 refer to miracles in a context of the prophetic topos of repentance. Yet wisdom rhetorolect also plays a role in Jesus' speech. Rather than viewing this material from the perspective of Q material, it will be discussed here from the perspective of Matthew and Luke respectively. Matt 11:20–24 opens with editorial comment:

Case: Then he began to reproach the cities in which most of his deeds of power had been done,
Rule: because they did not repent (v. 20).

The prophetic topos of "repentance," introduced as a rationale for Jesus' "reproach" (*oneidizein*) of the cities, sets the stage for Jesus' statements that follow. Adopting the form of "Woe" pronouncement, Jesus says that Chorazin, Bethsaida, and Capernaum will receive curses rather than blessings from God, because they did not repent in the context of mighty works done in their midst. In contrast, Tyre and Sidon (Gentile cities) would have repented long ago. Prophetic rhetorolect blends with apocalyptic rhetorolect as Jesus asks Capernaum:

Case: Will you be exalted to heaven? No, you will be brought down to Hades.
Rule: For if the deeds of power done in you had been done in Sodom, it would have remained until this day.
Case: But I tell you that on the day of judgment it will be more tolerable for the land of Sodom than for you (vv. 23–24).

The reasoning in this passage is that Jesus' performance of deeds of power should result in people's repentance. The presupposition is that if people repent in the context of the miraculous deeds, they will be blessed. If they do not, they will be cursed. The concept of curse moves to an apocalyptic picture of the day of judgment, when people will either be exalted to heaven or cast down to Hades. Thus Jesus' sayings blend miracle rhetorolect with prophetic and apocalyptic rhetorolect. This blend of miracle, prophetic, and apocalyptic rhetorolect, then, moves beyond the topos of "taking offense [*skandalisthēi*] at Jesus" (Luke 7: 23 || Matt 11:6) to "repenting" (*metenoēsan*) in the context of Jesus' deeds of power. While being scandalized keeps the focus on Jesus as a miracle worker, repenting moves the focus to movement "within the inner mind" of the person who observes the miraculous deeds. The topos of repentance, then, stands at the interface of prophetic and wisdom rhetorolect. Matthew 11:20–24 blends miracle, prophetic, and apocalyptic rhetorolect in a manner than moves inwardly in its cognition, rather than outwardly to the identity of Jesus, to God, or to demons and their network of power. Indeed, Matt 11:25–30 continues with the topic of "things hidden from the wise and intelligent" but revealed to infants. In Matt 11:20–24, then, we see a movement of miracle rhetorolect toward "inner processes" of redemption and renewal that create an "emergent structure" that invites wisdom rhetorolect dynamically into miracle rhetorolect.

Luke 10:11b–16 also blends miracle, prophetic, and apocalyptic rhetorolect, but in a slightly different way from Matt 11:20–24. Luke 10:11b, occurring in the midst of Jesus' instructions to the Seventy, presents Jesus asserting:

> **Case:** You know (*ginōskete*) this: the kingdom of God has come near.
> **Result:** I tell you, on that day it will be more tolerable for Sodom than for that town [that does not welcome you: 10:10].

These verses introduce a blend of wisdom, prophetic, and apocalyptic rhetorolect prior to the statement that refers to Jesus' deeds of power in 10:13. Thus they establish the blended frame into which Jesus' further statements blends miracle rhetorolect:

> **Case:** Woe to you, Chorazin! Woe to you, Bethsaida!
> **Rule:** For if the deeds of power done in you had been done in Tyre and Sidon, they would have repented long ago, sitting in sackcloth and ashes.
> **Case:** But at the judgment it will be more tolerable for Tyre and Sidon than for you (Luke 10:13–14).

In this instance, the assertion that Jesus' deeds of power should have resulted in repentance occurs only once, in the middle of Jesus' statement, rather than in narration at the beginning and then in speech of Jesus, as it does in Matt 11:20–21. The single reference to Jesus' deeds of power in Luke 10:13 contributes to a movement through prophetic, apocalyptic, and miracle rhetorolect to wisdom rhetorolect focused on the topos of "rejection":

> **Case:** Whoever listens to you listens to me,
> **Contrary Case:** and whoever rejects you rejects me,
> **Contrary Result:** and whoever rejects me rejects the one who sent me.

This tripartite saying of Jesus is, on the one hand, clearly early Christian wisdom rhetorolect. In the context of "knowing" that the kingdom of God has come near (10:11), Jesus transmits to the Seventy wisdom regarding being listened to and rejected. On the other hand, this wisdom blends the realms of discipleship, Christology, and theology. "Disciples" who accept Jesus' exhortation to "Go on your way" (10:3) will be listened to by some and rejected by others (10:16). Jesus teaches these "disciples" that people's acceptance or rejection of them is also an acceptance or rejection of Jesus as prophet, apocalyptic seer, and miracle worker. The final statement in the saying, however, moves beyond the Seventy and Jesus to the conceptual network of God's activity. The God of Israel, who brings the kingdom of God near and who calls and empowers Jesus to heal and to speak prophetic and apocalyptic wisdom, is the one whom people ultimately reject, if they reject those whom Jesus sends out as "laborers into his harvest" (10:2). This is early Christian wisdom, which contains prophetic, apocalyptic, and miracle rhetorolect thoroughly blended into its reasoning and its content. In this context, then, early Christian discourse is dynamically transforming miracle rhetorolect into wisdom rhetorolect through the media of early Christian prophetic and apocalyptic rhetorolect.

A significant number of miracle stories features "controversy" that pits the wisdom of Jesus against a range of people who take issue with his healing activity. One of the major issues is Jesus' performance of healings on the sabbath. These stories feature Jesus' wisdom as negotiating larger issues of life than "what is lawful" in the minds of Pharisees, lawyers, and chief priests. Jesus never responds to these issues of "lawfulness" by citing words from Torah. Rather, he responds with "wise sayings" that turn what otherwise might be "legal" discourse into a public "battle of wits." While Jesus always wins the argument, the narration indicates that he will not, in the end, escape the political "plans" against him. Thus, wisdom rhetorolect in these stories blends with prophetic rhetorolect in a manner that negotiates Jesus' rejection by political authorities as a judgment against those authorities rather than against Jesus himself.

The healing of the blind and lame in the temple in Matt 21:14–16 introduces controversy over Jesus' identity.[46] Again, faith is not a topic in this context:

Case: And the blind and the lame came to him in the temple,
Result/Case: and he healed them (v. 14).
Result/Case: But when the chief priests and the scribes saw the wonderful things that he did, and the children crying out in the temple, "Hosanna to the Son of David!" they were indignant (v. 15);
Result/Case: and they said to him, "Do you hear what these are saying?"
Result: And Jesus said to them, "Yes;

---

46. Cf. the focus on Jesus' identity in the healing of the lame man in John 5:1–18.

Rule: have you never read, 'Out of the mouth of babes and sucklings thou hast brought perfect praise'?" (v. 16).

In this instance, the controversy is embedded in narration that describes the reaction of people to Jesus' healing of the blind and lame people who came to Jesus in the temple. Attribution to children of praise of Jesus in the name of the Son of David introduces wisdom rhetorolect, which is grounded in the transmission of wisdom from parents to children. The topos of the children's speech, however, is internal to prophetic rhetorolect. When the chief priests and scribes confront Jesus about the children's praise of him as Son of David, he answers that he is aware of the content of their praise and articulates a premise (Rule) for the children's speech. Jesus' response to the chief priests and scribes recontextualizes the LXX form of Ps 8:2. There is no comment either in the narration or in Jesus' statement that attributes the statement to David. Rather, in the mode that appears in the Q account (Luke 7:18–23 || Matt 11:2–6) of Jesus' response to John's disciples, which was discussed above, words traditionally attributed to a personage in the Hebrew Bible are attributed to Jesus himself. The "Davidic" response defines newborn and suckling babies as those who (on the basis of un-adult-erated wisdom) speak perfect praise. Priestly rhetorolect stands in the background of the story with the presence of Jesus in the temple and with the speech of the chief priests and their scribes. Wisdom and prophetic rhetorolect blend with miracle rhetorolect as children praise Jesus in relation to the kingdom of Israel, and Jesus defends the "praise" of the children with words from the psalms of David. The story exhibits a sharp divide between the "priestly" wisdom of the chief priests and scribes and the "prophetic miracle" wisdom of Jesus. "Children," in their wisdom, respond with "perfect praise" of Jesus when he heals the blind and lame who come into the temple. Jesus replies to chief priests and scribes with a statement that defines them as either unaware or having forgotten how the psalms of David, the one who established Jerusalem as the place for God's temple, praise the speech that comes out of the mouths of newborn and suckling babies. When chief priests and scribes object to Jesus' performance of miraculous deeds of healing in the temple, they exhibit, according to the story, an absence of wisdom that children possess "naturally" from the time of their birth.

Yet another form of "wisdom" encounter occurs in Mark 3:1–6 || Matt 12:9–14 || Luke 6:6–11. In this story, Jesus heals a man with a withered hand in a synagogue. Jesus' characteristic activity in synagogues is teaching, as Luke 6:6 indicates (cf. Mark 1:21; 6:1 par.). In the context of his teaching, Jesus heals the man. When Pharisees (and "scribes" in Luke 6:7) object that Jesus is doing something "unlawful" by healing on the sabbath, priestly rhetorolect blends with wisdom rhetorolect as a result of a focus on sacred time. Instead of responding with something written in Torah, Jesus responds with "his own" wisdom: "Is it lawful on the sabbath to do good or to do evil, to save a life or to kill/destroy?" (Mark 3:4 || Luke 6:9). Matthew 12:11–12 features Jesus' response as: "Suppose one of you has only one sheep and it falls into a pit on the sabbath; will you not lay hold of it and lift it out? How much more valuable is a human being than a sheep!" Jesus does not enter into a legal debate based on what is written in the Torah. Rather, he responds with an insight based on "wisdom," people's "intelligent" actions in daily life. Like the story immediately above, this story ends with ominous conflict between the "wisdom" spoken by leaders in the context of a synagogue and the "wisdom" spoken by the one who performs miraculous deeds of healing, even on the sabbath.

Another version of the controversy between the wisdom of leaders of synagogues and the wisdom of Jesus who heals occurs in Luke 13:10–17. Again Jesus heals in a synagogue on the sabbath, but this time he heals a woman who had been bent over for eighteen years:

> **Case:** And when Jesus saw her, he called her and said to her, "Woman, you are freed from your infirmity" (v. 12).
> **Result/Case:** And he laid his hands upon her,
> **Result/Case:** and immediately she was made straight,
> **Result:** and she praised God (v. 13).

As in the stories above, there is no emphasis on faith. Also, there is no query about Jesus' identity. Rather, as soon as the woman is healed, she praises God. But this is not the end of the story. The ruler of the synagogue presents a contrary Result, which launches a controversy dialogue about healing on the sabbath:

> **Contrary Result/Case:** But the ruler of the synagogue,
>   **Rule:** indignant because Jesus had healed on the sabbath,
>   **Case:** said to the people,
>   **Rule:** "There are six days on which work ought to be done; come on those days and be healed, and not on the sabbath day" (v. 14).

> **Result/Case:** Then the Lord answered him, "You hypocrites!
> **Case:** Does not each of you on the sabbath untie his ox or his ass from the manger, and lead it away to water it? (v. 15).
> **Result:** And ought not this woman, a daughter of Abraham whom Satan bound for eighteen years, be loosed from this bond on the sabbath day?" (v. 16).
>
> **Result:** As he said this, all his adversaries were put to shame;
> **Contrary Result:** and all the people rejoiced at all the glorious things that were done by him (v. 17).

The ruler of the synagogue accuses Jesus of acting improperly on the sabbath, reciting the premise (Rule) that all healing must be done on the six days when people work, and not on the sabbath. Jesus does not counter the ruler's premise with another premise (Rule). In other words, Jesus does not counter a deductive argument with an opposite deductive argument. Also, Jesus does not cite a verse from Torah to counter the "wisdom" of the ruler of the synagogue. Rather, Jesus presents a Case of the activities of leaders of the Jewish people with their own ox or ass on the sabbath, and he draws an inductive conclusion (Result) from it. Then the narration interprets the effect of Jesus' response as "shame" for "all of Jesus' adversaries" in a context where "all the people" were celebrating all the things Jesus was doing. Malina and Rohrbaugh call attention to the manner in which Jesus identifies the woman as a legitimate member of the community—a daughter of Abraham (v. 16)—and restores her to her group. When the people respond positively to Jesus' restoration of the woman to the community in a public context where the ruler of the synagogue challenges Jesus' honor, the ruler suffers "a serious loss of face."[47] Again, there is no focus on faith in this story. The implicit controversy concerns Jesus' identity: Who is Jesus that he has the authority to perform deeds on the sabbath that are not considered appropriate by other religious authorities? Neither Jesus nor the people formulate an explicit premise (Rule) for Jesus' authority to do this. Rather, Jesus presents an inductive argument based on the activities of Jewish leaders with oxen and donkeys, and the people respond positively to it. Once again, wisdom rhetorolect becomes

---

47. Malina and Rohrbaugh, *Social-Science Commentary*, 363.

dominant in Jesus' speech, resulting in serious conflict between a leader of sacred place and time in the tradition of Israel.

Luke 14:1–6 exhibits yet another example of the function of early Christian wisdom rhetorolect in stories that feature controversy over Jesus' healing on the sabbath rather than a focus on Jesus' identity. In this instance, Jesus himself initiates a controversy with lawyers and Pharisees in the house of a ruler of the Pharisees and heals a man with dropsy as a public challenge to the premise (Rule) he presupposes they hold for judging the appropriateness of healing a person on the sabbath:

> **Case:** And Jesus spoke to the lawyers and Pharisees, saying,
> **Rule:** "Is it lawful to heal on the sabbath, or not?" (v. 3).
> **Result:** But they were silent.
> **Case with the Healed Man:** Then he took him and healed him, and let him go (v. 4).
> **Case with the lawyers and Pharisees:** And he said to them,
> **Case:** "Which of you, having a son or an ox that has fallen into a well, will not immediately pull him out on a sabbath day?" (v. 5).
> **Result:** And they could not reply to this (v. 6).

In this instance Jesus initiates a controversy by stating a premise (Rule) that he is sure the lawyers and Pharisees will consider authoritative, then healing a man with dropsy on the sabbath. The narration depicts the lawyers and Pharisees as unwilling to speak throughout the entire episode. In the house of a ruler of the Pharisees, Jesus issues a public challenge to lawyers and Pharisees that puts them in a position where the narration depicts them as either unable to speak successfully or unwilling to risk speaking in this public setting for fear of loss of face. Willi Braun has presented a detailed sociorhetorical analysis of the healing and its elaboration in Luke 14:1–24.[48] The overall controversy addresses the issue of social exclusivism at meals among the elite in Mediterranean society and inclusive fellowship among early Christian movement groups.[49] The Lukan episode negotiates the controversy with skillful wisdom rhetorolect that challenges the exclusion of the lame, maimed, and blind from one's religious community.

---

48. Willi Braun, *Feasting and Social Rhetoric in Luke 14* (SNTSMS 85; Cambridge: Cambridge University Press, 1995).

49. Malina and Rohrbaugh, *Social-Science Commentary*, 367–68.

Again, neither the healing nor the wisdom discourse following it raises the topic of faith.

Early Christian wisdom rhetorolect functions in a somewhat different way in the account of the possessed man in the Capernaum synagogue in Mark 1:21–28 || Luke 4:31–37 (no Matthew account).[50] The story begins with Jesus' teaching in the synagogue and the people's amazement at the authority of his teaching (Mark 1:21–22 || Luke 4:31). Then it turns abruptly to a possessed man who cries out to Jesus, "Why are you bothering us, Jesus of Nazareth? Have you come to destroy us? I know who you are, the Holy One of God" (Mark 1:24 || Luke 4:34).[51] The title "the Holy One of God," by which Jesus is identified in this confrontation, is language at home in the conceptual domain of the prophetic miracle worker Elisha.[52] The Result of the public identification of Jesus in this manner leads to the following sequence:

> **Result/Case:** Jesus rebuked him, saying, "Be silent, and come out of him!" (Mark 1:25 || Luke 4:35a).
> **Result/Case:** And the unclean spirit, convulsing him and crying with a loud voice, came out of him (Mark 1:26 || cf. Luke 4:35b).
> **Result/Case:** They were all amazed, and they kept on asking one another,
> > **Rule:** "What is this? A new teaching with authority!
> > **Case:** He commands even the unclean spirits,
> > **Result:** and they obey him" (Mark 1:27 || cf. Luke 4:36).
> **Result:** At once his fame began to spread throughout the surrounding region of Galilee (Mark 1:28 || cf. Luke 4:37).

The opening focus on Jesus' teaching and the question about the authority of Jesus' words to command unclean spirits in the closing blend Jesus' healing of the man with wisdom rhetorolect. In turn, the identification of Jesus as "the Holy One of God" blends prophetic rhetorolect with the wisdom and miracle rhetorolect in the story. The presence of the unclean spirits probably indicates the presence of apocalyptic rhetorolect in the background. There is no reference to faith in the account. Rather,

---

50. Cf. Matt 4:13; 7:28–29.
51. Luke 4:34 begins the attributed speech of the man with "Let us alone" (*ea*).
52. See 2 Kgs 4:9: "She said to her husband, 'Look, I am sure that this man who regularly passes our way is a holy man of God.'"

the story blends wisdom, miracle, prophetic, and apocalyptic rhetorolect as it focuses on the identity of Jesus and the source of his authority (and power) in the context of unclean spirits/demons.

The most fully developed "wisdom" discussion of Jesus' performance of miraculous deeds occurs in response to an assertion that Jesus casts out demons by the prince of demons, whom the tradition names as Beelzebul. There is, on the one hand, the account of the healing of the dumb man in Matt 9:32–34, which simply introduces the controversy without developing the topic with wisdom rhetorolect. The story focuses on the identity of Jesus and the source of his power, without emphasis on faith:

> **Case:** As they were going away, behold, a dumb demoniac was brought to him (v. 32).
> **Result/Case:** And when the demon had been cast out,
> **Result:** the dumb man spoke; and the crowds marveled, saying, "Never was anything like this seen in Israel" (v. 33).
> **Contrary Result:** But the Pharisees said, "He casts out demons by the ruler [*archonti*] of demons" (v. 34).

This story ends simply with a statement by the Pharisees that disagrees with the statement of the crowds. Instead of blending Jesus' activity with the story of Israel, which includes the God of Israel and God's prophets, the Pharisees blend Jesus' healing activity with apocalyptic rhetorolect. As we have seen above, early Christian discourse could blend its apocalyptically energized miracle rhetorolect in two basic ways. First, it could blend it with prophetic and wisdom rhetorolect in such a manner that Jesus' "word" has authority "to command even the unclean spirits and they obey." Second, it could blend it with a form of priestly rhetorolect that features Jesus as "the Son of God" or "Son of the Most High God," before whom unclean spirits fall down and worship. The story in Matt 9:32–34 intercepts both traditions of blending by introducing "an agent of evil" who is "the ruler" of demons. It is noticeable that no one in Matt 9:32–34 mentions God or uses the title Son of God. Pushing the conceptual network of the God of Israel into the background with a reference simply to "Israel," the story brings the apocalyptic conceptual domain of "demons" into the foreground through a repetitive texture that refers to the dumb man as "demonized" (v. 32), asserts that Jesus successfully cast out the demon (v. 33), then features the Pharisees asserting that he casts out demons by the ruler of demons (v. 34). The repetitive texture of the story displaces the "multiple" ways early

Christians blended apocalyptically energized miracle rhetorolect with a blend that focuses on a "ruler" of demons and aligns Jesus with that ruler, since he has such overwhelming power over them.

Early Christians used wisdom rhetorolect to address the "controversy" about the possibility that Jesus was aligned with the ruler of demons. Mark 3:22–30 and Luke 11:14–23 || Matt 12:22–30 (Q) present alternative versions of the "wisdom controversy."[53] It is important to notice that none of the discussions mention the topos of faith. Rather, the focus is on the identity of Jesus and the source of his power. For purposes of space, it is necessary to limit the discussion here to the version in Matt 12:22–37:

> **Case:** Then they brought to him a demoniac who was blind and mute (v. 22a);
> **Result/Case:** and he cured him, so that the one who had been mute could speak and see (v. 22b).
> **Result/Rule:** All the crowds were amazed and said, "Can this be the Son of David?" (v. 23)
> **Countercase:** But when the Pharisees heard it, they said, "It is only by Beelzebul, the ruler of the demons, that this fellow casts out the demons" (v. 24).
> **Argument from Analogies for the Implausibility of the Pharisees' Definition:** He knew what they were thinking and said to them, "Every kingdom divided against itself is laid waste, and no city or house divided against itself will stand. If Satan casts out Satan, he is divided against himself; how then will his kingdom stand? (vv. 25–26).
> **Argument from Quality in Common:** If I cast out demons by Beelzebul, by whom do your own exorcists cast them out? Therefore they will be your judges (v. 27).
> **Counterdefinition:** But if it is by the Spirit of God that I cast out demons, then the kingdom of God has come to you (v. 28).
> **Restatement of the Counterdefinition by Analogy:** Or how can one enter a strong man's house and plunder his property, without

---

53. Vernon K. Robbins, "Rhetorical Composition and the Beelzebul Controversy," in *Patterns of Persuasion in the Gospels* (ed. Burton L. Mack and Vernon K Robbins; Eugene, Ore.: Wipf & Stock, 2008), 161–93; idem, "Beelzebul Controversy in Mark and Luke: Rhetorical and Social Analysis," *Forum* 7.3–4 (1991): 261–77.

first tying up the strong man? Then indeed the house can be plundered (v. 29).
Inference: Whoever is not with me is against me, and whoever does not gather with me scatters (v. 30).
Argument concerning Gravity: Therefore I tell you, people will be forgiven for every sin and blasphemy, but blasphemy against the Spirit will not be forgiven (v. 31).
Statement of the Law: Whoever speaks a word against the Son of Man will be forgiven, but whoever speaks against the Holy Spirit will not be forgiven, either in this age or in the age to come (v. 32).
Diairesis through Analogy: Either make the tree good, and its fruit good; or make the tree bad, and its fruit bad; for the tree is known by its fruit (v. 33).

Conclusion:
Direct Address: You brood of vipers! (v. 34a).
Quaestio: How can you speak good things, when you are evil? (v. 34b).
Rationale: For out of the abundance of the heart the mouth speaks. The good person brings good things out of a good treasure, and the evil person brings evil things out of an evil treasure (vv. 34c–35).
Judgment with Rationale: I tell you, on the day of judgment you will have to give an account for every careless word you utter; for by your words you will be justified, and by your words you will be condemned" (vv. 36–37).[54]

One can easily see that the argumentative mode of wisdom rhetorolect has become dominant, in contrast to the inductive narrational mode of miracle rhetorolect. It is informative, however, to see how "picturesque" the argumentation is. Rhetography continually grounds the rhetology in a mode of argumentation that "seeks analogies" in multiple experiential domains.[55]

---

54. Robbins, "Rhetorical Composition and the Beelzebul Controversy," 178–85.
55. See Elizabeth E. Shively, "The Story Matters: Solving the Problem of the Parables in Mark 3:22–30," in *Between Author and Audience in Mark: Narration, Characterization, Interpretation* (ed. Elizabeth Struthers Malbon; Sheffield: Sheffield Phoenix, 2009), 122–44.

Matthew 12:22–37 begins with apocalyptically energized miracle narration (v. 22), to which crowds respond by blending a mode of prophetic rhetorolect that focuses on Jesus as "Son of David" (v. 23). Pharisees counter the response of the crowd with apocalyptically energized miracle rhetorolect that focuses on "Beelzebul, the ruler of demons" (vv. 24). Jesus responds with analogies from the domains of prophetic rhetorolect (kingdom) and wisdom rhetorolect (city and house) to describe Beelzebul in terms of "Satan divided against himself" (vv. 25–26). Then Jesus returns to miracle rhetorolect by comparing himself with an exorcist with "exorcists among the Pharisees" (v. 27). After this, Jesus introduces "the Spirit of God" as the counterforce against demons and blends the activity of this "spirit" with the topos of "the kingdom of God," which is central to prophetic rhetorolect (v. 28). Then Jesus returns to the topos of "house," which is central to wisdom rhetorolect but focuses on the house as a "storehouse" guarded by a strong man (v. 29). This move turns "the house of wisdom" into "a central storehouse" containing goods that people attempt to plunder for their own benefit. Moving into the realm of wisdom rhetorolect, Jesus draws an inference that people are either "with" him or "against" him (v. 30) and defines a stance against him as "blasphemy against the Spirit" that will not be forgiven, which is a topos of priestly rhetorolect energized by apocalyptic conceptuality (v. 31). At this point, Jesus introduces yet another personage from the conceptual domain of apocalyptic rhetorolect, the Son of Man. Instead of featuring the Son of man as God's "highest agent" of apocalyptic judgment, however, Jesus speaks of him as lower in rank than "the Holy Spirit." One can speak against the Son of Man and be forgiven, but any statement against the Holy Spirit is unforgivable (v. 31). At this point, the argumentation attributed to Jesus makes an unusual move in the arena of apocalyptically energized miracle discourse. In contrast to "miracle narration," which regularly features Jesus as "the Son of [the Most High] God" against the demons, Jesus' wisdom argumentation features "the Holy Spirit" or "the Spirit of God" (vv. 28, 31–32) as the ultimate power against the demons. In this way Jesus' argumentation, in response to the domain employed by his opponents, moves deeply into the domain of apocalyptic rhetorolect. Jesus' statements counter the charge of alignment with Beelzebul with a counterargument that raises the status of "the power" within Jesus (which could come forth) to "the Holy Spirit" or "the Spirit of God," which is the ultimate power against demons, unclean spirits, evil spirits, and all other spirits that cause dumbness, deafness, epilepsy, and other kinds of ailments. After the introduction of the Holy Spirit as the ultimate power against the demons, the argumentation returns to analogies characteristic of wisdom rhetorolect: (1) people are either like good fruit-bearing trees or bad fruit-bearing trees (v. 33); (2) people who speak evil things are snakes (v. 34a); and (3) words come out of the heart of a person like good or bad things come out of a treasure box (vv. 34b–35). Then the argumentation returns to apocalyptic rhetorolect as it features people who speak careless words as being condemned on the day of judgment (vv. 36–37).

In summary, Matt 12:22–37 features wisdom rhetorolect from the mouth of Jesus that negotiates apocalyptically energized miracle rhetorolect in such a manner that it identifies all apocalyptic "agents of evil" in the personages of demons, Beelzebul, and Satan as against "agents of God" in the personages of the Son of David, the Spirit of God, the Son of Man, and the Holy Spirit. No "miracle story," which keeps inductive narration as its rhetorical base, negotiates all of these personages in this manner. Only "wisdom argumentation," which negotiates questions, assertions, rationales, analogies, opposites, contraries, and authoritative judgments, is able to introduce this many "agents" of power into the discussion and define their activity in relation to God and to forces of evil.

As has been mentioned throughout this section, it is important to notice that none of the stories and summaries of Jesus' healings discussed above contains a reference to faith. Yet one can see how faith could become an important topos in early Christian narration of miracle discourse. If large numbers of people bring people to Jesus to be healed, then it can be reasoned that those people believe there is a good chance Jesus will be able to heal them. In other words, a series of stories about people bringing sick persons to Jesus can evoke the inference (Rule) that these people believed Jesus could heal them. Yet, as we have seen above, there are a significant number of summaries and stories in the Synoptic Gospels that do not mention faith as an explicit topos. Rather, they focus on Jesus as a healer, and they raise various possibilities about Jesus' relation to the God of Israel and to demons without giving specific answers concerning what those relationships might be. The focus of the narration, then, is epideictic: praise of Jesus and the God of Israel in contexts that sometimes blame demons or unclean spirits for people's afflictions. This miracle narration blends with apocalyptic, prophetic, and wisdom rhetorolect as the discourse provides various alternatives for identifying who Jesus is.

7. Miracle Stories Emphasizing Faith

In the midst of the narrational summaries and stories featuring the miraculous deeds of Jesus in the Synoptic Gospels, there are twelve stories that introduce the topos of "faith" (*pistis*) or "lack of faith" (*apistia*). Multiple versions of two of the stories refer to faith or lack of faith only in a narrational comment.[56] The remaining ten stories feature the topos of faith on the lips of Jesus, and sometimes faith is described as "great" or "little."[57] This paper concludes that the topos of faith blends wisdom rhetorolect with miracle rhetorolect in an especially dynamic manner in early Christian discourse. Faith resides in the inner recesses of the heart, mind, and body, where tradition conventionally places wisdom. Early Christian discourse programmatically reconfigures Mediterranean miracle discourse into wisdom discourse, and the topos of faith is a primary means by which this reconfiguration occurs. In the process, miracle discourse becomes sapiential faith discourse. This means that early Christian miracle discourse becomes wisdom discourse of a very particular kind in Mediterranean culture and society.

7.1. Faith in Narration

Two of the twelve miracle stories that mention faith or lack of faith present the topos in narration only, and not in speech attributed to Jesus. In Mark 2:1–12 || Matt 9:1–8 || Luke 5:17–26, Jesus interprets the exceptional effort of the people who bring the paralytic to Jesus—namely, their lowering of him through the roof when they could not get through the door—as faith.[58] This occurs in narration that asserts that Jesus, "seeing their faith" (*idōn*),

---

56. All three versions of the story where four men dig a hole in the roof of a house to let a paralytic down to Jesus (Mark 2:1–12 || Matt 9:1–8 || Luke 5:17–26) assert that Jesus "saw the faith" of the men, and there are two versions of Jesus' rejection at Nazareth (Mark 6:1–6 || Matt 13:53–58) that make a narrational assertion about "lack of faith" in a context where Jesus does not perform any "powerful deeds" (*dynameis*).

57. One of the stories is in Q tradition (Luke 7:1–10 || Matt 8:5–13); one is only in Luke (17:11–19); and one is only in Matthew (9:27–31). Five more are in triple tradition, and two are in Mark-Matthew tradition with no mention of faith in the Markan version and no parallel in Luke.

58. See Cotter, *Christ of the Miracle Stories*, 79–105. In her view (101–5), this story exhibits Jesus' *philanthrōpia*, *praos*, and *epieikia* (an understanding of the desperation of the needy that goes beyond any other consideration).

makes his pronouncement of healing. The narration, then, presents Jesus as interpreting actions of four men that all people can see in terms of faith that he "sees" in the inner recesses of their hearts and minds. In sociorhetorical terms, this action by Jesus blends wisdom rhetorolect with miracle rhetorolect. The Matthean account is particularly interesting for rhetorical analysis and interpretation, since it contrasts the faith Jesus sees in the four men with the "enthymemes" (inner reasonings) he sees in the scribes (9:2, 4). The contrast helps to define the location of faith in the place where people reason. In Matt 9:4, after the narrational assertion about Jesus "seeing [*idōn*] their *enthymemes* [*enthymēseis*]," Jesus asks the scribes why they "*enthymeme* [*enthymeisthe*] evil in their hearts."[59] This sequence counterbalances good reasoning, namely, faith that moves people toward Jesus for healing, against bad reasoning, namely, "enthymemes," supporting the proposition that Jesus blasphemes when he forgives sins. Jesus' statements about faith and *enthymeme* move the discourse decisively into the domain of early Christian wisdom rhetorolect, which is grounded in God's creation of the world as "good" (Gen 1) and in the ability of humans to distinguish between good and evil (Gen 3). But this story does more than blend miracle and wisdom rhetorolect. It blends miracle, wisdom, priestly, and perhaps apocalyptic rhetorolect when it identifies Jesus as "the Son of man who has authority on earth to forgive sins." Also, narration in Luke 5:17 specifically evokes the network of God's activity when it asserts that "the power of the Lord was with Jesus to heal." Miracle and wisdom rhetorolect, then, create an "emergent blend structure"[60] in which multiple conceptual domains and networks dynamically interact with, blend with, and reconfigure one another.

In the context of the multiple blending in the story of the healing of the paralytic, the endings of the different versions are particularly interesting. All three versions include "glorifying [*doxazein*] God" at the end of their accounts. The Markan version ends with an assertion that all were amazed (*existasthai*) and glorified God, saying, "We have never before seen anything like this!" (2:12). Here the people refer to God in relation to the overall event of the healing of the paralytic in a context of forgiveness of sins. The Matthean version blends the people's glorifying of God with

---

59. Matthew also uses the verb *enthymeomai* in 1:20, when Joseph *enthymemes* that he will divorce Mary quietly, and in 12:25, where Jesus knows the *enthymemes* of the Pharisees about Jesus' casting out of demons.

60. Fauconnier and Turner, *The Way We Think*, 42–50.

"being afraid" as they reflect on God's giving of "such authority to humans" (*anthrōpois*: 9:8). Here, then, fear and praise blend together as people direct their attention to God as the source of authority in humans both to forgive sins and to heal. The Lukan version both expands and reconfigures conceptual domains and networks as it shows a sequence that begins with the healed man's "glorifying of God" in his home and continues with all being seized (*elaben*) with amazement (*ekstasis*), glorifying God, being filled with fear, and saying, "We have seen a paradox [*paradoxa*] today" (5:26). Each version, in its own way, exhibits "inner processes of reasoning" that evoke multiple topoi in a "double-scope network" focused on Jesus as a miracle worker and God as one who empowers and authorizes certain humans on earth. While the Markan version shows the people responding to "the whole event," the Matthean version focuses attention on God's giving of authority to humans both to forgive and to heal, and the Lukan version introduces the concept of "paradox" to describe the conceptual challenge the story presents to people who try to understand the dynamics of the story. Wisdom rhetorolect therefore blends dynamically with miracle, priestly, and perhaps apocalyptic rhetorolect both throughout and at the end of this story in its multiple versions in the Synoptic Gospels.

Another story that features the concept of faith in narration is Mark 6:1–6 || Matt 13:53–58. In this story, however, the topos is "lack of faith" (*apistia*) rather than "faith" (*pistis*). The beginning of the story features Jesus teaching in his hometown synagogue. (Mark 6:2 adds that it was on the Sabbath.) The story blends wisdom with miracle rhetorolect when the people wonder out loud,

> **Rule:** "Where did this man get all this? What is this wisdom that has been given to him?
> **Case:** What deeds of power are done by his hands!
> **Case:** Is not this the carpenter, the son of Mary and the brother of James and Joses and Judas and Simon, and are not his sisters here with us?"
> **Result:** And they took offense (*eskandalizonto*) at him (Mark 6:2–3; cf. Matt 13:54–57).

Here the people in Jesus' hometown respond in exactly the way Jesus asks people not to respond in Luke 7:23 || Matt 11:6. When people are scandalized by Jesus, they fulfill the dynamics of prophetic rhetorolect that Jesus introduces when he says, "A prophet is not without honor except in his homeland, among his kinfolk, and in his home" (Mark 6:4).[61] In the Markan version, blending of wisdom, prophetic, and miracle rhetorolect features Jesus' inability (Mark 6:5) to do any "miracle" (*dynamis*) in the context of the people's rejection of him in Nazareth. He does, however, lay his hands on a few people and heal (*therapeuō*) them. Matthew 13:57 avoids a statement that Jesus was unable to perform miracles in a context where no faith is present, asserting in contrast to Mark that Jesus "did not do many miracles there." Markan narration in 6:6 asserts that Jesus, in the context of his inability to do any "miracle" (*dynamis*) there, "marveled" (*ethaumazen*) at their lack of faith (*apistian*). It is important to note that the Markan account does not say that Jesus was unable to perform any *dynamis* there "because" of the people's lack of faith, though the narration may be interpreted to imply this. Luke 4:16–30, which appears to be Luke's version of the account, features the people's rejection of Jesus, but it never features the topos of faith.

There are only two instances in miracle stories in the Synoptic Gospels, then, where faith or lack of faith is a topos in narration. In the story of the paralytic in Mark 2:1–12 || Matt 9:1–8 || Luke 5:17–26, wisdom, priestly, and perhaps apocalyptic rhetorolect blend together with miracle rhetorolect to create a dynamic emergent structure in early Christian discourse that focuses on people's reasoning about things in a manner that implies that faith is good reasoning. Narration in the story of Jesus' rejection at Nazareth works in a somewhat different way as it introduces lack of faith into discourse that blends wisdom, miracle, and prophetic rhetorolect dynamically with one another. In this instance, the prophetic topos of rejection creates a context in which the narration correlates either Jesus' "inability to perform any miracles" or simply his "not doing any miracles" with "lack of faith." The end result is a strengthening of the topos of faith through the presence of its opposite, lack of faith, in early Christian miracle discourse.

7.2. Jesus Says Their Faith "Made Them Well"

Three of the ten miracle stories that mention faith or lack of faith in speech attributed to Jesus present Jesus asserting to people that their faith has made them well. All three versions of the healing of the woman with the

---

61. Cf. Matt 13:57; Luke 4:24; John 4:44.

flow (Mark 5:24b–34 || Matt 9:19–22 || Luke 8:42b–48) contain only one occurrence of the word faith, and in all instances the word occurs in Jesus' statement, "Your faith has made you well [*sesōken*]." In this story, "faith" seems to refer to the confidence of the woman that there was power in Jesus that could and would come forth from Jesus and heal her disease. As I indicated in 1987, "Her motivation could be understood either as 'simplemendedness or silliness' (*euēthia*), 'boldness' (*tolmān/tolmein*), 'faith' (*pistis*), 'hope' (*elpis*), 'courage' (*andreia*), 'despair' (*apognōsis*), or some other state of mind or action."[62] In all versions, however, Jesus interprets the inner reasoning that motivated her as faith, and he asserts that this faith has made her well.

Rather than blending various rhetorolects together, this story locates Jesus' miracle activity in a context where physicians in the Mediterranean world regularly offer healing. The dynamic blending occurs in Jesus' interpreting of the reasoning of the woman, which he identifies as faith. Jesus asserts that this "faith reasoning" has motivated her to act in a manner that caused her healing to occur. Here again, then, we see a miracle story that portrays Jesus interpreting the inner reasoning of a person, in this instance the afflicted person herself, as faith. The end result, again, is a dynamic blending of miracle and wisdom rhetorolect.

Another story in which Jesus states that a person's faith has made him or her well is only in Luke. Luke 17:11–19 contains an account of Jesus' healing of ten lepers. As a group, they call Jesus by name, address him as Master (*epistata*), and ask him to have mercy on them. He tells them to go and show themselves to the priests, and as they go they are cleansed (v. 14). Thus the story blends miracle and priestly rhetorolect, and, as we also know from above, the healing of leprosy evokes prophetic rhetorolect in relation to Elisha. One of the lepers, a Samaritan, when he sees that he has been healed, turns back, praising God with a loud voice (v. 15), falling on his face at Jesus' feet, and giving Jesus thanks (v. 16). After Jesus rhetorically asks if ten were not cleansed and where the other nine are, and if no one has returned to praise God except this foreigner, he says, "Rise and go your way; your faith has made you well" (v. 19). Faith is associated in this story with appropriate embodying of action of inferiority in relation

---

62. Vernon K. Robbins, "The Woman who Touched Jesus' Garment: Socio-rhetorical Analysis of the Synoptic Accounts," *NTS* 33 (1987): 506 (502–15); repr. in *New Boundaries in Old Territory: Form and Social Rhetoric in Mark* (ESEC 3; New York: Lang, 1994), 191 (185–200).

to Jesus. Also, the story associates faith with praising God. An interesting question the story leaves unresolved is the means by which the other nine lepers were healed. Were the others healed, even though they did not have faith? Should one presuppose that the other nine enacted faith in their cry to Jesus to have mercy on them (v. 13)? The story leaves these questions unanswered. The focus is on a foreigner who praises God, prostrates himself at Jesus' feet, and thanks Jesus (vv. 15–16). Jesus defines this priestly activity and honoring of Jesus as faith, and Jesus asserts that this faith made him well.

The third story featuring an assertion by Jesus to the healed person that his faith made him well serves to introduce interpreters to ways in which Matthean miracle stories are particularly distinctive among the Synoptic Gospels. Overall, Matthean miracle stories feature more speech by Jesus than in Markan and Lukan miracle stories.[63] In the instance of the third story, the healing of the blind man in Mark 10:46–52 || Luke 18:35–43, Matthew presents a very special circumstance. The Matthean story with the closest relation to the Markan and Lukan version, Matt 20:29–34, does not feature Jesus saying anything about faith. Another story about the healing of two blind men, in Matt 9:27–31, however, so prominently features Jesus speaking about faith in relation to healing that it will be discussed in the next section of this paper.

The healing of the blind man (named Bartimaeus only in Mark) in Mark 10:46–52 || Luke 18:35–43 and the two blind men in Matt 20:29–34 feature a double cry to Jesus for mercy in a context where people are trying to stop their crying out.[64] Both times the blind men address Jesus as Son of David. In response to their cry, Jesus asks what he or they want him to do. The answer is to receive sight. In Mark, Jesus responds to the blind man:

Case: "Go,
Rule: your faith has made you well."
Result/Case: And immediately he received his sight
Result: and began to follow him on the way (v. 52).

---

63. H. J. Held, "Matthew as Interpreter of the Miracle Stories," in *Tradition and Interpretation in Matthew* (ed. G. Bornkamm, G. Barth, and H. J. Held; trans. Percy Scott; Philadelphia: Westminster, 1963), 165–299.

64. See Cotter, *Christ of the Miracle Stories*, 42–75. In her view, this story exhibits not only Jesus' *philanthrōpia*, *praos*, and *epieikia*, but also the boldness of Bartimaeus (74–75).

In this story, faith is persistence that brings the blind beggar face-to-face with Jesus, where he can tell Jesus he wants him to heal him. This story also presents a phenomenon discussed in a previous section, where people who experience Jesus' deeds of power "follow" him.

Luke 18:42–43 omits "Go" and "on the way" from the Markan ending, and has *parachrēma* rather than *euthys* for "immediately." With these changes, the Lukan ending presents the three items of (1) "your faith has made you well"; (2) immediately he received his sight; and (3) he began to follow. But Luke 18:43 presents a sequence of action that shows a tendency in Lukan miracle stories we have seen above. In addition to the man's "following" of Jesus at the end of the story:

Case: he glorified God.
Result: And when the people saw it, they gave praise to God (v. 43).

As we have seen above, Lukan miracle stories often feature "public witness" in the form of glorification of God. Also, we saw a sequence of glorification of God in the Lukan version of the healing of the paralytic in Luke 5:17–26. In the Lukan version of the healing of the blind man there is a "chain reaction" at the end, where the healed person's glorification of God causes others to praise God. Thus early Christian miracle rhetorolect not only generates a special kind of wisdom rhetorolect but also nurtures a special kind of priestly rhetorolect in locations outside of sacred places and sacred times. On the road, in a house, or virtually anywhere at any time, early Christians could break forth into "worship" speech characteristic of priestly rhetorolect. This means that miracle rhetorolect also helps to nurture a special kind of priestly rhetorolect, highly blended with wisdom rhetorolect, in the Mediterranean world.

Surprisingly, as mentioned above, Matt 20:34 does not feature Jesus saying anything about faith. Instead, moved with compassion, Jesus touches the eyelids of the men, immediately they see, and they follow Jesus. This is a surprise, because an overall tendency of Matthean storytelling is to add statements by Jesus about faith, which leads us to the miracle stories in the next section.

7.3. Matthew Features "Let It Be" and "Great Is Your Faith"

There are three Matthean miracle stories that feature Jesus saying some version of "Let it be done to you according to your faith." Each of these has a distinctive place in the context of miracle stories in the Synoptic Gospels. The first one is Matt 9:27–31, which is another version of Jesus' healing of two blind men in Matthew that contains only a few similarities with the Markan and Lukan versions of the healing of the blind man discussed above. In Matt 9:27–31, two blind men cry out only once to Jesus as Son of David (rather than twice, as in all other versions). Then they enter a house, and the following exchange takes place:

> **Rule:** Jesus said to them, "Do you believe that I am able to do this?"
> **Case:** They said to him, "Yes, Lord."
> **Result/Case:** Then he touched their eyes, saying, "According to your faith let it be it done to you."
> **Result/Case:** And their eyes were opened.
> **Result/Case:** And Jesus sternly charged them, "See that no one knows it."
> **Result:** But they went away and spread his fame through all that district (9:28–34).

In this story one sees the overall tendency for wisdom rhetorolect to be expanded in Matthean miracle stories, and for the topos of faith to play a role in that expansion. In this story, Jesus' speech introduces the verb "to believe" (*pisteuein*) when he asks the men if they believe he is able to heal them. Their affirmative response followed by Jesus' statement, "According to your faith let it be it done to you," establishes a specific logic of reasoning about faith and healing in the speech of Jesus, which becomes central to early Christian miracle-wisdom rhetorolect. The nature of Jesus' statement as wisdom is evident in Jesus' additional statement that they should let no one "know" (*ginōsketō*: v. 30). What happens to the men in this story becomes "knowledge" that can be transmitted to others. Despite what Jesus says, in verse 31 the men go out and "spread" (*diephēmisan*) this knowledge throughout the whole district. One of the characteristics of miracle rhetorolect is that people cannot resist narrating it to others, even if Jesus tells them not to! This "faith knowledge" must be told to others when it produces healing. Again, the underlying rhetoric of miracle rhetorolect is storytelling, which is "inductive" argumentation. Rehearsal of a series of stories of healing, however, produces "reasoning" about the stories that transforms miracle rhetorolect into a special kind of wisdom rhetorolect in early Christian discourse.

The second story featuring Jesus saying "Let it be done" on the basis of his perception that faith is present in the afflicted person is Matthew's version of the healing of the daughter of the Syrophoenician/Canaanite woman (Matt 15:21–28 || Mark 7:24–31).[65] The account of the story in Mark 7:24–31 has no reference to faith. Jesus' identity is an issue in the story as it begins with his entering a house, because he does not want anyone to know he is there (v. 24). When the Syrophoenician woman begs Jesus to cast a demon out of her daughter (v. 26), Jesus responds with:

Case: "Let the children be fed first,
Rule: because it is not fair to take the children's food and throw it to the little dogs." When she answers,
Contrary Rule: "Sir, even the dogs under the table eat the children's crumbs," Jesus says,
Contrary Case: "Go, the demon has left your daughter."

Wisdom rhetorolect blends with miracle rhetorolect in the exchange between Jesus and the Syrophoenician woman. This is the only story in the New Testament where someone's dispute with Jesus results in Jesus' changing his mind. This means that the woman's speech is exceptionally good wisdom. The presence of the substantive wisdom in the woman results in the healing of the woman's daughter. Wisdom rhetorolect becomes the catalyst that activates the healing miracle, and the daughter is healed simply through "the word" of Jesus. Thus, both the woman's dialogue with Jesus and Jesus' word of healing blend wisdom rhetorolect dynamically with miracle rhetorolect in the story. But this Markan version never mentions faith.

The account of the Canaanite woman in Matthew 15:21–28, which is parallel to Mark 7:24–31, also features wisdom rhetorolect blended with miracle rhetorolect. The Matthean version, however, portrays Jesus referring specifically to faith and saying "Let it be done" on the basis of faith, and it also nurtures early Christian priestly rhetorolect. At first the woman shouts at Jesus, "Have mercy on me, Lord, Son of David; my daughter is tormented by a demon" (v. 22). The ritualized nature of this approach introduces priestly rhetorolect blended with the prophetic topos of the

---

65. See Cotter, *Christ of the Miracle Stories*, 137–60. In her view, this story exhibits Jesus' *ēpios* in the form of a readiness to listen (160).

Son of David. When Jesus does not answer her and the disciples urge Jesus to send her away, because she keeps shouting at them, Jesus tells her: "I was sent only to the lost sheep of the house of Israel" (v. 24). When the woman comes to Jesus, kneels before him, and says, "Lord, help me" (v. 25), Jesus responds with a version of the Markan saying about throwing children's food to the dogs that does not contain the statement, "Let the children first be satisfied," but adds that the crumbs fall from the table of "their masters." After this exchange Jesus answers:

Rule: "O woman, great is your faith!
Case: Let it be done for you as you want."
Result: And her daughter was healed instantly (v. 28).

This version of the story features Jesus' defining the wisdom of the woman as "faith" and evaluating the "skill" of her faith wisdom as "great." In this story, Jesus "grades" the woman's faith much like a teacher grades a student's wisdom. The woman receives an A! But Jesus does not say, "How great is your wisdom!" Rather, he says, "Great is your faith!" Here, then, is yet another level of logic in early Christian miracle wisdom: the greater the faith, the more likely that healing will occur. On the basis of her high level of wisdom, Jesus gives her a high grade on her faith and grants the woman her wish for a miraculous healing.

The third healing story featuring "Let it be" on the basis of faith is the Matthean version of the Q healing story in Luke 7:1–10 || Matt 8:5–13, which features the centurion at Capernaum.[66] In this story, the narration focuses on the faith of a Roman centurion (Luke 7:2 || Matt 8:5), namely, a Gentile living in a city inhabited primarily by Jewish people. In the Matthean version, the sick male in the centurion's household could be his son or a servant (*pais*: Matt 8:6, 8, 13), while in the Lukan version, he is clearly a slave (*doulos*: Luke 7:2–3, 10 || *pais*: Luke 10:7). The material common to Luke and Matthew features an appeal by the centurion either in person (Matt 8:5) or through emissaries (Luke 7:3, 6) that signals substantive honor of Jesus. The centurion uses the language of "sufficiency" (*hikanos*: Luke 7:6 || Matt 8:8) to compare himself as one "insufficient" in relation to Jesus. In the context of this insufficiency, the

---

66. See Cotter, *The Christ of the Miracle Stories*, 106–34. In her view, this story exhibits Jesus' *eipieikia* (understanding) and compassion without any resentment or prejudice (134).

centurion communicates to Jesus that he should simply "say the word," and healing will occur. Jesus interprets as faith the centurion's request from a position of social insufficiency and of confidence that Jesus is able to function as a broker or patron of healing. This is a reorientation of faith in the tradition of Israelite belief, since faith was a special characteristic of Israel's relationship to God rather than a characteristic of members of "the nations." The centurion is careful not to issue a challenge to Jesus as an equal. Rather, he communicates to Jesus that even though he himself is a broker with authority, he readily accepts a position of client to Jesus as a broker or patron (Luke 7:6-8 || Matt 8:8-9).[67] Toward the end of the story, Jesus asserts that he "has never found such faith even in Israel" (Luke 7:9 || Matt 8:10). Beyond these observations, it is necessary to discuss each version of the story on its own terms.

In the Lukan account of the healing of the centurion's slave (7:1-10), Jesus and the centurion never come face-to-face with one another. Narration at the beginning of the story tells about a centurion who had a slave who was about to die, whom he valued highly (vv. 1-2). Hearing about Jesus, he sent "elders of the Jews" to him to ask him to come and heal his servant (v. 3). There is no dialogue between the elders and Jesus. Rather, they simply come to Jesus and appeal earnestly to him by saying:

Case: "He is worthy [*axios*] to have you do this for him,
Rule: for he loves [*agapāi*] our nation,
Case: and he built us our synagogue" (v. 5).
Result/Case: And Jesus went with them.

In the Lukan version of the story, the elders' beseeching of Jesus does not necessarily presuppose that they believe Jesus can heal the slave. The centurion has sent them, and they have been willing to go. Their faith or lack of faith never becomes a topos in the story, except through the ironic dimension that Jesus has never found faith "even in Israel" (of which they are members) like the faith of the centurion. The remarks of the Jewish elders focus entirely on the virtues of the Gentile centurion. He is "worthy," since he embodies "love" for the people and nation of Israel, which he has exhibited as a patron who has built a synagogue for them. The Jewish elders in the story gratefully accept their position as clients of

---

67. Ibid., 74-76, 326-29.

the centurion, and they reciprocate generously by communicating their praise of their patron to Jesus. Jesus goes with the elders as a result of their description of the centurion, but when Jesus is not far from the house the centurion sends "friends" to speak for him. They address Jesus as *kyrie*, tell him not to bother, since he (the centurion) is not sufficient for Jesus to come under his roof and does not consider himself worthy to come to Jesus. Jesus should simply "say the word" and his servant will be healed, since the centurion is also a man set under authority, with soldiers under him, and the soldiers go and come when he tells them, and his slave also does what he tells him (vv. 6–8). At this point Jesus turns to the crowd following him and says he has not found such faith even in Israel (v. 9). The story ends with narration asserting that when those who were sent returned the slave was in good health (v. 10).

According to Malina and Rohrbaugh, when Jesus is getting closer to the house, the centurion sends out "friends" and "signals to Jesus ... that he does not intend to make Jesus a client..., but considers him a superior."[68] In this account, the faith of the centurion is clearly embedded in his laudable virtues, which are based primarily on his knowledge of who is superior to whom. There is no prophetic or apocalyptic rhetorolect in the Lukan version. Also, there is no dialogue between Jesus and the centurion. Rather, wisdom rhetorolect blends with miracle rhetorolect through "emissaries" who carry information from the centurion to Jesus. Jesus speaks only once in the story, asserting that the centurion has more faith than anyone he has found in Israel. As David B. Gowler writes: "The narrator juxtaposes two people with different but analogous social roles: Both are in positions of authority, whether in the Roman Empire or God's empire. The centurion acknowledges and Jesus demonstrates the supremacy of God's empire. God's empire can accomplish what the Roman Empire can only claim to accomplish."[69]

In contrast to the Lukan version, Matt 8:5–13 begins as a dialogue between Jesus and the centurion. Coming to Jesus, the centurion describes the ill person as a paralytic who is lying at home in distress (vv. 5–6). Jesus tells the centurion he will come and cure him (v. 7). The centurion

---

68. Malina and Rohrbaugh, *Social-Science Commentary*, 329.
69. David B. Gowler, "Text, Culture, and Ideology in Luke 7:1–10: A Dialogic Reading," in *Fabrics of Discourse: Essays in Honor of Vernon K. Robbins* (ed. D. B. Gowler, L. G. Bloomquist, and D. F. Watson; Harrisburg, Pa.: Trinity Press International, 2003), 97.

responds with a long statement that begins by addressing Jesus as *kyrie* and continues by stating that the centurion is insufficient for Jesus to come under his roof and by asserting that soldiers under him go and come when he tells them and his servant also does what he tells him to do (vv. 8–9). At this point, Jesus marvels and tells those who are following him that he has never found such faith in Israel, that many will come from east and west to recline at table with Abraham, Isaac, and Jacob in the kingdom of the heavens, but the sons of the kingdom will be cast into outer darkness and there will be weeping and gnashing of teeth (vv. 10–12). Then Jesus tells the centurion, "Go, as you believe, let it be done to you," and the servant (or child) was healed that very hour. This version blends miracle, wisdom, prophetic, and apocalyptic rhetorolect in a sequence in which Jesus and the centurion respond to each other and Jesus refers twice to the faith of the man, first in relation to "Israel" (v. 10) and second in the context of his command to "let it be done" (v. 13). In accord with the tendency in Matthew to emphasize the role of faith in healing, the Matthean version of the healing of the centurion's son features faith in the middle and the closing of the story and contributes to a logic in early Christian discourse that healing occurs in people in direct relation to the presence of faith in them.

7.4. Qualifying Faith, Opposing It to Doubt, and Nurturing Worship

The four remaining miracle stories in the Synoptic Gospels that refer to faith show how multiplicity in the tradition creates an environment where faith can be qualified as "little" rather than "great," where faith that is very little can do incredible things, where faith can be understood as opposite to doubt, and where faith can lead to prayer and worship.

The first remarkable instance of this multiplicity is present in Mark 9:14–29 || Matt 17:14-20 || Luke 9:37–43a, which features the father of an epileptic boy with a spirit that makes him unable to speak.[70] The Markan account features Jesus introducing the topic of "lack of faith" early in the story in verse 19; it features a syllogistic exchange about faith and what is possible in verses 22–24; then it concludes in verses 28–29 with a discussion between Jesus and the disciples about how it is possible to cast out

---

70. See Cotter, *Christ of the Miracle Stories*, 161–91. In her view, this story exhibits Jesus' *philanthrōpia*, *eipieikia* ("understanding"), and *meekness* (189–91).

such a spirit. This sequence of attributed speech creates repetitive texture in the story that features four occurrences of a term for faith or lack of faith, and five occurrences of a term discussing "what is possible":

> Jesus: "You *faithless* generation!" (v. 19).
> Father: "If it is *possible* for you to do anything…" (v. 22).
> Jesus: "If it is *possible* for you! All things are *possible* for one who *has faith* (v. 23).
> Father: "I *have faith*; help my *lack of faith*" (v. 24).
> Disciples: "Why was it not *possible* for us to cast it out?" (v. 28).
> Jesus: "It is not *possible* for this kind to go out except by prayer" (v. 29).

In this story, Jesus introduces the topos of lack of faith in his response to the father's account of how he brought his son to Jesus' disciples for them to cast out the spirit that makes him unable to speak. Jesus' response is: "O faithless generation!" After the spirit convulses the boy in the presence of Jesus, Jesus creates a context for the father to narrate what the spirit regularly does to the boy. As the father is finishing the story, he says to Jesus, "If it is possible for you to do anything, be moved with compassion and help us" (v. 22). This produces an immediate response from Jesus about "what is possible" and creates a context in which Jesus introduces a dictum that was vigorously discussed among philosophers and widely attributed to Christians in the Mediterranean world: "All things are possible with God."[71] The exchange between Jesus and the father creates syllogistic reasoning about healing on the basis of faith: Since all things are possible for him who believes (major premise) and the father believes (minor premise), the father's son can be healed on the basis of the father's belief (conclusion). The Markan version embeds this syllogism (vv. 22–24) between Jesus' opening reference to a "faithless generation" (v. 19) and the closing discussion, where Jesus asserts that it is possible only through prayer for this kind of spirit to come out (vv. 28–29). The irony of the story, of course, is that the narration does not portray Jesus using prayer to cast the spirit out. Yet this story presents a link between prayer and Jesus' deeds of power that Jesus embellishes in Mark 11:22–24, which will be discussed below.

---

71. See Robert M. Grant, *Miracle and Natural Law in Graeco-Roman and Early Christian Thought* (Amsterdam: North-Holland, 1952).

The Markan exchange between Jesus and the father is neither in the Matthean nor Lukan account. The Lukan account of 9:37–43a, which is very short in comparison with the Markan account, also emphasizes the "faithless and perverse generation" that cannot heal (v. 41), and, in characteristic Lukan fashion, at the end of the account emphasizes that "all were astounded at the greatness of God" (v. 43). The Matthean account of 17:14–20 also features Jesus' assertion about the "faithless and perverse generation" that cannot produce healing (v. 17). Then, in characteristic Matthean fashion, Jesus tells the disciples they could not cast the spirit out because of their "little faith" (v. 20). This leads to special syllogistic reasoning in the Matthean account that becomes well known in Christian discourse:

Case: "If you have faith as a grain of mustard seed,
Result/Case: you will say to this mountain, 'Move from here to there,'
Result/Case: and it will move;
Rule: and nothing will be impossible for you" (v. 20).

In contrast to the Markan and Lukan accounts, the Matthean account ends in a brief wisdom discourse by Jesus about miracles. It is noticeable that this discourse does not talk about miracles of healing, which are the dominant focus of miracle rhetorolect in early Christian discourse. Talk about moving a mountain actually seems out of place in the context of the miracle stories in the Synoptic Gospels, since such a deed of power would appear to be a sign, like the Pharisees would like to see and which Jesus refuses to perform in Mark 8:11–12.[72] Nevertheless, we will see below that Jesus' discussion about faith's moving a mountain occurs in other contexts as well in the Synoptic Gospels.

In contrast to the placement of the statement about faith like a grain of a mustard seed at the end of the Matthean version of the healing of the epileptic boy (Matt 17:20), the Gospel of Luke features the saying in a context that has nothing to do with miraculous deeds of power. After Jesus discusses "occasions for stumbling" with the disciples in Luke 17:1–4, the apostles say, "Increase [add to] our faith!" Jesus says in response:

---

72. Vernon K. Robbins, "*Dynameis* and *Semeia* in Mark," *BR* 18 (1973): 1–16.

Case: "If you had faith the size of a mustard seed,
Result/Case: You could say to this mulberry tree, 'Be uprooted and planted in the sea,'
Result: and it would obey you" (17:5–6).

Jesus' speech presents miracle reasoning in a characteristic Case/Result manner based on inductive narration. Instead of telling a story about such an instance, however, Jesus puts the Case/Result sequence in the form of conditional wisdom: "If..., [then] ..." In Luke, then, Jesus' discussion of faith as a grain of mustard seed is wisdom discourse with miracle content, without any story of a miraculous deed in its context. This is a notable example of early Christian miracle rhetorolect transformed into wisdom rhetorolect.

A second and third story in the Synoptic Gospels show other dimensions of multiplicity that emerge in early Christian miracle rhetorolect. We saw above in the Matthean version of the healing of the Canaanite woman's daughter how Jesus could evaluate faith as "great." In other stories in Matthew, Jesus evaluates faith as "small" (*oligē*). Jesus' evaluation of faith as lesser than it should be does not occur in stories in which he heals bodies. Rather, it occurs in stories that somehow feature a "threat" to the body that is not an affliction but some other kind of crisis. In the story of the stilling of the storm in Mark 4:35–41, after Jesus rebukes and stills the wind, he says to the disciples: "Why are you cowards? Do you not yet have faith?" (v. 40).[73] In a similar manner, Luke 8:25 features Jesus as saying, "Where is your faith?" The Matthean version, in contrast to the Markan and Lukan versions, places Jesus' response about faith early in the story. When the disciples awaken Jesus by saying, "Lord, save us! We are perishing!" Jesus says to them, "Why are you afraid, you of little faith?" (8:26). In the Matthean version, then, Jesus defines fear in a context of danger as "little faith." Again faith is located in the place of reasoning in humans, but in this instance fear confuses or disturbs the reasoning in a manner that makes it weak or "small" reasoning. As the topos of faith blends with miracle rhetorolect, then, it acquires characteristics of wisdom in the Mediterranean world and enters a sphere where it can be evaluated as "small" or

---

73. See Cotter, *Christ of the Miracle Stories*, 195–232. In her view, this story exhibits Jesus' acceptance, compassion, understanding, and "meekness" (232).

"great," like one could encounter in a saying like, "Great was the wisdom of Solomon," or, perhaps, "Small was the wisdom of Croesus."

Yet another instance of Jesus' evaluation of faith as "little" occurs in the Matthean version of walking on water.[74] The topos of faith is not present in the Markan version (6:45-52), but there is a narrational comment at the end of the story that blends the miracle rhetorolect in the story with wisdom rhetorolect. When the disciples see Jesus walking on the sea and are terrified, Jesus says, "Take heart, it is I: do not be afraid" (v. 50). At this point, Jesus gets into the boat and the wind ceases (v. 51). Then there is the narrational comment: "And they were utterly astounded, for they did not understand about the loaves, but their hearts were hardened" (vv. 51-52). This final narrational comment blends wisdom rhetorolect with the miracle rhetorolect in the story. Fear and astonishment in the disciples, in a context of danger to their bodies, blends with wisdom rhetorolect when the narration relates fear and astonishment to other deeds of power the disciples have seen Jesus perform. There is a responsibility, then, in early Christian discourse for followers of Jesus to "understand" miracle rhetorolect. If followers do not understand it—namely, if they do not blend wisdom rhetorolect with it—there is something notably insufficient about their discipleship.

The Matthean version of Jesus' walking on water (14:22-33) explicitly brings the topos of faith into the story. Verse 29 adds to the story a moment when Peter gets out of the boat to walk to Jesus. When Peter sees the wind and is afraid, he begins to sink and cries out, "Lord, save me" (v. 30). Jesus reaches out his hand, catches him, and says, "O man of little faith, why did you doubt [*edistasas*]?" In this version, then, Jesus evaluates Peter's fear both as "little faith" and as "doubt." The terminology of doubt adds a dimension to this wisdom rhetorolect that is not present in any other story discussed above. In addition to the presence or absence of faith ("faith" or "lack of faith") and the size of faith as "great" or "small," early Christian discourse develops a concept of "forceful nonfaith" ("doubt"). This form of doubt is not "against faith." Rather, in this context it is "strong fear" based on what would conventionally be considered to be "good wisdom." A person who does not perceive a strong wind on the sea to be dangerous could appropriately be described as "foolish." Fishermen know

---

74. See Cotter, *Christ of the Miracle Stories*, 233-52. In her view, this story exhibits Jesus' "meekness" (*praos*) in respecting the limitations of his disciples and helping them (252).

this danger and are appropriately afraid of it. But there is more at stake in the Matthean version of Jesus' walking on water. In an imitative manner, Peter tries to walk on water like Jesus does. At first, from the perspective of the story, he is successful. But then, noticing the strong wind he becomes frightened and begins to sink (v. 30). At this point Peter cries out, "Lord, save me!" which is reminiscent of the cry of afflicted people to Jesus when they want him to heal them. The logic of the narration is that Peter's fear of the strong wind puts him in a position similar to people who have been afflicted by something that causes their body to malfunction, and they need Jesus to restore their body so it will function properly. Jesus immediately reaches out his hand (v. 31), just like he does in stories where he heals people or raises them from death. Instead of saying, "Your faith has saved you," however, he says, "You of little faith, why did you doubt?" Here is another important moment in early Christian discourse. The stories of Jesus' healing miracles do not try to show a "moment" when a person became afflicted. Rather, they show afflicted people, and they may narrate the story in a manner that "blames" the affliction on demons or unclean spirits, or perhaps on sin. In the Matthean version of walking on water, the story shows how a person can move into an "affliction" of "little faith" through "doubt" that arises in a context of fear. In this context, little faith caused by doubt has the nature of an affliction that needs to be cured, and Jesus is the one ready at hand to cure the "disease." Jesus' action of taking Peter by the hand and pronouncing his affliction to be little faith caused by doubt functions like a healing action and word. Jesus' "naming" of the affliction in the context of his taking of Peter's hand functions like Jesus' confrontation of an unclean spirit or demon in a healing story. Instead of Peter's being healed so he can walk again, as one might see at the end of a story in which a lame man is healed, Jesus and Peter successfully get into the boat together and the wind ceases, like it does in the stilling of the storm, when Jesus "rebukes the winds and the sea" (Matt 8:26). Then the closing of the story blends priestly rhetorolect dynamically with miracle rhetorolect as those in the boat "worship" Jesus, saying, "Truly you are the Son of God" (Matt 14:33). The structure of this story, interpreted through the blending of rhetorolects in early Christian discourse, shows how Peter became "afflicted" by little faith caused by doubt in a context of threat to his body that produced fear. The presence of Jesus saves Peter from this affliction as Jesus takes him by the hand, names his affliction as little faith, and questions him in a manner that moves his mind to the source that caused his affliction, namely, doubt. The end result is worship of Jesus as

Son of God by those in the boat. Once again we see a dynamic blending of miracle and wisdom rhetorolect that generates early Christian priestly rhetorolect at the close of the story. Early Christian miracle stories not only become wisdom stories. They also become stories of early Christian worship.

The final story in the Synoptic Gospels that shows how multiplicity emerges in early Christian miracle rhetorolect is Jesus' cursing of the fig tree in Mark 11:12-14, 20-25 || Matt 21:18-22. In this story, God's power destroys life in a plant, in a context of Jesus' prophetic assault on practices in the Jerusalem temple. Jesus curses the fig tree, because it has no fruit to feed his hungry body (Mark 11:12-14 || Matt 21:18-19). This establishes a context for Jesus' criticism that the temple is not a house where people can come to pray (Mark 11:17 || Matt 21:13),[75] which in turn establishes a context where faith, doubt, and prayer become topoi in prophetically energized wisdom rhetorolect that discusses miracle. In response to Peter's observation that the fig tree had withered, Jesus says:

> **Rule:** "Have faith in God.
> **Case:** Truly I tell you, if you say to this mountain, 'Be taken up and thrown into the sea,' and if you do not doubt in your heart, but believe that what you say will come to pass,
> **Result:** it will be done for you.
> So I tell you, whatever you ask for in prayer,
> **Case:** believe that you have received it,
> **Result:** and it will be yours" (11:22-24).

Jesus' wisdom discourse after the miracle of the withering of the fig tree sets forth a remarkable argument about the power of "faith in God" to perform miraculous deeds. In the Markan version, Jesus does not address the withering of the fig tree. Rather, he speaks about "throwing a mountain into the sea," which is the example that Jesus addresses at the end of the Matthean version of the epileptic boy who could not speak (17:20). Nor does Jesus compare faith to "a grain of mustard seed." Rather, Jesus juxtaposes faith to "doubt in one's heart," and merges faith with prayer in his assertion. The end result is a logic that asserts that "whatever" persons asks

---

75. This does not solve the problem with the Markan assertion that Jesus cursed the fig tree even though "it was not the season for figs" (Mark 11:13).

for in prayer, if they believe they have received it, it will be theirs (Mark 11:24). The Matthean version makes the sequence even more logical. The disciples ask Jesus, "How did the fig tree wither at once?" Jesus' answer merges the fig tree and the mountain together: "Truly I tell you, if you have faith and do not doubt, not only will you do what has been done to the fig tree, but even if you say to this mountain, 'Be lifted up and thrown into the sea,' it will be done. Whatever you ask for in prayer with faith, you will receive" (Matt 21:21–22). At this point, then, wisdom, miracle, and priestly rhetorolect blend together in a logic of miracle working that places "a believer" in a position not only to cause a fig tree to wither but also to move a mountain! It is difficult to imagine a more dramatic transformation of miracle rhetorolect into wisdom rhetorolect. In this context, the power of "faith wisdom" has become so great that it moves dramatically beyond restoration of malfunctioning bodies, or even beyond keeping bodies from danger in contexts of crisis. With a focus on destroying or moving trees and mountains, this "faith wisdom" has been granted powers that one sees most clearly in apocalyptic rhetorolect. Have powers of God that one sees only in God's destruction of things in apocalyptic rhetorolect blended with miracle, wisdom, and priestly rhetorolect in this "totalistic" claim about the power of faith linked with prayer? The logic is astonishing, but perhaps these verses give us some of the clues concerning how totalistic miracle logic could emerge in early Christian discourse.

8. Special Miracles in Relation to Jesus in Synoptic Miracle Discourse

There are a few events concerning God's power in the Synoptic Gospels that focus on Jesus in ways that have not yet been discussed in this essay. The star that appears at Jesus' birth, the transfiguration of Jesus in the middle of his ministry, the three-hour period when darkness covers the earth before Jesus' death, and the splitting of the curtain of the temple at the time of Jesus' death come immediately to mind. It is not possible to discuss these episodes in detail here, but the ones surrounding Jesus' death at least should be briefly mentioned.

The period of darkness over the earth during the time in the Synoptic Gospels when Jesus is dying establishes the context in which God's power of life goes out of the body of Jesus. Recognizing that God's power of life is weakening in his own body, in Mark and Matthew Jesus cries out, "My God, my God, why have you forsaken me" (Mark 15:34 || Matt 27:46), and in Luke Jesus cries out, "Father, into your hands I commend my spirit" (Luke 23:46). The three-hour period of darkness is, if you will, an antimiracle. It is a time when God's power withdraws from the human realm, in contrast to times when God's power imposes itself in an unusual manner in the human realm. The Synoptic accounts of the transfiguration of Jesus present an informative counterpart to the darkness over the earth at Jesus' death. While on the highest point of a mountain, Jesus is transfigured into a dazzling white form (Mark 9:3 || Matt 17:2 || Luke 9:29). Matthew emphasizes that Jesus' face "shone like the sun and his clothes became as white as light" (17:2; cf. 13:43). In addition, the cloud out of which God speaks is full of light (17:5).[76] In the transfiguration account, God's power imposes itself fully on the body of Jesus in the form of light, in contrast to the crucifixion, where light withdraws from the cosmos as life withdraws from Jesus' body.[77] In addition, at the moment when the power of life actually leaves the body of Jesus in Mark and Matthew, God's power splits the curtain of the temple from top to bottom (Mark 15:38 || Matt 27:51). In Luke, Jesus gives the power of his life back to God after the light of the sun fails and the curtain of the temple is torn in two (23:44–45). Perhaps in these phenomena one can see how the focus on the body of Jesus in the Synoptic Gospels presses toward resurrection of Jesus' body, appearances after death, and ascension into heaven in the Gospel of Luke. In any case, in the Synoptic Gospels the time of Jesus' life is so filled with miracle power that the time of his death is a time of "antimiracle" that calls for resolution in a miraculous restoration of his body, somehow related to the ways in which he miraculously restored other people's bodies.

---

76. Ulrich Luz, *Matthew 8–20: A Commentary* (trans. James Crouch; Hermeneia; Minneapolis: Fortress, 2001), 398.

77. Cf. John 12:23–30, where a voice from heaven says, "I have glorified it, and I will glorify it again" (v. 28) in response to Jesus' explanation that the death of the Son of Man is analogous to a grain of wheat that must fall into the earth and die in order to bear fruit (12:23–24). In contrast to the Synoptics, where the transfiguration "is really the only manifestation of glory during the public ministry (Luke ix 32)..., John ... stress[es] that the divine *doxa* shone through Jesus' miraculous signs (ii 11, xi 40, xvii 4)": Raymond E. Brown, *The Gospel according to John (i–xii)* (AB 29; Garden City, N.Y.: Doubleday, 1966), 503.

9. Conclusion

There is a remarkable amount of miracle discourse in the Synoptic Gospels. In addition, there is a remarkable amount of miracle discourse that does not feature faith as an explicit topos. The rhetorical force of the narration either of individual miracles or of large gatherings where many people are healed is inductive in force. This means that the narratee again and again hears that people bring afflicted people to Jesus, he heals them, and people respond with questions about the identity of Jesus and the source of his power, or respond with praise and glorification of God.

It is remarkable to see how many miracle stories introduce controversy without reference to the topos of faith. In these instances again, miracle narration works inductively, moving the story forward from Case to a Result that becomes a Case that produces another Result. In the midst of this inductive narration, both attributed speech and argumentative narration produce enthymematic and argumentative discourse about topics ranging from the authority to forgive to the right to heal on the sabbath.

In the context of the inductive force of miracle discourse throughout the Synoptic Gospels, faith emerges as a specific topos in the transformation of miracle rhetorolect into early Christian wisdom rhetorolect that focuses on miracle. In the Synoptic Gospels, Jesus interprets a wide range of activities by people who come into his presence as faith. What ordinary people might see as extraordinary effort, special ways of honoring Jesus, remarkable courage, or keen wisdom, Jesus sees as faith. This creates a perspective on Jesus that generates multiple ways of transforming miracle rhetorolect into wisdom rhetorolect that defines faith as "great" or "little," juxtaposes faith to lack of faith and doubt, and links prayer with faith to bring the fullness of God's power into the realm of human life.

In rhetorical terms, miracle discourse generates its major topoi primarily in relation to human personal afflictions, ailments, and crises.[78] A major Rule underlying miracle discourse is: "All things are possible with God."[79] Robert M. Grant's extensive investigation of miracle discourse, which appeared in 1952, indicates that while the view that "all things are

---

78. Emma J. Edelstein and Ludwig Edelstein, *Asclepius* (2 vols.; Baltimore: Johns Hopkins University Press, 1945); Theissen, *Miracle Stories of the Early Christian Tradition*; idem, *The Gospels in Context: Social and Political History in the Synoptic Tradition* (Minneapolis: Fortress, 1991); Cotter, *Miracles in Greco-Roman Antiquity*.

79. Grant, *Miracle and Natural Law*, 127–34.

possible for the gods" already existed in Homer's *Odyssey* 10.306,[80] during the first century B.C.E. "the idea of power became a leading conception, especially because of the increasing concentration of power at Rome."[81] Posidonius's system asserted that "there is nothing which God cannot do, and that without any effort."[82] The view that "all things are possible with God" seems close at hand in many contexts in the Synoptic Gospels.[83]

While the major focus of miracle discourse in the Synoptic Gospels is on the bodies of afflicted persons, various portions of this discourse focus on the bodies of the disciples in danger. Luke uses this context distinctively to present discipleship as a result of miraculous transformation of individual people. In addition, however, portions of miracle discourse focus on the body of Jesus. Jesus' ability to walk on water, and the transformation of Jesus' body in the transfiguration accounts press toward a focus on the resurrection of Jesus by the power of God. The Synoptic Gospels feature God's miraculous power at work in particular ways at Jesus' death, and Matthew and Luke extend this miraculous work of God back to the birth of Jesus.

It is remarkable, given the large amount of miracle discourse in the Synoptics, how little there is throughout the rest of the New Testament, except in the Gospel of John and the Acts of the Apostles. Analysis of miracle discourse in the Synoptic Gospels shows how early Christians used it to support multiple kinds of functions beyond simply epideictic persuasion. Rather, they used it to create an entire system of reasoning about God, about Jesus, and about the inner recesses of the hearts and minds of people. This transformation of miracle rhetorolect into wisdom rhetorolect moves even further in the Gospel of John and the writings of Paul.

---

80. Cf. Homer, *Od.* 4.237.
81. Grant, *Miracle and Natural Law*, 128.
82. Cicero, *Nat. d.* 3.92 (cf. 2.77); cf. miracle discourse in the Qur'an: Robbins and Newby, "A Prolegomenon," 33–36.
83. Mark 10:27 (par. Matt 19:26; Luke 18:27); 14:36; cf. Luke 1:37.

The Role of Argumentation in the Miracle Stories of Luke-Acts: Toward a Fuller Identification of Miracle Discourse for Use in Sociorhetorical Interpretation

L. Gregory Bloomquist

My exploration of argumentation in Lukan discourse began with my 1996 presentation to the Malibu rhetoric conference concerning the argumentation underlying Lukan apocalyptic discourse.[1] I continued this exploration in my 1999 Society of Biblical Literature presentation on the intertexture of apocalyptic discourse in Luke-Acts and in my 2000 Lund conference examination of the role of the audience in the argumentation of Luke-Acts.[2]

I continue this exploration here by presenting my findings on the role of argumentation as exemplified in three examples of miracle discourse in Luke-Acts. I do so in hopes of being more fully able to identify what miracle discourse looks like in general in its rhetorical form but also specifically what that argumentation looks like as we find it in Luke-Acts.[3]

---

1. "Rhetorical Argumentation and the Culture of Apocalyptic: A Socio-Rhetorical Analysis of Luke 21," in *The Rhetorical Interpretation of Scripture: Essays from the 1996 Malibu Conference* (ed. Stanley E. Porter and Dennis L. Stamps; JSNTSup 180; Sheffield: Sheffield Academic Press, 1999), 173–209.

2. "The Intertexture of Lukan Apocalyptic Discourse," in *The Intertexture of Apocalyptic Discourse in the New Testament* (ed. Duane F. Watson; SBLSymS 14; Atlanta: Society of Biblical Literature, 2002), 45–68; "The Role of the Audience in the Determination of Argumentation: The Gospel of Luke and the Acts of the Apostles," in *Rhetorical Argumentation in Biblical Texts* (ed. A. Eriksson, T. H. Olbricht, and W. Übelacker; ESEC 8; Harrisburg, Pa.: Trinity Press International, 2002), 157–73.

3. This material was originally presented in the Rhetoric and the New Testament section of the Society of Biblical Literature Annual Meeting held in Nashville, Novem-

1. Miracle Discourse

Miracle stories can be and have been variously described. Those found in the New Testament have long been the subject of form-critical classification, beginning with Dibelius's identification of them as "tales."[4] Shortly thereafter, a major turn away from social setting and from the social origins of biblical forms to the identification of the forms as such occurred. Bultmann's reformulation of form-criticism began with only two categories of forms—"sayings" and "narratives"—and divided narratives into miracle stories and historical stories. Of these, miracle stories were intended to demonstrate Jesus' messianic authority or divine power and could take the form of healing miracles (including exorcisms) and nature miracles.[5]

Recently authors have attempted to move beyond the study of Gospel miracle stories understood on their own and have attempted to locate New Testament miracle stories within the larger context of Greco-Roman miracle stories. An excellent example of this move can be found in Wendy Cotter's collection of miracle stories of the Greco-Roman period.[6] Specifically, Cotter is interested in identifying among Greco-Roman stories "those narratives in which a wonderful rescue or salvation of someone takes place by the overturning of the 'canons of the ordinary' through the intervention of a deity or hero."[7] Cotter's work has now progressed significantly, and her insights will be important for any future reflection on this material.[8]

However, given that my goal here attempts to further Vernon Robbins's approach,[9] I will first of all show the point to which Robbins has brought his analysis and then show how his work helps us to identify what

---

ber, 2000, and was thus a first attempt at identifying the rhetorical argumentation underlying miracle discourse.

4. Martin Dibelius, *From Tradition to Gospel* (trans. B. L. Woolf and Martin Dibelius; New York: Scribner's, 1935), 70.

5. Rudolf Bultmann, *History of the Synoptic Tradition* (trans. John Marsh; New York: Harper and Row, 1963).

6. Wendy J. Cotter, *Miracles in Greco-Roman Antiquity: A Sourcebook* (London: Routledge, 1999).

7. Ibid., 2. Cotter here cites Harold Remus, *Pagan-Christian Conflict Over Miracle in the Second Century* (Patristic Monograph Series; Cambridge: Philadelphia Patristic Foundation, 1983), though gives no page for the citation.

8. Wendy J. Cotter, *The Christ of the Miracle Stories: Portrait Through Encounter* (Grand Rapids: Baker Academic, 2010).

9. Vernon K. Robbins, "The Dialectical Nature of Early Christian Discourse,"

he calls miracle discourse and its argumentation in Luke-Acts. I will then use material collected and subsequently analyzed by Cotter to shed further light on Robbins's insights.

1.1. THE GOAL OF SOCIORHETORICAL ANALYSIS:
IDENTIFYING RHETORICAL CULTURES (RHETOROLECTS)

Since the mid-1990s, Vernon Robbins has constructed an approach he calls "sociorhetorical analysis." Contrary to the opinion of some, this approach does not simply and haphazardly bring existing methods into play[10] but, as Robbins shows in his two 1996 works,[11] enables researchers to explore the "textures" of New Testament texts in a "programmatic" way by using methods that explore different textures of the text. Robbins's two 1996 works remain the most complete exposition of the essential elements of the approach to date, though how the approach has continued to develop can be seen in a variety of later works, including Robbins's overview of it,[12] a major programmatic volume that points sociorhetorical interpretation (SRI) in new directions,[13] and most recently an important collected series of programmatic essays on SRI, including Robbins's "The Present and Future of Rhetorical Analysis."[14]

Central to this programmatic study is the attempt to provide an analysis of the "textures" of Mediterranean religious texts with a view to identifying rhetorical cultures, or as Robbins's terms it—following the work of Benjamin Hary—"rhetorolects."[15] As Robbins describes it, "A rhetorolect

---

Scriptura 59 (1996): 353–62, http://www.religion.emory.edu/faculty/robbins/SRS/vkr/dialect.cfm.

10. Vernon K. Robbins, Response to the reviews of Culpepper, Dean, and Newby, *JSNT* 70 (1998): 101–7.

11. Vernon K. Robbins, *Exploring the Texture of Texts: A Guide to Socio-Rhetorical Interpretation* (Valley Forge, Pa.: Trinity Press International, 1996); idem, *The Tapestry of Early Christian Discourse: Rhetoric, Society and Ideology* (London: Routledge, 1996).

12. Vernon K. Robbins, "Socio-Rhetorical Interpretation from Its Beginnings to the Present" (paper presented at SNTS, Pretoria, 1999), http://www.religion.emory.edu/faculty/robbins/Pdfs/SNTSPretSocRhetfromBeginning.pdf.

13. Vernon K. Robbins, *The Invention of Christian Discourse: Volume 1* (Rhetoric of Religious Antiquity; Blandford Forum, U.K.: Deo, 2009).

14. Vernon K. Robbins, *Sea Voyages and Beyond: Emerging Strategies in Socio-Rhetorical Interpretation* (ESEC 14; Blandford Forum, U.K.: Deo, 2010).

15. Robbins, "Dialectical Nature"; Benjamin H. Hary, *Multiglossia in Judeo-Ara-*

is a form of language variety or discourse identifiable on the basis of a distinctive configuration of themes, topics, reasonings, and argumentations."[16] Or again, basing himself on the assertion of Clifford Geertz that culture is organized in a "logico-meaningful" way, while society is organized in a "causal-functional" way, Robbins asserts that

> rhetorolects contain reasoning that reveals the logico-meaningful integration of a culture. In fact, one could argue that the focus of sociorhetorical analysis is the identification of rhetorical cultures and the way in which different forms of those cultures are interwoven with or embedded into others in order to create precise, audience-specific discursive cultures.[17]

These "rhetorolects," however, do not exist in a "pure" form in normal discourse; rather, "by their nature, rhetorolects interpenetrate one another and interact with one another like dialects do when people from different dialectical areas converse with one another."[18] The work of sociorhetorical analysis, then, becomes not simply the positing of unique rhetorolects but more significantly the identification of how separate and unique rhetorolects are interwoven to create discourse.

There are clearly various ways that such identification could proceed. Following Robbins, I have suggested that there are two primary criteria that enable us to identify rhetorical modes: (1) the rhetorical topoi regularly found in such discourses, and (2) the way those topoi are configured argumentatively in the textures of the text.[19]

---

bic with an Edition, Translation and Grammatical Study of the Cairene Purim Scroll (Études sur le Judaïsme Médiéval 14; Leiden: Brill, 1992), xiii.

16. Robbins, "Dialectical Nature," 356.

17. Robbins, "Dialectical Nature," 356; Clifford Geertz, "Ritual and Social Change: A Javanese Example," *American Anthropologist* 59 (1957): 35. On this point, see also my work, "Role of the Audience."

18. Robbins, "Dialectical Nature," 356.

19. "Paul's Inclusive Language: The Ideological Texture of Romans 1," in *Fabrics of Discourse: Essays in Honor of Vernon K. Robbins* (ed. D. B. Gowler, L. G. Bloomquist, and D. F. Watson; Harrisburg, Pa.: Trinity Press International, 2003), 165–93.

1.2. Christian Rhetorical Discourses and Their Configuration

The most complete, published presentation of the different discourses and their respective argumentative forms is found in Robbins's recent work *The Invention of Christian Discourse*. Here, Robbins more fully describes and analyzes the six major rhetorolects that he had earlier identified in early Christian discourse and their defining features: wisdom, miracle, apocalyptic, prophetic, priestly (formerly identified as "suffering-death"), and precreation discourse.

As noted above, however, what one finds in early Christian discourse is not any pure rhetorolect, but rather the interaction of rhetorolects in early Christianity. While it is no doubt true that some early Christian speakers or writers operated primarily within the context of one rhetorolect, more often than not they energetically intermingled various rhetorolects in their discourse. Thus, whether it be the privileging of one rhetorolect over another or the distinctive intermingling of rhetorolects, such choices introduced distinctive sociorhetorical features to their discourse. Furthermore, the overall differences in privileging one rhetorolect over another, as well as unique interminglings, created a marvelously rich rhetorical environment that we can indeed call "Christian discourse."

Within this environment, what role does so-called miracle discourse or miracle rhetorolect play? Early on, Robbins had identified "miracle discourse" as a discourse that "presupposes that God responds to humans in contexts of danger or disease and that Jesus is the mediator of these benefits to humans."[20] More specifically, he had identified within this discourse certain common topoi that we regularly find: "fear," "cowardice," and the response of "belief."[21] He then went on to show how these topoi were interwoven into the narrative in the Markan miracle stories,[22] observing that human emotions, associated with words of "fear," "cowardice," "faith," and "touching," are prominent in many miracle stories.

These observations are consistent with Cotter's overall approach to both the miracle stories of Mark and the earlier pre-Markan form of the stories. For example, Cotter notes that the petitioners of miracles in the pre-Markan material, as well as in Mark, "provide a very challenging ideal

---

20. Robbins, "Dialectical Nature," 358.
21. Ibid.
22. Vernon K. Robbins, "Interpreting Miracle Culture and Parable Culture in Mark 4–11," *SEÅ* 59 (1994): 59–81.

to the ordinary person. Interestingly, the narrator/s seem to choose bold, brash, outrageous, rude petitioners to approach Jesus."[23] Given Robbins's characterization of these petitioners, however, it becomes clear why they are such ideal rhetorical characters both to display the true need and subsequently, and as Cotter also notes, to highlight the action of Jesus.

Robbins also highlighted Cotter's point about Jesus' action when he noted that the sacred texture picture of Jesus that is developed falls within the context of the Jewish cultural presentation of God as Creator, Sustainer, and Redeemer.[24] These topoi are interwoven by means of an argumentative form that is based on a central, and what we probably would best call "sacred" and "ideological," premise, namely, "that all things are possible for God." From this premise, however, flow "various conditions which people must fulfill in order to receive extraordinary benefits in times of crisis, special need, or affliction," including faith, prayer, fasting, and so on.[25] In other words, while everything *is* possible for God, particular human actions are requisite as well.

This led Robbins to conclude, in the case of Mark, that the argumentative goal of miracle discourse is shaped by sacred texture elements: "If a person asks out of belief, that plea is a prayer to God," for "God cares whether or not humans perish or are afflicted with disease," a caring that is reflected in Jesus.[26] Robbins intuits from this that God's concern for "individual people's lives"—with Jesus as "the person through whom the powers of God work to answer their needs and fears"—will be a central characteristic of early Christian miracle discourse.[27] Cotter further confirms this insight.[28]

As an illustration, Robbins considers the cursing of the fig tree (Mark 11:12–25), to which the miracles in Mark have led. To the reader of Mark all of the pleas (spoken or unspoken) for healing are in fact "prayers"; accordingly, "the logic seems to be this: if a person asks out of belief, that plea is a prayer to God."[29] For Robbins, then, "miracle discourse is primarily epideictic and deliberative rhetoric. Through praise and censure, the

---

23. Cotter, *Christ of the Miracle Stories*, 7.
24. Robbins, "Interpreting Miracle Culture," 74.
25. Robbins, "Dialectical Nature," 358.
26. Robbins, "Interpreting Miracle Culture," 66.
27. Robbins, *Tapestry of Early Christian Discourse*, 167–71.
28. Cotter, *Christ of the Miracle Stories*, 7.
29. Robbins, "Dialectical Nature," 358. A similar logic appears in Jas 5:15–18.

stories of Jesus' healing nurture a worldview in which God offers relief and restoration to people in contexts of belief and prayer. People must follow certain guidelines for these special acts of benevolence to be granted."[30]

But Robbins also believes that the argumentative logic here, along with the topoi and their configuration, evidence the social environment within which miracle discourse functions. In order to discover this setting, Robbins follows Bryan Wilson's identification of how religious sects respond to evil in the world. In the case of miracle discourse, Robbins adopts Wilson's understanding of a thaumaturgical response:[31]

> The thaumaturgical response focuses on the individual's concern for relief from present and specific ills by special dispensations. The request for supernatural help is personal and local, and its operation is magical. Salvation is immediate but has no general application beyond the given case and others like it. Salvation takes the form of healing, assuagement of grief, restoration after loss, reassurance, the foresight and avoidance of calamity, and the guarantee of eternal (or at least continuing) life after death.

The centrality of the sacred texture in Markan miracle discourse is crucial for Robbins's conclusions about the fuller identification of the social and cultural texture of miracle discourse, an identification that should eventually lead us to a better understanding of the discursive culture within which miracle discourse works. Toward this end, and building on the identification by Paul Achtemeier of a chain of miracle stories in Mark 4–8[32] and by Burton Mack of the projection of a picture of Jesus as perpetuating the tradition of Moses and Elijah in Mark,[33] Robbins sees that early Christian miracle discourse picks up themes from both Jewish and Greco-Roman culture and reuses them in new and fruitful ways. Thus the Markan "variation of dominant Jewish and Greco-Roman traditions that feature the great healers of the past like Moses, Elijah, and Asclepius"[34] evidences subcultural rhetoric in the form of "the presence of well-nurtured

---

30. Robbins," Dialectical Nature," 359.
31. Robbins, *Exploring the Texture of Texts*, 73; Bryan R. Wilson, *Magic and the Millennium* (Frogmore, St. Albans, Herts: Paladin, 1975), 24–25.
32. Paul J. Achtemeier, "Toward the Isolation of Pre-Marcan Miracle Catenae," *JBL* (1970): 265–91.
33. Burton L. Mack, *A Myth of Innocence: Mark and Christian Origins* (Philadelphia: Fortress, 1988).
34. Robbins, *Tapestry of Early Christian Discourse*, 170–71.

miracle social rhetoric within certain early Christian circles" and its integration with other social rhetorics,[35] namely, "Jewish dominant culture rhetoric" and "dominant Hellenistic-Roman rhetoric."

Robbins argues that Markan miracle rhetoric is subcultural in relation to Jewish, dominant culture rhetoric, which "contains strong miracle rhetoric," because Markan miracle rhetoric uses "great traditions" from Torah and Deuteronomic History—that is, from the lives of Moses, Elijah, and Elisha—to show not how "the values of life and salvation espoused by dominant Jewish culture" are wrong but to show how followers of Jesus can claim special access to the divine powers through Jesus.[36]

It is a nuanced subcultural rhetoric, however, because the scene of the cursing of the fig tree—where the goal of fulfilling the prophetic expectation that the temple should be a house of prayer for all peoples (Isa 56:7)—sits in tension with the prophetic denunciation of the priests and scribes, who have made the temple a den of robbers (Jer 7:11). Markan miracle discourse, therefore, spans both subculture and contraculture (i.e., a culture in which behavior found in the dominant culture is inverted, though "without providing a clear rationale for an alternative system of action and thought," which would be the case in a "counterculture").[37]

Markan miracle discourse has a very different relationship to Hellenistic-Roman rhetoric and the stories such as those that Cotter assembles and analyzes. Robbins suggests, somewhat hesitantly I think, that because Hellenistic-Roman miracle rhetoric "exhibits significant restraint about individual action by divine powers to remove illness and affliction," Markan miracle discourse must be understood to be a subcultural element within that dominant, Greco-Roman rhetoric, even though "miraculous healing and portent was widespread."[38] He even sees a similar tension to the one noted above when he argues that Markan miracle rhetoric also has contracultural elements aimed at the Hellenistic-Roman culture in the form of the statement of the woman having wasted her wealth on physicians (Mark 5:26) and the name of the demon being "legion": "Instead of going to a physician, one should go to a religious healer who works with divine powers.... Instead of a legion of the army bringing peace and sanity in a

---

35. Robbins, "Interpreting Miracle Culture," 69.
36. Ibid., 70.
37. Ibid., 70–71.
38. Ibid., 72–73; Howard Clark Kee, *Miracle in the Early Christian World: A Study in Sociohistorical Method* (New Haven: Yale University Press, 1983), 78–145.

region, it brings the most insane kind of violence and brutality."[39] Robbins believes "most non-Jewish and non-Christian people in Mediterranean society could hear and understand Markan miracle rhetoric as a particular ethnic form of Hellenistic-Roman subculture rhetoric."[40]

Subsequently, Robbins focused on sensory-aesthetic texture and the underlying cultural meaning associated with bodies and body actions in an attempt to identify rhetorical discourse more precisely. This focus led him to assert that

> the primary topos underlying biblical miracle discourse is the power of God. The hands and the mouth, the same two body parts implicit in God's creation of the world (Gen 1: God's mouth; Gen 2: God's hands), are the primary agents for miracles to occur in early Christian miracle rhetorolect (God's mouth in Gen 1 and God's hands in Gen 2). Much like Moses' hands and mouth were the primary agents of God's power when he confronted Pharaoh and the challenges in the wilderness after leading the people out of Egypt, so Jesus' hands and mouth are the agents of the body through which the finger of God miraculously works in the Gospels, and followers of Jesus receive these abilities as successors to Jesus' miraculous activities. Yet the Elijah-Elisha tradition is more of a resource for early Christian miracle discourse than the Moses tradition. The manner in which Elijah and Elisha use their hands, mouth, and feet in relation to other people establish primary patterns for early Christian miracle rhetorolect.[41]

In expectation of the second volume of *The Invention of Christian Discourse*, in which Robbins lays out more fully what miracle discourse might entail, I would like to offer some suggestions as to what else will need to be kept in mind as we proceed.

1.3. A FULLER IDENTIFICATION OF MIRACLE DISCOURSE: TWO DIFFERENT KINDS OF MIRACLE DISCOURSE

In spite of Robbins's significant contribution to the exploration of the notion of miracle discourse culture, I would suggest that more needs to

---

39. Robbins, "Interpreting Miracle Culture," 73.
40. Ibid., 73.
41. Vernon K. Robbins, "Recent Developments in Socio-Rhetorical Interpretation" (paper given at the meetings of the SNTS, Bonn, July 29–August 1, 2003).

and can be said. In fact, in asserting this, I am following Robbins's own lead: he concludes his initial exploration of miracle discourse by noting that "a full socio-rhetorical exploration of this discourse in its contexts in the Gospels awaits interpreters who are equipped to analyze and interpret it."[42] I believe that the papers in this volume, and their responses, are a significant step in that direction.

To start with, I would reaffirm that Robbins has successfully identified miracle discourse, at least in terms of what we might call primarily "thaumaturgical" (following Wilson's taxonomy) topics and of an argumentation that fits such a discourse. But it appears to me that there is another form that a miracle rhetorolect also takes, both in terms of the topoi and their argumentative configuration. I would suggest that it is the form we find most commonly referred to as "magic," exemplary Greco-Roman texts of which are found in Cotter.[43]

It seems to me that part of the problem for us in identifying rhetorical miracle discourse lies in the unclear lines of definition concerning, on the one side, what is called magic, and on the other, miracle, both of which are often gathered together under what I would call miracle discourse. The attempt to distinguish the phenomena associated with these two general terms is not new. Lucy Mair, for example, illustrated the distinction when she noted that a person or group that seeks resolution through manipulation of forces is doing magic, while a person or group that seeks resolution through communication with spiritual beings is doing something religious, something we might call "miracle."[44]

This begins to get at an important distinction, but Cotter notes that "older scholarship presumed that there were certain elements of 'magic' that clearly distinguished it from miracle. Today, we recognize that the subject of magic is far more complex."[45] Curiously, though, she continues the distinction by creating a separate category in her work for "miracle"

---

42. Robbins, *Tapestry of Early Christian Discourse*, 171.

43. Cotter, *Miracles in Greco-Roman Antiquity*, 173–200. I presented this distinction at the Rhetorics of Healing conference, held in Claremont and Redlands, California in 2002. L. Gregory Bloomquist, "First Century Models of Bodily Healing and Their Socio-Rhetorical Transformation in Some NT Traditions," *Queen*, special issue (2002), http://www.ars-rhetorica.net/Queen/VolumeSpecialIssue/Articles/Bloomquist.pdf.

44. Lucy Mair, *An Introduction to Social Anthropology* (Oxford: Clarendon, 1972), 229, cited in Kee, *Miracle*, 212.

45. Cotter, *Miracles in Greco-Roman Antiquity*, 175.

stories and those that one could identify as "magic" without explaining how, other than generically or canonically, one can make that distinction. I agree with her about the distinction and want to suggest that in fact a better understanding of what we have identified as a rhetorolect called "miracle discourse" allows for a better differentiation than those of a previous era.

A common understanding of *magic* is drawn from the merely pejorative use of the word, which uses it as a catchword or "negative label to explain the successful supernatural deeds of any hero" who is not part of one's own tradition.[46] More helpfully, Marcel Mauss and Gerardus van der Leeuw identified magic as the combination of ritual acts that are correctly performed, pronouncements that are efficacious when using exact formulas, and consequent coerced actions and outcomes.[47] According to Howard Clark Kee, fifth-century C.E. Roman "magical" texts show that "the efficacy of magic depended on the recitation of multiple divine names, on the forcefulness of orders to the gods, on elaborate recipes for magical foods and extensive ritual, on observing the proper times as derived from phases of the moon or special days, and on the use of secret magical words, many of which are nonsense."[48] One cannot but help note here the resonance between Kee's understanding of this late understanding of magic and Robbins's statements regarding miracle discourse in Mark. Cotter's collection of "magical" texts seems to confirm the accuracy of both of these assessments, suggesting a broad, transtemporal, cultural model rather than mere historical instances.

I believe it is possible to expand on Kee's exploration by identifying these features of miracle discourse. We can do so by remarking that Robbins's appeal to Wilson's categories of cultural response to evil sought to identify miracle culture by appealing to only one form of sectarian approach to evil in the world, namely, thaumaturgical. I would suggest

---

46. Ibid., 176.
47. Marcel Mauss, *A General Theory of Magic* (trans. R. Brain; New York: W. W. Norton, 1972), 55–60; Gerardus van der Leeuw, *Religion in Essence and Manifestation* (ed. B. Nelson; trans. J. E. Turner; New York: Harper & Row, 1963), 2:423, cited in Kee, *Miracle*, 212–13.
48. Kee, *Miracle*, 214. As Kee notes, "magical" texts suggest that the main preoccupation of the performers is defense against evil spirits, enemies, or disease, as well as the desire for eternal life. His conclusion is that their aim is "to coerce the powers, to force one's way into the consciousness of a distant and inaccessible god … to manipulate the powers so that one can achieve one's goal."

that a gnostic-manipulationist response to evil is central to some miracle discourse but in a very different way.

According to Wilson, gnostic-manipulationist responses to the world are not first of all about changes in social or cultural goals (as is the case in introversionist or revolutionist responses to culture) but about changing the *means* whereby goals are attained. The primary goal is a "transformed set of relationships—a transformed method of coping with evil."[49] Robbins summarizes Wilson's point by focusing on the sacred aspect of gnostic-manipulationist goals: "Salvation is possible in the world, and evil may be overcome if people learn the right means, improved techniques, to deal with their problems."[50] Because of the emphasis on technique, gnostic-manipulationist approaches to evil also create a self-consciousness that practitioners are part of a small cadre that has received "special instruction about the enigmatic wisdom in the message, and the success of the truth of the message even though its success itself is a mystery."[51]

As this quote from Robbins indicates, Robbins himself suggests that gnostic-manipulationist language is not alien to Mark, and he in fact identifies it in Mark by contrasting it with thaumaturgical topics there! Thus, following Mack, he specifically points to the parables and their interpretation in Mark 4:1–34 as evidence of gnostic-manipulationist emphases: the Twelve are given the secret to the interpretation of parables, while those outside remain confused.[52]

Furthermore, as in the case of thaumaturgical culture, gnostic-manipulationist responses occur in relation to the surrounding Jewish and Hellenistic-Roman cultures, but that relation is different from the thaumaturgical response. For example, gnostic-manipulationist responses in Mark can be seen to be subcultural, not in relation to Jewish dominant culture rhetoric of the "great" traditions as thaumaturgical culture had been, but subcultural to *specific* Jewish subcultural rhetorics evidenced in apocalyptic, wisdom, and prophetic literature. Specifically, it is a relation that "claims to be in a position to receive special benefits articulated as values within Jewish tradition."[53]

---

49. Wilson, *Magic and the Millennium*, 24.
50. Robbins, *Exploring the Texture of Texts*, 73.
51. Robbins, "Interpreting Miracle Culture," 77.
52. Mack, *A Myth of Innocence: Mark and Christian Origins*, 150–65.
53. Robbins, "Interpreting Miracle Culture," 78–79.

In relation to Hellenistic-Roman culture, on the other hand, Markan gnostic-manipulationist responses are subcultural to the dominant Hellenistic-Roman culture of paideia. The latter, associated with wisdom discourse, has its focus on "nurturing one's mind and action through disciplined attainment of wisdom." It is also an "ethnic form of reasoning" that "isolates a few discrete items in an overall cultural environment that it attacks vigourously to establish its boundaries and identity" while leaving people free to "participate in a wide range of presuppositions and behaviors in the surrounding cultural environment." The result of gnostic-manipulationist discourse is thus very different from the attempt to create a kind of Hellenistic Christian "academy" based on wisdom discourse, but would in fact be a possible setting for an "academy" based on a gnostic-manipulationist understanding of Jesus' words.[54]

Nevertheless, a major question that arises in light of Robbins's work on Mark and our discussion of miracle is whether we need to limit this "gnostic-manipulationist" response to the "sayings" of Jesus. Is it not possible that such a response can also be seen in the "deeds" of Jesus, and thus possibly in the miracle discourse of Mark, that is, in the rhetography of Mark? Indeed, Mark does seem to have "magical" elements in the story of Jesus, elements that are excluded from Matthew and Luke, as in the case of Mark 8:22–26.[55]

Accordingly, while one does not end up in Mark with the highly elaborated, formulaic responses found in the so-called magical literature, one does end up with an embryonic picture of the interweaving of various kinds of miracle into the material. Specifically with regard to gnostic-manipulationist elements, if such responses can be found as a crucial element of at least some forms of miracle discourse, then one should expect

---

54. Ibid., 78–79.
55. Cotter, *Miracles in Greco-Roman Antiquity*, 192. Furthermore, is not this then also an "academy" of practitioners "in the know," including their knowledge of miracles? For it seems quite clear—at least at first reading—that in Mark, "salvation" is very much a part of the "miracles" of Jesus, and thus of miracle discourse. Healing is clearly not something that is available to everyone; it appears to have an "inner logic" and to have resided in a shared power in his followers. Elements of "gnostic-manipulationist" responses to evil can, of course, also be found also in Matthew and Luke. I am thinking here not only of the "magical" responses found in the Matthean and Lukan accounts of Jesus' logomachia with Satan in the wilderness nor of the apostolic thaumaturgia in Acts, but also of the further attempts by apostles to master thaumaturgia (Matt 10:8; 14:28–31) and Jesus' concern that they do (Luke 22:19).

to find a fundamental focus on mastering means, whether "primitive" or elaborate, to achieve ends. This is in fact what I assert we find in some strata of early Christian miracle discourse, including Mark.

Now, paradoxically perhaps in the eyes of some we also find texts that underscore the fundamental inability to master a technique that will lead to a healing (e.g., Mark 9:14–29). But, as I have suggested, one reason for this apparent paradox is the interweaving of other forms of miracle discourse, namely, the thaumaturgical kind, in which "healing … relies on topics of the unexpected, of inability to describe fully what has happened, and of the ineffable and numinous element of the sacred entering in some sort of uncontrolled way."[56] The cultural transformation that "thaumaturgical discourse" seeks to effect is one that has no prescriptive form, no diagnostic or remedy that Jesus passes on to those who will continue the cultural transformation. What Jesus passes on to his followers in the rhetorical tradition of the Gospels is both gnostic-manipulationist prescription and thaumaturgical clues, namely, that proximity to the divine is the key both to rhetorical presentation and social transformation as understood by Jesus.[57]

Various texts in Cotter's collection seem to affirm that the thaumaturgical approach to miracles did exist in first-century Mediterranean discourse. Not only are various miracle scenes found in Aelius Aristides characteristic of this form of miracle,[58] but so are texts like the one found in Dio Cassius's *Roman History* (8.65.8) concerning the miracles reportedly performed at the hands of Vespasian. The goal is clearly not to emulate Vespasian, but to acclaim him, or, as happens with the Alexandrians, to despise him.[59]

2. Sociorhetorical Attention to Argumentative Texture

The recent work of Kee, Robbins, Cotter, and others helps us to put on the table the common, social, and final topics that miracle discourse will incorporate uniquely and that will allow us to identify one form of the discourse from another on the basis, at least in part, of that incorporation. However, the other part of the equation is how these topics are intertwined

---

56. Bloomquist, "First Century Models of Healing."
57. See ibid.
58. Aelius Aristides, *The Complete Works* (trans. C. A. Behr; Leiden: Brill, 1981).
59. Cotter, *Miracles in Greco-Roman Antiquity*, 42.

toward particular argumentative ends. So, before we proceed to discover miracle discourse in Luke-Acts, we need to look at a final significant piece of our attempt to identify more fully what we can still call "miracle discourse," namely, the role of argumentative texture in rhetorical discourse. The particular argumentative ends to which the intertwining of topics are put will, I believe, provide us with an even fuller picture of miracle rhetorical discourse in both its forms.

2.1. TYPES OF ARGUMENTATION

Argumentation is at the root of both classical rhetoric and modern neo-Aristotelian rhetorical analysis. In both, two forms of argumentation are dominant: deductive or logical argumentation and inductive or qualitative argumentation.[60] Aristotle, who names these two forms as the basic forms of rhetorical persuasion, also argues that the deductive approach, with the enthymeme at its root, is the stronger of the two, while the inductive approach, based on the paradigm, is the more entertaining but less powerful (*Rhet.* 1.2.8).

Deductive or logical (enthymematic) argumentation, from which Robbins develops his notion of rhetology, can take a variety of forms. Basically, however, as Robbins notes, it "presents assertions and supports them with reasons, clarifies them through opposites and contraries, and possibly presents short or elaborate counterarguments."[61] *Assertions* are statements like "If anyone wants to follow me, he or she must be ready to give up his or her life." *Rationales* attempt to provide reasons for the assertion, such as "The reason you must be ready to give up your life if you want to follow me is because, if you seek to save your life, you will lose it." *Clarifications* are sometimes made by presenting the opposite from

---

60. One might also include here the logical form called "abduction." See Richard L. Lanigan, "From Enthymeme to Abduction: The Classical Law of Logic and the Postmodern Rule of Rhetoric," in *Recovering Pragmatism's Voice: The Classical Tradition, Rorty, and the Philosophy of Communication* (ed. L. Langsdorf and A. R. Smith; SUNY Series in the Philosophy of the Social Sciences; Albany: State University of New York Press, 1996), 49–70, and my response to the use of "abduction" in L. Gregory Bloomquist, "A Possible Direction for Providing Programmatic Correlation of Textures in Socio-Rhetorical Analysis," in *Rhetorical Criticism and the Bible: Essays from the 1996 Malibu Conference* (ed. Stanley E. Porter and Dennis L. Stamps; JSNTSup 195; Sheffield: Sheffield Academic Press, 2002), 61–96.

61. Robbins, *Exploring the Texture of Texts*, 21.

the case or the contrary from the case; a clarification of the assertion "No one can say that Jesus is Lord unless he or she is in the power of the Holy Spirit" and its rationale "because the Holy Spirit alone gives one knowledge of Jesus as Lord" might be "as you can see in that not everyone who calls Jesus Lord is one of his." Strengthening the assertion that forms the basis of logical argumentation are often *counterarguments* that undermine alternate or competing assertions; for example, in support of Paul's assertion that Christ is all that the Gentiles need to be pleasing to God, and the extensive rationales he invokes to support the assertion, Paul also provides counterarguments as to why the law is unable to save in the way Christ is able to save (see Rom 2:25).

In this deductive form of argument, one notes above all the logical tightness of the argument and the way in which supporting argumentative elements make the conclusion compelling. In fact, in works such as Paul's Letter to the Romans, the logical argumentation is so tight that if one misses any premise in the argument the reader may easily misunderstand the whole.[62]

Inductive or qualitative (paradigmatic) argumentation is the ground from which Robbins speaks of rhetography. Such argumentation provides the reader with a "quality of images and descriptions" that encourage "the reader to accept the portrayal as true and real. This occurs when analogies, examples, and citation of ancient testimony function in a persuasive manner."[63] Qualitative argumentation does not provide a statement, back it up with good reasons, and suggest why alternatives are no alternative to that position at all; instead, the reader or hearer is given a series of images and descriptions that presents a tableau before the reader, who, as in a dramatic presentation, not only assents but also "feels" that what he or she is hearing and seeing is true. It does so using analogies (e.g., "Your neighbor is something like the person in the following story…"), examples ("a good leader? well, take JFK for example…"), or citation of ancient testimony ("who is a friend? well, as the book of Proverbs says…"), or some combination of these.

Excellent examples of inductive argumentation that we associate with rhetography in biblical rhetorical address can be found in parables. One notes, for example, in Nathan's story to David (2 Sam 12) that, through the

---

62. Bloomquist, "Paul's Inclusive Language," 178–92.
63. Robbins, *Exploring the Texture of Texts*, 21.

use of analogy, dramatic tension is produced and the conclusion becomes compelling, not due to any rationale provided, but to the power of the analogy alone. However, in this case, Nathan must eventually explicitly name David as the culprit in the crime, since the "argument" itself only leads to the conclusion as to what one should do about someone who is like the person Nathan has alluded to, not who it is exactly who is like that. Paradigmatic, or qualitative, or inductive argumentation leaves the door open both to application and to exclusion. Had David asked Nathan why he was the one alluded to in the story, then Nathan would have been forced to engage David rhetologically (e.g., "You are the man, because…").

2.2. The Argumentative Texture of Miracle Discourse

Robbins helpfully and carefully lays out these two forms of argumentation in relation to early Christian discourse in his 1996 works.[64] More recently, however, and as noted, he has created the "neologisms" of *rhetography* for the development of topoi in pictorial-narrative elaboration (i.e., the communication of a mental picture) and *rhetology* for the development of topoi in enthymematic-syllogistic elaboration

One helpful way in which these neologisms assist analysis is to note that there are some rhetorolects in which rhetology is dominant, and some in which rhetography is dominant. I have already suggested that rhetology is dominant in some forms of discourse when compared with others, for example, apocalyptic compared with wisdom.[65]

I would now suggest that in that form of miracle discourse that is dominated by gnostic-manipulationist responses and its desire to gain a certain control of evil by someone who desires to be free of it or inflict it on another, we will likely find logical argumentation or "rhetology" to dominate. In magical formulas, including rites, gestures, mixtures, and so on, the logic must be clear and it must be tight:

General premise (unexpressed but assumed): My use of particular formulaic actions x [saying the following words / mixing the following potion / doing the following gestures / etc.] will result in a person doing y.

---

64. Ibid., 21–29; Robbins, *Tapestry of Early Christian Discourse*, 77–89.
65. Bloomquist, "Role of the Audience."

Minor premise: I did prescribed actions x.
Therefore: The person will do y.

Or, as it would be stated in common discourse, "The person or situation that is the object of the formula will do y because the one who performs the formula did x."

In this approach, nothing is left to chance or surprise. That this is the case is of course clear in the magical texts, which set forth prescriptions for maladies, though they do not normally set forth the "general premise" as to why the prescription will work. Enthymematically, they do not need to do so. This is why in the magical texts themselves rhetology is expressed in a succinct, manual-like form of instructions: "This is what you do, if you want y to happen" (or "If you do x, you will receive y" or "You will receive y because you did x").[66] The fuller explanation of the "enthymeme" can be found and is found in scientific descriptions of magical formulas and actions (e.g., in the several texts of Pliny's *Natural History* found in Cotter[67]), as one might expect from science, in which all the premises and conclusions must be spelled out.

In the case of what I have called thaumaturgical miracle discourse, however, qualitative argumentation, or rhetography, will likely be more common, as it is in some other forms of rhetorical discourses, such as, for example, wisdom discourse. In the case of wisdom discourse, rhetography is dominant because of the place of story and analogy.[68] Qualitative discourse is a defining feature of thaumaturgical miracle discourse because here enthymematic rationales would undermine the very discourse itself and turn it into gnostic-manipulationist miracle discourse.

Thus, not surprisingly, a reader is often hard-pressed to identify the rationale in some "miracle" stories but not in others. While in gnostic-

---

66. See, e.g., the examples given in Cotter, *Miracles in Greco-Roman Antiquity*, 191–99, especially that of the PGM 12.160–178 (Cotter, *Miracles*, 199). There are, however, occasions in which qualitative argumentation will also be used in this form of miracle discourse. I would suggest, however, that it is used here primarily as a means of effecting in an audience a leap to the conclusion that the power at work should be heeded. The use of qualitative argumentation is, in this way, a *captatio* or a *probatio* for an audience, but not the primary means whereby the argument progresses. An excellent example of this phenomenon is found in Philostratus's *Vita Apollonii* (Cotter, *Miracles*, 43–45).

67. Cotter, *Miracles in Greco-Roman Antiquity*, 178–82.

68. Bloomquist, "Role of the Audience," 160–63.

manipulationist miracle discourse, there should be no doubt about the source and cause of the "miracle," in thaumaturgical miracle discourse the result is often confusion and wonder and uncertainty about how exactly the miracle came about (e.g., see the scholarly discussions that attempt to identify the "mechanism" of the miracle in either Mark 5:24–34 or John 2:1–12).

Yet, though enigmatic, thaumaturgical discourse is not simply a picture but discourse. For example, the story of Jesus' action of healing the demoniac in the synagogue (Mark 1:23–28) is told in such a way as to suggest that it is not first of all an event or a "deed" done by Jesus but a "teaching." It is a teaching through deed; that is, the event is narrated in a way that is compellingly real for both a narrative audience *and* for an implied audience. As happens throughout qualitative argumentation, the narration is so affectively compelling that no logical counterargument is needed or even possible, by the narrative characters present or by the implied reader!

Now, as in the New Testament, so too in some of the literature surveyed by Cotter, these two forms of argumentation are interwoven in miracle stories. While the reason for this interweaving is not always clear in the fragmentary episodes in Cotter's texts, in the New Testament texts, there appears to be a clear reason for the interweaving. Take, for example, a story in which rhetology has a predominant role: the story of the woman with the flow of blood (Mark 5 and par.). Robbins notes that rhetology is clear in the woman's rationale: "If only I touch the garment, I shall be healed."[69] To express this more fully, one might propose the following:

General premise (unstated): One who touches Jesus' garment can be healed
Specific premise: I touched Jesus' garment.
Conclusion: I have been healed because I touched Jesus' garment.

---

69. Robbins, "Interpreting Miracle Culture," 67; idem, "The Woman Who Touched Jesus' Garment: A Socio-Rhetorical Analysis and the Synoptic Accounts," *NTS* 33 (1987): 502–15. Robbins relates the logic of Mark 9 to this rhetorical syllogism in Mark 5. There, on the basis of the petition of the father of the demoniac boy, who asks Jesus, "If it is possible, help us," and Jesus' response, "All things are possible to the one who believes," Robbins argues that there is a logical syllogism ("Interpreting Miracle Culture," 68), which, though he does not explicate it, can be suggested as: (1) General premise: All things are possible to the one who believes; (2) Specific premise: The father believes; (3) Conclusion: The father will receive even this seemingly impossible request for healing because he believes.

Closer attention to this story, however, reveals that it successfully does interweave the rhetology of gnostic-manipulationist miracle discourse and its expected results (on the part of the woman) but that it does so together with the rhetography of thaumaturgical miracle discourse and its surprising results. These are apparent in Jesus' words.[70] In other words, the woman's rhetologically driven motive contrasts with the words of Jesus. These words enigmatically place what happens in a qualitatively different framework from what her purely logical expectation would have led her to believe.

What is the reason for this interweaving? While clumsy construction is always a possibility, attention to redactional technique throughout Mark might also suggest that the author or a redactor may be cautioning a constructed audience against a strict dependence on the clarity and linearity of logical argumentation that is present in gnostic-manipulationist miracle discourse. Thus, while an author like Mark may indeed be establishing models of petitioners for subsequent readers,[71] it is also likely that these readers are being cautioned rhetorically against a simple reduction of petitions to a series of formulas drawn from the Gospel miracle accounts.

It is even possible that the author or redactor is using that discourse in the story as a foil for his warning. So-called magic is easily visualized: incantations, formulas for potions, gestures, and so on all accomplish assured results when performed correctly. True, not just anyone can perform them or achieve the results, for their "internal" nature is part of their essential character.[72] Nevertheless, miracle discourse that depends on thaumaturgical topics privileges simplicity, directness of expression, and, while none of the clarity and linearity of logical argumentation, a clear assessment of the drama of the situation and the dramatic need to address it. True, results may vary, and even then not necessarily as expected, or unexpected, but the result will likely be as dramatic and surprising as the need is dramatic and serious. Rational explanations of unexpected results will thus become very difficult, if not impossible![73]

---

70. Robbins confuses the fact that the underlying premise he identifies is in the woman's mind when in fact it is part of Jesus' response.

71. Cotter, *Christ of the Miracle Stories*, 8–9.

72. In fact, one of the reasons for what Kee calls "nonsense" in magical incantations is precisely so that not just anyone can repeat them.

73. An interesting example of the contrast between these two cultures is found in *Ta'anit* 3.8 regarding Honi (Onias) the Circle-Maker. At the outset of the story, when

As a result, when these two forms of discourse are blended, it may be in order to further one or the other, to correct one or the other, or to provide an entirely new avenue for reflection.[74] For an understanding of why an author or redactor may have done this, sociorhetorical interpretation looks to the analysis of the ideological texture of the text specifically in order to answer the question, why would an author do such a thing?[75]

2.3. Three Working Hypotheses Regarding the Argumentative Texture of Miracle Discourse

In light of our assumption that rhetorical discourse can be identified on the basis of topics and of argumentative texture, and in light of initial observations on "miracle" and "magic" (two catchwords for the two different forms of the miracle rhetorolect discerned by Robbins), I want to suggest three working hypotheses for what follows.

First, building on Robbins's initial insight and explorations, we can assert that the discovery of the presence of certain common textures and topoi is indeed evidence for and enables identification of rhetorical discourse or rhetorolects, including miracle discourse.

Honi is approached by the people who request that he pray in order that it rain, he prays but nothing happens; then, however, he takes the unusual and probably unexpected step of importuning God by placing a circle on the ground whence he will not move until God causes it to rain (which it does and which, via his communication with God, Honi must modulate from light to severe to moderate to cessation). I would suggest that in this example, what we have is the contrast between gnostic-manipulationist culture on behalf of the people and the relatively rare rabbinic portrayal of thaumaturgical culture in Honi's eventual success. The fact that this is thaumaturgic, rather than gnostic-manipulationist, is confirmed in the final words of R. Simeon b. Shetah, who would have condemned Honi's actions had it not been that Honi was like a "son" to God who was like "father" to him. I think that such an assertion underscores the propriety of Robbins's identification of a characteristic of thaumaturgical culture being personal communication. I would contend that miracle discourse that is primarily of thaumaturgical evidences personal communication, and its ebbs and flows, more frequently.

74. In this latter form, one can see the "emergent structure" that appears when these two, complex network blends are themselves brought together. The use of "conceptual blending" in sociorhetorical interpretation derives from the work of Gilles Fauconnier and Mark Turner, *The Way We Think: Conceptual Blending and the Mind's Hidden Complexities* (New York: Basic, 2003), 42–50.

75. Bloomquist, "Paul's Inclusive Language."

Second, rhetorical discourse (including miracle discourse) can be even more carefully identified on the basis of the artful interweaving of textures, topoi, and intertextures through particular argumentative forms, primarily logical-deductive argumentation (rhetology) and qualitative-paradigmatic argumentation (rhetography).[76] In the case of miracle discourse, this interweaving will utilize both gnostic-manipulationist miracle discourse and thaumaturgical miracle discourse.

Third, specific interweavings in nuanced and culturally embedded local ways create specific, local (i.e., cultural) rhetorolects that we can identify even more closely in their contexts. Thus we find uniquely Jewish gnostic-manipulationist and thaumaturgical miracle discourse, Isis gnostic-manipulationist and thaumaturgical miracle discourse, and Jesus gnostic-manipulationist and thaumaturgical miracle discourse, as well as a variety of other, local forms. Some features will of course be common among all of these local forms, but some will be different, since the ideological purpose will be different. This is true even within the different local forms.

---

76. Following Robbins's lead, I would suggest that both thaumaturgical and gnostic-manipulationist miracle discourse can be artfully interwoven with other discourses. For example, gnostic-manipulationist discourse can easily be interwoven with features of wisdom discourse when it comes to "law," in which the focus is on purposeful action, both for diagnosis and for control. The role of wisdom discourse as law is not specifically to exalt God's beneficence in the world (though that is an underlying presupposition behind it) but to provide an accurate assessment of why someone is in the situation that she or he is in and to afford an intelligible ritualized solution. Thus, law provides the same kind of diagnostic and control that analysis of medical symptoms does. Over against this gnostic-manipulationist approach stands that kind of miracle discourse that transcends diagnosis, and may or may not necessitate it. This form of discourse may, however, intersect with wisdom discourse as gnostic-manipulationist discourse does, but it does so where it becomes clear that what is at stake is the well-being and *shalom* of creation over against the chaotic and turbulent elements that leave people passive prey. In this way, the unexpected nature of thaumaturgical miracle discourse, as opposed to the routinized and ritualized response of gnostic-manipulationist discourse, also brings miracle discourse into connection with apocalyptic discourse and the code-breaking, countercultural element of the latter. On the nature of apocalyptic rhetoric, see L. Gregory Bloomquist, "Methodological Criteria for Apocalyptic Rhetoric: A Suggestion for the Expanded Use of Sociorhetorical Analysis," in *Vision and Persuasion: Rhetorical Dimensions of Apocalyptic Discourse* (ed. G. Carey and L. G. Bloomquist; St. Louis: Chalice, 1999), 181–203.

While these three points are suggested or developed in Robbins's own work, I want to explore now more fully the evidence for a rhetorolect of miracle discourse that is associated with Jesus and that privileges gnostic-manipulationist responses (a discourse in which argumentation takes place via a more or less strict logical and proper use of techniques to overcome or manipulate evil) and for a rhetorolect associated with Jesus, which privileges what I call thaumaturgical responses and thus one in which argumentation depends on qualitative movements that are reflective of the give and take of communication (as opposed to formulas) and that privilege possibly hoped for but not entirely expected and therefore qualitatively different results, much as communication itself does. I believe that in the specific case of Luke-Acts these two forms of miracle discourse are artfully interwoven for specific ideological goals that become evident through their analysis.[77]

3. Argumentative Texture of Miracle Discourse Found in Luke-Acts

3.1. Previous Discussions of Miracle in Luke-Acts

In his discussion of Luke-Acts, Kee argues that "miracles" have a prominent role. He also asserts that miracles, though varied, are governed by one primary theme: the fulfillment of prophecy in the context of a cosmic conflict "in which God through Jesus regains control of his errant creation."[78] Kee shows that Jesus' miraculous action in Luke-Acts promote (1) the involvement of the disciples, (2) the privileged position of the community of followers, and (3) the nature of the new age itself in which these all find themselves. Concerning the first point, Christian mission, "if it is carried out in obedience to and reliance upon Jesus," will be replicated in the lives of Jesus' disciples.[79] Second, and closely related to this, Kee observes the privileged position of the community, which finds demons subject to it (10:17–20) as to members of the elect community of God and recipients of divine revelation.[80] Third and finally, Kee notes, the followers of Jesus

---

77. Whether it was evident to "Luke" is not my point, only that the rhetorical structures of the text evidence ideological goals.
78. Kee, *Miracle*, 202–3.
79. Ibid., 205.
80. Ibid., 207–8.

are shown to be aware that they are involved in the "turn of the ages," marked by Jesus' faithful and trustworthy prediction of the fall of Jerusalem and the destruction of the temple.[81] The "cumulative force of this series of accounts of visions, angelic visitations, and miracles" that one finds throughout Luke-Acts "is to show that *God demonstrates his approbation* of each new stage in the cosmic process of redemption by a divine manifestation."[82]

Kee observes that throughout Luke-Acts "magic" is interwoven into the presentation. He notes that characteristic features of magic can be found "in some of the healing stories and a kindred outlook behind the punitive miracles."[83] Nevertheless, on the basis of passages such as Acts 12:20–23 (the death of Herod Agrippa), Kee also concludes that magical elements are relativized by Luke. In these passages Luke portrays "God's control over history rather than an instance of magic (no technique is hinted at) or of a miraculous action on the part of any human being."[84] Thus, Kee argues, "for Luke miracle functions, not only to heighten the drama of the narrative, but also to show that at every significant point in the transitions of Christianity from its Jewish origins in Jerusalem to its Gentile outreaching to Rome itself, the hand of God is evident in the form of public miraculous confirmation." In other words, magic is relativized to show that victory is achieved via "God's hand," a divine power that cannot be co-opted by those who would "exploit its extraordinary power for personal gain" or "for the accomplishment of political ends," though it is only and always "effected for human benefit."[85]

Similarly, Philip Esler has concluded that what he calls "thaumaturgic" activities in Luke-Acts, by which he means what others and I have called "magical" or "gnostic-manipulationist," are especially relevant in Luke-Acts in that they are activities that are overthrown by God. This includes, for example, the thaumaturgic activities of Simon Magus (Acts 8:9–13, 18–24), of Elymas the Jewish sorcerer in Paphos (Acts 13:6–12), and of the books of magic at Ephesus (19:19).[86]

---

81. Bloomquist, "Rhetorical Argumentation."
82. Kee, *Miracles*, 210 (emphasis original).
83. Ibid., 215.
84. Ibid., 216.
85. Ibid., 220.
86. Philip Francis Esler, *Community and Gospel in Luke-Acts* (SNTSMS 57; New York: Cambridge University Press, 1987), 59.

Esler's approach is important for my study, since his conclusions (though not his terminology) reflect my own findings. As I will suggest, Luke-Acts is antimagical since Luke wants to point to the superiority of the gospel over the magical and to caution his readers against adopting magical approaches to the gospel.

In sum, the work of both Kee and Esler independently point in the direction that I do; however, I will now show the rhetorical nature of the interweaving of the two forms of rhetorical miracle discourse, gnostic-manipulationist and thaumaturgic, in Lukan writings by exploring pertinent passages in Luke-Acts to suggest that these two forms of miracle discourse are present there and why they might be there, that is, what their presence and use might indicate about Luke's overall ideological goals.

3.2. LUKE 5:1–11

Luke 5:1–11 is one of many examples of miracle discourse in Luke-Acts. This L story is clearly set apart as a unit, since it is differentiated in terms of time, setting, and characters from what went before and what comes after. "Opening texture" seems apparent in Luke 5:1–3, which opens the story by assembling the characters in the story and the necessary components for the story to proceed; "closing texture" seems apparent in Luke 5:11, which brings the story to a conclusion. This suggests that Luke 5:4–10 is the "middle texture" of the unit, that is, the challenge to Simon Peter (v. 4) through to Jesus' response to Simon Peter (v. 10b).

Attention to repetitive, progressive, and sensory-aesthetic textures suggests that the focus of the story is also threefold: there is the opening setting, the miracle and its response, and the result (found in the "closing texture," v. 11). In the opening setting (the "opening texture," vv. 1–3), Jesus is depicted as a superior who requests the placement of the boats for sitting (something we can determine culturally is a suitable teaching posture).

The miracle story and its response (the "middle texture," vv. 4–10) is considerably more complex but can be seen to develop as follows:

1. Jesus issues a challenge to Simon Peter (v. 4).
2. Simon responds by elaborating on the night's labors (v. 5).
3. Purposeful action, embodied in Jesus' challenge, is carried through fruitfully (vv. 6–7).

4. A parallel to Simon's response (in v. 5) occurs with a challenge now addressed by Simon to Jesus (v. 8), along with an important rationale (vv. 9–10a).
5. Jesus responds to Simon (v. 10b) in a way that parallels Jesus' initial challenge to Simon (v. 4).

That the plot hinges on the purposeful action found in (3) is clear from the way (4) and (5) mirror (2) and (1) respectively and even chiastically, though also in a reconfigured way. At the end, though, and somewhat perplexingly, not everything is resolved: the reader is left with the question concerning exactly what Simon Peter, who has asked Jesus to leave, will be doing henceforth following Jesus (instead of being absent from him as Simon Peter has requested) and fishing now for men. The lack of resolution beckons the reader to the next story, at the very least because of a hope of finding a resolution.

Narrationally this text is rich. There are several levels of characters: the crowds, Jesus, and Simon Peter have a clear and prominent role, the latter two as actors, the former as witnesses. Peter's partners, James and John, have a lesser role; the other fishermen have an even more distant and less complete depiction.

There are also several layers of audience: in addition to the author's "created audience," we note the "crowd" (in 5:3 and implied from Luke 4:15, 44), Simon Peter (who is addressed by Jesus in 5:3 [implicitly], 5:4, 10), Jesus (implicitly addressed in 5:1 and explicitly by Peter in 5:5, 8), and the partners of those in the boat with Peter (who are hailed in 5:6 to come and help).

The narrator's role is for the most part objective in that purposeful and self-expressive action are recounted. The exceptions to this are two sets of narrated emotion-fused actions: (1) Jesus' and Peter's "seeing" and (2) the narration of the emotion-fused action that argumentatively is seen to trigger Peter's words to Jesus: "Fear gripped him" (5:9).

The plot advances on the basis of speech and action, something we discover to be a culturally contextualized challenge-response.[87] After Jesus requests to use Peter's boat as a teaching platform, an action that grants Peter a certain status, Jesus issues a challenge to enter Peter's social "space" by issuing new fishing instructions to Peter, who is an apparent leader

---

87. Robbins, *Exploring the Texture of Texts*, 80–82.

among the fishermen. This challenge to Peter's leadership and skill is a classic example of honor-challenge that threatens to undo any status Peter has gained; it is "a threat to usurp the reputation of another, to deprive another of his reputation."[88] In response to Jesus, Peter attempts to preserve his honor as one who knows what he is doing as a leader among a group of equals. When Peter yields to Jesus (v. 5), in all likelihood it is not so much a surrender as a response to Jesus that will, in Peter's mind, deprive Jesus of any further ground for challenge. In other words, Peter's response is intended to say colloquially: "You think you're smarter than I am: okay, just watch what happens when we throw the nets out." Thus, instead of understanding Peter's words as a whining concession, we should see them as a culturally strong response to the challenge from Jesus.

It is into this socially contextualized, rhetologically grounded conversation that we find an event that has no expectation in the logico-meaningful (cultural) exchange to this point, namely, a miraculous catch (5:6–7). Luke 5:6–9 epitomizes the argumentation of what I have called thaumaturgical miracle discourse: there is no rationale and no stated conclusion or résumé, no statement that this has happened because of something Jesus has said or done, no statement by the narrator or any actors as to what the action means. There is the catch, and then Peter throws himself at Jesus' feet. Following the words of Peter (see below), Jesus responds with a *chreia* ("from now on you will be fishing for men"). The narrative concludes with the fishermen following Jesus presumably to cast their nets yet again, and as they have just done, but now "for men," with the presumption that their catch will be equally abundant and equally mysterious.

As noted, the miracle itself is absent any rhetology except Peter's words (v. 8) and the narrator's interpretation of Peter's words (vv. 9–10a) following the miraculous catch. Peter falling (purposeful action) at Jesus' feet is presumably a visual expression of both the emotion-fused action ("fear") and self-expression of Peter.[89]

That rationale that is in fact found on the lips of Peter leads to a conclusion that, like several such syllogisms in Luke, is hortatory (5:8b):[90]

---

88. Ibid., 81.
89. Though Cotter does not deal with the text, elements of what she says in *Christ*, 195–232, are relevant. For example, the fear of the disciples reveals clearly that they have not understood Jesus, even though they may think they have. The contrast with Peter's initial words here and his subsequent petition suggests something similar.
90. Bloomquist, "Rhetorical Argumentation," 189.

I am a sinner
THEREFORE, leave me.

If we ask what the logic is behind this rhetological command, we find something like the following:

Someone like Jesus should not be in the presence of a sinner.
I am a sinner
THEREFORE, leave me.

But why? It seems likely that it is an argument that would only work with an audience who would understand that "someone like Jesus," perhaps miracle workers of Jesus' kind, should not be found in the presence of sinful people. Such a conclusion would rest on certain cultural assumptions concerning the status of miracle workers as holy persons, as is clear from Peter's use of the word "Lord."[91] Nevertheless, what is not immediately clear, even with this understanding, is whether it is a bad thing for Peter or for Jesus, or for both, or for others, that Peter be in Jesus' presence? Does Peter want Jesus to depart for his own sake, or for Jesus' sake, or for the sake of others (perhaps, as the captain of his "ship," for the sake of his fellow fishermen)?

This rationale is immediately followed by another. The narrator now provides a rationale for Peter's statement, but it is hardly one that is expected: Peter said what he said because he, and the whole company of fishermen, was astonished at the catch (v. 9). It is the narrator who makes a logical connection for the reader between Peter's confession of sinfulness and the audience reaction to the miracle (which was likely the opposite of what Peter's original logic had led him to conclude would happen):

Peter was seized by terror (at the miraculous catch?)
THEREFORE, he said to Jesus to leave him (Peter) because he (Peter) was a sinner.

Again, if we look for cultural information that would enable this argumentation, like the earlier one, to work with a particular readership, we

---

91. Geza Vermes, *Jesus the Jew: A Historian's Reading of the Gospels* (London: SCM, 1983), 116–22.

will find a cultural expectation that concerns the willingness to accept this event as a terror-inducing event and the common, cultural practice of not embracing terrifying things, especially if there is a reason for the terror, such as, for example, guilt or shame or existing weakness of some kind:

> Terrifying events, or terror-inducing individuals, cause people to fear for their lives especially if they are at some risk—through guilt, through sin, through weakness, and so on.
> Peter was seized by terror
> THEREFORE, he said to Jesus to leave him because he (Peter) was a sinner, and (as we know from the first argument) someone like Jesus should not be in the presence of a sinner.

In this case, the abnormal events are tied directly to Jesus, who thus becomes both the cause of the events and the source of the terror. Peter's words reflect a common cultural expectation: it is not "a good thing" that Jesus, an apparent thaumaturge, be in the presence of sinners, probably because of the impending effects on them through emotion-fused flaws. Furthermore, the narrator's logical argumentation builds on a common social and psychological action: people seized by terror try to get rid of the cause of the terror in order to save their lives.

But what is important to note is that Jesus does not leave them; he actually draws Peter and the other fishermen closer by asking them to follow him. Thus, I would argue, rhetology here is intended to highlight not the point of the story but what the story wants to overturn, namely, Peter's knowledge and whether or not the holy person (Jesus) should be in the presence of sinners. This "overturning" is grounded rhetographically, which is characteristic of thaumaturgical miracle discourse. Accordingly, we can begin to see that in this narrative, the gnostic-manipulationist response, evident in the two rationales, is subordinated to a thaumaturgical response.

But let us again ask: why? What is gained in the telling of this story, other than to demonstrate Jesus' superiority to Peter? Is it Jesus' use of miracle to stun followers into obedience? But, if so, what about Peter's confession of sinfulness? Why not have Jesus remove that sinfulness so that Peter could in fact be with him in some regular way?

I believe that the ambiguous double possibility (Jesus can do harm to Peter the sinner, but Peter the sinner can also do harm to Jesus by defiling him in the same way that a leper could defile a nonleper), combined with the narrator's description of the immediate audience of the miracle (i.e.,

Peter), who is seized not with satisfaction at the miracle but horror, confirms the suspicion of qualitatively different results that thaumaturgical miracle discourse brings and which is often set over against gnostic-manipulationist miracle discourse. Jesus appears to overturn *both* Peter's initial bleak assessment of the prospect of getting fish after having labored all night in that enterprise *and* Peter's initial assessment that it is wrong for someone like Jesus to be in the presence of sinners. Jesus does so, however, not by denying the logical nature of either assertion (it *is* culturally logical *both* that there be no fish to catch *and* that Jesus not associate with Peter), but by creating new, qualitatively different possible conditions than those that existed before: there *are* fish where none are expected to be, *and* Peter and Jesus will not only not part ways but will also become traveling companions. Jesus' actions here, as elsewhere in Luke, challenge the canons of Peter's cultural knowledge (and perhaps, via the author, the reader's as well).[92] As such, this particular example of Lukan miracle discourse shows how Luke interweaves both forms of miracle discourse to create, in this case, a tapestry of contrasts: the narrative underscores *both* logico-cultural terror *and* the creation by Jesus of a qualitatively new and different cultural situation.

From this perspective, the reader is left with a question concerning the future shape of Jesus' action in the subsequent chapters: what is the role of such qualitatively different actions in the ministry of Jesus as are implied by the thaumaturgical miracle discourse? Will these actions become the norm, thus making thaumaturgical miracle discourse a kind of normative discourse in the text? Or are these actions more like a qualitative *captatio*, intended to grab attention and to bring adherents to Jesus, perhaps challenging "normal" expectations? Furthermore, the narrative leaves open-ended at this point what kind of group formation will result from these new possibilities. Will the resulting group be an "action set" (if the focus is on the "fishing for men") or a "gang" (if the focus is on Jesus, as in "follow *me*").[93] If the former, their tenure as followers may be quite brief; if the latter, then their tenure will endure as long as Jesus remains the "gang" leader.

---

92. Robbins, *Exploring the Texture of Texts*, 86–88. This, it should be noted, may suggest for Cotter's analysis that readers are intended not simply to be given direction for their own petitions but also to be jarred from expecting to petition in certain ways. It should also be noted that it does remain to be seen whether that challenge is countercultural or contracultural.

93. Ibid., 100–101.

My hypothesis leads me to suggest from the remainder of the Lukan narrative that Jesus' actions do *not* become formulaic; rather, nonformulaic, thaumaturgical responses become regular or normative. In other words, as the Lukan narrative progresses, one begins to *expect* the unexpected. There is no formula for the fulfillment of Jesus' statement about the miracle or the result ("fishing for men"). The text does not appear to be shaped by gnostic-manipulationist miracle discourse but rather to set up gnostic-manipulationist thinking and show how it is interrupted in significant ways by thaumaturgical miracle discourse. Cultural action-set patterns will, as we shall see, be regularly disturbed by the leader of the gang, and that is exactly the kind of unexpected action that happens throughout the rest of the narrative!

For the moment, let me engage the ideological texture of Luke-Acts to suggest one possible reason why this may be so. As the followers of Jesus (including Peter but also an array of others, like Simon the Samaritan) developed as a "group," the pull of gnostic-manipulationist responses was very strong, especially as an argument for control of competing forces. As any member of a thaumaturgically oriented group knows, reliance on thaumaturgical responses means that there are too many unanswered questions and too much "silence" of the divine when crises arise. A natural human religious tendency appears to be away from the thaumaturgical toward the gnostic-manipulationist, thus the rise of priestly rhetorical discourse and magical miracle discourse, which rely on gnostic-manipulationist dynamics. The counterintuitive nature of the Lukan account of Jesus is thus partially based on the regular intrusion of thaumaturgical discourse as an ideological reminder to the reader of the need for a "Jesus-centered" faith, rather than a ritualistic one.

3.3. Acts 3:1–10

The healing of the lame man in Acts 3:1–10 may be viewed as another example of miracle discourse in Luke-Acts. Though it is the opening unit of a much longer narrative unit that extends from 3:1–4:35, 3:1–10 has an internal consistency and, though it leads to the subsequent events, can also stand on its own.

Attention to the repetitive texture of the text suggests the prominence played not only by the characters (Peter, John, the man, and the crowd) but also of the setting, namely, the temple. The progressive texture also suggests a move from physical stasis and incapacity (i.e., the impossibility of the man's full-range of purposeful action) and from dependence on charity (which implies that the man is not only immobile but also bereft of both regular access to any regular income and also the mutual reciprocity of family or clan to provide for his needs) to purposeful movement and self-expressive praise, and presumably thus to social restoration, though that is not clear in the text.

The before-and-after contrast is further highlighted by comparing the sensory-aesthetic texture of the narrative characters around the man: at the beginning of the text all of the active purposeful action is accomplished by the people around the paralytic, including Peter and John, while at the end it is the healed paralytic who expresses purposeful action and self-expressive praise of God most fully. Ironically, and perhaps intentionally, at the end, the crowd is described only in terms of emotion-fused action, not in purposeful or self-expressive terms.

The narrator here is present in a way similar to Luke 5. We note, for example, that the narration of this story resembles the previous story in significant ways. Like the story in Luke 5, this story has five of the six elements necessary for a *diēgēma*, that is, for narrative elaboration as presented in the *Progymnasmata* of Aelius Theon:[94] (1) character(s), (2) acts done by the character(s), (3) the place in which the activity was carried out (see 3:1), (4) the time during which the act was done (see 3:1), and (5) the manner of the activity. The only element missing is the argumentative rationale for why these things were done. In fact, all these narrative elements, save the manner of the activity, are introduced in the first two verses of the Acts story (Acts 3:1–2) and in the first three verses of the Lukan story (Luke 5:1–3), that is, in the "opening texture" of both.

In both cases, the introduction of the only element omitted, "manner of the activity," is triggered by the emotion-fused action of "seeing" (in the case of Luke 5:2 Jesus; in the case of Acts 3:3 the lame man), which in both cases is communicated by the narrator. In both stories, as well, the "seeing" moves the story beyond its initial, narrative elements, to the action that will flesh out the "manner" of the activity. Finally, in both cases, the story progresses from there to a challenge: in Luke 5:4 it is issued by Jesus to Peter (and the company with him, which includes John); in Acts 3:3 a chal-

---

94. James R. Butts, "The Progymnasmata of Theon: A New Text with Translation and Commentary" (Ph.D. diss., Claremont Graduate School, 1986), 290–401.

lenge of a kind is issued again to Peter, and now also John, by one who is himself self-evidently culturally unclean and presumably a sinner.

Here, however, we begin to notice some significant differences. The social location of the challenger is very different in the two stories: Jesus challenges Peter in Luke 5, eliciting a rationale as to why he thinks Jesus' challenge to be a bad idea but then follows that up quickly with an action Peter hopes will restore his own honor; in Acts 3, the challenge is more like a plea for mercy from one who has no claim to honor from a cultural superior who may be expected to show him charitable mercy.[95] In each case, though, the results are unexpected miracles, and thus thaumaturgical: in Luke 5 the miraculous catch following Jesus' words; in Acts 3 the healing of the man following Peter's words.

As in the story in Luke, the miracle in Acts 3 also marks a turning point to a second episode in the unitary story, but there are significant narrational similarities in the first part of each story and narrational differences in the second. The second part of the miracle scene in Luke 5 essentially comprised a brief direct discourse between Jesus and Peter (with only the second rationale by the narrator intruding); however, in Acts 3 there is no dialogue, and though the narrator moves the narrative forward, neither are there rationales: the narrator tells the reader what the action was and what effect that it had on the "people," a reaction that appears very similar to the narrated reaction of Peter in Luke 5.

There is also the difference in the status of the issuer of the challenge: in Luke 5, it is Jesus who issues the challenge to Peter, as if to a rival; in Acts 3, it is the lame man, who is no rival, who issues the challenge also to Peter. Naturally, the words of Peter are different in each case; however, the difference is noteworthy: in Luke 5, Jesus challenged, Peter responded, the miracle occurred, Peter responded to the miracle, and Jesus spoke; in Acts 3 there is no such reversal: the paralytic begs, Peter responds, the miracle occurs, the paralytic responds, and then the narrator describes the crowd as gripped by terror at what has come over the man, just as the narrator had described Peter in Luke 5.

Nor is there anything in the healed paralytic's demeanor that makes him like Peter in the initial story: the paralytic, unlike Peter, rejoices in the great miracle that has taken place; it is the crowd, not Peter, that is ter-

---

95. To this extent, the "challenger" of Acts 3 is more like a "petitioner" in Cotter's language. Cotter does not deal with Acts 3.

ror-stricken. Here, as in Luke 5, the turning point is again marked by the emotion-fused action of seeing, but the characters involved in the action are different: in Luke 5:8, it is Peter's seeing that leads to his terror, while in Acts 5:9 it is the crowd's seeing. Furthermore, in Luke 5 Peter was terrified, while in Acts 3 it is the crowd that is terrified. One, then, begins to suspect that in the next stage of the narrative of Acts 3, Peter will adopt the role that Jesus appears to have played in Luke 5. That may be the case, but what in fact follows in Acts 3:11–4:35 reveals Peter's providing a more or less lengthy address that expands narratively on the thaumaturgical action.

In sum, this story, too, advances due to the qualitative argumentation characteristic of thaumaturgical miracle discourse. The fact that there is no logical argumentation urges a reader to consider this narrative very differently from one characterized by gnostic-manipulationist rhetorical discourse.

3.4. Luke 8:22–39

As a final example of the Lukan use of gnostic-manipulationist miracle discourse and thaumaturgical miracle discourse, we return to Luke, this time to 8:22–39, which appears as a unit in Mark 5:1–21 (cf. the *inclusio* of 5:1 and 21), but in Matt 8:23–34 as sequential miracle stories. In Luke, the enigmatic statement of Jesus in 8:22 connects the fearful water voyage (8:22–25) to the healing of the Gerasene demoniac (8:26–39) through the self-expressed intention of Jesus.

Attention to repetitive, progressive, and sensory-aesthetic texture underscores the purposeful action that characterizes this unit, as well as the role played by turbulent elements and turbulent spirits. Both stories are dominated by purposeful and self-expressive action. Luke 8:22–27 is dominated by purposeful action (vv. 23–24), and self-expressive elements of challenge and response are woven into that action: in verse 24, Jesus is challenged by his followers; Jesus responds by arising, commanding the wind and water (v. 24), and then responding directly to his followers (v. 25). The result, fear and amazement on their part, is the only emotion-fused action in this first part of the unit, and it mirrors the reaction of Peter in Luke 5 and the analogous reaction of the people to the miracle at Peter's words in Acts 3.

Luke 8:26–39 continues this presentation, dominated as it is by purposeful and self-expressive action. But it is here that we find an interesting comparison between the reversal of the fortunes of the lame man in

Acts 3 and the demoniac of Luke 8. In the case of Acts 3, the paralytic was immobile and could only beg, though at the end he was running around and shouting praises to God; in the case of Luke 8, the demon-possessed man is running around nude and crying out, though at the end he is sitting (as Jesus had been in the boat in both Luke 5 and 8, and as the lame man had been forced to do at the outset of Acts 3), quiet and dressed. There is nothing caricatured in the effect on these two men, since the effects are contraries of each other in terms of sensory-aesthetic texture. Nevertheless, here again, as in both Luke 5 and Acts 3, the final action is the emotion-fused reaction of witnesses to the miracle, and here again it is one of terror.

In this text, like Luke 5, but unlike the text of Acts 3, we find rhetology. Specifically there are three examples of enthymematic argumentation. First, in 8:29a, the man (or perhaps the spirit) begs Jesus not to torment or torture him. As the narrator notes, this request had come because Jesus commands the unclean spirit to come out. For this narrational rationale to work, a culturally intelligible argument like the following must be operative:

> When unclean spirits are commanded to exit the person they inhabit, they torment the person (or, if the spirit is called out, are themselves tormented).
> Jesus commanded the unclean spirit to exit the man.
> THEREFORE, the tormented man said: do not torment me!

Culturally, it is conceivable that this argument would have been constructed in light of the limited-good society of Jesus' day. In other words, the logic that may enable the audience to assent to this cry is that it would be the recognizable cry of dispossession on the part of someone who owns property (e.g., a considerable amount of land or only some possessions) and who is about to be dispossessed of his property (cf. the similar language in Matt 18:23–35, where the "unjust slave" is handed over by the king to the torturers). At the fear of being dispossessed, the one about to be dispossessed, in this case, the demon, cries out.

Interestingly, the narrator adds a second rationale in order to explain why the demon has this "possessive" hold on the man and what such a "possession" consists of: Jesus commands the spirit to come out of the man because the spirit has tormented the man for a long time. Again, for this argument to work, something like the following must be assumed:

In order to free someone from excessive or lengthy torment or torture, one should release the victim.
The spirit had tormented this man for a long time.
THEREFORE, Jesus commanded the spirit to come out of him.

The nature of this argument suggests a social and cultural acceptance of the limited value of torment, perhaps understood as punishment or torture. The narrator could simply have said that the man had been tormented; instead, the narrator adds the length of time, making the argument work only if it is understood that possibly a shorter period of torture and torment is not always and in every situation a bad thing. Long-standing torture, however, especially for someone who may not be deserving of it, is not a good thing.[96]

Finally, the narrator builds on Jesus' own speech to construct a rhetology that identifies this spirit. When, in answer to Jesus' address to him "who are you?" the demon (apparently) replies, "My name is Legion," the narrator, not the demon adds, the explanation: "because many demons had entered the man" (8:30). Now, while some scholars, including Robbins, have suggested that the name "Legion" holds at least an implicit, but still clear, sociocultural "slap" directed against the Roman forces of occupation, the lack of any corroborating evidence that would suggest counter- or contracultural rejection of Roman rule, combined with attention to the argumentative texture, reveals that the word is less likely to be subversive than dialectical slang, employed to describe an otherwise impossible display of overwhelming power in the first-century Mediterranean world ruled by Rome. If so, then something like the following is all that is required for the above argument to work:

(In the Roman world of the first century c.e.) Something that is overwhelmingly powerful and made up of many parts is called "Legion"
Many demons had entered the man.
THEREFORE, the demon said that his/their name was "Legion."

It is of course true that we are not talking about the many parts of the body or the many parts of a flower, language that could in fact have been used

---

96. Danielle S. Allen, *The World of Prometheus: The Politics of Punishing in Democratic Athens* (Princeton: Princeton University Press, 2000), 104–5.

to express multiple parts, but rather a "many-parted" thing that is powerful and most likely also destructive. Nevertheless, it is difficult to see the term as a culturally subversive reference to Roman power without further evidence for such an assertion.

The final example of logical argumentation is difficult to discern, because it is so embedded in the narration. When the herdsmen flee, they go into the city and the neighboring fields; their peers come to see what is happening and, as in the case of Peter in Luke 5, the people in Acts 3, and the disciples (who are apparently present here but invisible) in the first part of this story, terror seizes them. Consistent with the narration in Luke 5 (and perhaps suggested in Acts 3), they too ask Jesus to leave them. The argumentation here, then, which is very similar to that of Luke 5, may demand a similar premise to the one we saw above:

When people are seized with great fear, they will try to get rid of the cause of their fear.
The people of the region were afraid.
THEREFORE, they asked Jesus to leave.

The similarities here with Peter's request of Jesus in Luke 5 are patent; nevertheless, unlike the ambiguity in Luke 5, it appears quite clear why the people have asked Jesus to leave in Luke 8: it is for their own well-being, not for Jesus' sake (e.g., in order to keep him from becoming defiled by them).

But, as a result of this observation, we can note that the following questions still remain for all three texts that end with emotion-fused actions of fear and amazement. First, why were Peter, the people in Acts 3, the disciples in the boat, and the Gerasenes seized with terror? No answer is provided, even though, as Cotter shows with the Markan account of the disciples in the boat, intertextural references from, say, the psalms or prophets could easily be adduced as they are in Qumran texts.[97] Second, what does the presence of Jesus mean for them and for him? These important but unanswered questions suggest that underlying the whole narrative is a qualitative argumentation that, like logical argumentation, relies heavily on common, cultural knowledge, but that, unlike logical argumentation, seeks to move people in ways that defy merely logico-cultural

---

97. Cotter, *Christ of the Miracle Stories*, 213–15.

understandings and that perhaps seek to create new understandings and responses or at least their possibility.

Qualitative argumentation also underlies the disciples' query: if Jesus can still the wind and the water, then who is this? The answer of course is not clear but suggests that he is "somebody," whether that be a divinity in Greco-Roman form,[98] a spirit being, or a holy person. In the second part of the story, qualitative argumentation also underlies the events and is, if anything, even more elusive than in the first part. Thus several questions are left unanswered in the narrative, and several answers are made possible: Why do the demons not want to be sent to the abyss? Are they afraid? Why do they want to enter the swine? Is it because swine are unclean, or are they safe? Why do the swine rush to the lake? Is it because this is the proper abode of demons or because the swine, like Balaam's ass, know better than the demons where they belong?[99]

Finally, we note that the story in Luke 8, like that found in Acts 3, also contains the same five of the six elements of narrative elaboration in Theon's *Progymnasmata*; like Acts 3, the missing element here is a rationale.

It is my contention that in the logical argumentation of gnostic-manipulationist discourse, these matters, including the response to the miracle, would *not* have been omitted or left unanswered. To do so would have been to leave the connection between action and result unclear. Such a state is contrary to magical miracle discourse, for how can one successfully bring the powers under one's control if the way of doing so and the rationale for doing so are left unexpressed or unclear? In this respect, gnostic-manipulationist discourse, which is common to both ancient magic and modern science, has a clear place in the expression of both. Thaumaturgical miracle discourse, however, challenges logico-cultural perceptions and logical argumentative explanations of that control by leaving various questions and by omitting rationales and conclusions. This is the situation that we ultimately find in these three stories.

I would further suggest that the stories found in Acts 3 and Luke 8 evidence a feature of narrative in the Synoptic Gospels generally, but particularly in Luke-Acts—namely, that in the Gospels, narratives, like parables,

---

98. See Cotter's analysis of the Markan version of the story in *Christ*, 224–30.

99. In this story we find an array of qualitative argumentation that is not clear. In 8:24, that narrator has Jesus' disciples seek to awaken the sleeping Jesus, but why? Do they want him to save himself or them? That the latter is in mind is clear in both Mark 4:38 and Matt 8:25 but not in Luke.

do not so much contain argumentation as they *are* argumentation. Much the same can be said of parables as the logical form of dealing with ethical questions: too many questions arise from parables to suggest an easy, logical move from cause, through rationale, to conclusion. The rift between cause and effect is not bridged in thaumaturgical, miracle discourse, leaving it problematic even for readers in our day, even though it causes some profound effect in those characters in the narrative who witness it. In this respect, then, these miracle stories bear a strong resemblance to the parables of the Gospel traditions.[100]

4. Tentative Conclusions

In the next few years, sociorhetorical commentary on early Christian literature will present new ways for discussing rhetorical discourse. Until now, as in most beginning scientific enterprises of the modern era, the process has been inductive since hypotheses have been suggested in light of observations made using existing categories of interpretation. Inevitably, studies such as the one I have presented will seek to put the enterprise in the category of what Thomas Kuhn calls "normal science"[101] and thus to pursue further exploration along deductive lines. I have suggested that this is already happening in the case of sociorhetorical analysis.[102] Having identified the modes of discourse, we will seek to see how texts take their shape within environments created by such modes and how, in other environments, different modes of discourse can artfully be interwoven.[103]

What I hope to have presented in this paper is a small step in the process. In the paper, I have concluded that Robbins's discussion of rhetorolects is a major step forward, but also that more precision is required.

I have also suggested that when talking about miracle discourse, for example, sociorhetorical analysis itself provides the necessary tools and insights for such precision. For example, by considering the connection between rhetorical topoi, argumentation and social and cultural texture,

---

100. Note the inclusion of miracle stories by Robbins in his *Ancient Quotes and Anecdotes: From Crib to Crypt* (Foundations and Facets; Sonoma, Calif.: Polebridge, 1989), cited by Cotter, *Christ of the Miracle Stories*, 4.

101. Thomas S. Kuhn, *The Structure of Scientific Revolutions* (2nd ed.; Foundations of the Unity of Science 2/2; Chicago: University of Chicago Press, 1967).

102. Bloomquist, "Programmatic Correlation."

103. Bloomquist, "Criteria for Apocalyptic Rhetoric."

we can see that what Robbins has called "miracle" discourse is actually pluriform, that there are, in other words, at least two different ways in which that discourse functions in first-century C.E. Mediterranean literature, one that privileges logical argumentation and cultural rules and another that privileges qualitative argumentation and rule confusion.[104]

Furthermore, we can see how, in at least one body of early Christian literature, Luke-Acts, one form of rhetorical discourse—thaumaturgical miracle discourse—is ideologically used against another—gnostic-manipulationist miracle discourse—in order to achieve an ideological result. In this corpus, this contrasting use seems to be the tool that is used to move these stories beyond their logico-cultural limitations. These stories are cast in narrative form with the intent of drawing the audience in and leaving the conclusion anything but rationally sure, though existentially inescapable. Gnostic-manipulationist miracle discourse is thus used as a foil that enables thaumaturgical miracle discourse concerning Jesus to bring existing cultural logic into real question.

---

104. Note in this the way in which thaumaturgical miracle discourse approximates not only parables but also the same affective impact as apocalyptic discourse. See Bloomquist, "Criteria for Apocalyptic Rhetoric."

Res Gestae Divi Christi: Miracles, Early Christian Heroes, and the Discourse of Power in Acts*

Todd Penner

1. Opening Sleight of Hand: Miracles and the Nexus of Power

When confronted with the prospect of working his own miracle, the emperor Vespasian is described by Suetonius in this way: "Though he had hardly any faith that this could possibly succeed, and therefore shrank

---

* This essay was originally presented as a paper in the Rhetoric and New Testament section at the SBL annual meeting in Denver, Colorado, November 2001. I want to express my appreciation to Duane Watson for the invitation to present in this session and to Wendy Cotter for her encouraging response on that occasion. My thanks also goes to Kimberly Stratton for her enthusiastic engagement of an earlier written version of this piece, to Caroline Vander Stichele for her substantive and helpful feedback on its earliest incarnation, and to Michele Kennerly (an Austin College undergraduate at the time, now a university professor) for providing the scrutiny of her critical eye in the latter stages. It is regrettable that the final redaction of this essay was brought to completion before Wendy Cotter's fine work, *The Christ of the Miracle Stories: Portrait through Encounter* (Grand Rapids: Baker Academic, 2010), was published. My analysis here, particularly that related to the manifestation of power in the miracle narratives of Acts, appears to prefigure some of her subsequent discussion of the miracle stories in the Gospels. I have thus asked Professor Cotter to detail several aspects of her work in her response to my essay in this volume. The major work on this essay was completed with funding support from a National Endowment for the Humanities Summer Research Grant (2003) for a project titled: "Gendering Acts: Rhetoric, Gender, and Imperial Values in Early Christian Narrative." Finally, I dedicate the labor and the text-linguistic product herein to the memory of my doctoral compatriot at Emory University, Philip L. Graber (who passed away September 2003). Philip was one of those colleagues who helped nurture the joy of study(ing)—the world of scholarship would signify more (often) if he were here to participate: "Daily you must gaze upon the power of the city and become her lover" (Thucydides 2.43.1).

even from making the attempt, he was at last prevailed upon by his friends and tried both things [healing a lame and blind man] in public before a large crowd; and with success" (*Vesp.* 7.2).[1] Most striking in this portrayal of the erstwhile emperor is the way in which Suetonius characterizes him as timid, perhaps even shrinking back in fear. Similar features are found in Tacitus's parallel account (*Hist.* 4.81), where Vespasian at first expresses outright ridicule at the request for the healing power of his regal touch, followed by reticence, and then finally moving forward in confidence, seemingly spurred on by the surrounding crowd. What is noteworthy in these two accounts is not that miracles were ascribed to the emperor per se, but the way in which he is characterized in each instance: as scornful and timid, giving in to the superstition of the masses, and being egged on by the crowds.[2]

This image is not particularly flattering. At the same time, however, one cannot help but wonder how ancient readers perceived such stories. After all, the emperor was one of the premiere examples of power—political, social, cultural, and religious—in the first century C.E., and certainly many individuals in the ancient world would not have been surprised to learn that one so powerful in word and deed was also able to work wondrous acts for the public good. Although it has a negative slant with respect to the masses, Dio Cassius's account of Vespasian's healing ability is telling in this respect: "Yet, although Heaven was thus magnifying him, the

---

1. This translation is taken from Wendy Cotter, *Miracles in Greco-Roman Antiquity: A Sourcebook for the Study of New Testament Miracles* (New York: Routledge, 1999), 42 (1.49). For a recent and related collection that supplements Cotter's material, see Daniel Ogden, *Magic, Witchcraft, and Ghosts in the Greek and Roman Worlds: A Sourcebook* (New York: Oxford University Press, 2002).

2. In his portrayal of Vespasian, Tacitus throughout seems to be tying the emperor closely to the lower-ranked soldiers, suggesting that Vespasian has inadvertently adopted the perspective of the masses, abandoning the skepticism deemed appropriate for one of his social and military rank (see further Rhiannon Ash, *Ordering Anarchy: Armies and Leaders in Tacitus' Histories* [Ann Arbor: University of Michigan Press, 1999], 129–36). For a different interpretation of Vespasian's actions, which stresses his "appropriate" response of "modesty" to the request for healing, see the discussion of the variants of this story by Ulrike Riemer, "Miracle Stories and Their Narrative Intent in the Context of the Ruler Cult of Classical Antiquity," in *Wonders Never Cease: The Purpose of Narrating Miracle Stories in the New Testament and Its Religious Environment* (ed. M. Labahn and B. J. Lietaert Peerbolte; LNTS 288; New York: T&T Clark, 2006), 40–42.

Alexandrians, far from delighting in his presence, detested him so heartily that they were for ever mocking and reviling him" (*Roman History* 65.8).[3] The miraculous signs affirm the emperor as a locus of power in the ancient world, and not surprisingly, such a manifestation demands a response by those who come into contact with this numinous display. The close association in Dio Cassius between Vespasian's ability to heal and his freedom to impose a monetary levy on the Alexandrians (the cause of their disdain for the emperor) deserves particular note. The text is premised on complex power negotiations, navigating patronage and benefaction—human and divine. Political and religious manifestations of power exist side by side, both mutually supporting the other, both serving to characterize the emperor, both making implied arguments about proper order and placement in the *oikoumene*, both establishing claims on the reader's loyalty.

By contrast, when one moves to the miracles in Acts we find no timid or fearful (and certainly not scornful) apostles, who are basing the source of their strength on the "crowds." Rather, we observe these heroes making bold and assertive claims on divine power, frequently in the name of Jesus, working "signs and wonders" and demonstrating that the locus of power (and hence authority) resides in them, the progenitors of the early Christian communities. While we have little difficulty seeing the way in which power is manifested in each miraculous encounter, scholars are often reticent to situate this display in the context of other, more complex nexuses of power and dominance in the ancient world, such as we observe operative in the Vespasian accounts. Perhaps most importantly, scholars tend to overlook the connection of the emergent characterization of these individuals to the broader social and cultural world. In contrast, I would suggest a need exists to examine the sociocultural world encoded in the text as it is worked out in terms of the rhetorics of the narrative. Thus, when we examine miracles performed by the wonder-working apostles through the power of *christos* and *pneumatos*, we should explore precisely what those elements may have entailed for ancient readers in terms of their value systems and in what ways the language of power in Acts supports, modifies, or overturns those very systems.

Fundamentally at stake in such narratives, I would suggest, is the creation of character and the manifestation of an individual's *ethos* in positive or negative terms, or possibly a mixture of the two. Aristotle understood

---

3. Translation from Cotter, *Miracles in Greco-Roman Antiquity*, 42 (1.50).

ethos to represent those words or actions that illustrated a person's moral character (*Poet.* 1454a). For Aristotle, this largely entailed the depiction of an individual's choices that would expose his or her underlying aims, motivations, and basic nature.[4] This emphasis on characterization in narrative corresponds to patterns evident elsewhere in ancient literature, which in turn suggests that the display of miracles in narrative conveys substantive information about the subjects, the world they inhabit, and especially the interrelationship of the two. I would argue that this framework needs to inform any study of miracles in narrative discourse.[5] In the final analysis, miracles, as actions performed by narrative characters, represent an essential building block in the construction of rhetorical identity in the story, which in turn becomes a critical feature in developing patterns of persuasion and amplifying appropriate themes.

2. History of Interpretation and the Neglect of Power

In stark contrast to the important role that miracles seem to play in Luke's narrative, scholarship on miracles in Acts has actually been relatively sparse. In part, this absence has resulted from a certain reticence and discomfort scholars often have dealing with the issues of authenticity of miraculous elements present in biblical narratives.[6] In his classic form-critical classification of the various miracles in Acts, for example, Martin Dibelius concluded by stating that "I have intentionally not considered whether all these stories are authentic or not…. We are assessing only the story-teller's method of writing and not the authenticity of what he relates."[7] One will note how deftly Dibelius manages both to avoid the historical questions (despite his protestations that he is in fact laying out the groundwork for such study) and to protect the integrity of Lukan theology. Dibelius here reflects a long-standing approach that has developed

---

4. See Elizabeth S. Belfiore, *Tragic Pleasures: Aristotle on Plot and Emotion* (Princeton: Princeton University Press, 1992), 94–95; and Nancy Sherman, *The Fabric of Character: Aristotle's Theory of Virtue* (Oxford: Clarendon, 1989), 79–83.

5. For a more detailed discussion, see Todd Penner, *In Praise of Christian Origins: Stephen and the Hellenists in Lukan Apologetic Historiography* (ESEC 10; London: T&T Clark, 2004), 196–208.

6. See the brief assessment by Rick Strelan, *Strange Acts: Studies in the Cultural World of the Acts of the Apostles* (BZNW 126; Berlin: de Gruyter, 2004), 9–14.

7. Martin Dibelius, "Style Criticism of the Book of Acts," in *Studies in the Acts of the Apostles* (ed. H. Greeven; London: SCM, 1956), 25.

a dually focused strategy: miraculous material is placed in the sphere of "tradition," and it is subordinated to a writer's particular theological or literary agenda.

Looking at the discussion of miracles in Acts scholarship, one immediately notices that a great deal of emphasis has been placed on delineating and assessing the preexisting tradition and its subsequent redaction. The classic paradigm was established nearly thirty years ago by Paul Achtemeier, who argued that Mark used a preexistent miracle catenae in the composition of his Gospel.[8] Most recently, Achtemeier's thesis has been expanded by Roy Kotansky, who proffers that the *Sitz im Leben* for the pre-Markan material may be in those early Hellenistic communities attested to in the first half of Acts, asserting as well that the image of Jesus as "divine man" in the pre-Markan material may account for the use of similar collections in the composition of the book of Acts.[9]

Further, while the issue of preexisting miracle traditions can never be fully separated from the question of Lukan sources,[10] overall scholars have tended to focus more squarely on redactional issues in analyzing miracles in Luke-Acts. In this way, by addressing how Luke molded the miracle stories he received to serve his theological purposes, scholars have thereby avoided some of the more "unseemly" historical questions or implications.[11] Even the most recent study of miracles in Acts, by the eminent historian of

---

8. Paul J. Achtemeier, "Toward the Isolation of Pre-Markan Miracle Catenae," *JBL* 89 (1970): 265–91; and idem, "Origin and Function of the Pre-Marcan Miracle Catenae," *JBL* 91 (1972): 198–221. For a recent treatment, with more explicit emphasis on the orality of these preexisting lists, see David Frankfurter, "The Origin of the Miracle-List Tradition and Its Medium of Circulation," in *1990 Society of Biblical Literature Seminar Papers* (SBLSP 29; Atlanta: Scholars Press, 1990), 344–74.

9. Roy D. Kotansky, "Jesus and Heracles in Cádiz (*ta Gadeira*): Death, Myth, and Monsters at the 'Straits of Gibraltar' (Mark 4:35–5:43)," in *Ancient and Modern Perspectives on the Bible and Culture: Essays in Honor of Hans Dieter Betz* (ed. Adela Yarbro Collins; Atlanta: Scholars Press, 1998), 222–26.

10. See the summary in Frans Neirynck, "The Miracle Stories in the Acts of the Apostles," in *Les Actes des Apôtres: Traditions, rédaction, théologie* (ed. J. Kremer; BETL 48; Leuven: Leuven University Press, 1979), 188–95.

11. Matti Myllykoski ("Being There: The Function of the Supernatural in Acts 1–12," in *Wonders Never Cease* [ed. M. Labahn and B. J. Lietaert Peerbolte; LNTS 288; New York: T&T Clark, 2006], 147–54) makes a significant contribution to this discussion. In broad strokes, he traces some of the historical issues occupying modern scholarship on the miracles of Acts, especially in terms of "tradition" and "redaction," suggesting that focus on miracles as forming a constituent element of Lukan source

early Christianity Daniel Marguerat, reveals a similar pattern of interpretation. Marguerat readily admits the easy "slippage" of the miracles of Acts into the ambient religious world of antiquity[12] but asserts that Luke "saves" the miracles by developing a hermeneutic that attaches the act itself to the christological word of the apostles,[13] which, finally, places Luke's emphasis firmly on ethics and "doctrinal truth."[14] It certainly cannot be denied that Luke may have sought to "save" his miracle stories from "misunderstanding" by juxtaposing (or even infusing) them with "theological" interpretation. But it is also the case that modern scholars are equally concerned to "save" Luke from his ancient world.[15] While Marguerat "insists" on Luke's alignment of miracles with ethics and theology,[16] it is evident throughout that Marguerat, one of the most adept scholars at analyzing the connection of Lukan discourse with its broader sociocultural world, capitulates to "rescuing" Luke himself, neglecting the role of power in both presentation and performance as it unfolds in the text.

Thus it is primarily in the modern scholarly discussion of Luke's theological activity that one perceives an evident effort to *sanitize* the miraculous features of Luke-Acts. Simply put, to sanitize the miracles in Acts is to purify them of cultural or religious features that might bring their language or thought too close (for our comfort) to the "pagan" environment of the ancient world. With the exception of John Hull, who did draw close associations between Luke's conception of miracles and the supernatural world of antiquity,[17] the majority of scholars have moved in the opposite

---

tradition represents a *re*historicizing reaction to the Tübingen tendency to consider the miracles as a Lukan fictional element.

12. Daniel Marguerat, "Magic and Miracle in the Acts of the Apostles," in *Magic in the Biblical World: From the Rod of Aaron to the Ring of Solomon* (ed. T. Klutz; JSNTSup 245; London: T&T Clark, 2003), 103, 117–18. Also see his "Magie, Guérison et Parole dans les Actes des Apôtres," *ETL* 72 (1997): 197–208.

13. Ibid., 101, 109, 114.

14. Ibid., 113, 115, 120, 123.

15. As Ivoni Richter Reimer aptly notes, "There is an apologetic attempt to embed Christian miracles in the world of ideas of that time, but simultaneously to distance them from that world. The result is that what is uniquely Christian is emphasized at the expense of other experiences" (*Women in the Acts of the Apostles: A Feminist Liberation Perspective* [trans. L. M. Maloney; Minneapolis: Fortress, 1995], 56).

16. Marguerat, "Magic and Miracle," 113.

17. John M. Hull, *Hellenistic Magic and the Synoptic Tradition* (SBT 2/28; London: SCM, 1974), 87–115.

direction. An evident attempt to distance Luke from the ambient magical sphere permeating the ancient world thus emerges in the history of scholarship. One of the best illustrations of this point is provided in the following comment by Paul Achtemeier: "Luke has not subordinated his presentation of Jesus to a magical world-view.... He has not allowed, to the extent [John] Hull has proposed, the traditions of faith to be penetrated by magic."[18]

Moreover, one might add that the attempt to distance Acts from the ancient cultural milieu cannot be separated from the effort to drive a wedge between Acts and the comparable Christian apocryphal texts.[19] Although he has little to say about the miraculous episodes explicitly, Richard Pervo points out that the miracles in Acts and the apocryphal

---

18. Paul Achtemeier, "The Lukan Perspective on the Miracles of Jesus," in *Perspectives on Luke-Acts* (ed. Charles H. Talbert; Perspectives in Religious Studies, Special Studies Series 5; Macon, Ga.: Mercer University Press; Edinburgh: T&T Clark, 1978), 165 (see also idem, "The Lucan Perspective on the Miracles of Jesus: A Preliminary Sketch," *JBL* 94 [1975]: 558). The following comment, by Elisabeth Schüssler Fiorenza, illustrates this point further: "As a man of his time, Luke does not hesitate to conceive of this power *partly* in magical terms" ("Miracles, Mission, and Apologetics: An Introduction," in *Aspects of Religious Propaganda in Judaism and Early Christianity* (ed. Elisabeth Schüssler Fiorenza; Notre Dame, Ind.: University of Notre Dame Press, 1976), 13 (emphasis added). The qualification "partly" appears to downplay her earlier assertion that "for Luke the early Christian missionary possesses magic powers and exhibits miraculous capabilities which prove to be greater than those of the competition" (8). Indeed, it is hard to imagine that Luke would have been able to conceive of miracles in any other way but *wholly* magical. Howard Clark Kee's well-known objection to the association of the New Testament writings with the "magical world-view," and his attempt to create distance between this later Roman phenomenon and the world of early Christian and Jewish apocalyptic texts, establish category distinctions for the ancient world that are impossible to construct and to maintain in practice (*Medicine, Miracle, and Magic in New Testament Times* [SNTSMS 55; Cambridge: Cambridge University Press, 1986], 117–20; but cf. 128, where he seems more nuanced on this point). For further discussion, see Cotter, *Miracles in Greco-Roman Antiquity*, 176–77.

19. This tendency is evidenced explicitly in the study by Erkki Koskenniemi, *Apollonios von Tyana in der neutestamentlichen Exegese: Forschungsbericht und Weiterführung der Diskussion* (WUNT 2/61; Tübingen: Mohr Siebeck, 1994): "Die Magie, die mehrfach im Neuen Testament strikt verurteilt wird, gewinnt im 1. und 2. Jahrhundert unbestreitbar an Einfluss. Die zunehmende Bedeutung erklärt zweifellos den dramatischen Unterschied zwischen der lukanischen Apostelgeschichte und den apokryphen Apostelakten" (228–29).

works are relatively similar in form and function,[20] a position not shared by the majority of scholars. Indeed, most scholars have been reticent to recognize any explicit links between the miracle episodes in Acts and the cultural ethos of the apocryphal texts, which are saturated with miraculous features in connection with the various narrative characters[21] and which, to some degree, might appear more magical in orientation.[22]

In this same vein, while history of religions comparisons can be fruitful for analysis of miracles in early Christian discourse as a whole,[23] especially in terms of clarifying specific patterns of characterization and delineating the significance of particular topoi, they can also be used to sidestep some

---

20. Richard I. Pervo, *Profit with Delight: The Literary Genre of the Acts of the Apostles* (Philadelphia: Fortress, 1987), 126. Now also see Myllykoski, "Being There," 146–79.

21. See the summary in Rosa Söder, *Die Apokryphen Apostelgeschichten und die Romanhafte Literatur der Antike* (repr.; Darmstadt: Wissenschaftliche Buchgesellschaft, 1969 [1932]), 51–102.

22. Cf. Kee, *Medicine, Miracle, and Magic*, 130, as well as the following comments by Söder: "Von den Wundertaten Jesu selbst haben ja bereits die Evangelien vieles berichtet und Wundertaten der Apostel erzählt auch die Apg, aber in ganz anderer Weise als hier [apocryphal Acts]. Dort ist es überall der Geist, der aus den Handlungen spricht, und aus diesem Geiste werden sie geboren, nicht aber aus der Prahlsucht und dem Allmachtsdünkel der Jünger" (*Apokryphen Apostelgeschichten*, 73). Söder goes on to signal the use of the name of Jesus in the miracles of Acts as the feature that lends those miraculous episodes a more certain grounding in tradition (74). The strong reaction in scholarship *against* any interpretation that would promote a view of the apostles in Acts as wonder-workers in their own right should be situated in the (apologetic) trajectory of scholarship that seeks to separate the canonical from the apocryphal Acts. The comments by Susan M. Praeder are typical: "Nowhere [in the canonical Acts] is Paul portrayed as a miracle worker simply for the sake of 'personal glorification' or in order to transform a *Geistesheld* into a *Wundertaeter*" ("Miracle Worker and Missionary: Paul in the Acts of the Apostles," *1983 Society of Biblical Literature Seminar Papers* [SBLSP 22; Atlanta: Scholars Press, 1983], 128). See also Anton Fridrichsen: "Cases are rare [in Acts] where aretological and popular interest prevails, so that miracle serves directly and particularly to glorify the hero" (*The Problem of Miracle in Primitive Christianity* [trans. R. A. Harrisville and J. S. Hanson; Minneapolis: Augsburg, 1972 (1925)], 61–62).

23. Illustrative in this respect are the results of the recent study by Rick Strelan, "Recognizing the Gods (Acts 14.8–10)," *NTS* 46 (2000): 488–503. Also see Susan R. Garrett, "Light on a Dark Subject and Vice Versa: Magic and Magicians in the New Testament," in *Religion, Science, and Magic: In Concert and Conflict* (ed. J. Neusner, E. S. Frerichs, and P. V. M. Flesher; New York: Oxford University Press, 1989), esp. 153–59.

of the more important issues related to the function of miracles in Lukan narrative construction or the rhetorical dimension of miracle claims in ancient literature.[24] Here one can easily get caught up in collecting parallels, assessing meaning, or, as is frequently the case, nuancing interpretation, while failing to note the overt function of manifestations of power in the text, which must necessarily shape any understanding of textual meaning in the first place.

Given some of these broader considerations, then, it is not surprising to find that scholars studying the use of miracles in Acts generally seem to make every effort to subordinate the role and character of the miracles to the "more important" features of the narrative. To list just a few interpretations in this vein, the miracles in Acts have been understood to bring about faith in the hearer;[25] to legitimate the preaching of Paul[26] and/or the theological themes of Luke associated with Paul's missionary journeys;[27] to characterize the prophets in the narrative as legitimate messengers of God (which carries with it as well an implicit apologetic function in terms of comparison with competitors in the narrative);[28] to demonstrate the divine providentiality of God in the Lukan narrative;[29] to establish a *Heilsgeschichtliche* correlation with the exodus event through Christ and now beginning anew in Paul;[30] to possess a social-liberationist function

---

24. An example of such side-stepping is aptly illustrated by Bernd Kollman, *Jesus und die Christen als Wundertäter: Studien zu Magie, Medizin und Schamanismus in Antike und Christentum* (FRLANT 170; Göttingen: Vandenhoeck & Ruprecht, 1996).

25. Mary E. Mills, *Human Agents of Cosmic Power in Hellenistic Judaism and the Synoptic Tradition* (JSNTSup 41; Sheffield: JSOT Press, 1990), 116.

26. Jacob Jervell, "The Signs of an Apostle: Paul's Miracles," in *The Unknown Paul: Essays on Luke-Acts and Early Christian History* (Minneapolis: Augsburg, 1984), 84–88; cf. Bert Jan Lietaert Peerbolte, "Paul the Miracle Worker: Development and Background of Pauline Miracle Stories," in Labahn and Peerbolte, *Wonders Never Cease*, 181–87, who stresses the function that miracles have in authenticating Paul "as an envoy" of Jesus.

27. Praeder, "Miracle Worker and Missionary," 107–29.

28. Wolfgang Weiss, "Zeichen und Wunder:" Eine Studie zu der Sprachtradition und ihrer Verwendung im Neuen Testament (WMANT 67; Neukirchen-Vluyn: Neukirchener, 1995), 73–119; and Strelan, *Strange Acts*, 28–29.

29. John T. Squires, *The Plan of God in Luke-Acts* (SNTSMS 76; Cambridge: Cambridge University Press, 1993).

30. Stefan Schreiber, *Paulus als Wundertäter: Redaktionsgeschichtliche Untersuchungen zur Apostelgeschichte und den authentischen Paulusbriefen* (BZNW 79; Berlin: de Gruyter, 1996). Cf. Graham H. Twelftree, *In the Name of Jesus: Exorcism among*

that underscores the power of relationships;[31] or to combine several of the above options.[32] One might also add to this list those studies emphasizing that miracles provide the narrative and theological bridge unifying the missionaries of Acts with Jesus.[33]

In one of the early, now classic studies on miracles in the New Testament, Anton Fridrichsen aptly summarized these essential categories that have come to dominate the conceptual framing:

> The miracles manifest that divine power which sustains the mission, acts through it, and has created all things new in the ethical and material realms ... if this is the main and higher point of view ... miracle serves to *legitimate* God's messenger and his preaching ... [and] the canonical book of Acts still remains at such a level that the miraculous is subordinated to the great religious purpose. Purely aretalogical features are rarely encountered there.... However varied, even offensive the miracles of the Acts might be, the narrative is still far from disappearing in the miraculous. What dominates is the basic religious thought of spreading salvation. This is all the more remarkable since several of the narratives in Acts recount miracles which originally were told only for the miracle's sake. [Luke] ... subordinated them to a superior view: they must accent the great purpose of his work, viz., to further the triumphal and irresistible march of the gospel.... We may assume that this fine religious tact in regard to miracle is found with most of the eminent personalities of the ancient church. For all its enthusiasm, primitive Christianity had a very sure sense of the fundamentally moral character of religion.[34]

Early Christians (Grand Rapids: Baker Academic, 2007), 129–55, who emphasizes the function of Jesus' bringing eschatological salvation, now through the apostles.

31. Richter Reimer, *Women in the Acts of the Apostles*, 60. Although Richter Reimer argues against explicit theological interpretations of the miracles in Acts (see n. 15 above), viewing herself as promoting a more social mode of analysis, I would argue that her specific "liberationist" reading is as theologically motivated as those others she criticizes.

32. Marilyn McCord Adams, "The Role of Miracles in the Structure of Luke-Acts," in *Hermes and Athena: Biblical Exegesis and Philosophical Theology* (ed. E. Stump and T. P. Flint; Notre Dame, Ind.: University of Notre Dame Press, 1993), 237–38.

33. See most recently Andreas Lindemann, "Einheit und Veilfalt im Lukanischen Doppelwerk: Beobachtungen zu Reden, Wundererzählungen und Mahlberichten," in *The Unity of Luke-Acts* (ed. J. Verheyden; BETL 142; Leuven: Leuven University Press, 1999), 237–50.

34. Fridrichsen, *Problem of Miracle*, 61–62 (emphasis in original). See also the expression of this same sentiment by Hans-Josef Klauck, *Magic and Paganism in Early*

The above statement is illuminating for its positioning of miracles not only in Acts, but also in early Christianity as a whole. Clear in this programmatic assessment is that the miracles are not only subordinated to the "mission" message of Acts, but that in fact Luke has helped sanitize some of the traditional pieces he took over, making sure to tone down the purely miraculous elements in the service of advancing his gospel. Moreover, serving to distinguish Christianity from this environment of "pagan magic" is the former's ethical and moral emphases that restrain the adherent's mind from capitulating to the "magical" worldview pervasive in the broader Mediterranean milieu.

It may be fair to suggest that Acts itself might inadvertently encourage this impression: its heroes work miracles in the name of Jesus in support of their mission over and against the magical practices of their opponents. Yet this view also represents a fairly simplistic rendering of the rhetoric of the narrative. When Hans-Josef Klauck asserts that "Luke fears above all the survival of remnants of popular religiosity in his communities, and that he does not regard his Christians as secure from occasional lapses into magical practices,"[35] an argument that he frames in light of Luke's ability to reflect the (postconversion) rational critique of such expressions of ancient religious imagination, one receives the distinct impression that the sophisticated narrative strategies of argumentation used by Luke have, at a fundamental level, been neglected (but have thereby also proven themselves effective!). Rather than examining more broadly how Luke may be using these features of miracles/magic in his narrative, one is simply left with a Christian triumphalist sentiment that bears little relation to the discourse of power mediated in and through the text.[36]

In light of this neglect outlined above, I believe a reassessment of the sociorhetorical function of miracle discourse in the Lukan story would be helpful in terms of better situating his work in its ancient sociocultural context. By distancing miracles from the cultural world of Acts, by

---

Christianity: The World of the Acts of the Apostles (trans. B. McNeil; Edinburgh: T&T Clark, 2000), 120.

35. Klauck, *Magic and Paganism*, 120.

36. I would include in such triumphalist readings those that focus on Luke's "superior" ethical stance in relation to his depiction of miracles (cf. Marguerat, "Magic and Miracle," 120, 123; and Andy M. Reimer, "Virtual Prison Breaks: Non-escape Narratives and the Definition of 'Magic,'" in *Magic in the Biblical World* (ed. T. Klutz; JSNTSup 245; London: T&T Clark, 2003), 137–38.

emphasizing the traditional nature of the accounts, the history of religions typologies, or the theological redactional emphases of Luke, scholars have managed to overlook or misrepresent the core aspect of miracle stories in Acts: the manifestation of power in narrative form.[37] Indeed, it is precisely the interpreter's discomfort with this rhetorical force of power that has resulted in the attempt to sanitize the miracles in the first place. *Power*, as I use that term here, refers to a broader category than merely miraculous manifestations.[38] For it is a complex nexus of power relationships that one encounters in the ancient world, and narratives form one avenue for negotiation in the struggles and contests spawned by this structure, wherein one person gains identity enhancement at the expense of another's loss. Thus, while we can speak of "numinous power" in the form of miracles, this category cannot be separated from all other forms of related manifestations of political, social, and cultural force. But this interconnection has largely been overlooked in modern scholarship precisely because of the latter's failure to consider miracle stories on their own (narrative) terms: as mighty acts that negotiate and identify the locus of power in narrative.

---

37. In this context, I would also note that cultural-anthropological and sociological studies dealing with miracles tend to produce the same effect in terms of reducing attention to rhetorical aspects of the text (see most recently John J. Pilch, *Visions and Healing in the Acts of the Apostles: How the Early Believers Experienced God* [Collegeville, Minn.: Liturgical Press, 2004]). In moving from narrative to experience it can be relatively easy to overlook or minimize the textually embedded ideologies and literary strategies that provide *cultural* meaning for the events depicted.

38. In what follows, I am indebted more broadly to some of the groundbreaking work by Michel Foucault on the relationship of power to discourses that are situated within and defined by particular sociocultural and historical communicative practices. Much of Foucault's work has been preoccupied with this theme more generally, but for a short introduction see especially "The Subject and Power," in *The Essential Foucault: Selections from Essential Works of Foucault 1954–1984* (ed. P. Rabinow and N. Rose; New York: The New Press, 2003), 126–44. Foucault's rich discussion links power to historical-cultural institutions that situate and subject individuals within specific discursive practices, which thereby possess the power to force persons into subjection but also to enforce (more subtly) a form of self-recognized subjectivity on persons—power in this sense both *confines* and *defines* (or, as Foucault states, this "form of power ... subjugates and makes subject to," 130). Also see the helpful discussion of Foucault's diverse emphases in Elizabeth A. Clark, *History, Theory, Text: Historians and the Linguistic Turn* (Cambridge: Harvard University Press, 2004), 113–19. Also see Todd Penner and Caroline Vander Stichele, *Contextualizing Gender in Early Christian Discourse: Thinking beyond Thecla* (London: T&T Clark, 2009), 18–19.

Indeed, at the same time that we distance miracles from the discourse of power in Acts, we also tend to downplay the radicalism of the political and cultural power perspectives of that same Lukan discourse.[39] These are not two separate spheres (politics/culture versus literature), but are, as I will argue, intricately related.

3. The Politics of Miracles: Recovering the Power in/of Narrative

It is constructive to begin this analysis with a reassessment of the relationship between miracle and magic in Acts. These two features, as noted above, are frequently separated out as a practice of scholarship, resulting in a framework in which miracles in Acts are interpreted to be nonmagical in their essence. This view helps solidify the equation of "magic" with "pagan" versus "miracle" with "Christian," reinscribing in the process the binary opposition between these two fields of reference. As Wendy Cotter claims, "There is no suggestion in any Christian material that magic was considered as anything but completely negative, no matter where it occurred. If our purpose is to interpret the intended meaning of the Jesus miracle stories, then, a suggestion of magical power, such as was understood in the Greco-Roman world, is completely unsupported."[40]

By contrast, my starting premise is that miracles and magic (the latter used here in a nonpejorative sense) represent a fused category in the ancient religious imagination.[41] In short, I suggest that the book of Acts is permeated by what we label as "magic."[42] Of course, one must keep

---

39. The downplaying of this radicalism is seen particularly in those interpretations supporting either the classic sense of "political apologetic," where Luke is assumed to be appealing to the Roman overseers for tolerance (rejected by Richard J. Cassidy, *Society and Politics in the Acts of the Apostles in the Acts of the Apostles* [Maryknoll, N.Y.: Orbis, 1987], 145–55), or its more nuanced (and more common) form in which Luke is viewed as tacitly affirming Roman legitimacy and authority (see, e.g., Douglas R. Edwards, "Surviving the Web of Power: Religion and Power in the Acts of the Apostles, Josephus, and Chariton's *Chaereas and Callirhoe*," in *Images of Empire* [ed. L. Alexander; JSOTSup 122; Sheffield: JSOT Press, 1991], 187–88).

40. Cotter, *Miracles in Greco-Roman Antiquity*, 177.

41. Graham H. Twelftree (*Jesus the Exorcist: A Contribution to the Study of the Historical Jesus* [WUNT 2/54; Tübingen: Mohr Siebeck, 1993], 190–91) summarizes some of the major studies on this point.

42. Morton Smith's assessment in *Jesus the Magician* (San Francisco: Harper &

in mind that "magic" was frequently used to label that with which one did not agree.[43] "Magic" as a conceptual category is therefore often used as a form of slander that describes in negative terms the miracles of the "other."[44] This judgment is reminiscent of E. E. Evans-Pritchard's observation contrasting Azande tribal witches and sorcerers with those practicing so-called good magic: "You will never meet a Zande who professes himself a sorcerer."[45] "Magic," then, becomes difficult to define in the ancient world in large part because it is used in such highly relativistic ways. Still, there were some general issues at stake in such designations,[46] and in part

---

Row, 1978) is dead-on in this respect. It is thus no surprise that in earliest Christian representations Jesus is depicted in the guise of a magician, with wand at the ready. See further Thomas F. Matthews, *The Clash of Gods: A Reinterpretation of Early Christian Art* (rev. ed.; Princeton: Princeton University Press, 1999), 54–91.

43. See Cotter, *Miracles in Greco-Roman Antiquity*, 176–77.

44. See the finely nuanced discussion in Fritz Graf (*Magic in the Ancient World* [trans. F. Philip; Revealing Antiquity 10; Cambridge: Harvard University Press, 1997], 61–88), who essentially affirms the classic formulation of Marcel Mauss—that most often what we are dealing with in these ancient discussions is the marginalization, or, one might say, "magicalization," of a perceived outsider. Also see Alan F. Segal, "Hellenistic Magic: Some Questions of Definition," in *Studies in Gnosticism and Hellenistic Religions: Presented to Gilles Quispel on the Occasion of His 65th Birthday* (ed. R. van der Broek and M. J. Vermaseren; EPRO 91; Leiden: Brill, 1981), 349–75; Kimberly B. Stratton, *Naming the Witch: Magic, Ideology, and Stereotype in the Ancient World* (Gender, Theory, and Religion; New York: Columbia University Press, 2007), 1–38; McCord Adams, "Role of Miracles," 245–47; and Mihwa Choi, "Christianity, Magic, and Difference: Name-Calling and Resistance between the Lines in *Contra Celsum*," *Semeia* 79 (1997): 75–92.

45. E. E. Evans-Pritchard, *Witchcraft, Oracles and Magic among the Azande* (London: Oxford University Press, 1937), 391.

46. See the discussions by Naomi Janowitz, *Magic in the Roman World* (Religion in the First Christian Centuries; New York: Routledge, 2001), 9–26; and Jonathan Z. Smith, "Trading Places," in *Ancient Magic and Ritual Power* (ed. M. Meyer and P. Mirecki; RGRW 129; Leiden: Brill: 1995), 13–20; as well as the lengthy treatment by Stratton, *Naming the Witch*. More recent studies (e.g., Matthew W. Dickie, *Magic and Magicians in the Greco-Roman World* [New York: Routledge, 2001], 124–41) continue to perpetuate the hard and fast line between "magic" and perceived legitimate forms of religious expression in antiquity. Andy M. Reimer (*Miracle and Magic: A Study in the Acts of the Apostles and the* Life of Apollonius of Tyana [JSNTSup 235; London: Sheffield Academic Press, 2002]) pushes the traditional assessments further by seeking a broader sociological basis for the designation "magician" (cf. the more theoretical and useful contextualization by Jonathan Z. Smith, "Here, There, and Anywhere," in *Prayer, Magic and the Stars in the Ancient and Late Antique World* [ed. S.

these have to do with the perceived legitimate or illegitimate use of numinous power.[47]

One should not be surprised, then, to find that charges of practicing magic abound in the competitive and combative environment of the ancient world. For instance, Josephus refers to Theudas as a "magician" trying to replicate the wonders of Moses, whom, from Josephus's perspective, seems to have received his just deserts for those grandiose claims (*Ant.* 20.5.97). Such negative characterization predominates in the examples from ancient literature. Tacitus describes the conniving Agrippina as inventing the charge against Lollia that she conferred with astrologers and magicians (including consultation of the Clarian Apollo). The end result of the charge was dramatic: she was forced into suicide (*Ann.* 12.22). Elsewhere, "accusers" of Scaurus combine the charges of adultery with the practice of magical rites (*Ann.* 6.29). Deception is one of the key negative elements in the characterization of magic and its practitioners (see Plato, *Resp.* 381e; 598c; Tacitus, *Ann.* 2.27; Josephus, *Ant.* 2.284, 320 [where reference is made to the negative assessment of Moses' deeds by the Pharaoh]; 20.141; Plautus, *Amph.* 814), with the concomitant charges of being treacherous or of causing harm following close behind (Tacitus, *Ann.* 4.22; 12.59; Euripides, *Hel.* 1100). Further, in an environment in which almost every reference to magic and its practice occurs within the rhetorical framework of accusation, denigration, and negative characterization, it is difficult to know, for instance, whether the labels "astrologers" and "magicians" in the Senate expulsion order from Italy reported by Tacitus (*Ann.* 2.32) refer to political, religious, or some other cultural transgression, or if they represent the fabrication of a charge to justify the expulsion of a group resented for entirely different reasons. In other words, the *function* of the language is often highly ambiguous.

Noegel, J. Walker, and B. Wheeler; Magic in History; University Park: Pennsylvania State University Press, 2003], 21–36). Also see the brief but helpful discussion by Scott Shauf, *Theology as History, History as Theology: Paul in Ephesus in Acts 19* (BZNW 133; Berlin: de Gruyter, 2005), 178–90.

47. C. R. Phillips III ("*Nullum Crimen sine Lege*: Socioreligious Sanctions on Magic," in *Magika Hiera: Ancient Greek Magic and Religion* [ed. C. A. Faraone and D. Obbink; New York: Oxford University Press, 1991], 260–76) provides a sound assessment of the broad scope but also ambiguous nature of the legislation against "magic," and identifies the problem with respect to determining the precise nature of that expression of religious sentiment and ritual that was perceived to move beyond what was deemed "legitimate" by the dominant cultural authorities.

Charges of magic are thus illustrative because they demonstrate the means of gaining sociocultural power by associating one's opponent with a negative category. In the end, terms of such overt negative association are difficult to use for social-historical reconstruction; at best, they delineate the rhetorical strategies of particular writers.[48] Miracles, such as we find in early Christian texts, similarly negotiate power, but from a so-called positive perspective, but they are no more reliable for being that. In both cases a "magical worldview" is assumed, and the associated language is used to navigate the complexity of relationships therein. Thus, while miracle discourse in the New Testament belongs to the broader, shared cultural view of manifestations of power in the ancient world, there also exists within this context a vying for position and identity relative to those same terms. One thus finds charges of malice, greed, and general bad character associated with particular expressions of religious power; or, conversely, ascriptions of mercy, faith, and purity with others. Indeed, at the very moment some manifestation of power is attested, it is also contested, thereby being negotiated relative to other overt or implied claims.

Coming back to Acts, then, I believe it is misleading to separate too sharply (if at all) the sociocultural world and discourse reflected in Acts from that of its sociocultural environment. On the one hand, there seems to be substantive merit in the conception of the ancient world as being inundated with expressions of the divine. Ramsay MacMullen's description of just how pervasive religious images were and how they could impinge on even the most seemingly disinterested individual is apropos:

> Their senses were assaulted by messages directing their attention to religion: shouts and singing in public places, generally in the open air ... and to an accompaniment as loud as ancient instruments could sound; applause for highly ornate prose paeans in theaters ... while the idols looked on from seats of honor; the god-possessed swirl of worshippers coming down the street to the noise of rattles and drums ... so obtrusive upon the attention of the least interested was the world of the divine.[49]

---

48. Marguerat ("Magic and Miracle," 115–17) recognizes this rhetorical aspect, yet suggests that the ancient author in question can be a reliable guide in distinguishing between "magic" as a technical art (e.g., divination) and its use in polemic. It is unlikely, however, that we have such "absolute" perspectives in any ancient texts (or modern ones for that matter).

49. Ramsay MacMullen, *Paganism in the Roman Empire* (New Haven: Yale University Press, 1981), 27.

On the other hand, one cannot assume some sort of unified perception of ancient religion and the supernatural.[50] It was a world permeated by numinous elements, but then it was also a world of "sound reasoning" and "sober thinking." One need only recall, for example, the extensive comments in Polybius and Lucian regarding the use of supernatural explanations in historical compositions. Both writers eschew the description of episodes that include such causes because they detract from the usefulness of these stories for the polis. Polybius dismisses such accounts as sensational; they appeal to the inclinations of the passions and defy that which is "natural or generally happen[s] in the world" (15.36.8), being "contrary to reasonable probability" (3.48.8-9).[51] In this light, Plutarch could describe one goal of historical composition as "purifying Fable," making "her submit to reason and take on the semblance of History" (*Thes.* 1.3).[52] For these various writers, then, the rational basis of historical composition rests in reflecting the daily reality of the civic dimension of the polis,[53] standing in stark contrast to the description of the world proffered by MacMullen, which these ancient writers would label as "superstitious," and which Lucian parodies in his *True History* thus: "I shall at least be truthful in saying that I am a liar ... be it understood, then, that I am writing about things which I have neither seen, nor had to

---

50. Dale Martin (*Inventing Superstition: From the Hippocratics to the Christians* [Cambridge: Harvard University Press, 2004], 14) rightly challenges the use of the term *supernatural* as a useful category of interpretation for the ancient world, pointing out that "for ancient people whatever does exist exists in 'nature.'" In other words, we need to be cautious about constructing "otherworldly realms" of significant divine action (relevant to our modern world) in thinking about ancient configurations of numinous power—the locus of divine action is in the "real" world. My use of *supernatural* in this context should not be taken to connote such, but rather refers more broadly to "divine action."

51. Cf. "probable reasoning" in Plutarch (*Thes.* 1.1); or "improbability" in Sextus Empiricus (*Adv. Math.* 1.267-68). Unless otherwise noted, citations from ancient writers are taken from the Loeb Classical Library.

52. For further discussion of the tension with respect to including miraculous accounts in ancient historiography, see Eckhard Plümacher, "TEPATEIA: Fiktion und Wunder in der hellenistiche-römischen Geschichtsschreibung und in der Apostelgeschichte," *ZNW* 89 (1998): 66-90.

53. See further Todd Penner, "Civilizing Discourse: Acts, Declamation, and the Rhetoric of the *Polis*," in *Contextualizing Acts: Lukan Narrative and Greco-Roman Discourse* (ed. Todd Penner and Caroline Vander Stichele; SBLSymS 20; Atlanta: Scholars Press, 2003), 72-78.

do with, nor learned from others—which, in fact, do not exist at all and, in the nature of things, cannot exist" (1.4).

Acts falls somewhere in the midst of this diverse and seemingly mutually exclusive terrain. Loveday Alexander has noted the problems with the cultural contextualization of Acts, a work of ancient historiography that in many respects works against the stream of that genre in terms of its commitment to supernatural explanations. Yet, at the same time, Alexander notes that Luke affirms the "broadly factual status of his narrative."[54] Since one key aspect of ancient historiographical composition is the commitment to plausible narration,[55] it is evident that Luke at the very least must believe that the broad pattern of events described in his narrative correlates with the cultural and religious environment out of which he is writing. Moreover, as a historian, Luke negotiates the commitment to the manifestation of numinous display in the world early Christianity inhabits while tacitly affirming the civic dimension of the historian's discourse (i.e., the commitment to the values of and topoi related to the polis), which itself involves a navigation of political, social, and cultural power structures. It would be imprudent to separate these two spheres in Acts, as the two are fundamentally integrated into the fabric of Lukan narrative. This affirmation implies, then, that one ought to examine the evident displays of miraculous power in Acts as an expression of magical, numinous power, but simultaneously to keep in view that this feature cannot be isolated from the tasks of the historian to negotiate and to structure civic and cultural relationships. Paying close attention to the rhetorical function and placement of miracles in Acts thus cannot help but move us beyond the merely religious to the much broader integrative landscape of the ancient world, where politics, religion, and society represented varying components of a larger equation.

One need only turn to the increasing role that "divine men" were playing in the later Greco-Roman era in order to grasp more fully the complexity of this picture. From the general reflection on and characterization of "divine men" in Greek and Jewish literature[56] to the connection of Moses

---

54. Loveday Alexander, "Fact, Fiction and the Genre of Acts," *NTS* 44 (1998): 399.

55. Robert G. Hall, "Josephus, *Contra Apionem* and Historical Inquiry in the Roman Rhetorical Schools," in *Josephus'* Contra Apionem: *Studies in Its Character and Content* (ed. L. H. Feldman and J. R. Levison; AGJU 34; Leiden: Brill, 1996), 236.

56. David L. Tiede (*The Charismatic Figure as Miracle Worker* [SBLDS 1; Missoula, Mont.: Scholars Press, 1972]) has marshaled the extensive evidence for this

to magic in pagan literature,[57] there is enough evidence to suggest that in both the Greco-Roman and Jewish cultural contexts there was an increased interest in the intersections of heaven and earth in the actions and speech of cultural wonder-workers, philosophers, prophets, sages, and kings.[58] In his epilogue to the translation of his classic study on missionary propaganda in early Christianity, Dieter Georgi moves beyond the more formalized assessment of the "divine man" as a type toward an approach that emphasizes the dynamic qualities of the agonistic cultural ethos that is permeated with divergent images of humans as representative of and infused with the divine.[59] His assessment that the "main characteristic of Hellenistic culture between Alexander and Constantine ... was committed to experiment with transcendence, literally as well as metaphorically" (with the "divine man" as the "foremost representative of that culture's experiment with transcendence")[60] represents a particularly apt summary portrayal of the cultural environment in which Acts is to be situated.

---

view. Also see the classic and still useful study by Ludwig Bieler, *Theios Anēr: Das Bild des "Göttlichen Menschen" in Spätantike und Frühchristentum* (1935–1936; repr., Darmstadt: Wissenschaftliche Buchgesellschaft, 1967); as well as Gail Corrington Streete, *The "Divine Man": His Origin and Function in Hellenistic Popular Religion* (New York: Lang, 1984).

57. John G. Gager, *Moses in Greco-Roman Paganism* (SBLMS 16; Nashville: Abingdon, 1972), 134–61.

58. See further Koskenniemi, *Apollonios von Tyana*, 206–29. Gerd Theissen argues that after the Hellenistic period there was less separation between rational and irrational viewpoints, resulting in an increase in and greater mass appeal of a so-called magical worldview (*The Miracle Stories of the Early Christian Tradition* [ed. J. Riches; trans. J. McDonagh; Philadelphia: Fortress, 1983], 269–70).

59. Dieter Georgi, *The Opponents of Paul in Second Corinthians* (Philadelphia: Fortress, 1986), 390–415. This affirmation of Georgi's position does not negate the assessment by Carl R. Holladay (*Theios Aner in Hellenistic-Judaism: A Critique of the Use of This Category in New Testament Christology* [SLBDS 40; Missoula, Mont.: Scholars Press, 1977], 233–42) and others (e.g., Koskenniemi, *Apollonios von Tyana*, 228; and Eugene V. Gallagher, *Divine Man or Magician: Celsus and Origen on Jesus* [SBLDS 64; Chico, Calif.: Scholars Press, 1982], 27, 178–79) regarding the problematic nature of the overformalization and conceptualization of the category of "divine man" in New Testament scholarship. Rather, I mean to stress that one should be thinking in terms of a broadly conceived and highly variant culture of perceived divine interactions with humans. Whatever the precise origins of early Christian stories are, certainly they are to be intricately situated in this larger environment.

60. Georgi, *Opponents of Paul*, 390–91.

Perhaps the phenomenon of the "divine man" as a convergence of "religion" and "politics" is best illustrated in the development of the image of the emperor in the first century.[61] In this light, one of the most important cultural and political references for understanding the discourse of power in Acts may well be the inscription of Augustus written in Latin and Greek on (presumably) numerous temples throughout the empire. The superscription to that text at the temple of Rome and Augustus at Ancyra begins thus: "Below is a copy of the acts of the Deified Augustus by which he placed the whole world under the sovereignty of the Roman people, and of the amounts which he expended upon the state and the Roman people" (*Res Gestae* 1). What follows is the "personal" account of Augustus's great acts, celebrating on the one hand his power of *imperium* and on the other his magnanimous expressions of *philia* toward both Roman and conquered peoples. Given the assumed widespread availability of this lengthy inscription throughout the empire,[62] there is a strong possibility that a writer such as Luke was familiar with the contents of the text, and most certainly the ethos it reflected: the combination of the lethal influence of the sword with the sway of beneficence, both having the aim of securing and maintaining the loyalty of conquered peoples (and their territories). In large part, this coupling is significant because we see herein the emperor being characterized as a political and social hero, perhaps even as *Kulturbringer*,[63] negotiating the power structures of the ancient world

---

61. The suggestion by Dieter Zeller ("The *Theia Physis* of Hippocrates and of Other 'Divine Men,'" in *Early Christianity and Classical Culture: Comparative Essays in Honor of Abraham J. Malherbe* [ed. J. T. Fitzgerald, T. H. Olbricht, and L. M. White; NovTSup 110; Leiden: Brill, 2003], 49–69) that in the Hellenistic and Roman imperial period a shift was made away from an emphasis on "divine nature" in this terminology to a stress on "character" (virtue and piety) as determinative of participation in divinity would actually lend further support to the integrative nature of the conception at this time.

62. See further Gary Gilbert, "The List of Nations in Acts 2: Roman Propaganda and the Lucan Response," *JBL* 121 (2002): 497–529; and idem, "Roman Propaganda and Christian Identity in the Worldview of Luke-Acts," in Penner and Vander Stichele, *Contextualizing Acts*, 233–56.

63. This feature brings the emperor in line with famous epic heroes such as Hercules, Osiris, Odysseus, and Aeneas. See Doran Mendels, "Pagan or Jewish? The Presentation of Paul's Mission in the Book of Acts," in *Geschichte—Tradition—Reflexion: Festschrift für Martin Hengel zum 70. Geburtstag* (ed. H. Cancik, H. Lichtenberger, and P. Schäfer; 3 vols.; Tübingen: Mohr Siebeck, 1996), 1:431–52.

through the recitation of mighty deeds. Yet this image was also closely connected to representations of the emperor's religious/numinous power. Paul Zanker, in his treatment of the pervasive impact of Augustan cultural images, describes a particular relief thus:

> Augustus in the guise of Jupiter is enthroned beside Roma, but instead of a thunderbolt he holds the augur's staff. His gaze is directed toward Tiberius as he descends from a chariot driven by Victoria. The *lituus* in Augustus's hand thus indicates that Tiberius's victory was won under the auspices of Augustus. The young Germanicus stands armed next to Roma, ready for the next campaign. The two princes are emissaries of the universal ruler; his invincibility is transferred to them like a discreet entity. This is why Roma looks admiringly at Augustus and not at the actual victors. Victory is as predictable as the movement of the stars through the heavens. Above Augustus's head, the Capricorn shines against a disk (the sun?) and a star in the background, all three symbols of mythic and cosmic predestination. From behind Augustus's throne representatives of this blessed world look up toward him, Italia, wearing around her neck the *bulla* (actually the token of a *freeborn* youth!), sits on the ground, surrounded by children and holding a cornucopia. Behind are Oceanus and Oikoumene, the latter crowning Augustus with the *corona civica*. The personification of the inhabited world wears a mural crown, thus representing the flourishing cities of the Empire.[64]

This description demonstrates how readily political images of power and conquest could be elided with those depicting the emperor as the medium/locus of divine power, not only in terms of his providence in overseeing battles but also with respect to his supplying the basis for military virility. And we should not forget that all of this political and religious power stands in the service of establishing civic and political order in the *oikoumene*, a notion that proved to be a vital feature of Roman imperial ideology and propaganda.[65] The rhetorical impact of the image thus establishes the extremely potent force of Augustus (and the empire he embodies). One should also not lose sight of the fact that predominant in such con-

---

64. Paul Zanker, *The Power of Images in the Age of Augustus* (trans. A. Shapiro; Ann Arbor: University of Michigan Press, 1988), 230–31.

65. For a detailed development of this theme, see the assessment by Eberhard Faust, *Pax Christi et Pax Caesaris: Religionsgeschichtliche, traditionsgeschichtliche und sozialgeschichtliche Studien zum Epheserbrief* (NTOA 24; Göttingen: Vandenhoeck & Ruprecht, 1993), 280–314.

texts are men, male power, and masculine virtue, a gendered feature not inconsequential for the cultural and social impact of these images.

The framework established here is crucial for understanding Acts since Luke quite possibly wrote his volumes at the pinnacle of the emperor cult in the Greek East under the Flavians,[66] and the complex web of power negotiations that pervades Luke's narrative carries all the more significance as a result. Already much earlier, Adolf Deissmann noted that "the cult of Christ goes forth into the world of the Mediterranean and soon displays the endeavor to reserve for Christ the words already in use for worship in the world, words that had been transferred to the deified emperors or had perhaps even been newly invented in emperor worship. Thus there arises a polemical parallelism between the cult of the emperor and the cult of Christ."[67] This particular framework for understanding early Christian discourse has frequently and perhaps unfairly been sidestepped in the history of discussion. In a more recent move, however, Gary Gilbert has undertaken an extensive and innovative examination of the language and conceptual framework of Acts 2 (the list of nations) in light of features related to imperial and territorial conquest found in texts like the *Res Gestae*, arguing that Luke has deliberately shaped Christian discourse in this instance not as an apologetic response in the traditional sense but as a co-option of Roman imperial rhetoric.[68] This insight provides a context for reconsidering the ways in which Roman language of imperial authority could be taken over by early Christians and used in both subtle and explicit ways not only to subvert the conceptions of the dominant culture but also in many respects to outmaneuver that culture at its own "language game."

---

66. The date of Acts is undergoing renewed scrutiny, with special focus being placed on its use in second-century polemics. It may thus well be that Acts needs to be resituated in the early to mid-portion of the second century, although the argument developed here is not substantially altered as a result. See especially Christopher Mount, *Pauline Christianity: Luke-Acts and the Legacy of Paul* (NovTSup 104; Leiden: Brill, 2002); Andrew Gregory, *The Reception of Luke and Acts in the Period before Irenaeus: Looking for Luke in the Second Century* (WUNT 2/169; Tübingen: Mohr Siebeck, 2003); Joseph B. Tyson, *Marcion and Luke-Acts: A Defining Struggle* (Columbia: University of South Carolina Press, 2006); and Richard I. Pervo, *Dating Acts: Between the Evangelists and the Apologists* (Santa Rosa, Calif.: Polebridge, 2006).

67. Gustav Adolf Deissmann, *Light from the Ancient East* (trans. L. R. M. Strachan; 2nd ed.; London: Hodder & Stoughton, 1911), 346.

68. Gilbert, "List of Nations in Acts 2"; idem, "Roman Propaganda."

Apologetic discourse hereby becomes much more than simply "defending" one's marginal position; it may actually suggest a rhetorical form of counterattack. If one considers the dual foci found in Augustus's famous lines cited earlier—the power of the sword and the binding obligation of *clementia*—both of which involve social and rhetorical placement and positioning, then, given that much of the narrative in Acts concerns the demonstration of *clementia* and the expansion of the gospel, we find rhetorically charged tropes both in the exhibition of early Christian *philanthropia* and *philia*[69] and in the incursion of the gospel into imperial terrain. Yet miracles evidently cannot be separated from that manifestation either, as they aim to characterize the apostles, their communities, and their deity as merciful representatives par excellence. At the same time, one cannot dismiss the impinging rhetoric of the "sword," which equally forces our attention on miracle discourse in Acts as the forum for contest and conquest. The early Christian heroes are intentionally typified as manifesting the locus of power in the world, and Luke appears to have a vested interest in demonstrating that this power is not a static entity but rather a *conquering* force.

In Acts 14, for example, there is a claim on the power of the gods Zeus and Hermes, while Acts 13 and 19 evidence a demand on the authority of magicians and magic, and still elsewhere we see the appropriation of the power of a pagan prophetess (16:16-24) and control over the devil (10:38; 26:18). There are many more subtleties as well in terms of this overall appropriation of traditions and figures. For instance, in a significant study of the language of healing in the ancient world, Louise Wells has demonstrated that Luke, over against Matthew and Mark, uses the terminology for healing that is more closely associated with Asclepius, suggesting, again, a possible appropriation of the status of this ubiquitous deity through imagery reconfigured and redeployed.[70] While this out-

---

69. See further Penner, *In Praise of Christian Origins*, 262–87.

70. Louise Wells, *The Greek Language of Healing from Homer to New Testament Times* (BZNW 83; Berlin: de Gruyter, 1998), 227–28. In line with this emphasis, one might also be tempted to read an oblique reference to the deity in the narrative in which Paul is bit by a snake (28:3-6). On the association of snakes with Asclepius, see James A. Kelhoffer, *Miracle and Mission: The Authentication of Missionaries and Their Message in the Longer Ending of Mark* (WUNT 2/112; Tübingen: Mohr Siebeck, 2000), 365–73 (although, admittedly, Luke uses a different Greek word for "snake" in this story than the one usually used to designate the Asclepian reptiles).

line is brief, it does illustrate that in Acts there are complex negotiations and claims being established in and through the narrative. These facets resonate in large part with the shared value system of Luke's readers, and whatever their broad and sometimes convoluted religio-cultural structures may be, we can presume that the manifestations of power evident throughout Acts would have certainly suggested to (if not convinced) the ancient reader that the locus of supreme power is evidenced (only) in Luke's narrative characters (and, by extension, presumably also the "real"-world correspondent communities and ideologies they would have been perceived to represent/promote).[71]

In light of the foregoing observations, I would suggest that a reassessment of the miracles in Acts is in order. We have a world permeated by the miraculous and magical, yet at the same time we also find an environment that encourages rational, civic discourse—and an investigation of the miracles in Acts should not be isolated from either of these discursive spheres. In particular, a sociorhetorical investigation that takes seriously the intersection of the cultural intertexture related to miracles in Acts with the civic nature of Lukan discourse may end up yielding important insights. Rather than seeing Luke *qua* historian simply in conflict with the supernatural ethos infusing the ancient world, it might be more profitable to examine the interrelationship between miracles and the polis in terms of Lukan narrative dynamics. This approach suggests taking Luke seriously as a true *author* of these episodes, refusing to distance the miraculous elements manifested in the text from Luke's explicit and implicit compositional process.

We thus need to give full attention not just to the role that miracles perform in Lukan discourse, but even more specifically to the way in which they are enmeshed in and inseparable from the Lukan narrative itself. Analyzing miracle/power discourse in Acts in conjunction with Luke's emergent political interests reveals a resultant ideology that lays claim to the polis of the Greeks and Romans for Christ and underscores the apostles as heroes for both emulation and adulation. Furthermore, in contrast to a wide spectrum of previous scholarship on Acts, the method developed here also promotes assessing and understanding miracles as a manifestation of power fully integrated with other cultur-

---

71. For further assessment of the interconnection of Lukan divine images with the broader Greco-Roman world, see Lynn Allan Kauppi, *Foreign but Familiar Gods: Graeco-Romans Read Religion in Acts* (LNTS 277; New York: T&T Clark, 2006).

ally coded images of strength and domination/dominion evidenced in the Lukan narrative and elsewhere in the wider literary landscape of antiquity.[72] Thus the miracle narratives in Acts form an integral part of a larger, more complex negotiation of power relationships, with gains in Christian identity garnered at the expense of the loss for others in the text. Last, the narrative itself—both the process of composition and final rhetorical construction—cannot be viewed as an innocuous by-product: it is the medium of power for Lukan discourse, the vehicle by which the culturally complex negotiation of power is manifested and carried out for and over the reader.

4. Pious and Imperious Manifestations of Power in Acts

4.1. Power and Character

As noted at the outset, miracles in Lukan narrative function to characterize the "wonder-workers" as loci of divine numen in the world. The miracles are thus part of the construction of heroic identity in the Acts narrative, be it apostles, Hellenists, or Paul. While miracle accounts provide an overarching structure in terms of linking the various narrative threads together, including the creation of parallels between the diverse characters,[73] the most striking emergent aspect is the culturally resonant nature of the presentation of the miracle worker. The most overt features may be the healing power of Peter's shadow (5:15) and the magical qualities associated with the fabric that has come into contact with Paul (19:11-12). The point is not too difficult to grasp: a tremendous outworking of power is attributed to Peter and Paul, which, for the ancient reader, would have signaled these two figures as eminently potent. Peter and Paul thus

---

72. While I have focused throughout on the Greco-Roman cultural background of Acts, I do not thereby intend to imply that the Jewish threads should be neglected. I would suggest, however, that the Judaism of the Hellenistic and Roman periods should be understood in a similar way in its relationship to the Greco-Roman environment (see further Penner, "Contextualizing Acts," 19–20).

73. On the nature and extent of the evident parallels, see David P. Moessner, "'The Christ Must Suffer': New Light on the Jesus-Peter, Stephen, Paul Parallels in Luke-Acts," in *The Composition of Luke's Gospel* (ed. D. E. Orton; Leiden: Brill, 1999), 117–53.

possess the rational power of *logoi*, which is balanced by the miraculous *ergoi* they perform throughout the text.[74]

Leaving the function of the explicit parallels to one side, I would simply emphasize for the moment that Luke clearly portrays these two key figures in a similar light: they both heal at a distance (5:15 || 19:11-12), cure the lame (3:1-10; 9:32-25 || 14:8-10), raise the dead (9:36-42 || 20:7-12), are miraculously delivered from prison (12:3-17 || 16:25-34), receive visions (10:9-17 || 16:9-10), transfer the power of the Holy Spirit to others (8:17 || 19:6), and pronounce words of judgment that result in action taken against the accused (5:1-11 || 13:9-12). For Luke, both characters embody the power of God/Christ.[75] In the cultural world of Acts, this discourse signals these figures as "divine men," whose mighty deeds are matched by the force of their words. If we take this rhetorical construction of Peter's and Paul's identity seriously (cf. the characterization of the Jerusalem apostles in general [2:43; 5:12, 17-21]; Stephen [6:8]; Philip [8:6-7, 13]; and Barnabas [14:3]), then further examination of the function of this representation may help illuminate aspects of Luke's larger literary and cultural agenda.

Simply put, the characters of Peter and Paul signify potent, authoritative, dominant men (and the gender identity, as noted earlier, is not insignificant in this context). In comparing men of power to those with wealth, Aristotle describes the character of the former in this way:

> The powerful [*hoi dynamenoi*] are more ambitious [*philotimoteroi*] and more manly [*andrōdesteroi*] in character [*ēthē*] than the rich, since

---

74. There are varying ways of assessing the relationship of word and miracle in Acts. Earlier I noted that Marguerat ("Magic and Miracle") viewed these two elements as essential in Luke's effort to save the miracles from coalescing with the more ambiguously open religious environment of antiquity. I would suggest, conversely, that the two work in tandem to promote a broad and potent cultural image of the Lukan heroes. In this view, the narrative function of the combination is more important than any theological relationship that can thereby be established.

75. Throughout the narrative, bodies become both the medium/locus of power and the location for the manifestation of control. One must keep in mind, as Maud W. Gleason asserts, that the Greco-Roman culture was one in which "autonomy and social control were articulated in the language of the body." See her "Mutilated Messengers: Body Language in Josephus," in *Being Greek under Rome: Cultural Identity, the Second Sophistic and the Development of Empire* (ed. S. Goldhill; Cambridge: Cambridge University Press, 2001), 84. I am indebted to Gleason's exemplary study on the semiotics of the body in Josephus for some of the following observations with respect to Acts.

they aim at the performance of deeds [*ergōn*] which their power [*dia tēn dynamin*] gives them the opportunity [*exousia*] of carrying out. And they are more energetic; for being obliged to look after their power, they are always on the watch. And they are dignified rather than heavily pompous; for their rank renders them more conspicuous, so that they avoid excess; and this dignity is a mild and decent pomposity. And their wrongdoings are never petty, but great. (*Rhet.* 2.17.2-4)

The linguistic-conceptual designations "power" and "powerful" are particularly noteworthy features in Aristotle's description of these "great men." Even more to the point, Aristotle here describes the nature of rulers, their superiority over the ruled, and the "manly" dimension presumed inherent in these characteristics, which is confirmed by the rulers' "authority"[76] to carry out deeds of power.[77] Indeed, it should not be lost on us that *virtus* (manliness) encapsulated the essential nature of the competitive environment and its aim of (virile) virtuousness.[78] Thus, manifest within this description of "power" is the aim to demonstrate the superiority of the person so portrayed. These are the real "men," the "rulers," those who

---

76. I translate *exousia* as "authority" instead of the LCL translation of "opportunity."

77. See Craig A. Williams (*Roman Homosexuality: Ideologies of Masculinity in Classical Antiquity* [New York: Oxford University Press, 1999], 125–42) for an application of this predominant stereotype to the Roman perception and construction of masculinity. One thus cannot underestimate the importance of a figure like Hercules for interpreting the early Christian portrayal of manliness in the performance of "conquering"/"controlling" acts and manifested in "mighty deeds." Hercules, probably the most important and prominent hero in the ancient world well into the late Hellenistic and early Roman periods, in many respects defines quintessential "manhood." Early Christian narrative images tend to play up the potent aspect of their heroes while downplaying (or, perhaps, sublimating) the subjection of the individual to the passions and the subversion of manliness by women. On the depiction of Hercules, see Nicole Loraux, "Herakles: The Super-Male and the Feminine," in *Before Sexuality: The Construction of Erotic Experience in the Ancient World* (ed. D. M. Halperin, J. J. Winkler, and F. I. Zeitlin; Princeton: Princeton University Press, 1990), 24–30. For a more ambivalent portrait of early Christian masculinity read in light of the colonial context, see Eric Thurman, "Novel Men: Masculinity and Empire in Mark's Gospel and Xenophon's *An Ephesian Tale*," in *Mapping Gender in Ancient Religious Discourses* (ed. Todd Penner and Caroline Vander Stichele; BIS 84; Leiden: Brill, 2007), 185–229.

78. Karl Galinsky, *Augustan Culture: An Interpretive Introduction* (Princeton: Princeton University Press, 1996), 84.

palpably demonstrate their "power" in forceful words, in their display of mighty deeds, and through their embodiment of excellence in civic virtues.

Moreover, one cannot separate this attempt to rhetoricize the character of Peter and Paul as great and powerful men, working "signs and wonders" like the Jewish heroes of old (see 7:36), from the agonistic context of ancient discourse.[79] Christian identity is constructed positively precisely through the loss of identity for others in the text.[80] Three interrelated scenes stand out with respect to this ancient contest over character: the showdowns between Peter and Simon Magus (8:18-24), Paul and Elymas (13:9-12), and Paul and the prophesying slave girl (16:16-21).[81] In two of these episodes, the first and the last, Peter and Paul both confront adversaries characterized as greedy. In terms of the character of the opponents, one is reminded, especially in the first two instances, of Aristotle's description of the rich: they "are insolent and arrogant, being mentally affected by the acquisition of wealth.... They are luxurious and swaggerers.... In a word, the character of the rich man is that of a fool favored by fortune.... Their unjust acts are not due to malice, but partly to insolence, partly to incontinence" (*Rhet.* 2.16). Thus, given the importance of *synkrisis* in ancient narrative composition,[82] one should not be surprised to find the

---

79. On the importance of the agonistic feature for negotiating identity and for "making men," particularly in the eastern part of the Roman Empire, see Onno van Nijf, "Local Heroes: Athletics, Festivals and Elite Self-Fashioning in the Roman East," in Goldhill, *Being Greek under Rome*, 306–34. Cf. Georgi, *Opponents of Paul*, 404.

80. Gleason's study of the use of comportment in oratory in this combat for identity-construction is immensely helpful for analyzing these similar facets of early Christian literature. See Maud W. Gleason, *Making Men: Sophists and Self-Presentation in Ancient Rome* (Princeton: Princeton University Press, 1995). Also see the shorter summary of her argument in "The Semiotics of Gender: Physiognomy and Self-Fashioning in the Second Century C.E.," in Halperin, Winkler, and Zeitlin, *Before Sexuality: The Construction of Erotic Experience in the Ancient World*, 389–415.

81. In the latter story, the conflict is really between Paul and the owners of the girl. See Todd Penner and Caroline Vander Stichele, "Gendering Violence: Patterns of Power and Constructs of Masculinity in the Acts of the Apostles," in *A Feminist Companion to the Acts of the Apostles* (ed. A.-J. Levine with M. Blickenstaff; FCNTECW 9; London: T&T Clark, 2004), 207.

82. Aristotle defines *synkrisis* thus: it "is concerned with things that are closely related and about which we discuss which we ought preferably to support ... if one or more points of superiority can be shown, the mind will agree that whichever of the two alternatives is actually superior is the more worthy of choice" (*Top.* 3.1). On *syn-*

heroes of the narrative confirmed to be superior to the various opponents of questionable character whom they encounter.

These heroes, then, are enhanced in status as others lose their culturally valued identity markers: they are portrayed as avaricious, unrighteous, lovers of money, faithless, and malicious.[83] Most significantly, these "others" are frequently made impotent in the narrative. The story of Elymas and the sons of Sceva (19:13-19), for example, demonstrates that both Greek and Jewish "imitators" do not possess the divine numen evidenced by the narrative heroes.[84] These potent Lukan characters are, as Douglas Edwards refers to them, the "cosmic power brokers," who, in confrontation and competition with their rivals,[85] are seeking to appropriate the honor, standing, and territory of the latter. This phenomenon also relates to the overall affect of the prison "escape" scenes, which appear at critical junctures in the Acts narrative (12:3-17; 16:25-34). In these episodes, the authorities are incapable of holding or containing the narrative heroes, demonstrating the ineffectual nature of the former and the strength and dominance of the latter.[86] The miracles in Acts thus form an essential

---

krisis in ancient historiography in general and Acts in particular, see Penner, *In Praise of Christian Origins*, 203–6, 288–301.

83. It is in a similar context that accusations against the philosophers in Lucian find their rhetorical home: being "greedy," "loving money," and "selling philosophy" present ways of characterizing an opponent (including, not least, charges of being a "charlatan" and a "magician"; see esp. *Alex.* 1–5, 8, 12, 14, 16–17, 20, 22–24, 26, 36, 49). See the excellent discussion of this phenomenon in Luke T. Johnson, "The New Testament's Anti-Jewish Slander and the Conventions of Ancient Polemic," *JBL* 108 (1989): 430–34. Focusing on the ethical aspects of Luke's characterization, Marguerat ("Magic and Miracle," 113–15, 118–19) implicitly and Reimer ("Virtual Prison Breaks," 138) explicitly assume a degree of reality for the images Luke constructs: early Christian apostles (or writers!) were not as "greedy" or as interested in "self-advancement" as were the so-called magicians (and the many other opponents) whom they encountered. This *is* Luke's point, of course, but failure to attend to the Lukan cultural ideology operative in the narrative leads quite naturally to a reinscribing of the binary oppositional rhetoric embedded therein. For a helpful comparison, see the discussion of Lucian's interaction with Alexander "the false prophet" in Erik Gunderson, "Men of Learning: The Cult of *Paideia* in Lucian's *Alexander*," in Penner and Vander Stichele, *Mapping Gender in Ancient Religious Discourses*, 479–510.

84. See Penner and Vander Stichele, "Gendering Violence," 204–8.

85. Douglas R. Edwards, *Religion and Power: Pagans, Jews, and Christians in the Greek East* (New York: Oxford University Press, 1996), 110–15.

86. Reimer ("Virtual Prison Breaks") reads the episode in Acts 16, dealing with

component of the larger demonstration of the dominion of early Christian heroes over all facets of their cultural, social, political, and religious environment.[87] Miraculous displays by the apostles therefore provide

---

the imprisonment of Paul and Silas, as indicating that the Lukan characters are ethically superior and hence not real "magicians," since they do not flee when they are miraculously freed from prison (see 5:17–42). This interpretation, of course, is undermined by the earlier instance in which Peter in fact does escape from prison under supernatural circumstances (Acts 12:6–18)—it is unlikely that Luke would be promoting two different "values" in this respect. Rather, one has to situate "prison breaks"—real or virtual—in terms of the broader image Luke seeks to develop for his characters throughout the narrative. Narratively, raw power is displayed either way, and spectacular representation seems to be an end in itself in terms of the dominant aim of these stories (see further John B. Weaver, *Plots of Epiphany: Prison-Escape in the Acts of the Apostles* [BZNW 131; Berlin: de Gruyter, 2004], who argues that these miraculous escape stories [divine epiphanies] function as elements of cultic foundation legends, a position that coheres well with the interpretation offered here; see also n. 88 below; cf. Richard I. Pervo, *Acts: A Commentary* [Hermeneia; Minneapolis: Fortress, 2009], 409–11).

87. As noted earlier in this essay with respect to Augustus, even when these heroes evidence the cardinal virtue of *clementia* or mercy toward the ailing and infirm (3:1-10; 9:36-42; 20:7-12), one has not yet left the realm of power discourse (on the significance of *clementia*, see Andrew Wallace-Hadrill, "The Emperor and His Virtues," *Historia* 30 [1981]: 302; and Helen F. North, "Canons and Hierarchies of the Cardinal Virtues in Greek and Latin Literature," in *The Classical Tradition: Literary and Historical Studies in Honor of Harry Caplan* [ed. L. Wallach; Ithaca, N.Y.: Cornell University Press, 1966], 178). As Diodorus notes, "The spirits of civilized men are gripped ... most perhaps by mercy, because of the sympathy which nature has planted in us" (13.24.2). Thus, on the one hand, the mark of civilization and certainly civic duty is represented in "mercy" displayed toward those in need, enhanced not least in that, unlike the "greedy" opposition, the apostles do not charge for their persuasive words of freedom or their miraculous deeds of healing (cf. the contrasting portraits of Simon and Peter/John in Acts 8:9–23). On the other hand, one should not lose sight of the rhetorical slant of the acts of *clementia* in the narrative: they place the apostles in a position of dominance. In part, this feature is related to the securing of obligations in the ancient social structure (as Galinsky notes, "*clementia* obligates both the holder of power and those in his care" [*Augustan Culture*, 85]), while also functioning to construct rhetorical identity in the contest for superiority before the spectator. Within even the most virtuous language of compassion in Acts, then, imperial connotations always lay nearby, especially since *clementia* was the virtue frequently identified with Julius Caesar himself (Stefan Weinstock, *Divus Julius* [London: Oxford University Press, 1971], 233–45). Similarly, when Augustus maintains his own acts of mercy and "giving" (*Res Gestae* 15–17), these characterize the emperor precisely as someone beneficent and magnanimous, embodying fundamental ancient virtues.

narrative threads that delimit the puissant nature of the heroes of Luke's foundation narrative. At stake is the characterization of Peter and Paul as "great men"—the "type" who rule, being ideal founders of the expanding Christian *politeia*.[88] On certain occasions their persuasive words manifest their essentially virtuous character; on others their mighty deeds perform that same function. Both work in tandem to demonstrate the unity of *logos* and *ergōn* in the founder figures, in whom resides ultimate control, authority, and power. And this power is something that Simon cannot buy, Elymas cannot protect against, Herod and the authorities in Philippi cannot contain, and the sons of Sceva cannot channel.[89]

Throughout Acts the responses to these mighty manifestations also perform a critical role in characterizing the power itself. In almost every instance of divine encounter in Acts, various groups or individuals respond with amazement followed by conversion (2:43; 3:9-10; 5:11; 5:13; 8:8, 13; 9:35, 42; 13:12; 14:11; 19:17; 28:6, 10). The response of the people heightens the rhetorical ethos of the apostles, as well as affirms this narrative numen to be one that originates from an "authentic" source.[90] This observation applies in a variety of ways to Acts. For instance, in the confrontation between Paul and Elymas, the latter of whom is twice called a *magos* (13:6, 8),[91] the end result is that the proconsul becomes a believer

---

But the characterization is not in small part a power play in the ancient competition for securing manly virtue (and, as a result, it helps solidify the loyalty of individuals and cities; see J. E. Lendon, *Empire of Honour: The Art of Government in the Roman World* [New York: Oxford University Press, 1997], 156–60). Thus, when we observe mercy and compassion embodied in the acts of Luke's narrative heroes, we should not be surprised to find similar dynamics at work: the use of miraculous powers in the service of mercy demonstrates the apostles' superior nature and virtue over their narrative opponents.

88. On the connection of miraculous/divine activity and the founding of colonies in the ancient world, see Walter T. Wilson, "Urban Legends: Acts 10:1-11:18 and the Strategies of Greco-Roman Foundation Narratives," *JBL* 120 (2001): 85–86; as well as David L. Balch, "ΜΕΤΑΒΟΛΗ ΠΟΛΙΤΕΙΩΝ. Jesus as Founder of the Church in Luke-Acts: Form and Function," in Penner and Vander Stichele, *Contextualizing Acts*, 155–57.

89. See Twelftree, *In the Name of Jesus*, 142–53.

90. In many respects, then, the response of the spectator validates the competing truth claims that are either explicit or implicit in the text. See further Maud Gleason, "Truth Contests and Talking Corpses," in *Constructions of the Classical Body* (ed. J. I. Porter; Ann Arbor: University of Michigan Press, 1999), 290–94.

91. This scene echoes the classic battles between biblical heroes and magicians

(13:12). The way in which this phenomenon is described is significant: the proconsul witnesses the powerful action taken against Elymas and the ineffectiveness of the latter's magic, and "believes" as a result of being "amazed at" the teaching about the Lord. For the present argument, it is important to emphasize the acknowledgment of the "magical" superiority of Paul over Elymas, and the proconsul's attesting to this victory by switching his allegiance from the ineffectual power represented by Elymas to that displayed palpably before his eyes by Paul.[92]

Moreover, scholars such as Susan Garrett, who suggest Elymas in this instance possesses the "power of the devil,"[93] misconstrue the larger picture. The situation with the sons of Sceva is similar, in that the inhabitants of Ephesus recognize that it is only in Paul that true authority and force reside.[94] The relinquishing of their magical practices (19:18-19) is narrative confirmation of this point. Indeed, in the case of the seven sons it is the evil spirit that has the power over them. So the sons come in the name of the "Lord Jesus" (19:13; *to onoma tou kyriou iēsou*) and

---

found in Jewish traditions: Moses and the magicians of Egypt (Exod 7:11, 22; 8:7, 18, 19; 9:11), Joseph and those of Egypt (Gen 41:8, 24), and Daniel and those of Babylon (Dan 1:20; 2:2, 27; 4:7, 9; 5:11).

92. It is difficult to reckon how some interpreters can completely ignore the features of "magical contest" in this story. John J. Kilgallen, for example, argues that "the *magos* story is not concerned with pagan magic, but with the persistent conflict with certain Jews" ("Acts 13:4-12: The Role of the *Magos*," EstBib 55 [1997]: 236). In his view, the sole function of the story is to demonstrate Jewish opposition to the advance of the Christian gospel. No doubt the story could perform double duty for Luke's larger agenda (and the reference to Elymas as a "Jewish false prophet" [13:6] may thus be significant), but Luke shows interest in such magical encounters throughout the narrative, and this story should be situated within that broader pattern.

93. Susan R. Garrett, *The Demise of the Devil: Magic and the Demonic in Luke's Writings* (Minneapolis: Fortress, 1989), 79-87. Her move from "magicians" to "Satan" overstretches the evidence for Acts. The point of all the "magician" stories seems to be that these wonder-workers are ineffectual; they have no power. In this way, the characterization is more in line with the rhetorical polemic of "charlatan": they make claims to power, but it takes a "true" power broker to expose them for the "fakes" they are (see Lucian, *Alex.* 17). Also see Garrett, "Light on a Dark Subject," 153-56, where she brings together the Jewish evidence for associating magic with Satan (arguing that this is the background to be assumed for the episode in Acts 13).

94. The possibility that this story might be intended to be humorous fleshes out further the darker side of the Lukan apostolic construction in Acts. Also Pervo, *Profit with Delight*, 61-63.

are "lorded over" (19:16; *katakyrieusas*) instead. The discursive reversal furthers one of Luke's main narrative aims: to demonstrate that the name of the "Lord" is in fact the root of all "power," but only characters like Paul possess that authority and can make the demons submit; the demons will "lord" over all others. And while it might be tempting to adopt Garrett's proposal that again we see here the victory of Jesus over Satan,[95] and that it is this event that motivates people to turn to Christ, in fact the story pivots on the premise that people want power (wherever it happens to reside) in order to control demons. The sons of Sceva know that the name of Jesus is numinous, but they are not members of *his* community, so this power will not work for them. That kind of control over demons, the desire for which the magical papyri attest to in abundance, resides only with the narrative heroes. Hence, the magic books are burned precisely because they are ineffectual; they do not work. One is *not* dealing with "true" versus "false" or "pure" versus "demonic" power. Rather, for all intents and purposes, there is only one true force in this world, one which everyone desires to possess, but which only Christians in "reality" do.[96]

---

95. See Garrett (*Demise of the Devil*, 95), who argues that here we see the "defeat of magic." It is difficult to imagine, however, how an ancient reader would perceive the text in this manner, especially since "magic" in the nonpejorative sense is not abandoned—rather, one powerful magician simply puts the others to shame. Lest there be any doubt about that slant, Luke intentionally characterizes Paul in a heightened "magical" fashion immediately preceding the story of the seven sons: Paul is so powerful that fabric that touches him transmits healing power at a distance (see further Strelan, *Strange Acts*, 195–98; cf. the similar effects of Peter's shadow in Acts 5:15). Scholars often neglect to see that this image of Paul frames the following story, for it is precisely the magical powers of Paul that the seven sons covet (see 19:13). The same goes for Simon Magus and Peter: Simon yearns to have Peter's power, but he thinks he can purchase it (8:18–19). The point in this earlier story is that total allegiance must be given to the Power in order for it to be effective. For a thorough critique of Garrett's position in this respect, see the detailed assessment by Shauf, *Theology as History*, 196–226.

96. In this way, the typical distinction that the narrative heroes of Acts were "divine men" opposed by "magicians" (as a socially and culturally "acceptable" type versus a "negative" one) is not the whole picture (see Pervo, *Acts*, 207–9). There are definitely shades of this perspective evident in the text. At the same time, however, Luke is also (seemingly at least) more complex (playful?) in his cultural articulations, in that his narrative heroes embody some very strong magical qualities and manifest direct results thereof. It is not clear that ancient readers of Acts would have made the

Finally, one should include in this discussion the two stories in which there is a direct connection between the working of a miracle and the attempt to deify a Lukan hero. In the first instance, after healing the lame man in Lystra, the people are ecstatic that Zeus and Hermes have come down for a visitation, and the priest of Zeus ventures forth in order to offer sacrifices to Paul and Barnabas (14:11-13). Paul and Barnabas plea for restraint (14:15), yet the people can hardly contain their excitement (14:18). Not surprisingly, the people are called on to turn away from "worthless things" (14:15). In the narrative, however, despite claiming to be "mere" mortals, very much the opposite appears to be the case: Paul and Barnabas actually manifest numinous force,[97] while the people are portrayed as honoring and valuing that numen. Indeed, Luke here plays on what is a culturally appropriate reaction to such power, suggesting, however, that the response should be directed to the "living God" rather than to his representatives (14:15; cf. 17:29, where Paul directs his hearers away from human-made images in order to achieve a similar end). In light of this focus, it is no wonder that Paul and Barnabas reply in the way they do: if you want such power, if you honor such power, then you ought to turn from your worthless, useless, and futile avenues for gaining power, and seek him in whom the only real and true power rests—the Creator of the universe (and Jesus Christ, his representative raised from the dead [17:31]).[98] Thus the people are urged to leave behind ineffectual means

---

distinction as readily as we modern scholars do. Precise terminological differentiations are thus not likely to help clarify much in the end.

97. On the sociocultural features that evidence Paul's numinous characterization, see the assessment by Strelan, "Recognizing the Gods." At least in part, one is dealing here with the characterization of the *theios anēr*, where the hero possesses or is possessed by *numen*. While the category distinctions with respect to divine characterization are somewhat fluid in antiquity, one would note that such an identification of Barnabas and Paul as actually being gods (Hermes and Zeus "in human form"; cf. 28:6) as opposed to being *like* gods suggests that Luke is pushing the Lystran "recognition" one step further: the two are considered by the people to be *numen*, a designation usually accorded to deity itself (see Duncan Fishwick, "*Genius* and *Numen*," HTR 62 [1969]: 364–65; and esp. Ittai Gradel, *Emperor Worship and Roman Religion* [Oxford Classical Monographs; New York: Oxford, 2002], 245–49; cf. Paul Veyne, *Bread and Circuses: Historical Sociology and Political Pluralism* [trans. B. Pearce; New York: Penguin, 1990], 310–12).

98. One should not overlook, of course, that refusal of divine honors by culturally powerful individuals (such as the emperor) were taken as signs of their *moderatio* (Gradel, *Emperor Worship*, 233). Thus, these scenes in Acts may also play on this

of power, centered here not on magical books as in Acts 19, but in the explicit worship of Zeus and sacrifices in his temple. In other words, the story in Acts 14 has the same rhetorical function as the story in Acts 19: such potent manifestations of the divine only reside in the narrative community of Christ.[99]

In this vein, it is intriguing that in the second example of this type of story Luke makes no reference to Paul's actually refusing the attempt of the people to deify him (28:6). Indeed, the narrator asserts that, when they departed from the island of Malta, the local people "honored them greatly" (28:10; *hoi kai pollais timais etimēsan*), which quite possibly resonates with the language of cultic worship. Here again, the display of signs and wonders results in honor and esteem for the apostles, with undercurrents of deification in the text.[100] This stress confirms what has been evident throughout: the heroes of Acts are glorified and shown to be exemplary in every respect, providing motivation for ancient readers to align themselves with the Christ communities these characters represent. It is in *this* community, after all, that the potent force manifested throughout Acts resides; not in the practice of magic, not in the worship of Zeus and Hermes, not in the temple of Zeus, not in the sanctuary of Artemis, not even in the temple of Jerusalem itself (see 7:48-50). Traditional media and loci of power are thus supplanted in favor of the community as the center through which the power and control in the world operates/flows, and the responses of the various groups and individuals to the manifestations depicted by Luke assure his readers that these narrative claims are true.

---

topos as well, further enhancing the positive characterization of Paul and Barnabas as a result. Luke thus gets double duty out of this story: it is an honor they are considered to be gods, and it is honorable that they refuse such honor (from both an emergent Christian and Greco-Roman perspective).

99. Amy L. Wordelman makes a strong argument for viewing the Lystran episode as fundamentally in line with the aim of other miracle stories in Acts, suggesting that the Lystran response is not something that Luke intends to signal as unique per se, as is sometimes suggested by scholars ("Cultural Divides and Dual Realities: A Greco-Roman Context for Acts 14," in Penner and Vander Stichele, *Contextualizing Acts*, esp. 217–19).

100. Cf. F. Scott Spencer ("Paul's Odyssey in Acts: Status Struggles and Island Adventures," *BTB* 28 [1999]: 157), who notes that Paul "proceeds to act very much like a 'god' or at least like a chief client/broker of an invincible Heavenly Patron." Spencer also stresses the extraordinary status enhancement that Paul acquires as a result of this characterization.

4.2. Power and Space

One of the obvious features with respect to miracles in Acts is that they are manifested in the open and public domain. Everywhere there is an audience, from Roman proconsuls, to various groups of people, to whole cities; and the wondrous activities occur in public forums, near temples, in "every corner" of the Roman Empire. Scholars have paid some attention to the body zones of the healing miracles,[101] but much less scrutiny has been given to the public space of the polis, which is progressively (and successfully) being claimed by the heroes in Acts through word and deed.[102] Here one can compare the progression from the Gospel of Luke, with its increasing claim on the household,[103] to the intensifying engage-

---

101. With respect to Acts, see especially John J. Pilch, "Sickness and Healing in Luke-Acts," in *The Social World of Luke-Acts* (ed. J. H. Neyrey; Peabody, Mass.: Hendrickson, 1991), 181–209; Bart J. Koet, "Purity and Impurity of the Body in Luke-Acts," in *Purity and Holiness: The Heritage of Leviticus* (ed. M. J. H. M. Poorthuis and J. Schwartz; JCPS 2; Leiden: Brill, 2000), 93–106; and, more generally, Jerome H. Neyrey, "Miracles, In Other Words: Social Science Perspectives on Healings," in *Miracles in Jewish and Christian Antiquity: Imagining Truth* (ed. J. C. Cavadini; Notre Dame, Ind.: University of Notre Dame Press, 1999), 19–55.

102. I would add that more attention should also be given to the relationship between displays of numinous power and the symbolic cartography in the Lukan narrative. For instance, Wordelman points out that it is rather intriguing that miracles and belief therein are located primarily in the East, while in the West (particularly Athens, Rome, Corinth) *logos* seems to dominate the interaction ("Cultural Divides," 219; for a similar analysis of Luke's colonial construction of his geography, see Penner and Vander Stichele, "Gendering Violence," 199–201; and Jeffrey L. Staley, "Changing Women: Toward a Postcolonial Postfeminist Interpretation of Acts 16:6–40," in Levine and Blickenstaff, *Feminist Companion to the Acts of the Apostles*, 184–85).

103. On the importance of the household as a spatial area for Lukan rhetorical claims in his Gospel, see Vernon K. Robbins, "The Socio-Rhetorical Role of the Old Testament in Luke 4-19," in *Z Noveho Zakona/From the New Testament: Sbornik k narozeninam Prof. Th. Dr. Zdenka Sazavy* (ed. H. Tonzarova and P. Melmuk; Praha: Vydala Cirkev ceskoslovenska husitska, 2001), 86–91. John H. Elliott ("Temple versus Household in Luke-Acts: A Contrast in Social Institutions," in Neyrey, *Social World of Luke-Acts*, 211–40) has noted a similar type of shift in spatial focus between the Gospel and Acts, but in the reverse (temple/*polis* in the Gospel, household in Acts; see 238). See also Halvor Moxnes, "Kingdom Takes Place: Transformations of Place and Power in the Kingdom of God in the Gospel of Luke," in *Social Scientific Models for Interpreting the Bible: Essays by the Context Group in Honor of Bruce J. Malina* (ed. J. J. Pilch; BIS 53; Leiden: Brill, 2001), 176–209.

ment of the polis in Acts, which, finally, becomes a demand on the empire as a whole. Thus, rather than viewing Luke as someone who more or less accepts the role and legitimacy of the Roman Empire, I would argue that Acts represents a more aggressive assault on Roman imperium, and manifestations of numinous power form an integral component of this literary and political enterprise.[104]

The locus of power in the empire now inhabits the nascent Christian community as represented in the narrative by its heroes. And we should not lose sight of the basic principle that, even though the emperor only surfaces at the end of Acts (and then in name only), all these cities, shrines, and spaces are in effect *his*. While the opening of the Gospel may begin with the emperor's "decree" (Luke 2:1; cf. 3:1), the ending of the two-volume work concludes with Paul's, as he appeals to the emperor (Acts 25:11–12, 21; 26:32; 27:24; 28:19). This framing of the two-volume work with explicit references to the emperor is intriguing, especially since, as noted earlier, in this cultural world the emperor is understood to be the locus of both divine and political power. Therefore, in a text that is from beginning to end about power—those who have it, those who do not—reference to this culturally powerful symbol in the narrative ought to be given serious attention, even when the emperor himself is explicitly missing. Indeed, *absence* is a noteworthy feature of Acts, as the Christian narrative counterpart to the emperor—Christ—is similarly missing (in a physical sense at least). Thus, both the emperor and Christ are absent, but are mediated through their respective representatives. The fact that everywhere we see

---

104. While perpetuating the long-standing tradition that Luke did not intend to present Christianity "as anything but politically innocuous," Martin (*Inventing Superstition*, 137–38) nonetheless affirms that the Gospel and Acts contain material that would be rather affronting to a Roman reader. I wonder, however, if a reading like the one offered here does not challenge Martin's sense of Luke's *un*intentionality—political propaganda often (and by necessity!) carries a subtle, perhaps even sublime, edge to it. Helpful in this respect is Shadi Bartsch, *Actors in the Audience: Theatricality and Doublespeak from Nero to Hadrian* (Revealing Antiquity; Cambridge: Harvard University Press, 1994). Also see Todd Penner and Caroline Vander Stichele, "Script(ur)ing Gender in Acts: The Past and Present Power of *Imperium*," in *Mapping Gender in Ancient Religious Discourses* (ed. Todd Penner and Caroline Vander Stichele; BIS 84; Leiden: Brill, 2007), 231–66; idem, "Le territoire corinthien: point de vue et poétique dans les Actes des Apôtres," in *Regards croisés sur la Bible: Etudes sur le point de vue* (Lectio Divina; Paris: Cerf, 2007), 197–204; and idem, *Contextualizing Gender in Early Christian Discourse*, 209–14.

God in control and Christ in authority through their selected delegates proves quite revealing in terms of Luke's understanding of the nexus of *real* power in Roman space.[105]

This claim on space moves quite naturally into other spheres that are similarly controlled through the use of power in the narrative, a feature often overlooked, as most interpreters generally limit their focus to the explicit geographical advances being established in the text. But as Maud Gleason notes in her research on Josephus, "To mark the body of another in the ancient world was to signal that ownership and agency rested not with the one who bore the mark but with the person who imposed it."[106] This component is critical for the understanding of the Paul-Elymas contest, for example, in which the latter's temporary blindness attests not only to the superior force of Paul, but even more importantly to the "mark" of Paul on Elymas's flesh. Metaphorically speaking, Elymas is blind to "Paul's gospel," but he is literally blinded by Paul's magic. Ultimately, this event attests to the ownership of Elymas by the power that Paul brokers. Taken one step further, this emphasis opens up the possibility that miracles in Acts are very much about the control of bodies in both the narrative and perhaps the extratextual world as well.[107]

In this light, we can more fully appreciate what is at stake in the characterization of a figure like Stephen, who is mighty in miraculous powers (6:8), tempered in equal measure by persuasive words that cannot be matched or withstood (6:10): the narrative hero controls the bodies of those around him. Not surprisingly, the only response to this phenomenon is simply to take the life/body of the one in control, which Stephen's opponents promptly do (7:54-60). Thus the display of miraculous force in Acts is through the control of bodies, whether marking those in terms of establishing ownership or, more predominantly, demonstrating the presence of authentic numen through the control of sick, infirm, and possessed bodies. Further, there is an additional cultural association in this

---

105. Vernon K. Robbins's earlier treatment of the Peter/Cornelius episode shows a move in this direction: "In the final analysis, then, God is the one who oversees the symbiotic relationship of the structures of power in the Roman empire and in Christianity" ("Luke-Acts: A Mixed Population Seeks a Home in the Roman Empire," in *Images of Empire* (ed. L. Alexander; JSOTSup 122; Sheffield: JSOT Press, 1991), 210.

106. Gleason, "Mutilated Messengers," 79.

107. On control as a critical component of ancient discourse generally, see Gleason, "Truth Contests," 292.

latter form of control. Gleason's suggestions with respect to "mutilated messengers" holds true also for the "mutilated" in body, mind, and spirit in Acts: "Greco-Roman aristocrats were expected to display a body free from the scars of mutilating punishment or manual work; for aristocratic Jews, the stakes were even higher."[108] In the miracles of Acts, we frequently observe a reversal of such scars of "mutilation," as bodies are healed and restored to ideal form, which, in this Roman cultural world, reinstates such ones to full civic and social status.[109] The force we observe at work in Acts, then, both "mutilates" flesh if there is opposition to it and possesses a "healing" effect, reversing the marks of "mutilation" inflicted on the bodies of the empire.

Additionally, one cannot separate the rhetoric of action from the rhetoric of response demanded by that action: in both cases one is dealing with control of bodies, with successive layers of control moving from the purely physical to that of social, cultural, and religious obligation. Thus there is every bit as much a claim on the body that results from the benevolent action evidenced in a healing as there is from punitive miraculous displays.[110] Bodies are therefore controlled throughout Acts, and, as a result, authentic power is not only manifested and established but in turn also

---

108. Gleason, "Mutilated Messengers," 84.

109. On the marginalization caused by physical imperfection (especially in the Roman period), see Robert Garland, *The Eye of the Beholder: Deformity and Disability in the Greco-Roman World* (Ithaca, N.Y.: Cornell University Press, 1995), 45–58. Also see the discussion in Chad Hartsock, *Sight and Blindness in Luke-Acts: The Use of Physical Features in Characterization* (BIS 94; Leiden: Brill, 2008); and Mikeal C. Parsons, *Body and Character in Luke and Acts: The Subversion of Physiognomy in Early Christianity* (Grand Rapids: Baker Academic, 2006).

110. Although his recent book on Luke-Acts and physiognomy (*Body and Character in Luke-Acts*) contains much interesting detail, Parsons, along with the many other scholars (such as Garrett) who insist on seeing the Lukan rhetoric as subversive (in an absolute and theological way), are overlooking pivotal cultural and social features of the ideology manifest in the text. Subversion through restoration of a body in healing is premised on the following: (1) the clemency of the healer (and the absolute right of such a person to determine who lives and who dies); (2) the acknowledgment that deformity is a type of abjection (the people are, after all, healed of their afflictions); and (3) the power that heals now has a claim on the body of the afflicted individual. As I have argued throughout this essay, such a framework represents a transference of power relations rather than subversion in the true sense of that term.

lays claim to the loyalty of these same bodies.[111] The people of Lystra provide a negative example in this respect: they see the power at work, they authenticate that power by seeking to worship the "brokers" as gods, but then, at the slightest urging of the Jews from Antioch and Iconium, they are willing to turn against these representatives of the divine (14:19). Their response ought to have been like that of the Greeks and Jews in Ephesus, who switch their allegiance to the power they witnessed as operative among them (19:17-20).

In view of this analysis, then, one should keep in mind that these various individuals who are "controlled" and "claimed" by the narrative power are in fact subjects of and subject to the emperor. Further, the emperor's representatives are ubiquitously present throughout the narrative, whether proconsuls, officials of provinces and cities,[112] Roman legions and tribunes, governors, or client kings. Indeed, everywhere we meet the subjects of Roman imperium, and it is these subjects of the emperor who, throughout the narrative, are switching allegiance to another power. One cannot ignore the potent imperialistic discourse into which the miracles of Acts naturally flow: control of bodies in Lukan narrative implies authority over the emperor's bodies, and operative, at the very least, is an implicit co-option of the latter's dominion. Further, this switch in allegiance is not just (if at all) about moving from being adherents of Zeus, for example, to being adherents of Christ; it is, rather, a total transfer of loyalty from the polis and its relationship to the emperor to the "living God," who is the creator of the *kosmos*—the "Lord of heaven and earth" (17:24).

---

111. Alongside the analysis in Penner and Vander Stichele, "Gendering Violence," see also idem, "All the World's a Stage: The Rhetoric of Gender in Acts," in *Luke and His Ancient Readers: Festschrift for A. Denaux* (ed. R. Bieringer, G. van Belle, and J. Verheyden; BETL 182; Leuven: Leuven University Press, 2005), 373–96; Mary Rose D'Angelo, "The ANHP Question in Luke-Acts: Imperial Masculinity and the Deployment of Women in the Early Second Century," in *A Feminist Companion to Luke* (ed. A.-J. Levine with M. Blickenstaff; FCNTECW 3; Sheffield: Sheffield Academic Press, 2002), 44–69; and Colleen Conway, *Behold the Man: Jesus and Greco-Roman Masculinity* (New York: Oxford University Press, 2008), 127–42.

112. In this connection, it is noteworthy that temples, such as the famous sanctuary of Artemis in Ephesus, were often under the control of the emperor as well (see Fergus Millar, *The Emperor in the Roman World 31 BC–AD 337* [Ithaca, N.Y.: Cornell University Press, 1977], 447–48). Thus, in terms of officials, one should also include priests in this list.

Moreover, throughout the narrative we see the various bearers of the emperor's imperium facing off against those who possess the imperium of the "Lord," with the latter inevitably winning the contest. It is Jesus/the Lord who liberates the bound and renegotiates the boundaries; it is he who has the power over life and death, over slavery and freedom. This force is normally the prerogative of the emperor in the cultural images projected by Roman authority, but the only ones in the narrative who possess this imperium are the apostles and other Christian delegates, those vice-gerents of the power that none of the emperor's authorities seem to be able to control. Miracles go a long way in establishing the authority and control of this power in Roman space, as the unfolding supernatural force demonstrates the unsurpassing nature of the claim and achievement of this divine manifestation in and on the empire, as it moves from margin to center.[113]

It is within this context that one should interpret the Lukan notifications that the miracles are done in the "name" of Jesus (3:6, 16; 4:10, 30; 16:18), since, throughout Acts, power—actual or ineffectual—resides in specific titles, designations, and appellations. This feature is one of the major foci in the account of the Jewish exorcists' inability to access the power of the name (19:13). In the story of Paul and Barnabas at Lystra, for instance, they proclaim the "living God" (14:15). In the story of Paul and Elymas, *kyrios* is the one who "teaches" through the display of superior magic (13:12). After the miraculous escape from prison in Jerusalem, the apostles declare that Jesus is the *christos* (5:42). In Peter's sermon after the miracle of Pentecost, Jesus is said to have been "made" both *kyrios* and *christos* (2:36). Ancient readers would hardly have missed the royal language inherent in these categories.[114] When combined with the rhetorical force of the very public claims on Roman space we see throughout Acts, it is easy to see here again the rhetorics of power being turned against the Roman Empire itself.[115]

---

113. In this light, the suggestion (see esp. Steven J. Scherrer, "Signs and Wonders in the Imperial Cult: A New Look at a Roman Religious Institution in the Light of Rev 13:13–15," *JBL* 103 [1984]: 599–610) that "signs and wonders" were in some cases associated with the imperial cult (perhaps even "faked" by priests) reveals more features of the Lukan cultural overlay that may potentially have been operative in characterizing the narrative heroes.

114. See further, Penner and Vander Stichele, "Script(ur)ing Gender in Acts," 261–66.

115. See especially Allen Brent, "Luke-Acts and the Imperial Cult in Asia Minor," *JTS* 48 (1997): 111–38; and idem, *The Imperial Cult and the Development of Church*

After all, Jesus is a truly divine man, authenticated by "deeds of power" and might (2:22), and, in a cultural environment where the emperor is being honored and worshiped everywhere for the same,[116] it is tempting to see here a reversal of the claims and venues of authority in this world. Should we miss this point, Luke demonstrates what happens when anyone else in the narrative assumes divine pretensions: they are struck down and horribly "mutilated" by God (12:22-23)—"There can be only one!"

This rhetoric of Acts can be considered subversive to the extent that it makes these dramatic claims *for* Jesus, and in that the delegitimation of Roman imperial power proceeds in implicit ways, as Luke appropriates and reconfigures the language of the polis and the empire to his own ends. But it is also a prima facie case of colonial mimicry, with relatively little space opened for the challenge of hybridity. Thus, in line with the mimicry, in this claim on Roman imperial discourse one should not be surprised to find the blurring of religious and political language; after all, such intermixing was the genius of rulers from the Hellenistic era onward.[117] While the precise relationship of the emperor to the gods was not rigid and stan-

---

Order: Concepts and Images of Authority in Paganism and Early Christianity before the Age of Cyprian (VCSup 45; Leiden: Brill, 1999), 73–139. For a similar interaction operative elsewhere in early Christian literature, see Todd Penner and Caroline Vander Stichele, "Bodies and the Technology of Power: Reading *The Gospel of Peter* under Empire," in *Das Petrusevangelium als Teil spätantiker Literatur* (ed. T. Nicklas and T. J. Kraus; TUGAL 158; Berlin: de Gruyter, 2007), 349–68.

116. The importance and pervasive impact of the cult of the emperor in the first century should be read as one of the backdrops for Luke's imperial discourse in Acts. See most recently Steven J. Friesen, *Imperial Cults and the Apocalypse of John: Reading Revelation in the Ruins* (New York: Oxford University Press, 2001). For an extensive list of the various known imperial temples in Asia Minor (attesting to the cult's ubiquitous presence), see Simon R. F. Price, *Rituals and Power: The Roman Imperial Cult in Asia Minor* (Cambridge: Cambridge University Press, 1984), 249–74. Alongside Price's evidence, one must also reckon with the assessment of Philip A. Harland that much of the ritualistic activity related to the emperor actually went on in local associations outside of purely official imperial channels (*Associations, Synagogues, and Congregations: Claiming a Place in Ancient Mediterranean Society* [Minneapolis: Fortress, 2003], esp. 125–36, 148–60), an observation that further attests to the ubiquitous presence of the emperor (cf. Gradel, *Emperor Worship*, 212–33).

117. Still useful for presenting the broad history of development is Fritz Taeger, *Charisma: Studien zur Geschichte des antiken Herrscherkultes* (2 vols.; Stuttgart: Kohlhammer, 1957–60).

dardized in the first century,[118] there was an indisputable pervasive ethos of religious rhetoric mixed with political language in this period.[119] The established relationship between the emperor and Zeus/Jupiter[120] provides one useful configuration for understanding the specific blurring in Acts, where language related to the "God of Heaven" becomes politicized and the language of the emperor becomes sacralized. This linguistic dexterity offers an important rhetorical reservoir and a strategic launching point for resistance for a writer like Luke.

This proposed framework helps one appreciate more fully the constant interplay between the language of the gods and that of humans in Acts, and the amorphous relationship that is thereby established in the narrative. In Acts 14, the authentication of the power of the "living God" is compared to that of Zeus, just as in Acts 13 the power of Paul is displayed before and over the proconsul, the representative of the emperor. In both cases we are in the same territory, and in both cases we find imperial space and bodies claimed for Jesus. For this reason the reference in 26:18, where Paul recounts his call before Agrippa, is of such importance.

---

118. This point is stressed in Daniel N. Schowalter, *The Emperor and the Gods: Images from the Time of Trajan* (HDR 28; Minneapolis: Fortress, 1993).

119. Price, *Rituals and Power*, 239–48. On the political implications of emperor worship, see Lendon, *Empire of Honour*, 161–68.

120. On this connection, see Weinstock, *Divus Julius*, 300–305; Zanker, *Power of Images*, 230–38; and Adela Yarbro Collins, "The Worship of Jesus and the Imperial Cult," in *The Jewish Roots of Christological Monotheism: Papers from the St. Andrews Conference on the Historical Origins of the Worship of Jesus* (ed. C. C. Newman, J. R. Davila, and G. S. Lewis; JSJSup 63; Leiden: Brill, 1999), 249–50. See also the more nuanced study by John Pollini, "Man or God: Divine Assimilation and Imitation in the Late Republic and Early Principate," in *Between Republic and Empire: Interpretations of Augustus and His Principate* (ed. K. A. Raaflaub and M. Toher; Berkeley and Los Angeles: University of California Press, 1990), 334–57. Pollini argues that Augustus is portrayed not as Jupiter but *like* the god (338) (i.e., there is not a complete fusion of identity, but rather an interplay between the two; cf. Fishwick, "*Genius* and *Numen*," 365, who suggests, with respect to Augustus, that such fusion took place largely in the "popular imagination" of the lower classes). This assessment flows into Pollini's argument that in ancient discourse the gods tend to take on features of human leaders, while humans tend to assimilate aspects associated with deities (356). Cf. Steven J. Friesen (*Twice Neokoros: Ephesus, Asia and the Cult of the Flavian Imperial Family* [RGRR 116; Leiden: Brill, 1993], 165–67), who demonstrates the parallels between the emperor and Zeus in the temple of the Sebastoi in Ephesus, where Olympian deities provided a model for the worship of the imperial family.

Here Paul states that he was commanded to aid in the movement of the world from under the authority of Satan to the control of God. Paul's statement, used by those scholars who read in this account justification for viewing the main battle in Acts as being waged between the devil and Jesus, is sandwiched between explicit references to Paul's appeal to the emperor (25:8, 10, 11, 12, 21, 25 || 26:32; 27:24, 28:19). Thus, in Luke's not-so-subtle framing, and in accordance with the narrative argument of Acts up to this point, the identity of the emperor in effect is coalesced with the mythic demonic creature of Jewish/Christian legend. And lest there be any doubt, in two of the references that Paul makes he does not use the term "Caesar," but rather the more religiously charged titular *sebastos* (25:21, 25).[121]

With respect to the miracles, then, this larger nexus of imperial power cannot be separated from the role and function of the displays of divine numen in the Lukan narrative. They not only lay claim to and on imperial space, but the very structure of miracle discourse is also imbued with the religio-political language attached to the emperor in the Roman world. This conclusion does not necessarily imply that early Christians like Luke are touting a new emperor in Jesus (although that possibility cannot be excluded), but it does suggest that, if one is to describe or display (in narra-

---

121. It is difficult to imagine that Luke's readers would not associate this linguistic framing, at least in part, with the emperor cult. One can compare, for instance, the language associated with the temple of the Sebastoi at Ephesus, which was under Flavian patronage. See Friesen (*Twice Neokoros*, 34, 38), who argues that identification of Domitian as a Sebastos in temple dedications designates the former as an object of worship (cf. idem, "Myth and Symbolic Resistance in Revelation 13," *JBL* 123 [2004]: 291; and Lendon, *Empire of Honour*, 163). Indeed, the place for the worship of the emperor could be called a *Sebasteion* (David W. Pao, "The Sebasteion in Aphrodisias: Structure and Meaning of a Temple Complex for the Imperial Cult," *Jian Dao* 6 [1996]: 55–56) and the image bearers in the cult were designated by the term *sebastophoros/Sebastophant*. See further, Allen Brent, "Ignatius of Antioch and the Imperial Cult," *VC* 52 (1998): 41; Joyce M. Reynolds, "Ruler-Cult at Aphrodisias in the Late Republic and under the Julio-Claudian Emperors," in *Subject and Ruler: The Cult of the Ruling Power in Classical Antiquity* (ed. A. Small; Journal of Roman Archaeology Supplement Series 18; Ann Arbor: Journal of Roman Archaeology, 1996), 48; and Philip A. Harland, "Honours and Worship: Emperors, Imperial Cults and Associations at Ephesus (First to Third Centuries C.E.)," *SR* 25 (1996): 331–33. Compare the use of *sebastologos* for the official in charge of praising Gaius in the cult at Miletus, detailed by Simon R. F. Price, "Gods and Emperors: The Greek Language of the Roman Imperial Cult," *JHS* 104 (1984): 90.

tive) manifestations of power in this world, the conceptual framework that is to be used will resonate with imperial imagery.[122] Power in this sociocultural matrix is not separated easily into supernatural and human categories, but rather is integrated in divergent ways and to varying degrees in specific individuals and communities. Thus it becomes difficult to disentangle the web of power in Lukan discourse or even to have justification for doing so. Yet we do know that miracles wrought by early Christian heroes in the name of Jesus are one means of laying narrative claim on the authority of empire and the loyalties of its citizens. Thus miracles in Acts are inseparable from the broader rhetoric of power pervasive in the ancient world. Restoring the raw, brute force to this cultural discourse and applying it as such to an analysis of Acts represents a step forward toward a fuller appreciation of just how truly incarnational the "theological" message of Acts in fact is.

5. "Not Done in a Corner": Concluding Imperial Reflections

In the preceding discussion I set forth the following argument. First, I began with assessing some of the past trends in miracle research on Acts, with the aim of revealing patterns in the way that miracle discourse has been appraised and interpreted that indicate an attempt to sanitize (and indeed to save!) the miracle stories themselves, distancing them from the ancient cultural world and, at the same time, subordinating the miracles to various theological and narrative features found in Acts. My overriding concern was to restore a sense of the ancient feel of the narrative, working not with the history behind the story, but taking the narrative as *historia* in its own right, arguing that the account must be read and understood in light of ancient perceptions of miracle stories as those intersect with conceptions and images of power in the Roman world. I suggested that

---

122. In this connection, the recent work on Roman imperial iconography and imagery in conversation with Paul's writings is illuminating. See especially Davina Lopez, "Before Your Very Eyes: Roman Imperial Ideology, Gender Constructs and Paul's Inter-Nationalism," in Penner and Vander Stichele, *Mapping Gender*, 115–62; idem, *Apostle to the Conquered: Reimagining Paul's Mission* (Paul in Critical Contexts; Minneapolis: Fortress, 2008); Neil Elliott, *The Arrogance of Nations: Reading Romans in the Shadow of Empire* (Paul in Critical Contexts: Minneapolis: Fortress, 2008); and Joseph A. Marchal, *The Politics of Heaven: Women, Gender, and Empire in the Study of Paul* (Paul in Critical Contexts; Minneapolis: Fortress, 2008).

using a nonpejorative conception of "magic" would be a useful starting point for analysis, and that Luke intends his narrative to evoke that sense in his readers. This move represents an important first step in recovering the function of miracle discourse in Acts. By repositioning the miracles *behind* the text or by subordinating them to something "higher" *in* the narrative, scholars have frequently neglected the ideological and cultural power of Luke's presentation of the apostles as miracle workers and bearers of divine/numinous power. Indeed, by largely avoiding serious discussion or even recognition of power and control in the narrative of Acts, especially failing to engage how these cultural notions are displayed in the contests and competitions that direct the flow of action in the narrative, scholars have tended to overlook the fundamental agonistic (and indeed also antagonistic) edge of Lukan discursive practice, which is the larger context in which the miracles must be situated.

Second, I proceeded to argue for two interconnected uses of miracles in Acts (although I would not limit it to just these). In the first instance, miracles function to characterize the founders of the nascent Christian communities as powerful in word and deed. In the textual contest for identity, then, miracles are used to authenticate the apostles as the bearers of divine power, showing them to be superior in *ergon*, which matches their equal supremacy in *logos*.[123] In many respects, we can characterize this

---

123. See the recent discussion by Loveday Alexander on the apostles as ideal philosophers in their evolving role in Acts, particularly with respect to both their public and private comportment ("'Foolishness to the Greeks': Jews and Christians in the Public Life of the Empire," in *Philosophy and Power in the Graeco-Roman World: Essays in Honour of Miriam Griffin* [ed. G. Clark and T. Rajak; New York: Oxford University Press, 2002], 229-49; cf. Penner and Vander Stichele, "All the World's a Stage," 388-91). The verbal component emphasized in Alexander's characterization balances the features related to the portrayal of the apostles as wonder-workers developed in this essay (cf. John A. Darr, *Herod the Fox: Audience Criticism and Lukan Characterization* [JSNTSup 163; Sheffield: Sheffield Academic Press, 1998], 92-136, who develops a similar point with respect to the inclusion of both words and deeds in the type-scene relating the "showdown" between philosopher and tyrant; see also Penner, "Civilizing Discourse"). I should make clear that the argument proposed in this essay is not that there is only one "type" of ancient character that Luke has in view when he crafts his narrative heroes. Rather, we ought to be thinking more complexly in terms of intersecting vectors of images and ideologically loaded topoi upon which Luke and his ancient readers drew, both consciously and unconsciously (see further Todd Penner, "Madness in the Method? The Acts of the Apostles in Current Study," *CurBS* 2 [2004]: 256-57).

discourse as the language of the polis, the competitive edge of citizenship in a world dominated by the maintenance and advancement of one's identity by and through the loss of another's. Thus, unlike the general trend in miracle research on Acts, I have argued that numinous displays are about the apostles' power and its raw exhibition and, in tandem, the demonstration of the powerlessness of those "opponents" who cannot withstand these divinely appointed and sanctioned individuals' words and deeds.

At the same time, this characterization of the apostles leads to another layer of interpretation in the narrative, which is parallel to the function of the first. Here we see that the miracles of Acts are carried out in "Jesus' name" (see Acts 3:6, 16; 4:10, 18, 30; 5:40; 16:18), which has traditionally been perceived as "theological" in its orientation, referring to the power of the resurrected Christ (see 2:21; 9:15–16; 15:17; 19:17; 21:13).[124] In part, this position may be affirmed, but there is undoubtedly a more radical edge to this nomenclature as well. Miracles demonstrate the claim of Christ on Roman space in the narrative, beginning in Jerusalem and culminating in Paul's arrival at Rome in the final chapter of the book. It is through his earthly representatives that Jesus' power is most palpably displayed, claiming not only territory but also the loyalty of "bodies." While the image is more subtle, everywhere we see an absent and impotent emperor, whose subjects are being won over in the contest for power and control being waged by/through the apostles. Miracle discourse in Acts must be seen, then, as extending from the polis to the larger landscape of empire, wherein numinous displays provide the main vehicle for the demonstration of Christ's beneficence but also his just revenge when appropriate. The book of Acts therefore represents Christ's *Res Gestae* in much the same way that we find in the Augustus inscription: an attempt to win the world through acts of power, through the extension of *both* "mercy" and "justice."

---

124. See Larry W. Hurtado's brief assessment of the use of Jesus' name for healing and exorcism in Acts (*Lord Jesus Christ: Devotion to Jesus in Earliest Christianity* [Grand Rapids: Eerdmans, 2003], 203–5). In this context, one should note that the deified emperor was similarly thought to have wielded efficacious power for those calling on his name (see Duncan Fishwick, "Prudentius and the Cult of Divus Augustus," *Historia* 39 [1990]: 483–84; and Price, "Gods and Emperors," 92), although it is unclear if anyone ever invoked the deified emperor expressly for purposes of healing (see Price, "Gods and Emperors," 91; and Fishwick, "*Genius* and *Numen*," 365).

If this move to reassess Lukan miracles in light of the language of imperial dominance and control proves fruitful, then the boundaries of Acts study will begin to shift as a result. The frequent characterization of Acts as promoting the image that Christians are "friends" of the Roman Empire—rather than a threat to the political order—allows the surface features of Luke's narrative to dominate and diverts the more substantive indications of a power struggle going on just beneath that surface. In light of the argument developed here, the discursive structures of Acts cannot be viewed as amicable toward the Roman Empire, and the Christians of Acts actually do pose a threat, especially insofar as the miracle discourse contained therein exerts a bold (and inimical—in mimicry) claim on the spaces and bodies subject to the emperor. In this cultural context, it is difficult to imagine getting much more radical than that.[125]

And one cannot ignore the effective history of this discourse either. Eusebius, that key player in the transfer of power during the time of Constantine, who created the mytho-ideological basis for this movement in his *Ecclesiastical History*, applied Acts as the main script for his narrative portrait of the expansion of Christianity.[126] Since the "origins" as delineated in Acts became the foundation for Eusebius's vision, it should not surprise one to find that power and control became the hallmark of Christianity in this period.[127] Is it any wonder that Eusebius should have heralded so

---

125. This imperial mimicry by Luke (on which see most recently Shelly Matthews, "The Need for the Stoning of Stephen," in *Violence in the New Testament: Jesus Followers and Other Jews under Empire* [ed. S. Matthews and E. L. Gibson; London: T&T Clark, 2005], 124–39) may need to take a more prominent role in the discussion of the subsequent use of the text, especially given the neglect (or lack of awareness) of Acts in the early second century (alongside Gregory, *Reception of Luke and Acts*; also see William A. Strange, *The Problem of the Text of Acts* [SNTSMS 71; Cambridge: Cambridge University Press, 1992], 178–83). As early Christians began to imitate "empire" in the interactions with and interrelations between their diverse communities spread out over the empire (as evidenced already quite early in the imperialistic claims of *1 Clement*), the broader and more radical scope of Acts may have become less problematic (or more useful).

126. See Ron Cameron, "Alternate Beginnings—Different Ends: Eusebius, Thomas, and the Construction of Christian Origins," in *Religious Propaganda and Missionary Competition in the New Testament World: Essays Honoring Dieter Georgi* (ed. L. Bormann, K. Del Tredici, and A. Standhartinger; NovTSup 74; Leiden: Brill, 1994), 505–11.

127. See Foucault's comments in this respect: "It has often been said that Christianity brought into being a code of ethics fundamentally different from that of the

enthusiastically the advent of one who could in fact play both roles: that of Christian hero and emperor? In the final analysis, this legacy may represent the surest testament to the potency and dynamism of Lukan narrative argumentation, because what was rhetoricized and imagined in narrative in the end became the very real stuff of history.

---

ancient world. Less emphasis is usually placed on the fact that it proposed and spread new power relations throughout the ancient world" ("Subject and Power," 131). Foucault defines this particular Christian manifestation as "pastoral power" (esp. 131–32).

Miracle Discourse and the Gospel of John

Gail R. O'Day

1. Introduction

In the history of New Testament scholarship, one can trace the major trends in interpretation by looking at the ways that miracle stories were discussed. In debates about the historicity of the Gospel accounts, for example, the miracle stories were often the places in the text where the claims of faith and the claims of reason came most into conflict. The clearest example of this can be seen in the work of David Friedrich Strauss,[1] but Strauss was hardly alone in noting the problems that Jesus' miracles caused interpreters in light of the birth and development of modern science. Form criticism, with its emphasis on the function of Gospel traditions within their communities of origin, made it possible to approach the miracle-story material from a perspective other than the strict historicity of the material. The classic treatments of Dibelius and Bultmann devote much attention to the miracle stories, although they do not categorize them in exactly the same way.[2]

The interest in communities of origin led easily into an interest in the sources of the traditions used and formed by these communities. The source-critical approach, a mode of study enhanced by an increased interest in the ancient Mediterranean world and its crosscurrents of religious traditions, was concerned to identify the sources that lie behind the New Testament traditions—sometimes understood to be written

---

1. David Friedrich Strauss, *The Life of Jesus Critically Examined* (German edition 1835–1836; ed. Peter C. Hodgson; trans. George Eliot; Philadelphia: Fortress, 1972).

2. Martin Dibelius, *From Tradition to Gospel* (trans. B. L. Woolf and M. Dibelius; New York: Scribner's, 1935); Rudolf Bultmann, *History of the Synoptic Tradition* (trans. John Marsh; New York: Harper & Row, 1963).

sources, sometimes oral. In either case, the emphasis on sources led to increased interest on what predated the Gospels in the form in which they are found in the canon. For the study of the Gospel of John in particular, miracle stories were among the key factors that shaped scholarly construction of sources.[3]

All of these approaches emphasized the building blocks out of which the Gospels were constructed, and redaction criticism developed as a way of attending to how the Evangelists, primarily conceived as editors ("redactors") of tradition, put the pieces together in the composition of their Gospels. Miracle stories played an important role in redaction-critical studies of the Gospels, as the placement of these stories in the Gospels were seen as indicative of an Evangelist's theological perspective.[4]

The approach to the study of miracle stories in this volume certainly draws on the work of these earlier approaches, but views these stories from the perspective of rhetorical criticism. History, form, and theology are all understood to be constitutive elements of the miracle-story discourse rather than components that can be examined individually. The synthetic approach of rhetorical criticism can be seen most clearly in the topics suggested for the Society of Biblical Literature panel that initially gave rise to these papers: attention to the nature of miracle discourse in explicit conversation with a collection of miracle stories from Greco-Roman antiquity.[5]

The direction of this paper is shaped by a suggestion from the New Testament and Rhetorical Criticism steering committee about possible angles of vision that rhetorical criticism offers to the study of miracle discourse, and two observations by Wendy Cotter in the introduction to her collection of Greco-Roman miracle stories. The steering committee suggested that panelists think about "the embedding of topics and arguments in miracle discourse to create a new Christian *paideia*." The study of embedded topics and arguments is particularly applicable to the Gospel of John, since

---

3. Robert T. Fortna, *The Gospel of Signs: A Reconstruction of the Narrative Underlying the Fourth Gospel* (Cambridge: Cambridge University Press, 1970); and idem, *The Fourth Gospel and Its Predecessor: From Narrative Source to Present Gospel* (Philadelphia: Fortress, 1988).

4. Gunther Bornkamm, Gerhard Barth, and Heinz Joachim Held, *Tradition and Interpretation in Matthew* (trans. Percy Scott; Philadelphia: Westminster, 1963).

5. Wendy J. Cotter, *Miracles in Greco-Roman Antiquity: A Sourcebook for the Study of New Testament Miracle Stories* (London: Routledge, 1999).

the storytelling style of the Gospel regularly blurs the distinction between narrative proper and discursive elaboration. Similarly, Cotter makes two comments about miracle stories that point away from strict consideration of their form and source, some of the more prevalent ways of studying miracle stories, especially in John,[6] and in the direction of their rhetorical function. The first comment occurs in a discussion of some of the difficulties caused by attempts to maintain the form-critical distinctions between miracle story and apophthegm. Cotter observes, "Any ancient author was free to tell the story his/her own way, turning it to whatever purpose might seem most attractive or advantageous.... The 'miracle-story' writer was creating a story, and s/he was free of such restraints."[7] Later, in describing one criterion she used in selecting material for the section of healing miracles, Cotter writes, "Since it is particularly helpful if a narrator comments about the significance of the hero or god's miracle, I also include any interpretive remarks attached to the story's presentation."[8]

To attend to the embedding of topics and arguments in miracle discourse suggests consideration of the ways in which attention to both the content and the function of miracle discourse can reconfigure categories that derive primarily from formal characterization of miracle discourse. To ask about topics and arguments that may be embedded in miracle discourse seems to ask about the ways in which miracle discourse functions to communicate something more or other than the surprising manifestation of divine presence and power, areas conventionally associated with miracle stories. Cotter's observation about the fluidity and malleability of the miracle-story form also engages that range of considerations, because what an author wants to accomplish in his or her narration of a miracle story becomes at least as important a factor as the particular requirements or expectations of form. Cotter's acknowledgment that it was important to include where possible an author's interpretive remarks about the significance of a healing miracle also suggests the limits of formal classification of miracle discourse apart from rhetorical function. The effect of a miracle

---

6. In Johannine studies, this emphasis of investigation is seen most clearly in source-critical studies that focus on the *semeia* source. So, for example, Rudolf Bultmann, *The Gospel of John: A Commentary* (trans. G. R. Beasley-Murray, R. W. N. Hoare, and J. K. Riches; Philadelphia: Westminster, 1971); Fortna, *Gospel of Signs*.

7. Cotter, *Miracles in Greco-Roman Antiquity*, 3.

8. Ibid., 11.

story is not coterminous with the narration of the story proper, but can inform the surrounding narrative in which it is embedded.

These framing observations are suggestive for studying miracle discourse in the Gospel of John. They point to ways in which conventional expectations of form can become malleable in the face of a wide range of rhetorical functions. This is especially appropriate for John, and a potentially rich avenue of exploration, because the narrative style and mode of the Gospel of John regularly redefines and recasts conventional formal expectations.[9] An examination from this perspective of the function of miracle discourse also may provide fresh access to larger Johannine questions.

2. Topics Embedded in Miracle Discourse: John 2:1–11

I will begin with an examination of the wine miracle at Cana. Cotter's collection of Dionysus stories is a reminder that a miracle revolving around a superabundance of wine would have been recognizable as a story of a divine manifestation to listeners and readers in the first-century Mediterranean world.[10] And moving beyond the resources offered by Cotter, rabbinic haggadah also reported miraculous provisions of wine, indicating that the motif would resonate with Jewish and Gentile readers.[11]

The Cana wine miracle is the first miracle narrated in John, as well as the shortest, so provides a good starting point for clues to ways in which miracle discourse may function in John. And as is well known, it is also the miracle story that introduces the word *sign* into the Gospel and into the lexicon of Johannine interpretation. This miracle story is also a useful starting point because it is a one-of-a-kind story in Gospel literature—no other Gospel narrates such a transformation miracle. Interestingly, the John 2 story is also one of a kind in another way—not only does it recount an event distinct in the canonical literature, but also it is the only time

---

9. See Harold W. Attridge, "Genre Bending in the Fourth Gospel," *JBL* 121 (2002): 3–21.

10. Cotter, *Miracles in Greco-Roman Antiquity*, 164–65.

11. See, for examples, the stories cited by Martin Hengel, "The Interpretation of the Wine Miracle at Cana: John 2:1–11," in *The Glory of Christ in the New Testament: Studies in Christology* (ed. L. D. Hurst and N. T. Wright; Oxford: Clarendon, 1987), 104–12.

there is a miracle story in one Gospel that does not have a corresponding story or type of story in at least one other canonical Gospel.[12]

Even before the details of the story are examined, the story's multifaceted uniqueness and its positioning in the Gospel narrative is intriguing—particularly if one allows oneself to examine the story from the perspective of rhetorical function and not primarily as the linchpin in reconstructing the *sēmeia* source or the signs Gospel. All the other miracle stories narrated in John either have parallels in the synoptic material (the healing of a centurion's son, John 4:46–54 || Matt 8:5–13 || Luke 7:1–10; the healing of a blind man, John 9:1–11 || Matt 20:29–34 || Mark 10:46–52 || Luke 18:35–43; the multiplication of loaves and fishes, John 6:1–14 || Matt 14:13–21 || Mark 6:30–44 || Mark 8:1–21 || Luke 9:10–17; Jesus' walking on water, John 6:16–21 || Matt 14:22–27 || Mark 6:45–52) or narrate a type of story that is also narrated in the Synoptic Gospels (the healing of a paralytic, John 5:1–9; see Matt 9:1–8 || Mark 2:1–11 || Luke 5:17–26; the raising of a dead person, John 11:1–44, see Matt 9:18–26 || Mark 5:21–43 || Luke 8:40–56; and the miraculous catch of fish, John 21:1–14, see Luke 5:1–11). It can hardly be mere coincidence that the narrative of John opens with this unparalleled story. The prologue of John 1:1–18 and the witness of John the Baptist and the disciples in 1:19–51 have talked about the revelation of God in Jesus, but with the possible exception of Jesus' recognition of Nathanael under the fig tree,[13] no epiphany of the divine has yet been narrated. The promise of seeing "greater things than these" (1:50) sets up the transition from the opening witnesses to the scene at Cana, and creates a readiness in the reader for an epiphany (as does 1:51, with its apocalyptic promise of the heavens opening and angels ascending and descending on the Son of Man).

In its formal contours, the wine miracle at Cana is, to quote Bultmann, "a typical *miracle story*," meaning that it adheres to the characteristics that

---

12. If we follow the Jesus miracles as given in Cotter's book, Matt 17:24–27 (3.63), "Jesus pays tax with a shekel from a fish's mouth," would be considered a singleton miracle. But it is not clear to me that this passage is a miracle *story* per se, as the miraculous is promised but never actualized in the Gospel narrative.

13. John narrates two manifestations of divine power that involve no physical changes—no healing, multiplication, or transformation—but that do display supernatural abilities: Jesus' recognition of Nathanael under the fig tree (1:46–49) and his knowledge of the Samaritan woman's marital history (4:16–19). One wonders if it is possible to think of a category of "miracle of cognition" to add to Bultmann's four categories (*History of the Synoptic Tradition*) that provide the outline for Cotter's work.

derive from his form-critical work on the Synoptic tradition.[14] What is this typical form? The setting (vv. 1–2), the situation of need, or in this case, lack (vv. 3–5), the miracle itself, here narrated indirectly (vv. 6–8), and the corroboration of the miracle by witnesses (vv. 9–10). When read from the form-critical perspective, there is nothing surprising or even distinctive about the John 2 miracle—its narrative flow and constitutive elements correspond to most of the miracles in the canonical Gospels. It is how the Fourth Evangelist uses the conventional form that makes the story interesting. If we look at the miracle story from the perspective of what topics or arguments might be embedded in it, we begin to see how the content reconfigures the form. The narrative weight of the story falls not on the miracle per se, but on the interpretation of the miracle embedded in the story proper. Here too, then, we begin to see hints that it may not always be possible to distinguish between a miracle and its interpretation.

2.1. CHARACTERS' DIRECT SPEECH AS INTERPRETIVE TOOL

Three characters speak in the story of the Cana wine miracle: Jesus' mother, Jesus, and the chief steward. Jesus' mother speaks to him (v. 3) and to the servants at the wedding (v. 5), Jesus speaks to his mother (v. 4) and to the servants (vv. 7, 8), and the steward speaks to the bridegroom (v. 10). The words of Jesus' mother establish the situation of lack/need, Jesus' words to the servants in verses 7 and 8 are the indirect narration of the miracle itself, and the steward's words in verse 10 testify to the occurrence of a miracle. Each of these speaking parts plays a necessary role in fulfilling the formal requirements of a miracle story. But an examination of the specific content of what each character speaks shows that their words move beyond this formal requirement.

The words that Jesus' mother speaks to him in verse 3 ("They have no wine") not only confirm the situation of need, a conventional element of the miracle-story form, but also indicate to the reader that this situation is somehow of concern to Jesus. This, too, is a standard element of miracle stories in the Gospels—the situation of need produces an appeal to Jesus for help (see for example, Mark 2:30, "Now Simon's mother-in-law was in bed with a fever, and they told him [Jesus] about her at once."). Nor is Jesus' seeming rebuff to his mother ("Woman, what concern is that to you

---

14. Bultmann, *John*, 115.

and to me?" v. 4a) completely without parallel in the miracle-story literature of the Gospels.[15] Yet even these conventional elements contribute on more levels than simply narrative flow. The comments on Jesus' mother put the narrative focus squarely on Jesus, even before Jesus has spoken, and Jesus' initial response to his mother similarly moves the focus away from her and onto himself.

The second half of Jesus' response to his mother completes this shift in focus. With the words, "My hour has not yet come," the role of embedded commentary and interpretation becomes clearer.[16] These words about Jesus' hour place this one individual story in the much broader context of the flow of the entire Gospel story.

To speak of Jesus' hour is to speak of the defining moment of Jesus' death, resurrection, and ascension, and so this reference to the hour places the opening act of Jesus' ministry in the context of the closing acts of that ministry.[17] Because this is the first occurrence of "hour" in John, the reader is not fully equipped to decipher this reference at this narrative juncture. Rather, this reference to Jesus' hour is the embedding of a topic that will grow in significance as the Gospel narrative progresses. This embedding suggests that one of the rhetorical functions of the Cana miracle is to begin the Gospel conversation about Jesus' death—and to show that in John, the miraculous is always tied to core christological questions. That Jesus' death is to be imported to the beginning of his ministry will be confirmed by the scene that follows the Cana miracle, the cleansing of the Jerusalem temple (2:13–22), in which the narrator will juxtapose a request for a sign (2:18) with Jesus' symbolic prediction of his death and resurrection (2:19, 21).

The embedding of the remarks about Jesus' hour tells the reader that the wonder enacted by the Cana miracle cannot be interpreted apart from the defining context of Jesus' hour. Importantly, this interpretive lens is embedded into the dialogue and direct discourse of the story itself, and is not offered as commentary on the story by the narrator. The conversation

---

15. Note, for example, Jesus' initial rebuff of the Canaanite woman who requests healing for her daughter in Matt 15.

16. Jesus' response to the Canaanite woman also embeds commentary into that miracle story, because it turns the reader's attention to the nature of Jesus' mission and whether it is to be extended to the Gentiles.

17. Another topic suggested by the steering committee was to consider "the eventual absorption of miracle discourse by death-resurrection discourse," and John 2:1–11 would be a fruitful place of study for that as well.

between Jesus and his mother provides interpretation of the miracle before it even occurs.

The words of Jesus' mother that follow this exchange provide a second example of interpretation embedded in direct discourse. Even though Jesus has spoken no word of assent to his mother's implied request that he should attend to the wine shortage, she nonetheless instructs the servants to do what Jesus tells them to do (v. 5). These words function as interpretation of the miracle for the reader, because they create a context in which whatever follows will now be linked for the reader to Jesus and his actions. Jesus is the main actor even before he acts, so that again, Jesus' identity (and the ways in which God is revealed in him) becomes a topic of the miracle story.

The steward's comments in verse 10 provide a third example of embedded interpretation. As noted, when read through the lens of the formal requirements of a miracle story, the steward's comments testify that a miracle has indeed taken place. It is marvelously indirect and ironic testimony, because the steward is speaking to the bridegroom, whom he assumes is the source of the wine. Yet as with the comments of Jesus and his mother, the steward's commentary moves beyond simple narrative requirements. Under the guise of a lesson on entertainment economics ("Everyone serves the good wine first, and then the inferior wine after the guests have become drunk"), the steward not only attests to the fact of the miracle but also provides commentary on the nature of the miracle. Even though the setup for the miracle seems to draw the reader's attention to the quantity of wine ("six stone jars ... each holding twenty or thirty gallons," v. 6), the steward's comments direct the reader to attend to its quality instead ("But you have kept the good wine until now," v. 10). The steward's comments turn the story away from the simple fact of a miracle to the meaning and value of the miraculous. The judgment that the wine is good (*kalos*) is evocative of several interpretive directions—Israel's eschatological expectations of hills dripping with sweet wine (Amos 9:13; Joel 3:18), a new creation, the work of the "good" shepherd—all of which will be tested and retested by the reader as the Gospel narrative progresses.

What is important in the context of rhetorical criticism is to note the ways in which interpretation—and through that interpretation, central Johannine topics and arguments—are embedded in the miracle story itself. Intrinsic to the Gospel's storytelling in this miracle story are narrative details that direct the story's interpretation toward Jesus' death, his identity as the one who makes God known, and the quality of Jesus' works. These are topics that will appear again and again in the Gospel of John, and the reader is first introduced to them through the embedding of topics in the narrative enactment of a miracle story.

In John 2:1–10, the miracle story occupies center stage; the narrator does not insert any explicit commentary that interrupts the flow of the story or that asks the reader to attend to something other than the story of the abundance of wine. Yet even without any explicit narratorial intervention, the story is implicitly embedded with the Gospel's larger concerns. John 2:1–10 is the story of the miraculous production of a superabundance of good wine, but the story is told in such a way that it also teaches the reader new ways to appropriate and approach the presence and power of God in their world.

2.2. The Narrator's Explicit Commentary as Interpretive Tool

The Johannine narrator does provide explicit comments about the miracle's significance at the end of the story. In verse 11, the narrator comments, "Jesus did this, the first of his signs in Cana of Galilee, and revealed his glory; and his disciples believed in him." This explicit commentary directs the reader to attend to four aspects of the story that has just been narrated: (1) It is the first, (2) of Jesus' signs; (3) Jesus revealed his glory (*doxa*) in this act, and (4) as a result of this act, his disciples believed in him. There is much for any reader and serious interpreter to grapple with in the narrator's commentary here. Even if we bracket from this discussion any source-critical questions (e.g., what is the source of the enumeration, since only two of Jesus' miracles in John are explicitly numbered), the significance of this verse for the interpretation not only of the miracle but also of the larger Gospel is staggering.

Three key topics that will recur throughout the Gospel are at play here: signs, glory, and coming to believe. Through this commentary, the wine miracle is reconfigured away from its local significance as an individual event in Jesus' ministry to its status as one element in a larger story. The explicit enumeration of the miracle efficiently accomplishes this, because it cues the reader to look for more signs, but the use of *doxa* and *pisteuō* also instruct the reader to move beyond this one story. Glory and belief figured prominently in the Gospel's prologue (1:7, 12, 14), and the return to those topics here firmly and explicitly links this miracle with the revelation of God in the Word become flesh. This is the first revelation of the *doxa*,[18] and it has its optimal effect—the witnesses to the revelation believe. Other revelatory moments in the Gospel will have less clear-cut results, and so this miracle is "first" in more than a chronological sense.

Through the commentary in verse 11, the narrator makes explicit what has been implicit in the narration of the story itself. The words of Jesus' mother in verse 5 already cued the reader to attend to Jesus as the main actor of the story; Jesus' words about his hour pointed the reader to the broader theological context in which this miracle should be read; and the steward's comments about the quality of the miracle anticipate the disciples' reaction of faith. The topics that concern the Evangelist are completely embedded in the narration of the miracle story, so that one cannot talk about the miraculous event apart from its interpretation. The fact of the wine miracle cannot be narrated without seamlessly narrating its meaning—each of the constitutive elements of the story simultaneously has a function in advancing the story line and in advancing the "meaning" line.[19] The narration of the Cana wine miracle communicates more than the power and presence of the divine at work in Jesus. It also guides the reader in the appropriate response to such a manifestation—belief—and gives this miracle a distinctive content by grounding it in the death of Jesus, and provides the reader with a lens for reading the rest of the Jesus story.

3. The Embedding of Miracle Discourse throughout John

There is a complementary perspective to attending to the ways in which topics and arguments are embedded in miracle discourse. That is to attend to the ways in which miracle discourse may be embedded in other topics and arguments that constitute the larger fabric of the Gospel of John. If, as we have seen in the analysis of the Cana miracle of John 2:1-11, topics as central to the Gospel of John as the death of Jesus can be embedded in miracle discourse, then it seems appropriate to examine where and how

---

18. Bultmann, *John*, 119.
19. Here I part company with the language used by Bultmann to describe Jesus' revelation of God in John. Bultmann insists that there is only the existential *das* in Jesus' revelation—it is the fact of the revelation that matters, not any content (*was*) of the revelation. But this analysis of the Cana story shows that as important as the *das* of revelation is, there is also a *was*—something is being communicated to which the narrator wants the reader to give assent.

miracle discourse might be embedded in topics and arguments that on the face of it do not deal with the miraculous. A reading of the entire Gospel from this perspective is by necessity a suggestive overview. I will give three examples that point to the complexity of distinguishing miracle story and interpretation, and miracle story and embedded topics throughout the Gospel of John.

3.1. Cross-Referencing and Self-Referentiality about Miracles in John

Throughout the Gospel of John there is a remarkable degree of cross-referencing and self-referentiality about miracles. Jesus and his miracles are a major topic of conversation—not only for the Gospel narrator but for Jesus himself and other Gospel characters as well.

A good example is the conversation between Jesus and Nicodemus in John 3. This conversation is introduced by the following observation by the narrator: "Many believed in his name because they saw the signs (*sēmeia*) that he was doing. But Jesus on his part would not trust himself to them." The narrator's comments here echo many of the themes we have just noted in 2:11, most especially the linking of faith with seeing signs. The narrator uses almost identical vocabulary here as in 2:11, where the link between seeing signs and believing is affirmed. But at 2:23–24, the narrator cites the perspective of Jesus and so calls the link between seeing signs and faith into question. (It is interesting that Jesus gives no response to the disciples' reported faith at 2:11.)[20] This commentary by the narrator about signs is followed almost immediately by commentary by Nicodemus about signs (3:2): "Rabbi, we know that you are a teacher who has come from God; for no one can do these signs apart from the presence of God." Here, embedded in the dialogue between Jesus and Nicodemus, is a working definition of miracle—an act worked in/with the presence of God—that one of the Gospel characters uses as a lens through which to interpret Jesus and his acts. Nicodemus is doing exactly what the embedding of topics in John 2:1–11 asked the reader to do: to be taught by the miracle story about the identity of Jesus and his relationship with God.

---

20. This seeming contradiction is an important point of departure for source critics, as well as the reference to multiple signs, even though the Gospel has so far only narrated one—but to go in this direction misses the possibility of thinking about the rhetorical function of miracle discourse.

Explicit references to Jesus' miracles or signs serve as touchstones throughout the Gospel. At John 6:2, the crowd's interest in Jesus is explained because "they saw the signs that he was doing for the sick." Jesus himself refers to the crowd's reaction to one of his miracles at 7:21 ("I performed one work and all of you are astonished"), and uses their reaction as the occasion to teach about proper interpretation at 7:24 ("Do not judge by appearances, but judge with right judgment"). The healing of the man born blind in John 9 is referred to at 10:21 ("These are not the words of a demon. Can a demon open the eyes of the blind?") and at 11:37 ("Could not he who opened the eyes of the blind man have kept this man from dying?"). Through these references, found not in the narrator's commentary, but in the words of Gospel characters, the Gospel characters enact the process of discernment and learning that is demanded of the Gospel readers.

3.2. The Vocabulary of the Miraculous

"Sign" is not the only vocabulary used to speak of miracles in John. The vocabulary of work, works, and working (*ergon*) is also used to refer to Jesus' miracles. In 7:21, Jesus refers to his earlier healing of the paralytic on the sabbath as a "work." In this regard, Jesus' speech about work to the Jewish authorities in chapter 5 after this sabbath healing is particularly suggestive in thinking about the rhetorical place and function of miracle discourse in John. Through the vocabulary of "work," the topic of Jesus' identity and relationship to God is explicitly embedded in his explanation of his miraculous act of healing: "My Father is working and I also am working" (5:18). Yet work is transformed in the rest of Jesus' speech in 5:19–45 from any limited meaning of that which violates sabbath rest to a more inclusive term for astonishing and miraculous acts of Jesus that reveal the presence of God.

The vocabulary of work simultaneously describes and interprets the miraculous in line with Johannine topics and themes: "The Father loves the Son and shows him all that he himself is doing; and he will show him greater works than these, so that you will be astonished. Indeed, just as the Father raises the dead and gives them life, so also the Son gives life to whomever he wishes" (5:20–21). Since Jesus will demonstrate the truth of his own teaching in John 11, when he, like God, raises someone from the dead, Jesus' words about life and death are not simply metaphorical here, but do point to the presence of the miraculous. Jesus' words, like those of

Nicodemus in 3:2, also contain within them a definition of the miraculous: works given by God to evoke astonishment. And works, like signs, are also linked to faith: "If I am not doing the works of the Father, then do not believe me. But if I do them, even though you do not believe me, believe the works, so that you may know and understand that the Father is in me and I am in the Father" (10:37–38). The vocabulary of "works" will recur throughout the speeches of Jesus in John, so that miracle discourse can be seen as providing the rhetorical frame for much of the theological perspective of the Gospel.

3.3. THE DEMONIC AND THE MIRACULOUS

My final example of the embedding of miracle discourse throughout the Gospel of John comes from what is not in John more than from what is. Cotter's collection is organized around four types of miracle story: healing, exorcism, nature miracle, raising from the dead. Exorcisms are prevalent in the sources Cotter surveys, as well as in the Synoptic Gospels, but there are no exorcisms at all in John. *Daimonion* occurs only as an epithet and never as an animate being. This absence of exorcism and of the narrative presence of demons is striking, because it cannot be said that evil does not fit into the worldview or theological perspective of the Gospel. John operates with a very stark cosmology, in which good and evil are clearly articulated and the lines sharply drawn. So, for example, the cosmology articulated in this key passage from John 3:19–21: "And this is the judgment, that the light has come into the world, and people loved darkness more than light because their deeds were evil. For all who do evil hate the light and do not come to the light, so that their deeds may not be exposed. But those who do what is true come to the light, so that it may be clearly seen that their deeds have been done in God." Moreover, variously referred to as Satan (13:27), the devil (13:2), or "the ruler of this world" (14:30), personified evil also plays an important role in the narrative and theological world of the Gospel. Satan or the devil is explicitly named as the active agent behind Judas's betrayal of Jesus (13:2, 27). Yet in this narrative and theological world in which evil is real, there are no exorcisms.

John 2:1–11 can help us address this puzzle. In response to his mother's (unspoken) request that he perform a miracle, he replies, "My hour has not yet come." As we noted, these words brought Jesus' death, resurrection, and ascension into the foreground at the very beginning of this Gospel, helping the reader to see that everything that is to follow, including the miraculous, is to be interpreted through the lens of Jesus' hour. But the hour is still in the future; the reader interprets through this lens, but the fulfillment of the hour still waits in the narrative future. Each reader can enact and anticipate the effects of the hour, but Jesus will fulfill this decisive moment only once. The community's role in participating in the conflict between good and evil is at the heart of the quotation from 3:19–21 cited above. What is good and what is evil in the world is determined by how one responds to the light, one of the Gospel's metaphors for the presence of Jesus in the world; it is not predetermined in advance of being in the presence of the light. But the cosmic conflict with the power of evil can and will only be resolved at Jesus' hour.

In the Johannine narrative and theological world, Jesus' power over evil is not localized in any single narrative event like an exorcism prior to the crucifixion in John. Jesus' language in the Farewell Discourse, in which he interprets the meaning of his death, resurrection, and ascension ("his hour") for his disciples, makes explicit this dimension of his death: "The ruler of the world is coming. He has no power over me" (14:30–31), and "I have overcome the world" (16:31).

Exorcisms are thus rendered superfluous in the Gospel of John. The conflict between good and evil is embedded in the more general topics and arguments about faith (e.g., 3:19–21), so that an exorcism narrative is not needed as a way of showing the Gospel readers the power and presence of evil in the world. Yet because the cosmic battle between good and evil in John will ultimately be resolved only in and through Jesus' hour, exorcism narratives would serve no narrative and rhetorical function.

All three of these examples suggest ways in which miracle discourse is embedded in the general rhetoric of the Gospel yet still retains distinct and recognizable elements. This is an important complement to the embedding of interpretive topics inside the more conventionally recognizable miracle discourse of the miracle stories. Attention to the varied forms and functions of miracle discourse provides a fresh perspective on the ways in which the words and works of Jesus cohere in the Gospel of John.

Miracle Discourse in the Pauline Epistles: The Role of Resurrection and Rhetoric

Duane F. Watson

The portrayal of Paul in the Acts of the Apostles demonstrates that he was remembered as a miracle worker. In that narrative, Paul is shown healing with a handkerchief (19:11–12), casting out demons (16:16–18), and raising the dead (20:7–12), thus aligning him with the apostles (5:12–16). However, that portrayal of Paul is not the concern here.[1] This essay focuses on the undisputed letters of Paul for self-reference as a miracle worker and for his understanding of the miraculous. It examines Paul's use of the miraculous in the narrative and argumentation of his letters.

1. Paul as a Miracle Worker

It is intriguing that Paul refers to himself as a miracle worker in his undisputed letters, but there are no references to Paul as a miracle worker in the disputed letters. Apparently the memory of Paul in the generation to follow did not include him as a miracle worker. Even Paul himself did not emphasize his ability to perform miracles, mainly only broaching the subject when he needed to defend his apostolic status. We will now examine his five references to miracles, as found in 2 Cor 12:11–12, Gal 3:1–5, Rom 15:17–19, 1 Thess 1:4–5, and 1 Cor 2:4–5.[2]

---

1. For a comparison of Paul as miracle worker in Acts and his own letters, see Stefan Schreiber, *Paulus als Wundertäter: Redaktionsgeschichtliche Untersuchungen zur Apostelgeschichte und den authentischen Paulusbriefen* (BZNW 79; Berlin: de Gruyter, 1996); Jacob Jervell, *The Unknown Paul: Essays on Luke-Acts and Early Christian History* (Minneapolis: Augsburg, 1984), 77–95.

2. See James A. Kelhoffer, *Miracle and Mission: The Authentication of Missionaries and Their Message in the Longer Ending of Mark* (WUNT 2/112; Tübingen: Mohr Sie-

In 2 Cor 12:11-12 the reference to miracles occurs within Paul's extended defense against the claims and accusations of rival apostles at Corinth (2 Cor 10-13).[3] It may be that the rival apostles were claiming that Paul was not a miracle worker, particularly because he had health problems that he could not heal (2 Cor 10:7-10).[4] Why can he not heal himself if he is a genuine miracle worker? The reference to miracles occurs within the portion of the defense based on spiritual manifestations (12:1-13). The rival apostles were boasting of their own visions and revelations of the Lord (v. 1). Paul bests them with his account of being caught up to paradise and hearing mysteries no mortal can repeat (vv. 2-7a), explaining his thorn in the flesh as a way for God to keep him humble in light of the vision and demonstrate how God's power is made perfect in weakness (vv. 7b-10). Paul concludes in verses 11-13 with "I have been a fool! You forced me to it. Indeed you should have been the ones commending me, for I am not at all inferior to these super-apostles, even though I am nothing. The signs of a true apostle were performed among you with utmost patience, signs and wonders and mighty works" (vv. 11-12).[5]

Here at the close of the "fool's speech," begun at 11:1, Paul mentions the signs of a true apostle in case he did not succeed in convincing the Corinthians that he was a genuine apostle. He points to evidence of his apostleship—signs, wonders, and mighty works—to create an argument from signs, a strong argument in the case of spiritual power. The same power of God that is made perfect through weakness (12:9) worked through Paul's weakness to perform miracles among the Corinthians.[6] He implies that these rival apostles could perform miracles, and he understands that miracles verify their apostolic status, and now points to his own performance of miracles to verify his same status. Having used the criterion of the ability to work miracles to conclude that Paul's rivals were authentic apostles,

---

beck, 2000), 271-79; idem, "Paul and Justin Martyr on the Miraculous: A Comparison of Appeals to Authority," *GRBS* 42 (2001): 163-75.

3. For an examination of the rhetoric of this section, see Duane F. Watson, "Paul and Boasting," in *Paul in the Greco-Roman World: A Handbook* (ed. J. Paul Sampley; Harrisburg, Pa.: Trinity Press International, 2003), 77-100.

4. Jervell, *Unknown Paul*, 93-94.

5. All biblical quotations are from the NRSV.

6. Jacob Jervell, "Der Schwache Christmatiker," in *Rechtfertigung: Festschrift für Ernst Käsemann zum 70 Geburtstag* (ed. J. Friedrich, W. Pöhlmann, and P. Stuhlmacker; Tübingen: Mohr Siebeck; Göttingen: Vandenhoeck & Ruprecht, 1976), 194-98.

the Corinthians should also evaluate Paul's performance of miracles and reach the same conclusion.

In Galatians 3:1–5, in his debate with those who sought to impose circumcision and observance of Jewish law, and his struggle with the Galatians who were heeding this different gospel, Paul writes,

> You foolish Galatians! Who has bewitched you? It was before your eyes that Jesus Christ was publicly exhibited as crucified. The only thing I want to learn from you is this: Did you receive the Spirit by doing the works of the law or by believing what you heard? Are you so foolish? Having started with the Spirit, are you now ending with the flesh? Did you experience so much for nothing?—if it really was for nothing. Well then, does God supply you with the Spirit and work miracles among you by your doing the works of the law, or by your believing what you heard?

At their initial conversion at the preaching of Paul, the Galatians received the Spirit (v. 2), and that same God-given Spirit worked miracles among them (v. 5). Thus it is the Spirit given by faith, not works of the law, that manifests the power of God first experienced at conversion. If these rhetorical questions are answered as Paul anticipates they should be, miracles become part of an inductive proof from experience that faith, not works, brings the Spirit and the power of God into the lives of believers.

In this letter-body closing of Romans in 15:17–19, Paul boasts of what Christ has done through him.

> In Christ Jesus, then, I have reason to boast of my work for God. For I will not venture to speak of anything except what Christ has accomplished through me to win obedience from the Gentiles, by word and deed, by the power of signs and wonders, by the power of the Spirit of God, so that from Jerusalem and as far around as Illyricum I have fully proclaimed the good news of Christ.

This kind of boasting is rhetorically acceptable in Judaism because the focus is on what Christ had done through Paul, and in essence is confession and doxology. It is also acceptable in Greco-Roman culture because power is attributed to someone other than the boaster.[7] Miracles are used here as worship and understood as part of the power of the Spirit of God that enabled Paul to bring the gospel to the Gentiles. Miracles accompa-

---

7. Watson, "Paul and Boasting," 77–81, 95–96.

nied his preaching, and Paul's reference to them gives further credence to his request for the Romans to support his planned missionary venture to Gentiles in Spain (15:28–29).

Besides the three places above where Paul explicitly refers to himself as a performer of miracles, on two occasions he alludes to the fact that miracles accompanied his preaching. In 1 Thess 1:4–5 Paul states, "For we know, brothers and sisters beloved by God, that he has chosen you, because our message of the gospel came to you not in word only, but also in power and in the Holy Spirit and with full conviction; just as you know what kind of persons we proved to be among you for your sake." I am assuming that the three terms of "power, Holy Spirit, and full conviction" in successive *en* phrases are not separate parallel terms but rather are arranged so that the last two are in apposition to the first, giving the source and effect of the power: the gospel came in power from its source, the Holy Spirit, with the effect of full conviction on the part of the Thessalonians.[8] Also, "in power" (*en dynamei*) most likely refers to miracles (cf. Rom 15:19).[9] Paul points to the miracles enabled by the Holy Spirit that accompanied his preaching and lead the Thessalonians to accept the gospel with full conviction as a proof that they were chosen by God.

In 1 Cor 2:4–5 Paul contrasts his proclamation, which was accompanied by demonstration of power, with the proclamation of others, which were based solely on human wisdom. "My speech and my proclamation were not with plausible words of wisdom, but with a demonstration of the Spirit and of power, so that your faith might rest, not on human wisdom but on the power of God." Paul recognizes that he was not as skilled an orator as other preachers at Corinth, so he turns to miracles to build his authority, considering their manifestation to be superior to eloquent words based on standard topoi and presentation alone.

In summary, Paul refers to his performance of miracles in proportion to his need to defend himself (2 Cor 12:11–12) and his gospel (Gal 1:1–5).[10] He also refers to such performance to legitimate his Gentile mission (Rom

---

8. Earl J. Richard, *First and Second Thessalonians* (SP 11; Collegeville, Minn.: Liturgical Press, 1995), 48, 64–65.

9. Jervell, *Unknown Paul*, 92–93; Kelhoffer, *Miracle and Mission*, 271–72; idem, "Paul and Justin Martyr on the Miraculous," 171. *Contra* Richard, *First and Second Thessalonians*, 64; Schreiber, *Paulus als Wundertäter*, 257–66.

10. Kelhoffer, *Miracle and Mission*, 275–76; idem, "Paul and Justin Martyr on the Miraculous," 170.

15:17–19). When he indirectly refers to his miracles, he assumes that the recipients of his letters know that miracles accompanied his preaching (1 Thess 1:4–5; 1 Cor 2:4–5).

We have to ask how effective Paul is in his argumentation when he refers to his ability to perform miracles as a way to affirm his status as an apostle. It is interesting that he gives his miracles such an important role in supporting the authenticity of his apostleship, since he assumes that rival apostles were also performing miracles. To compound the problem, in his discussion of spiritual gifts in 1 Cor 12:4–11, 27–30, the only other place that Paul mentions others performing miracles, he acknowledges that others besides apostles in fact did perform miracles. How can Paul use his demonstration of miracles to authenticate his apostleship when he recognizes that rival apostles and nonapostles also perform miracles? James Kelhoffer concludes that Paul's recognition of miracles performed by others makes his appeal to miracle a "moot point."[11]

But is Paul such an incompetent rhetor? This negative assessment fails to realize that miracles accompany Paul's forceful proclamation of the gospel as an apostle (Rom 15:17–19; 1 Thess 1:4–5; 1 Cor 2:4–5; Gal 3:1–5).[12] "Though Paul seldom and only on occasion speaks of his miraculous activity, he still states clearly that miracles occur *wherever* he preaches the gospel. This is in itself self-evident, because miraculous deeds were a part of his proclamation of the gospel, and for Paul, proclamation is inconceivable apart from deeds of power."[13] It is this combination of forceful proclamation and the working of miracles whenever he preached that distinguishes Paul the apostle from others that perform miracles.

2. Paul and Miracle Discourse

Paul never refers to any of the miracles of Jesus or give any account of the miracles performed by Jesus, himself, or anyone else. We can speculate that part of the reason for this is that references to miracles would be rhetorically effective in the initial proclamation of the gospel, but not in letters where Paul addresses specific exigencies. In the initial proclamation of the gospel, miracles would provide signs for proofs of the nature of Jesus and

---

11. Kelhoffer, "Paul and Justin Martyr on the Miraculous," 174; cf. idem, *Miracle and Mission*, 278–79.
12. Jervell, *Unknown Paul*, 91–94.
13. Ibid., 91.

the truth of his claims (Quint. *Inst.* 5.10.12–15).[14] However, once the audience was convinced of the nature of Jesus and were committed believers, miracles would not address their particular theological and ethical issues with the same efficacy. For example, an account of Jesus' healing of a leper does not address Corinthian immorality.

Paul also may not refer to the miracles of Jesus because, while Jesus used miracles to announce the coming of the kingdom, it was the resurrection that ultimately proved the truth of his proclamation of the kingdom. In Paul's theology, the main manifestation of the supernatural is the resurrection of Jesus Christ. The resurrection is a large part of Paul's ideology and an assumed premise in much of his argumentation, based on his experience of the resurrected Christ (1 Cor 15:3–9; 9:1; Gal 1:11–12). Specific miracles pale in comparison to the resurrection itself.

Another part of the reason Paul does not refer to the miracles of Jesus is that he utilizes the rhetoric of his day, and the miraculous did not play a strong role in Greco-Roman rhetoric. It mainly appears in the rhetorical handbooks under the rubric of prophecies, supernatural oracles, and answers from divination used in proof, typically proofs from example (Cic., *Part. or.* 2.6; Quint., *Inst.* 5.11.42; cf. *Rhet. Alex.* 1.1422a.25ff.). The handbooks indicate that it was conventional to use oracles in argumentation, but not full accounts of miracles. Cicero's discussion of evidence in proof is illustrative: "Divine evidence is for instance oracles, auspices, prophecies, the answers of priests and augurs and diviners." (*Part. or.* 2.6).[15] The handbooks also assume that even the use of such oracles is uncommon. In his discussion of external judgments used in proof, Quintilian says, "Some include under this head the supernatural authority that is derived from oracles.... Such authority is rare, but may prove useful" (*Inst.* 5.11.42).

When these oracles are used in argumentation, their natural form is a *chreia*, "a saying or act that is well-aimed or apt, expressed concisely, attributed to a person, and regarded as useful for living."[16] It is interesting

---

14. For full discussion of signs in argumentation, see *Rhet. Alex.* 12; Quint. *Inst.* 5.9.1–16. Heinrich Lausberg, *Handbuch der literarischen Rhetorik. Eine Grundlegung der Literaturwissenschaft* (2nd ed.; 2 vols.; Amsterdam: Hakkert, 1963), 1:195–97, §§358–65; Josef Martin, *Antike Rhetorik: Technik und Methode* (Handbuch der Altertumswissenschaft 2.3; Münich: Beck, 1974), 106–7.

15. All quotations of the rhetorical handbooks are from the LCL editions.

16. Vernon K. Robbins, "The Chreia," in *Greco-Roman Literature and the New Testament* (ed. David E. Aune; SBLSBS 21; Atlanta: Scholars Press, 1988), 2. For full

that a perusal of the index of the major source book of *chreiai*, under the rubrics of "oracle" and "prophecy," one discovers only five oracles found in the form of *chreiai*.[17] Three are from the Delphic Oracle, where one is cited and the other two are summarized.[18] Two others are from an unnamed seer whose oracles are cited.[19] Thus supernatural oracles were neither frequently used nor frequently found as *chreiai*, their most natural rhetorical form.

While supernatural oracles and the *chreiai* were conventional literary forms or subjects for elaboration in the *progymnasmata* (classroom exercises used to train future rhetoricians), larger miracle accounts were not.[20] Unlike supernatural oracles that could be a *chreai*, miracle accounts were not part of the Greco-Roman rhetor's standard arsenal. If we seldom see supernatural oracles as *chreiai* employed in rhetorical argumentation, we do not expect to ever see full accounts of a miracle.

As a skilled rhetorician, Paul does not utilize either the sayings and miraculous deeds of Jesus in *chreiai* form or full miracle accounts in his argumentation. The closest he comes to citing supernatural oracles is using Old Testament messianic prophecies in argumentation, assuming a divine plan of salvation that anticipates the messianic age whose arrival he is proclaiming.[21] Quite the opposite is true in regard to the writers of the Gospels, for they use a plethora of *chreiai* relating the words and deeds (obviously including miracles) of Jesus as central to the argumentation of the Gospels. These are elaborated in different formats as taught in the *progymnasmata*.[22] This was appropriate for the purpose of the Gospels to

---

discussion, see Ronald F. Hock and E. N. O'Neil, trans. and eds., *The Chreai in Ancient Rhetoric: Volume 1: The Progymnasmata* (Texts and Translations 27; GRRS 9; Atlanta: Scholars Press, 1986), 26.

17. Vernon K. Robbins, *Ancient Quotes and Anecdotes: From Crib to Crypt* (Sonoma, Calif.: Polebridge, 1989).

18. Ibid., cited in n. 903 and summarized in n. 4 and n. 464.

19. Ibid., n. 957 and n. 961a.

20. A point well made by Wendy J. Cotter, *Miracles in Greco-Roman Antiquity: A Sourcebook for the Study of New Testament Miracles Stories* (New York: Routledge, 1999), 1. For the use of *chreiai* in the progymnasmata, see Ronald F. Hock and Edward N. O'Neil, trans. and eds., *The Chreia and Ancient Rhetoric: Classroom Exercises* (SBLWGRW 2; Atlanta: Scholars Press, 2002).

21. For more details, see Christopher D. Stanley, *Arguing with Scripture: The Rhetoric of Quotations in the Letters of Paul* (New York: T&T Clark, 2004).

22. For a discussion of the chreia and its use, especially in the Gospels, see Duane

proclaim and evangelize. Miracle accounts are to be expected in the Gospels, literature emphasizing the nature and purpose of Jesus and aimed at eliciting a faith response.

Other than his references to his performance of miracles, Paul does not utilize miracle discourse in argumentation. Reference to miracles did not help him address theological and ethical issues, nor were miracle accounts a formal part of a Greco-Roman rhetor's training and arsenal or commonly experienced in public rhetoric. While supernatural oracles were included in rhetorical instruction, their use was limited in practice. While supernatural oracles were used as *chreiai* and these are elaborated in the Gospels for proclamation, their use was not as effective for Paul in addressing contextual issues beyond citation of Old Testament prophets. Paul's lack of use of miracle discourse is natural for one working to be rhetorically effective in specific rhetorical contexts.

F. Watson, "Chreia/Aphorism," in *The Dictionary of Jesus and the Gospels* (ed. Joel B Green, Scot McKnight, and I. Howard Marshall; Downers Grove, Ill.: InterVarsity Press, 1992), 104–6.

Toward a Sociorhetorical Taxonomy of Divine Intervention: Miracle Discourse in the Revelation to John[*]

David A. deSilva

1. Introduction

My primary goal for this essay is to identify how and where John invokes the "themes, topics, reasonings and argumentations"[1] constitutive of miracle discourse in Revelation, and to analyze the rhetorical use to which he puts them. A secondary task, however, is to test Vernon Robbins's definitions and delineations of a number of the six rhetorolects in light of the analysis of Revelation and the streams of discourse that therein converge. This dual focus will provide, I hope, something of a safeguard against the criticism that the rhetorolects themselves are subjective and arbitrary categories, subjecting them to scrutiny and thus the possibility both of correction and confirmation as useful categories for the rhetorical analysis of New Testament texts.

This second focus only emerges at all here because, by Dr. Robbins's definitions of the rhetorolects, there is little if any "miracle discourse" in Revelation, the book that gives perhaps the most space and attention of all New Testament texts to dramatic divine intervention in the affairs of this world. This analysis of Revelation, then, also seeks to understand more

---

[*] Reprinted here with slight revision and format changes from "Toward a Socio-Rhetorical Taxonomy of Divine Intervention: Miracle Discourse in the Revelation to John," in *Fabrics of Discourse: Essays in Honor of Vernon K. Robbins* (ed. D. B. Gowler, L. G. Bloomquist, and D. F. Watson; Harrisburg, Pa.: Trinity Press International, 2003), 303–13.

1. Vernon K. Robbins, "The Dialectical Nature of Early Christian Discourse," *Scriptura* 59 (1996): 353–62 (356).

precisely where the boundaries between miracle discourse and apocalyptic discourse, and between miracle discourse and prophetic discourse, appear. If it is miracle discourse for Jesus to cast out a demon, does John also invoke miracle discourse when an angel casts Satan bound into the abyss? If it is miracle discourse for Jesus to still a storm, is it still miracle discourse when God causes no winds to blow on the earth while God's servants are sealed on the forehead? If so, how has John transformed miracle discourse near the end of the first century? If not, what kinds of topics and overall discourse is John invoking as God breaks in on the world in marvelous and unusual ways throughout Revelation? Hopefully, this paper will make a small, positive contribution to sociorhetorical analysis by answering questions such as these along the way.

2. Miracle Discourse: Drawing the Boundaries

In the essay that introduced the term *rhetorolect* to the English language, Robbins provided his initial discussion of each of the six modes of discourse he has identified within early Christian discourse. He identifies the basic premise behind miracle discourse as the conviction that "God responds to humans in contexts of danger or disease and that Jesus is the mediator of these benefits to humans."[2] A corollary is that "all things are possible for God," but that certain conditions must be met in order for God to intervene, such as prayer, trust, anointing with oil, confession of sins, and the like. Miracle discourse is distinguished from wisdom discourse (which stresses God's beneficence in general to all humankind) first in the particularity of the intervention envisioned and second in the attention to the conditions under which God provides special benefits.[3] A very important observation closes this discussion: "There is no significant social conflict in this discourse. In the context of the burdens of life, people turn to leaders who intercede to God for special help."[4] I highlight this specifically because of the context of high social conflict in which Revelation was written, and which John envisages escalating as people respond positively to his message.[5] A setting of social conflict may explain many

---

2. Robbins, "Dialectical Nature," 358.
3. Ibid., 358–59.
4. Ibid., 359.
5. See David A. deSilva, "The Revelation to John: A Case Study in Apocalyptic Propaganda and the Maintenance of Sectarian Identity," *SA* 53 (1992): 375–95; idem,

occasions in which a topic that could potentially invoke miracle discourse actually invokes prophetic or apocalyptic discourse, both of which are more at home in settings of social conflict.

In an unpublished paper prepared for the editorial board of the Rhetoric of Religious Antiquity series, Robbins speaks of miracle discourse as

> a rehearsal of unusual and dramatic displays of God's power to restore life and health, furnish food, or remove personal crisis. In this discourse, Jesus and holy spirit function as agents of God's power in various contexts in God's created world. The goal of the discourse is to increase the intensity of adherence to belief in God's power as so great that it can, under the right conditions, function unusually and dramatically in the human realm.[6]

Miracle discourse appears in the Epistles and the Apocalypse "as part of God's general work of redemption, which exhibits itself most dramatically in resurrection."

Wendy Cotter has helpfully gathered together Jewish, Greco-Roman, and early Christian stories about the timely intervention of the divine to meet human needs, or the unusual display of supernatural power over the elements of nature and the spirits that deceive or torment humankind.[7] By setting the New Testament stories within the larger literary environment of stories about the "miraculous," she has provided readers with a clear sense of what first-century people would have recognized and understood as "miracle discourse." Alongside stories about healings, in which a divinity directly or through an intermediary brings relief from some distressing condition, and exorcisms, Cotter chooses to include stories about control of nature and manipulation and transmutation of the elements.

Of all the material that Cotter has collected, it is only such stories as walking on water, or other such displays of superhuman power over the elements, that might not fit within Robbins's definitions of "miracle discourse." Walking on water does not manifest God's beneficence reaching out to

---

"The Construction and Social Function of a Counter-Cosmos in the Revelation of John," *Forum* 9.1–2 (1993): 47–61.

6. Vernon K. Robbins, "The Invention of Early Christian Paideia: Sociorhetorical Interpretation of the New Testament" (paper presented at the Society of Biblical Literature Annual Meeting, Nashville, Tennessee, November 17, 2000).

7. Wendy J. Cotter, *Miracles in Greco-Roman Antiquity: A Sourcebook for the Study of New Testament Miracle Stories* (London: Routledge, 1999).

relieve some specific human need. The expanded story of Jesus and Peter walking on the water (Matt 14:22–33) could be identified as an instance of miracle discourse being taken over by "cosmic" or "precreation discourse," since the story aligns well with the principle goal of precreation discourse, namely, "to heighten the Christological reasoning in the other discourses."[8] The present conclusion of the story in Matt 14:33 ("those in the boat worshiped him, saying, 'Truly you are the Son of God'") overshadows a conclusion more natural to miracle discourse, namely, the emphasis on "faith" as the precondition for doing the impossible (Matt 14:31). This is the same condition that, being present, would allow the disciple to pluck up a mountain and cast it into the sea (Mark 11:22–24). Because this illustration serves to foster an environment in which readers expect prayers to be answered by God (Mark 11:24), this hypothetical "nature miracle" could be considered to invoke topics of miracle discourse.

That Robbins's definition of miracle discourse can include (mutatis mutandis for the non-Christian literature) most of the material in the collection by Cotter goes a long way toward demonstrating that he has correctly identified a kind of discourse that would have been recognized as distinctive by first-century authors and audiences, and that he has well captured the essence of that discourse in his preliminary discussions. These ancient audiences would have related to the realm of "miracle discourse" topics that suggested

> (1) the intrusion of the divine in the personal affairs of specific human beings, particularly beneficent intervention to relieve distress of some kind;
> (2) the conditions that tended to precede or accompany such intervention, such as prayer or trust on the part of the human recipient;
> (3) the work of a human intermediary in directing divine power toward human need.

As we work through Revelation with these topics in mind, we will attempt to discern where John allows the invocation of these topics to move fully into miracle discourse and to what rhetorical use he puts miracle discourse; how, where, and to what end John moves potential topics of miracle dis-

---

8. Robbins, "Dialectical Nature," 361.

course in other directions; and how Robbins's delineation of the discourses might need to be modified in order to accommodate the data of Revelation.

3. An Analysis of "Miraculous Interventions" in Revelation

John opens with topics of apocalyptic discourse (the chain of "revelation," including the topic of "narration of the future," the "angelic intermediary," and the visionary experience in Rev 1:1–3), but quickly moves to interweaving topics of cosmic discourse (the topic of God's eternity in 1:4, 8), suffering-death discourse as he introduces Jesus and praises his accomplishments (1:5–6; see also 5:6, 9–10, 12), and apocalyptic discourse as he introduces the future coming of God's Messiah and the sorrow of his enemies as he appears (1:7). John introduces himself with topics of suffering-death discourse in 1:8, thus identifying himself with the pattern of Jesus, a pattern toward which he will seek to draw all his congregations. The opening vision of Jesus in 1:9–20 invokes topics of apocalyptic discourse to serve the goals of cosmic discourse, namely, the heightening of christological reflection. Jesus is now the apocalyptic "Son of Man," vested with the glory and characteristics of God (the details of the vision of the "Ancient of Days" from Daniel 7 being used now to describe Jesus) and with the life of eternity.

The oracles to the seven churches invoke prophetic discourse, both insofar as they recall the prophetic form of "thus says the Lord" in the new formula "these are the words of him who...," and insofar as they enact the goals of prophetic discourse, namely, calling the "chosen people" to set their lives in order and to fall more closely in line with the expectations and standards of God so as to attain the promised blessings and avoid the threatened punishments.[9] Key to identifying prophetic discourse is the context of a speaker, whose point of view is identified with that of God, addressing a group of people who consider themselves to stand in a relationship with God.

Within these oracles are several promises of dramatic intervention. First, the glorified Christ himself promises to strike down the Nicolaitans,

---

9. See "Opposition Discourse" in ibid., 360. In "Invention of Early Christian Paideia," Robbins describes "prophetic discourse" as enacting "both a deliberative and judicial function as it focuses on God's confrontation of people with an imminent decision to enact righteousness in a context where certain people's actions are condemned as disobedient."

Jezebel, and her followers unless they repent (2:16, 21–23). This intervention is reminiscent of the cursing of the fig tree in the Synoptic tradition, and even more especially of the deaths of Ananias and Sapphira in Acts 5:1–11. However unusual or "miraculous" such intervention would be, however, the context would not allow it to be heard as an invocation of miracle discourse. Rather, like the cursing of the fig tree and the striking down of Ananias and Sapphira, it remains a topic of prophetic discourse—the enaction of the consequences of disobedience within the "chosen people." On the other hand, the oracles are replete with promises of blessing for obedience. There are also certain conditions that must be met in order for the addressees to attain the promised goods. Nevertheless, the emphasis on these conditions does not move the speech from prophetic discourse into miracle discourse, all the more as the promised blessings all pertain to the eschatological future, and not the conditions of this life.

John's vision of the throne of God, the worshiping hosts of heaven, and the Lamb's triumphant reception of the scroll does nothing to introduce topics of miracle discourse into Revelation. This scene does, however, establish a premise of great importance for understanding the majority of the dramatic intrusions of God's wonders in human history described in the remainder of the book. That premise belongs to "wisdom discourse," and is specifically the topic of God's generosity toward all.[10] According to Rev 4:11, God merits honor and worship on account of God's creation of all things. Honor and gratitude are due God as the universal patron of all things living, and this is specifically what the heavenly hosts and other creatures "in heaven, on earth, and under the earth" properly enact. This topic will emerge again fully in Rev 10:6 and 14:6–7, the latter being a summons to all creatures to enact a proper response of reverence toward the Creator. In Revelation, this topic of wisdom discourse feeds apocalyptic discourse and its judicial concerns, as the speakers are convicting the world of injustice, neglecting to honor their Benefactor as he deserves,[11] offering worship instead to "demons and idols of gold and silver and bronze and stone and wood" (9:20–21), to God's enemies, the dragon and the beast.

The judicial environment of Revelation is advanced by the cry of the martyrs in 6:9–11, from the midst of a chapter that, as a whole, employs

---

10. Robbins, "Dialectical Nature," 357–58, discussing Jas 1:5; Matt 5:44–45.

11. David A. deSilva, "Honor Discourse and the Rhetorical Strategy of the Apocalypse of John," *JSNT* 71 (1998): 79–110, especially 87–99; Robbins, "Dialectical Nature," 359.

topics of apocalyptic discourse. God's chosen ones—those who have committed themselves to persevere in their witness to Jesus and their obedience to God—are assaulted and killed by the inhabitants of the earth, and their blood cries out for vindication. The honor of God's servants has been trampled, and God's own honor assaulted in their persons. They therefore call on the just God to judge their cause, and indeed to judge God's own cause, against their enemies, and are in fact assured that God will judge their cause when the time is fulfilled. A little further on, John will introduce the topic of prayer rather directly (8:1–5), one of the well-known prerequisites for miraculous intervention. Still, however, John will not develop this topic in the direction of miracle discourse, but rather apocalyptic discourse. The result of prayer is the ongoing enaction of God's judgments on the earth in the seven trumpets.

This provides the all-important context for understanding how God's unusual and marvelous interventions in Revelation are to be understood. John does not envision "the context of the burdens of life," under which "people turn to leaders who intercede with God for special help."[12] Rather, this is the context of God's judicial action against a world that has proven itself hostile to God's values, God's order, and God's servants. In this context, God's marvels will invoke the presuppositions and rationales of prophetic or apocalyptic discourse rather than those belonging to miracle discourse.

The impact of context on the hearers' or readers' perceptions of what realm of discourse the author invokes is especially apparent when one compares Revelation with one of its major sources, namely Exodus. Most of the trumpets and bowl plagues reconfigure the plagues that God sent on Egypt or other divine interventions surrounding the exodus event. An initial question of mine as I came to this paper was the following: Were God's plagues against Egypt and God's deliverance of the Hebrews at the Red Sea invocations of miracle discourse? If so, do the corresponding plagues and acts of deliverance in Revelation, drawn from Exodus, also invoke miracle discourse? The acts of God surrounding the exodus would seem to fit within miracle discourse. The majority of them came to pass through the agency of human miracle workers acting on God's behalf—namely, Moses and Aaron. Many directly reveal God's concern to respond to human distress and need (e.g., providing water and food in the desert and parting the Red Sea). Even those that bring disaster, notably the plagues sent against the Egyptians,

---

12. Robbins, "Dialectical Nature," 359.

served the end of securing deliverance for an oppressed people by miraculous means.

A "miracle discourse" interpretation of these events is preserved in the Wisdom of Solomon's midrash on the exodus in Wisdom 11:1–19:22. Even though one of the major themes the author wishes to stress is God's punitive action against the ungodly "by the very things by which one sins" (11:16), he gives equal place to the other major theme of the Israelites' receiving "benefit in their need" by means of "the very things by which their enemies were punished" (11:5). The topics of God's beneficence (11:24), ability to do all things (e.g., 11:17–20; 12:18), and timely intervention to provide aid in the thick of the burdens of this life (19:22) are all invoked throughout this section.

Revelation, however, has changed the interpretive context and thus cultivated an environment in which potential miracle topics (or topics that would have signaled miracle discourse in Exodus and Wisdom of Solomon) actually advance prophetic and apocalyptic discourse. The plagues are manifestations of God's "wrath" (Rev 6:16–17; 15:1), God's just anger at the inhabitants of the earth that have despised God and victimized God's servants. The plagues do not serve the goal of bringing temporal benefit to God's people (healing, exorcising, or otherwise ameliorating their condition in this world), but of righting the wrongs that have been perpetrated against God's people and God's name through punitive action. The Song of Moses and Song of the Lamb in 15:3–4, together with the pronouncement of the angel in 16:5–6, serve as a commentary on the signs and marvels of Revelation:

> Great and amazing are your deeds, Lord God the Almighty! Just and true are your ways, King of the nations! Lord, who will not fear and glorify your name? For you alone are holy. All nations will come and worship before you, for your judgments have been revealed. (15:3–4)

> You are just, O Holy One, who are and were, for you have judged these things; because they shed the blood of saints and prophets, you have given them blood to drink. It is what they deserve!" And I heard the altar respond, "Yes, O Lord God, the Almighty, your judgments are true and just! (16:5–7)

The *thaumasta* do not create thaumaturgical discourse: they express the outworking of God's judicial processes that are central to the definition of apocalyptic discourse. Indeed, these *thaumasta erga* fail to evoke repentance and conversion, and even spur people on to more crimes against God (see 9:20–21; 16:9, 11). While in the Synoptic tradition, a display of power over nature, such as the stilling of a storm, could evoke "fear" and "reverence" (Mark 4:35–41), God's command over the elements and God's causing them to work in unusual and unnatural ways do not effect conversion, but confirm eternal destiny[13] and enact judgment. The movement of the cycles of seals and trumpets climaxing ultimately in 9:20–21, where people confirm their commitment to idolatry and to refusing the universal Benefactor the honor and service that is God's due, reinforces the conviction that signs, wonders, and plagues all serve apocalyptic discourse's transmutation of wisdom discourse (the punishment of those who refuse to respond to God's beneficence appropriately).

There are more marvels in Revelation, however, than simply the punitive judgments of God. Chapter 11 presents a complex interweaving of discourses in which the miraculous or marvelous plays a prominent role. The chapter opens with topics that clearly sound notes of prophetic discourse. The measuring of the temple with a rod (11:1–2) is a familiar topic from the Old Testament prophets (see Zech 2:1–5), and the two witnesses (themselves described with images taken directly from Zech 4:3–14) are explicitly given authority to "prophesy" to the people who have enjoyed a tradition of God's revelation, namely, the Jerusalemites (11:8), calling them to repent and fall in line with God's ways. These two witnesses work wonders reminiscent of those performed by Moses and Elijah in the course of their ministries. Elijah called down fire from heaven upon those who came to arrest him (2 Kgs 1:10, 12), and the witnesses shoot fire from their mouths at those who would harm them (Rev 11:5); Elijah caused rain to cease for three years (1 Kgs 17:1; Rev 11:6); Moses turned water into blood and struck the land with all manner of plague (Exodus, *passim*; Rev 11:6). Here at least we find the topic of the wonder-working agent of divine power. Still, these wonders do not move the passage into miracle discourse: their goal is the confirmation and enhancement of a prophetic ministry, designed to call the inhabitants of God's Holy City to repentance, not the relief of disease, need, or other circumstances of personal distress. If anything, these witnesses are said to afflict rather than ameliorate (11:10).

---

13. A contrast thus well phrased by my colleague Dr. Russell Morton.

At this point, John reintroduces suffering-death discourse, prominent in his descriptions of the Messiah (1:5-6; 5:6, 9-10, 12) and in his description of the conditions of faithful discipleship (1:9; 2:9-10, 13; 6:9-11; 7:13-17). The witnesses are put to death and made to lie unburied, the most feared disgrace in the ancient world (to judge from Sophocles's *Antigone*), in the streets of Jerusalem (11:7-10). Even the prophetic ministry charged with signs and wonders still comes to this end in John's vision, as does all faithful witness to God and the Lamb in this world.[14] A new miraculous intervention follows: on the fourth day, the two witnesses are revived by the "breath of life from God" and are summoned to heaven by a "loud voice," whence they are borne upon a cloud to the astonishment of their enemies (11:11-12). Again John introduces a potential topic of miracle discourse, namely, the revivification of corpses, something prominent in the miracle narratives of the four Gospels and Acts.

Absent, however, is any mention of the preconditions for miraculous intervention (e.g., prayer or belief), as well as the absence of a miracle-working agent. Indeed, the revivification (it is unclear whether to call it a resuscitation, a topic of miracle discourse, or resurrection, a topic of apocalyptic discourse) and assumption of the witnesses seems to be related more to their vindication in the sight of their adversaries, and thus a divine confirmation of their prophetic word, than an act of God to relieve human need. This "miracle" on the streets of the Holy City, then, is used by John to inculcate the conviction that God vindicates God's faithful and obedient witnesses. It merges, then, either into apocalyptic discourse, with its emphasis on "victory over death," or possibly suffering-death discourse, if we were to modify our understanding of its goals ever so slightly.[15] The

---

14. Revelation 10:1-11:13 is a sign, as a whole, of John's ongoing interest in weaving together prophetic discourse and suffering-death discourse with apocalyptic discourse, for this whole section otherwise interrupts the progression of the apocalyptic judgments signaled by the seven trumpets. Revelation 11:14 should more naturally follow 9:21, but has been postponed by John so as to make room for a section very heavily invested with prophetic discourse and suffering-death discourse, and to embed this section within the apocalyptic discourse.

15. This seems to be one of the murkier areas in the evolution of the discourses. "Death-resurrection" discourse received the sketchiest treatment of all in Robbins's initial article on the six modes of discourse (Robbins, "Dialectical Nature," 360) and later emerged as "suffering-death" discourse. The emphasis shifts from a focus on Jesus' story and the importance of proofs from Scripture to support that story, to the story of Jesus and his followers as they accept suffering, and even death out of obedience

result of this intervention is the successful conclusion of the witnesses' prophetic ministry. After a rather modest disaster befalls the city (compared to the disasters about to overtake Babylon, that is), the survivors "gave glory to the God of heaven" (11:13). Once again, a potential topic of miracle discourse is actualized only within the framework, and to achieve the goals, of other discourses.

The cosmic drama of Rev 12 includes a few topics of miracle discourse. These are the sustenance of the woman in a place prepared for her by God in the desert (Rev 12:6, 14), directly reminiscent of God's sustenance of his prophet Elijah during his flight from Jezebel (1 Kgs 19:1–8), and the deliverance of the woman from the flood unleashed by the dragon (Rev 12:15–16). Even though the element of divine intervention is muted in the second instance (it is the "earth" that helps the woman), both of these instances nurture a basic premise of miracle discourse, namely, that "God responds to humans in context of danger or disease."[16] Miracle discourse as Robbins defines it, however, is far from fully developed here: there is no attention given to the conditions under which God will intervene to bring timely help, and no emphasis on Jesus or any other figure as the mediator of these timely benefits. Still, this is the closest John comes to inviting miracle discourse into Revelation.

In Revelation 13, John introduces another worker of *sēmeia*, namely, the "beast that rose out of the earth" (13:11). Already the recovery of the first beast's mortal wound had been greeted with amazement (13:3), and now the second beast adds to the aura of the extraordinary by "making fire come down from heaven to earth in the sight of all" (13:13) and making the image of the first beast seem to come alive (13:15). The first is an obvious parody of the Elijah story, where a prophet makes fire come down from heaven to prove who is the true God (1 Kgs 18), here put to the service of "deceiving" the people of the earth regarding the divinity of the first beast. Rather than introduce miracle discourse, however, these

---

to God's purpose ("The Invention of Early Christian Paideia"). Since suffering-death discourse in the New Testament (as well as a fair amount of intertestamental Jewish literature and even Greco-Roman philosophical literature) really rests on the premise that God vindicates God's faithful ones (see, e.g., 2 Macc 7), perhaps this discourse could have finally emerged as "suffering-vindication" discourse. The alternative, of course, is to see suffering-death discourse as consistently merged with apocalyptic discourse, in which vindication of the righteous is a prominent topic.

16. Robbins, "Dialectical Nature," 358.

wonders are part of John's creation of a parody of prophetic discourse. A prophet encounters people who have received a tradition of salvation history—from the point of view of the *pax Romana*—and seeks to motivate them to "righteous action" vis-à-vis the imperial god so that they may participate in the benefits that attend that system and avoid the punishments that attend disloyalty or ingratitude. Revelation 13:11–18 is a parody of Rev 11:3–13, where the witnesses of the true God exercise their prophetic ministry.

The last group of potential topics of miracle discourse appears in Rev 20. In place of an exorcism story, we find an angel binding Satan, the archenemy—a topic of the cosmic struggle between God and Satan and thus an apocalyptic counterpart to the more mundane exorcism of miracle discourse. Revelation 20:4–5 returns to the topic of resurrection, and this should be understood along the same lines as Rev 11:11–12. Those who were faithful to God, and accepted suffering and death to enact that faithfulness, are vindicated by God and rewarded through participation in "the first resurrection." The context of eschatological events and final rewards and punishments distances this from the resuscitation stories of miracle discourse. Similar statements would have to be made regarding the resurrection and judgment scenes of Rev 20:12–13. At one point, however, John speaks of miraculous deliverance. As Satan and his armies advance on the servants of God encamped around the "beloved city," "fire came down from heaven and consumed" the adversaries (Rev 20:9). Again, this topic is drawn from 2 Kgs 1:10, 12, where God miraculously delivers Elijah twice from arrest at the same time that God confirms Elijah's prophetic authority. In this context, once again, the topic yields to apocalyptic discourse: the deliverance of the chosen ones is assumed, but the just and unending punishment of God's enemies receives explicit treatment (20:10).

One final detail might be thought to invoke miracle discourse, namely, the presence in the new Jerusalem of a tree whose leaves "are for the healing of the nations" (Rev 22:2). The generality of this statement (no specific disease is mentioned), the absence of any attention to the conditions under which God will perform a healing, and indeed the almost naturalistic tenor of the remedy suggest that this image belongs to the apocalyptic "righting" of all wrongs rather than the realm of miracle discourse. Indeed, it might be viewed as an invocation of a wisdom topic (the knowledge of plants and their [medicinal] properties being a component of wisdom in Wis 7:20) in an apocalyptic setting. The remedy is there in God's new creation, and the nations are invited to seek it out and apply it to themselves.

4. Conclusion

Using Robbins's definitions of the six modes of discourse, there really is no significant miracle discourse in Revelation. John gives very little attention to nurturing the expectation that God intervenes amid the "burdens of life" to relieve disease, distress, or other typical conditions relieved by miraculous interventions in the Gospels, Acts, or even the corpus of Greco-Roman and Jewish literature gathered by Cotter. The place where miracle discourse emerges most clearly is Rev 12, which seems, however, to tell the story of events prior to the time of John's writing rather than events yet to come. The hints of miracle discourse there, then, testify to God's interventions in the past story of God's people, not expectations of how God will act in the forthcoming future.

Instead, the divine interventions envisioned in Revelation are to be explained by the basic premises and goals of other modes of discourse, apocalyptic discourse being the most prominent, with prophetic and suffering-death discourse the other major resources. Why should there be so little miracle discourse in the book most concerned with God's interventions in the realm of humanity? John's concern is not the amelioration of life in the midst of hardship. Tribulation is the lot of faithful disciples, and all expectation of reversal and reward for faithfulness has been transferred to the life beyond the present world. From John's perspective on what is wrong with the universe, the stories that enact miracle discourse would seem to apply Band-aids where radical surgery is required. God is about to perform that radical surgery, pouring out judgment and punishments on all who have resisted God's unique claim to worship and who have mistreated or marginalized those who bore witness to that claim. Apocalyptic discourse thus dominates Revelation. The way to attain the benefits God desires to bestow on the faithful is the way of suffering and death, the way pioneered by the Lamb, exemplified by the two witnesses, and embraced by all true disciples who would keep their witness and obedience pure. Here, the importance of suffering-death discourse emerges. Finally, God's own people must purge themselves of all the defilements of collusion with God's enemies, whether among the seven churches or in the Holy City, and enact righteousness in the midst of a world that is hostile to God's righteousness. This secures the place of prophetic discourse in Revelation.

From the foregoing exploration of Revelation, we find that indeed not every "marvel," "wonder," or "divine intervention" would qualify as miracle discourse. Many "wonders" belong much more naturally within the realms of prophetic discourse or apocalyptic discourse, and would probably have been seen to invoke those realms of discourse by the first-century audiences since the goals of those wonders are consonant with the goals of prophetic and apocalyptic discourse. If "miracle discourse" were redefined, however, to include the display of God's power in and over creation, then we would be able to discuss much more energetically the interweaving of miracle discourse with prophetic and apocalyptic discourse. It is a matter of boundaries. The fact that Cotter has been able to amass such an amount of material that coincides with Robbins's definition of miracle discourse, and so little in the way of "nature miracle" or "marvelous display" without human need in view, tends to suggest that the boundaries of miracle discourse are already well drawn.

MIRACLE DISCOURSE IN THE NEW TESTAMENT: A RESPONSE

Wendy J. Cotter

In this important collection of essays, rhetorical and sociorhetorical studies have crossed a form-critical boundary set down by Rudolf Bultmann in his *History of the Synoptic Tradition*, where the miracle accounts belong to the narratives, myth, and legends, while the anecdotes or "apophthegms" belong to sayings that also include the parables and other "wisdom" *chreiai*.[1] For Bultmann, each division can be identified by its focus. For the miracle accounts, the focus is on the deeds of Jesus, while for the apophthegms and wisdom sayings, it is on his words of wisdom. In this volume, scholars known for their expertise in the analysis of wisdom sayings and the rhetorical function of their composition and cultural context turn to discuss the "discourse" ongoing in the miracle accounts. In this way, they prove that Martin Dibelius was right in saying that all the materials, narrative and sayings alike, support Christian teaching and clearly survived because their message was effective.[2]

The work of Vernon Robbins and Gregory Bloomquist should be discussed together since Bloomquist shows in his essay the degree to which his own work flows from that of Robbins. These two essays are notable for the manner in which they move from an objective analysis for scholars on this side of the time line to the interpretation available to the first audiences on the other side of the time line, the world of Greco-Roman antiquity. Robbins first identifies the kinds of rhetorolects he sees isolated or

---

1. Rudolf Bultmann, *History of the Synoptic Tradition* (trans. John Marsh; New York: Harper & Row, 1963).

2. Martin Dibelius, *From Tradition to Gospel* (trans. B. L. Woolf and M. Dibelius; New York: Scribner's, 1935), 287–301.

blended in miracle narratives, or summary statements of the Evangelist, or their interpretive inserts. The rhetorolects are identified as wisdom, prophetic, apocalyptic, priestly, precreation, and miracle, and their presence in various literary forms supplies a rich array of "discourse," whether direct speech is present or not. Then, in his illustrative examples, Robbins discusses the intended allusions that fill out the message of the material pertaining to the miraculous in the Synoptic material.

Robbins breaks new ground here, since the miracles and references to them have not received a "rhetorical" hearing. As both he and Bloomquist state, these are the beginning steps in hearing miracle discourse, although these analyses strike one as anything but preliminary and tentative. Rather, they show the intensive erudition and focus that produces insightful interpretation of the pre-Gospel and Gospel tradition.

In my view, there are, however, two difficulties with this approach that impede its use for analysis, and I respectfully offer them for consideration. The first is the classification of the elements in miracle accounts and its interpretation from only a Jewish background and perspective. Second is assigning meaning to the elements in a miracle account by appeal to the redaction by a later Evangelist with his own particular theological agenda and from the perspective of later theological reflection.

Let us look first at the limited classification of the elements of miracle accounts according to Jewish categories. The rhetorolect of "prophetic" is applied only to those miracle accounts where either a deliberate allusion to Elijah and Elisha appear, as in Luke 7:11–17 and the summary statement in Matt 12:15–19. However, surely "prophetic" as we use it relates to the challenge to society on the grounds of prejudice against those of lower class and status, as in Jesus' respectful treatment of Bartimaeus. That challenge goes unnamed, and yet "prophetic" is the effect of Jesus respectful words, "What is it I can do for you?" and his modest assignment of Bartimaeus's reception of sight to his faith. Robbins's categories do not make room for that "prophetic" character of Jesus, which is prominent in both the rhetology and rhetography of the miracle accounts. It is necessary to find a designation for that message of Jesus which would have been familiar to the listeners who had never heard the Old Testament prophets read and did not know what the prophets had done.

The rhetorolect of "apocalyptic" is the classification presumed for all the material that deals with the presence and exorcism of demons. As Robbins states, "The perception in early Christian tradition that all demons are negative appears to be the result of the conceptual domain of Jewish apocalyptic literature and discourse,"[3] and again,

> This early Christian perception of demons as equivalent to unclean spirits has a close relation to the reasoning in passages in apocalyptic literature like 1 Enoch 8:2; 15:6–12; and Jubilees 5:2–3, 10; 7:20–21; 10:5, 8; 11:4; 50:5. It appears that most stories in the Synoptic Gospels that refer to demons and unclean spirits do so as a result of the conceptual domain of apocalyptic rhetorolect in the background.[4]

Only if demon possession and expulsions were unknown to the Greco-Roman world and located solely in Jewish apocalyptic documents could this classification hold. However, exorcisms were well known in the first-century Mediterranean world, a world that did not feature an apocalyptic cosmology. This is true for Jews as well. In Josephus's recounting of David's "exorcising" the tormented King Saul (*Ant.* 6.166–69), he writes that Saul "had no other physician than David." Josephus considers exorcism as a kind of healing for *this* life. Then he offers the contemporary example of Eliezer who exorcised men in the presence of Vespasian, his sons, tribunes, and a number of soldiers (*Ant.* 8.46–49). This story, written in a text that was supposedly directed to a non-Jewish audience, presumes that it is familiar with exorcism and understood it as an act of power. Again, exorcism is seen as a restoration for *this* life. Exorcism then calls for a rhetorolect not limited to "apocalyptic" and fits the ideas accessible in the larger world.

The rhetorolect of "priestly" is used to classify the healing of the leper account (Mark 1:40–45 || Matt 8:1–4 || Luke 5:12–16), primarily due to the man's prostration before Jesus as one would before a priest. Actually in Mark this element is a disputed reading, although independent redaction by Matthew, so that that man prostrates himself (most petitioners prostrate themselves before Jesus) and by Luke, so that the man falls on his face, show that the Evangelists' desired the man to demonstrate reverence for Jesus. However, prostration before Jesus does not indicate that he is a priest. In the account Jesus will send the man to the priests to be examined. If he were a priest, he himself could have told the man to go and join society. The accounts do not encourage us to conclude that Jesus is a

---

3. P. 34 above.
4. P. 34 above.

priest. Once a story like this is placed against a backdrop of other stories of petition where people asking a favor go down on their knees, the listener does not conclude that this person must be a priest but that the person has power to do something about the matter at hand.

So the prophetic, apocalyptic, and priestly rhetorolects seem confined and forced, and need to be broadened to accommodate elements of social challenge and redemptive authority that are part of the wider Mediterranean context. Also, one cannot help but notice that none of the presentations of miracle accounts discuss allusions to and associations with the wider Greco-Roman world, as though the narrators and their audiences could be presumed to be Jewish, and a Jewish audience that would only make allusions and associations with the Hebrew Scriptures and/or the intertestamental writings they knew.

Along with the singular appeal to Jewish material alone, the study seems to press the miracle accounts for affirmation that the miraculous power of Jesus is the expression of God's power in him. Jewish accounts of the prophets certainly do make sure that it is clear that God is the one who actually performs the miracle. Luke 7:11–17 is one such case, where the praise of God is given. However, the Jesus miracles do not feature him praying before he performs the miracles (except in the case of the miraculous loaves and fishes). Rather, the petitioner appeals to Jesus, and Jesus is shown to be the one who performs the miracle. We note that the narrators do not, as Luke does above, have the recipient praise God. Jesus usually tells the person that they can depart, and they do. This is to accept the miracle accounts as they are, that is, not Jewish in their lack of interest in directing the listener to the God who gave Jesus the power. The theme of directing the listener to God does not seem to be as important a point in the miracle accounts as it is to Robbins.

Also, Robbins emphasizes that faith is not usually explicitly mentioned in miracle accounts, but mention of faith is also not as important a point in the miracle accounts as it is for Robbins. Surely there are exceptions, for Jesus tells Bartimaeus that his faith saved him, and he remonstrates his disciples in the account of the stilling of the storm because they lacked faith. However, as Held showed long ago, it is Matthew who will redact the miracles accounts to bring out the theme of faith.[5] This is probably

---

5. Heinz Joachim Held, "Matthew as Interpreter of the Miracle Stories," in *Tradition and Interpretation in Matthew* (ed. G. Bornkamm, G. Barth, and H. J. Held; trans. Percy Scott; Philadelphia: Westminster, 1963), 178–81.

because, even as Robbins observes, it is obvious that the person has come with this determination, this confidence, this faith in Jesus to care and to rescue. Yet Robbins's many observations that faith is not mentioned signifies it as a special search of his own, one that was invited not by the miracle accounts but by subsequent theological discussions about the relationship between faith and miracles.

In spite of these points of disagreement, Robbins's explorations open new doors, and his ongoing decoding of the rhetoric of the miracle accounts continues to bring riches to the guild.

L. Gregory Bloomquist also employs rhetorolects in his discussion of the argumentation present in the miracle discourse of Luke-Acts, but he divides the miracle rhetorolect into "thaumaturgical discourse"—that is, the communication that derives from acts of power that have no expectation of associated rituals—and "gnostic-manipulationist discourse"—a communication derived from deeds of power that depend on step-by-step rituals, such as magical rituals. When the miracle accounts of Luke-Acts are classified by these two discourse categories, Bloomquist shows that the miracles of Jesus and his apostles are predominantly thaumaturgical discourse. The argumentation created is that the power of God is supreme over all manifestations of gnostic manipulations. In fact, as Bloomquist concludes, "Gnostic-manipulationist miracle discourse is thus used as a foil that enables thaumaturgical miracle discourse concerning Jesus to bring existing cultural logic into real question."[6]

This effort to categorize the miracle discourse by the way the power is generated, so to speak, is a fresh approach, and as Bloomquist notes, is in its initial development. I want to point out three things I think would bring greater clarity to the investigation. First, in trying to identify "magic" as gnostic-manipulationist, over against thaumaturgical, Bloomquist is setting up a distinction that would have been unknown to anyone in the Greco-Roman world, including the Christian narrators. All miracles, actions outside "the canons of the ordinary,"[7] were open to the label of "magic." Certainly all of Jesus' miracles were openly charged as magic by second-century men of letters, which only reflects the readiness of the culture to do the same. What we may say with confidence is that no writer of the New Testament collection presents any story where Jesus' miracle

---

6. P. 124 above.

7. Harold Remus, *Pagan-Christian Conflict over Miracle in the Second Century* (Cambridge: The Philadelphia Patristic Foundation, 1983), esp. 14–26.

is received with praises for his great magical power, or with cries of how great a magician he is. In Acts 8:9–24 Simon the Magician supposedly converts to the faith, and in Acts 19:19, the hearers of Paul's message who practiced magic burn their expensive books. Thus just by inference, and the total absence of the term *magic* for Jesus' miracles and those of the disciples, it is clear that in the circles represented by the writers and the subsequent communities of Christians all of Jesus' miracles were not magic, and not to be termed magic. Magic is clearly a negative label for any act that is outside the "canons of the ordinary." It is very difficult, then, to establish any criteria for magic.

Second, Bloomquist's analysis of individual miracle accounts is blurred, because, while he includes redaction the Evangelist added, he does not include the Evangelist's placement of the account in relation to other materials that clarify his meaning (Mark 1:23–28; Luke 5:1–11; 8:22–25, 26–39; Acts 3:1–10). As a result, Bloomquist attributes to the miracle accounts what belongs to the Evangelist's redaction, but does not allow the contextualization of the miracle account to inform its interpretation. Although his examples are meant to represent argumentation presented in the respective Gospels, by attributing to the miracle accounts what belongs to the Evangelist's redaction and ignoring the placement of the miracle accounts in the broader argumentation of the Gospel he truncates the discussion of argumentation. For example, in describing Mark 1:23–28, the exorcism in the synagogue, he identifies it as a thaumaturgic miracle with its own peculiar logic because verse 28 describes the exorcism as a teaching. However, that reference to teaching is a redactional addition of Mark to the pre-Markan exorcism account, which is shown by the fact that the Evangelist supplies an introduction in verses 21–22, where he contextualizes the event as Jesus' teaching in the synagogue where everyone was admiring his teaching. So Mark does not mean that the exorcism was what Jesus was teaching. Rather, he is trying to supplant the image of Jesus the exorcist with Jesus the teacher. So certainly Bloomquist is correct that verse 28 gives the impression that the exorcism is the teaching, but only if one fails to recognize that the pericope includes verses 21–22, and forgets that the theme of Jesus as teacher is found throughout Mark's Gospel.

Likewise, in the extensive discussion of Luke 5:1–11 and the great catch of fish, Bloomquist sets out a number of interpretations that conflict with the meaning the Evangelist has already supplied through the placement of the story. For example, Bloomquist understands Peter's acquiescence to Jesus' request to put out into the deep and cast the fishing nets out (v. 4) as "not so much a surrender as a response to Jesus that will, in Peter's mind, deprive Jesus of any further ground for challenge,"[8] and by so doing Peter hopes it will "restore his honor."[9] But Peter's respectful, if tired, agreement must be seen in its context in Luke's Gospel, in which Peter has just seen Jesus miraculously cure his mother-in-law of a fever. So the listener would suppose that Peter was respectful of him as a very holy man, not as one with whom he was engaged in an honor challenge.

Bloomquist also needs the Gospel context to answer his own questions about why Peter experiences fear at the huge catch of fish. For him, Peter tells Jesus to depart because he, Peter, is a sinful person, and because Jesus is so terrifying that Peter could fear harm. As Bloomquist states, "Terrifying events, or terror-inducing individuals, cause people to fear for their lives especially if they are at some risk—through guilt, through sin, through weakness, and so on."[10] It would help Bloomquist to notice that Jesus responds to Simon with the command, "Do not be afraid," which was used previously by the angel who appears to Zachariah (Luke 1:13) and to Mary (Luke 1:30). The listener is meant to understand the exchange between Peter and Jesus in this way: a traditionally human recognition of one's unholiness in the presence of one who is holy and from God.

Moreover, besides the psalms and Old Testament attributions of complete control over nature by God, the Greco-Roman examples of control of the sea boasted by Greco-Roman military leaders, which was well known to the first-century populace, would help fill out the scope of this miracle for Jew or Gentile. The obedience of nature's forces is their recognition of a human leader's divine empowerment to rule the earth. In the Lukan account, nature's forces obeyed Jesus immediately. Peter's fear is also a testimony that he is completely certain that Jesus is empowered by God and has been given authority over nature's forces. Actually, all the miracles of the Lukan Gospel are explained as soon as Jesus begins his public life, for in Luke 4:16–30, when Jesus visits the synagogue of his hometown, he opens the scroll and reads from Isaiah 61, "The Spirit of the Lord is upon me, because he has anointed me."

In Acts 3:1–10, the listener does not have to wonder why the man is healed, since, as Charles H. Talbert shows, the author of that book has

---

8. P. 111 above.
9. P. 117 above.
10. P. 113 above.

taken pains to show how the apostle's miracles repeat those of Jesus,[11] and in fact Peter tells the man that the healing is done "in the name of Jesus" (v. 6). Moreover, just as Jesus is anointed by the Holy Spirit and performs miracles, so too the apostles receive the Holy Spirit promised by Jesus (Acts 2:1–4), and this parallel action of healing is already expected by the listener. So if the task is to represent what the miracle account communicates for a Gospel, any redaction of the account by the Evangelist and his placement of the account in his Gospel needs to be considered.

Finally, Bloomquist would have the answers to some questions that he raises if he would note the kind of miracle under examination. For example, he asks why the reaction of the formerly lame man in Acts 3 is one of joy, while the reaction of Peter to the abundant haul of fish is one of fear. A healing is a restoration of health and not something unknown or uncommon in the first century. That is, while other healers were known, the command of Jesus over the sea is not at all common, and neither is the demand that nature's forces respond instantly. The uncommon nature of such a miracle explains the disciples' fear and awe when Jesus stops a sea storm. Their question explains it all, "Who then is this, that he commands even the winds and the water, and they obey him?" (Mark 4:41). The fear of the Gerasenes is another example. Luke 8:29 emphasizes how the people had tried to control the demon, and without any success, but the demons leave instantly when Jesus gives the command. Jesus' power scares them.

Bloomquist is certainly right that argumentation is taking place in miracle accounts and his work in developing scholarly ways to objectively identify the elements of that argumentation are very important to furthering the analysis of miracle accounts. I suggest that adding the context of the miracle accounts in their respective Gospels to these investigations will help to clarify the character and method of that argumentation.

Todd Penner gives a masterful analysis of the propaganda value of miracle accounts in the Acts of the Apostles. Beginning with the evidence of the political use of Vespasian's miracle as proof of Heaven's choice of him for emperor, Penner shows how this same value has not been granted to the miracles in Acts. He notes the scholarly isolation of Acts from the world to which it speaks through selective contextualization of the material with exclusively Jewish sources or other Christian texts. He also notes that

---

11. Charles H. Talbert, *Literary Patterns, Theological Themes, and the Genre of Luke-Acts* (Missoula, Mont.: Scholars Press, 1975).

a theologizing and spiritualizing of the miracle accounts in Acts in such a way as to divorce them from the regular function of miracle accounts in the first century cannot hope to represent the author's intent. Penner sees the miracles in Acts as proof that Jesus' rule is endorsed by Heaven. To make his point, he endeavors to allow the miracles to stand on their own and allow the most familiar associations of the first century to be active in the interpretation. He tries to use the term *magic* as a neutral term for the particular act of power, but recognizes that it too has its own associations, and settles for the simpler term *power*. He is trying to view the act of the miracle in a nonprejudicial way, to evaluate the message it would convey to the ordinary listener.

As Penner understands them, miracles in Acts function to contend with the claims of Roman imperial propaganda. They confront imperial power and systems that justify their oppression by appeal to the manifestations of divine approval given to the emperors. He sees Acts triumphing over this imperial power. Jesus' power confronts these futile expressions of worldly aggression and wins. For example, although Peter and Paul are imprisoned, they are each miraculously freed. Jesus is preeminent over any authority, and the Holy Spirit has ultimate control over the world. Thus Acts uses the miracles to show Jesus as the true and reliable Lord and Savior of the world. Penner's attention to the way in which miracles associated with a leader, hero, and Lord are used in the first-century material change our reconstructions of what these miracles of Acts would have meant to the listeners, whether they agreed to the claim or not. Miracle accounts in Acts are not to be viewed as charming vignettes designed to entertain in a pious way, but as providing a series of proofs that Jesus is the locus of real power, the true Savior on whom everyone may rely.

To Penner's magnificent work I would add that the miracle stories also function to affirm a way of life and a perception of others that would have been challenging to that day. They endorse the idea that God treats all people from every class as his dear children, and thus divisions of any kind are unsupported. The social vision of the miracles calls the hearers to imitate the prejudice-free behavior of Jesus, and in turn his disciples. We notice that the first miracle after the coming of the Holy Spirit (2:1–4) is the cure of the lame man (3:1–10), already discussed in Bloomquist's essay. Like Jesus, the apostles grant a miracle to a person ordinarily "invisible" and unimportant. The raising to life of Dorcas by Peter (9:40) and Eutychus by Paul (20:9–12) both occur in a context of community. We can see that the ideals supported are those of group concern, unity, and the importance of each person. So the ideals of Christian community are supported positively there, not only in the miracle of life restoration, but also in the description of everyone's concern and love.

Community unity is defended as God-willed in the negative miracle of Ananias and Sapphira's being struck dead for duplicity when they seek to hide their wealth (5:1-11). The author of Acts has Peter address Ananias, "How is it that you have contrived this deed in your heart? You have not lied to people but to God" (v. 4), and to Sapphira he says, "How is it that you have agreed together to tempt the Spirit of the Lord? Hark, the feet of those that have buried your husband are at the door, and they will carry you out" (v. 9). The story of their death concludes, "And a great fear came upon the whole church, and upon all who heard of these things" (v. 11). This account brings out the idea that it is God who wills the community aspect of the church, and faithfulness to one's participation is to be seen as a kind of reverence to God.

Penner's essay already leads the way to uncover these other messages in the miracle accounts, and the size of the challenges posed to the ordinary person of that world. Christian miracle accounts, like the miracle accounts used by the power establishments of the Greco-Roman world, are powerful vehicles of propaganda.

Gail O'Day's analysis of the rhetoric embedded in the Johannine miracle accounts seems to flag something of a trajectory. While Bloomquist notes in his examination of miracles in Luke-Acts that most are open-ended "thaumaturgic" expressions of power and few are accompanied by explanations of the miracle, O'Day illustrates throughout her essay how the meaning of the miracle is deliberately provided over and over again in the narrative. The meaning is embedded not only in the miracle account itself but also in the references to it throughout the Gospel. In her close reading of the miracle of Cana, O'Day observes that there are no signs of a secondary addition of explanation to what Bloomquist would call a "thaumaturgic" miracle story, but rather meaning occurs in the very basic components: (1) the problem (and with it the focus on the importance of Jesus), (2) the action the hero takes (and with it the connection between this act and Jesus' final hour), and (3) the demonstration (which also attests the intrinsic goodness that Jesus' arrival on earth signifies to the community). O'Day includes examples of how these telling "signs" are integrated into the Gospel so that the clues in the miracle accounts act as portents of what is to come, just as the later references back to the miracle accounts secure the significance of Jesus' person and message. Her examination demonstrates a sophistication in the rhetorical use of miracle in John's Gospel that is not matched by any other text in the New Testament canon. As she shows, the miracle cannot be told without the listener's being alerted to major themes ahead in the Gospel, while the rest of the Gospel requires those "signs" as support. Yet here is the irony: while the Gospel needs the miracle accounts to give the first-century listener confidence in the power of Jesus, the Gospel claims that belief in Jesus on that account is unworthy. Jesus' testimony is the only reason for belief. The listener is told that complete surrender to Jesus' words and to his person will bring life and light.

O'Day addresses the lack of exorcisms in the Johannine Gospel as perhaps too superfluous given Jesus' mission against all darkness. I would suggest that they are too small for the cosmic grandeur of Jesus' stature as the Logos made flesh. Individual stories of demons in people, and the idea of groups of demons setting up household in people, do not fit in this cosmically grand Gospel. Rather, to balance the status of Jesus as the Logos, it is the force of Satan's darkness that Jesus will overthrow: "The Light shines in the darkness, and the darkness has not overcome it" (1:5).

O'Day has opened up the Johannine miracles in a new way, and her work invites more intensive examination of each "sign" for the manner in which it functions rhetorically, both as a unit and as it communicates with the rest of the Gospel.

Duane Watson's discussion of miracle in Paul's letters points to the difficulty encountered when one is dealing with the form of the true letter. With the exception of Romans, the rest of Paul's authentic letters address communities already founded by him and to whom he writes on a regular basis for purposes of exhortation and problem solving. Thus there is no need for Paul to repeat any miracle stories he might have used in the initial stages of preaching and teaching with the group. Rather, Paul makes the occasional allusion to an experience of God's power among the group as he makes this or that argument. Watson's investigation into the rhetorical function of these allusions confirms what Penner found true for Acts. For just as Acts uses miracles as propaganda to assert the preeminence of Jesus' power, so too Paul's references are meant to reassert his own authentic apostleship from God, and hence the legitimacy of his teaching and decisions.

Very interestingly, Watson includes in this investigation of "miracle" the resurrection of Jesus, and he is surely right! Suddenly we recognize that simply because form critics such as Bultmann and Dibelius assign the resurrection to the separate category of "myth" we have no grounds to eliminate it as "miracle" for the populace of the Mediterranean world of the first century. Watson's cultural sensibility caused him to deliberately transverse these scholarly categories. In my own sourcebook, I confined myself to the categories of miracle prepared by Bultmann and observed by the scholarly guild. Watson's inclusion of Jesus' resurrection as a persuasive miracle would be enhanced by Roman apotheosis texts and the propaganda that flowed from it. For Paul uses references to Jesus' resurrection and his own experience of that Jesus to ratify his own credibility, and the foundations of belief for the community. Also, Paul asks the communities he addresses to recall their own miraculous experiences. So although Paul does not narrate miracle accounts of the historical Jesus such as would be found later in the gospels, Watson illustrates that Paul's allusions to the major miracle of Jesus' resurrection and the communities' own experience of a miraculous visitation of God's Spirit affirm that the foundations of their community faith are solid, as is his own identity as an apostle and his authority to teach. Watson's examination of the rhetorical use of Jesus' resurrection in Paul is an exciting new way to discuss the use of miracle in his letters.

With regard to the book of Revelation, genre again is the reason one cannot expect miracle accounts. As David deSilva makes clear, the apocalyptic visions belong to an overall cosmic transformation where the "canons of the ordinary" are completely overturned so that which is regarded as "normal" is destroyed. A new kingdom with its own order begins with judgment and retributions on a cosmic scale. So just as individual exorcisms are too small for the large scope of John's Gospel, where Jesus as Light will overpower Darkness, so too all individual miracle accounts of a person's being healed or raised from the dead are too confined for the gigantic sweep of the Apocalypse, which wants to converse on a grand scale. Individual nature miracles such as those in the Gospels (e.g., stilling a storm, walking on the sea, and cursing a fig tree) seem pale in comparison to the entire sky breaking apart and the sea disappearing. It is for this reason that I do not think that the Jewish listener, or the convert now acquainted with the unusual cosmology presented in the apocalypse, would connect the forensic/prophetic pronouncements and predictions with miracle discourse. The interpretation of this text requires other apocalypses to create a context and a conversation with like elements of a genre that is quite odd in comparison with all other literary production in the Greco-Roman world. A second necessity would be a conversance with the contemporary events and their powerful protagonists in order to decode what has been seen as a genre meant to respond to persecution in a climate that forbids free speech. Little wonder that the inclusion of the book of Revelation into the New Testament canon was disputed, for it requires massive decoding and thus holds the danger of unorthodox interpretation.

DeSilva then turns to the exclusively Jewish rhetorolects of Robbins to help set up the possible contexts, and hence, functions, of the eschatological promises and predictions in Revelation. However, these rhetorolects, while helpful for the classification of the function of the discourse, still require room for categories that may be suggested by exposure to ideas spawned in the non-Jewish Greco-Roman culture. The constant exposure of Jewish Christians to the world cannot help but have influenced their expectations of God and the new kingdom ready to descend out of heaven.

In my miracle source book, I make the point that early Christian composers were free to create their accounts as they saw fit, mixing forms and combining allusions. They seem to have been subject only to the approval of the communities whose faith they were striving to communicate. This means that our scholarship has to be ready to cross form-critical lines. This is what the Rhetoric and New Testament section has done in this erudite collection of essays. In a series of independent approaches, these scholars have listened for the rhetorical function in the miracle accounts and miracle discourse. The results of their work prove them wise to have done so, because it is clear that miracle accounts were intended to do more than prove that Jesus had power to do this or that marvelous deed. The way the miraculous serves the presentation of Jesus, and the message of salvation he was believed to bring, is uncovered in a new way. These newly hewn paths now supply our guild with fresh access to the early church and to further investigation of the way miracle and the miraculous served its proclamation.

Miraculous Methodologies:
Critical Reflections on
"Ancient Miracle Discourse" Discourse

Davina C. Lopez*

1. Introduction: Wonder(ing) in the Woods

Deep in the German forest, sometime in the latter part of the second century C.E., the Roman army was blessed with a miracle that hastened a decisive victory for their embattled emperor, Marcus Aurelius, over the "savage" Quadii nation. According to the narrative of Dio's *Roman History* (72.8.4), it was hot, and way too dry, and the Romans were wounded, overheated, and exhausted by thirst due to their being hemmed in away from the water supply. For their part, the Quadii, who outnumbered the Romans, had surrounded the cavalry and had stopped fighting in anticipation of an easy conquest over their severely weakened opponents. And then, so the story goes, the unexpected happened: the clouds gathered quickly, the heavens opened, and it poured rain on the battlefield. The Romans drank, first directly from the sky, and then from their helmets, which they filled with rainwater. In fact, Dio relates, the soldiers were so parched that they drank their own blood along with the rain, and they were so consumed with drinking the rain that they would have been defeated by the Quadii had another miracle not occurred. A sudden, massive downpour of hail

---

*I am grateful to Duane F. Watson for a most generous invitation to contribute to this volume, as well as the rest of the contributors for providing stimulating material on which to reflect. An auspicious exchange with Craig Keener inspired me to consider more deeply some important issues at stake in modern studies of miracle discourse. And Todd Penner, a wonder-worker in his own right, deserves special credit for his enthusiastic engagement of my questions and concerns about methodologies and ethics in biblical scholarship.

and thunderbolts made it look like it was raining flames down onto the enemy hoards, and many caught ablaze and wounded themselves to put out the fire with their own blood. Never mind how it could be the case that the Quadii would need to do so, given how stormy it must have been outside—only the Romans' rain was wet, it seems. In the end, the would-be captors were slain, and Marcus Aurelius, who had mercy upon the burning barbarians, was hailed as imperator yet again. The wonder in the woods made Roman victory possible.

The "rain miracle" of Marcus Aurelius appears numerous times in ancient literature of diverse genres. The content of these narratives differs primarily in naming who is to take responsibility for the miracle, and to what end.[1] Dio, writing at least two decades after the battle in question supposedly took place, claims that an Egyptian magician named Arnuphis, himself a companion of the emperor, caused the downpour with the help of the god Mercury. Julian the Theurgist, also called "The Chaldean," is mentioned as the bringer of the rain in Neoplatonic writers such as Porphyry, as well as in the Byzantine *Suda*.[2] According to a "biography" of Marcus Aurelius in the *Historia Augusta*, it is the emperor himself, a merciful leader, who brought much-needed rain to his troops through his own prayers on behalf of his men (*MAA* 24). That this emperor is responsible for raining (water and) lightning down upon his opponents is also alluded to in book 12 of the *Sibylline Oracles*, where the Germans, Spaniards, Assyrians, and Thracians join the Jews as those who will be destroyed by his potent warrior-king hand (12.94–100).

Christian interpreters, on the other hand, insisted that their people should be given credit for the convenient wonder of the rain—Christian soldiers fighting for Rome who prayed on behalf of the empire, no less.

---

1. For a comparative approach to the primary and secondary literature on this particular miracle story, see H. Z. Rubin, "Weather Miracles under Marcus Aurelius," *Athenaeum* 57 (1979): 357–80; Garth Fowden, "Pagan Versions of the Rain Miracle of A.D. 172," *Historia: Zeitschrift für Alte Geschichte* 36.1 (1987): 83–95; Michael Sage, "Eusebius and the Rain Miracle: Some Observations," *Historia: Zeitschrift für Alte Geschichte* 36.1 (1987): 96–113; and Ido Israelowich, "The Rain Miracle of Marcus Aurelius: (Re-) Construction of Consensus," *Greece & Rome* 55.1 (2008): 83–102. For a fuller treatment, see Péter Kovács, *Marcus Aurelius' Rain Miracle and the Macromannic Wars* (Mnemosyne Biblioteca Classica Batava Supplementum/History and Archaeology of Classical Antiquity 308; Leiden: Brill, 2009). Kovács places especial emphasis on the question of divine responsibility for the rain miracle.

2. Fowden, "Pagan Versions," 90–93.

In his *Apology*, Tertullian states that he has read as much in the "letters of Marcus Aurelius," and embeds the rain miracle in a larger argument about the injustice and savagery of Roman persecution. In Tertullian's argument, even when an emperor's reputation on the battlefield is saved by the prayerful action of the people, and even when the Roman army is chock full of Christian soldiers, an emperor chooses to treat Christians poorly (5.6).[3] Eusebius largely repeats the accounts of Dio and Tertullian. In the *Ecclesiastical History* he mentions that both Christian and non-Christian writers knew that the Christians knelt and prayed in their customary way for the rain and thunderbolts to occur, but that only the Christian writers understood that the miracle was an answer to their supplication (5.1–7). Similarly, Xiphilinus, Dio's eleventh-century Byzantine epitomator, just a few lines later than what is thought to be Dio's own (fragmentary) account of the attribution of the rain miracle to Arnuphis, states that it was a legion of soldiers who held allegiance to the Christian faith, and not to Egyptian magic, who saved the day in that German forest.[4]

The miraculous event that supposedly saved the Romans from defeat by the northern barbarians enjoyed a long and varied history of literary appropriation in late antiquity and beyond, wherein the rain miracle was variously attributed to Egyptian, Chaldean, Roman, and Christian actors. It is striking that the story traveled so far over so long a period of time,

---

3. But see also Tertullian, *Ad Scapulam* 4, where he writes that the people "paid tribute to our [Christian] God under the name of Jupiter" after the rain miracle, thus suggesting a complexity of understanding.

4. Xiphilinus states: "This is what Dio says about the matter, but he is apparently in error, whether intentionally or otherwise; and yet I am inclined to believe his error was chiefly intentional. It surely must be so, for he was not ignorant of the division of soldiers that bore the special name of the 'Thundering' Legion—indeed he mentions it in the list along with the others—a title which was given it for no other reason (for no other is reported) than because of the incident that occurred in this very war. It was precisely this incident that saved the Romans on this occasion and brought destruction upon the barbarians, and not Arnuphis, the magician; for Marcus is not reported to have taken pleasure in the company of magicians or in witchcraft" (*Roman History* 78.8.5, LCL translation). Much of the scholarship on the rain miracle has dwelt on the "thundering legion" as an important element of the narrative. I would posit that the inclusion of this linkage in the Christian appropriations of this story is an argumentative device, a detail meant to (further) convince a Roman audience of Christian responsibility for the rain. Outside of this purpose, it is not central to the story.

with no consensus as to "what happened." Whatever else one might make of the stories of the rain miracle and its role in helping the army of Marcus Aurelius to win a battle against the Germans, one who is familiar with the range of approaches to ancient rhetoric outlined in this volume will observe the differences in the literary accounts of the event—not toward a goal of making sense of the "real" procedural sequence, but for emphasizing the diversity, distance, and distinctiveness of the narratives themselves, as well as what these narratives indicate about their authors and audiences.

2. Hermeneutical Interventions: Miracles, Now and Then

Each of the accounts mentioned above, of course, is as much about the rhetorical programs and aims of the authors and the audiences' perceptions of the event as it is about the event itself. Even as the rain miracle might be mentioned numerous times in ancient narratives of varying genres (history, biography, oracle, encyclopedia, apology, and so on), those narratives are not necessarily constructed so as to reconfigure a preexisting "miracle discourse" toward differing rhetorical ends. Read synoptically, the accounts and interpellations of Dio/Xiphilinus, Tertullian, Eusebius, and the author(s) of the *Historia Augusta* do not have to be read as betraying a particularly linear trajectory by which an emergent miracle discourse can be measured. Rather, each narrative deployment of the rain miracle can be seen as that which becomes its own story with its own complicated history and baggage, a story responding to a story, all the while attempting to persuade an audience as to "what happened," with all the attendant social implications entailed therein.

Indeed, the primary point these narratives have in common—discussion of who is to take responsibility for the rain miracle—is at the same time the primary point of divergence. As such, the difference could be taken to signify a diversity, even an instability, inherent not in the ancient "reality" of miracles like this one but in the modern mode of representation itself. That is to say, it could very well be the case that contemporary New Testament scholarship on ancient miracle accounts and the attendant discourses surrounding miracles, in its efforts to classify, categorize, and "normalize" such stories as discursive forms and patterns, has produced a stable, bounded, coherent "miracle discourse" where there may not have been such distinctions, in the same manner as we would make them now, in the worlds where the accounts were initially produced and disseminated.⁵ Of course, one of the premises of rhetorical-critical analysis, such as is privileged in this volume, is that engaging the literature of the ancient world means appraising not its transparency as "truth" or reflections of reality, but its complexity through argumentative strategies, ethical programs, and ideological textures. In other words, such analysis should take as a given that literary representations are, in effect, constructions of particular realities that may or may not be persuasive in the multiple contexts in which such constructions are encountered.

Furthermore, all engagements with the extant literature of the ancient world in our contemporary context reflect more of the ideological configurations and commitments of the present day than those of the ancient past. Studying the literature of the New Testament in its ancient environment(s)—even if we admit that such landscapes are predominantly accessible through analysis of rhetorical forms and effects—has as much to do with negotiating the terms of a historical and contemporary relationship with the materials and their significations as it does with an interpreter's desire to negotiate and describe them. Along these lines, it is telling that, as famous as the rain miracle appears to be in ancient "Greco-Roman" or "pagan," "Jewish," and "Christian" literature, it is rarely, if ever, mentioned in New Testament scholarship on miracles as an event and/or form of early Christian discourse, even in scholarship that serves the function of collecting and organizing primary sources for interpretive projects that seek to illuminate the purpose and function of miracles in the ancient world.⁶ Perhaps this oversight is because it is not actually clear

---

5. On this point I resonate with Craig Keener's recent appraisal of the emergence of modern scholarly methods and discourses as they concern the veracity of miracle accounts. Modern assumptions must be named as that which influences contemporary understandings of miracles, and as such must be interrogated. While Keener's project on the reliability of the New Testament miracle stories is not quite aligned in scope or methodological outlook with the project undertaken in this volume, the proposal still stands: modern scholarly orientations necessarily shape the circumstances and frameworks in which analysis is undertaken. Therefore, scholarship is as much about naming the contours of our own interpretive context, as it is about that of the New Testament's world. See Keener, *Miracles: The Credibility of the New Testament Accounts* (2 vols.; Grand Rapids: Baker Academic, 2011), especially 1:85–106 and 2:645–711.

6. One might say the signal work in the area of collecting and categorizing miracle stories is still Wendy J. Cotter, *Miracles in Greco-Roman Antiquity: A Sourcebook for the Study of New Testament Miracle Stories* (The Context of Early Christianity; New York: Routledge, 1999). Cotter includes a variety of ancient miracle accounts from

in the various narratives who is responsible for the rain miracle, and such ambiguity or inconsistency does not serve the historian's aim. Or perhaps the rain miracle does not work well with modern analysis of miracle stories because a Roman emperor and the activities of the state are involved, thus putting the event into the realm of what we call the "political," as opposed to the "religious." Emperors and other "political" figures have not, in the modern scholarly imagination, regularly been placed in the same space as "religious" or "holy" figures such as Jesus, the apostles, or Apollonius of Tyana, even if, as some might have it, we cannot discern meaningful differences between religion and politics in the ancient environment in which the texts of the New Testament were produced.[7] In Marcus Aurelius's world, though, it appears to have been advantageous for an emperor to become a "holy man" in his own right, in part through gaining a reputation as one who could work wonders—whether through bringing rain to his troops, food to his people, or peace to his frontiers.[8] It was important

---

the time of Jesus well into the third century CE in her sourcebook, and, while there is a section titled "Gods and Heroes Who Control Nature" (131–74), the rain miracle is unfortunately not to be found among the second- and third-century sources. Cotter claims that the purpose of this sourcebook is to "recapture evidence about the Greco-Roman view of miracles of various kinds" (6) and admits that the material is meant to "help the reconstruction of the miracle story writer's own intention as found in his story from the early first century" (7). The terms of contemporary relationship with ancient material, then, are predicated on special importance given to the miracles of Jesus and the ancient authors who narrated them—which then sets the terms and scope of comparison with other stories.

7. There is a considerable bibliography, going all the way back to Adolf Deissmann, on the "polemical parallelism" between the New Testament and the Roman Empire. For a brief contemporary discussion, see John Dominic Crossan, "Roman Imperial Theology," in *In the Shadow of Empire: Reclaiming the Bible as a History of Faithful Resistance* (ed. Richard A. Horsley; Louisville: Westminster John Knox, 2008), 59–74; Richard A. Horsley, *Jesus and Empire: The Kingdom of God and the New World Disorder* (Minneapolis: Fortress, 2002); and Neil Elliott, *The Arrogance of Nations: Reading Romans in the Shadow of Empire* (Paul in Critical Contexts; Minneapolis: Fortress, 2008). For an appraisal of Roman imperial religiosity as it is intertwined with political matters from the disciplinary perspectives of classics and ancient history, see Clifford Ando, *The Matter of the Gods: Religion and the Roman Empire* (Transformation of the Classical Heritage; Berkeley and Los Angeles: University of California Press, 2009) as well as Mary Beard, John North, and Simon Price, *Religions of Rome, Volume I: A History* (New York: Cambridge University Press, 1998), especially 73–113.

8. This observation is not at all new in studies of the New Testament and Christian origins, at least not in the history of scholarship exhibiting Marxist hermeneutical

for those who narrated the emperor's deeds to construct him as one who could do amazing things on a grand scale. Whether one was persuaded (or "believed") that he did or could work miracles perhaps meant something in terms of one's religiosity and national identity—a point that could signify that the emperor's link with the miraculous was a site of contestation for his subjects. Similarly, it does make a difference whether contemporary scholars are persuaded (or "believe") that stories attributing the capacity to work miracles to emperors have any analytical value beyond the political and propagandistic.[9] Such orientations to this material make a difference for how we reconstruct the ancient contexts for the New Testament's miracle stories, a task that is only important insofar as those stories continue to serve as a source for meaning-making in the present. Hermeneutically, then, larger political, social, and religious issues are always tangled up with interpretations of miracles, in the past and in the present.

Thus, as far as method is concerned, it is the case that the resources and procedures deployed to assess miracle discourses are always indebted in some sense to the assumptions of the scholars making decisions about what "counts" or is "relevant" for constructing and reifying categories and processes by which ancient literary representations may be compared, analyzed, and interpreted. As we aim to make meaning in the present, we decide what material we use, and how we use it, as well as what is *not* useful. In the end, method is about us. And here is where the scholarly and otherwise professional analysis of miracle discourses can certainly be complicated further—where we might turn our attention to our interpretive choices as the object of our studies, as such choices afford consequences that are worth our consideration. For example, it is not just that we have tended to downplay the significance of Roman (political) sources alongside canonical New Testament (religious) literature as resources for understanding the origins and invention of early Christian discourses. We have also decided that students of the religious discourses such as we think the New Testament adduces must ultimately be students of writ-

---

orientations; see, for example, Karl Kautsky, *The Foundations of Christianity* (trans. Henry Mins; New York: S.A. Russell, 1953), 100–104.

9. For example, Daniel Ogden's sourcebook on "magical" discourses in the Greek and Roman contexts contains very few entries concerning emperors as agents of the miraculous (or magical); Augustus is a notable exception. See Ogden, *Magic, Witchcraft, and Ghosts in the Greek and Roman Worlds* (New York: Oxford University Press, 2002).

ten words. Literary representation, then, is that which must be used as a *primary* source for examination, with nonliterary representation as that which illustrates and supports the texts or otherwise reifies and vivifies the historical character of the world in which the literature was produced, even if that world is solely rhetorical in nature.[10] Such methodological assumptions produce the effect of naturalizing and stabilizing ancient and modern discourses, all the while obscuring the basic instability and unnaturalness of the categories we use and assign to the ancients.

3. Visualizing Miracle Discourse: Enter the "Rain Man"

One of the avenues open to scholars of the New Testament and early Christianity as a means to challenge some of our interpretive assumptions and methods is a turn toward visual representation. Moving from managing literary representations alone to exploring visual resources as equally important exposes an important operative methodological assumption, namely, when it comes to miracles or any other kind of ancient Christian discourses, we desire to construct categories and narratives that provide us with a certain stability and coherence with respect to the ancient world, as well as our relationship to it. However, we must remember that visual representation constitutes a vital arena for the negotiation of power relationships in both the ancient past and contemporary context and, hence, brings instability to the forefront in the interpretive enterprise. That is, while we might be quick to think that oral or written rhetoric can summon corresponding visual imagery in the minds of hearing or reading audiences, we tend to be more reticent to admit that visual representations constitute communicative systems, or "discourses," in their own right, beyond mere illustrations and proofs for words and events.[11]

---

10. For more on this point in particular, and for a brief consideration of what difference it might make to use visual representation in a manner beyond the illustrative in New Testament studies, see Davina C. Lopez, "Visual Perspectives: Imag(in)ing the Big Pauline Picture," in *Studying Paul's Letters: Contemporary Perspectives and Approaches* (ed. J. A. Marchal; Minneapolis: Fortress, 2012), 93–116.

11. Peter Burke (*Eyewitnessing: The Uses of Images as Historical Evidence* [Ithaca, N.Y.: Cornell University Press, 2001], 10) notes this process of illustration thus: "When they do use images, historians tend to treat them as mere illustrations, reproducing them in their books without comment. In cases in which the images are discussed in the text, this evidence is often used to illustrate conclusions that the author has already reached by other means, rather than to give new answers or to ask new questions."

For further consideration of the potential questions facing modern rhetorical analysis of ancient miracle discourses, it is worth glancing at the most famous representation of the rain miracle, that of its portrayal on the second-century Column of Marcus Aurelius (see fig. 1 below). This relief depicts the falling rain as a large winged male figure spreading his watery arms over what looks like a battle scene. The otherwise unidentifiable "rain man" hovers over the advancing Romans—some of whom are holding their shields above their heads, as if to catch the water—and soon-to-be-vanquished barbarians, whose bodies pile up on the right side of the scene to the point of overlapping with the next chapter in the column's visual narrative. Neither Marcus Aurelius nor Egyptian or Chaldean magicians make an appearance in this relief. Further, if viewers are to understand that some of the Roman soldiers depicted are Christians, as Tertullian or Eusebius might have it, then visual clues to that effect are no longer decipherable to gazing eyes. In fact, far from managing public perception of this supposedly pivotal event in a Roman war against northern enemies, or telling the story of "what happened," this particular image leaves much about the story of the rain miracle to the imagination of those who see it.

The rain miracle relief on the Column of Marcus Aurelius serves as a site where the significations of miracle discourse can be interrogated, the basic instability of such discourse noted, and different horizons for investigation articulated. One reason this image is critical for the examination of ancient miracle discourse is that this particular visual narrative is rare—even singular—in Roman art, for it is one of the only extant depictions of an ancient miraculous event. Classical art historians and archaeologists often note two other aspects of this monument: first, that it is intimately related to (and even could be derived from) the Column of Trajan, which is stationed nearby; and second, that its sole purpose is to serve as a narrative of war, with the reliefs spiraling about its shaft serving as historical depictions of two military campaigns against the Germans and Sarmatians.[12] Scholars often presume that the reliefs are arranged in

---

12. The Column of Marcus Aurelius has received much less professional attention than that of Trajan, perhaps due to the pervasive scholarly assumption that it is derivative of the "better" column. For discussion of the issues, see the classic collection edited by Eugen Petersen, Alfred von Domaszewski, Guglielmo Calderini, *Die Marcus-säule auf Piazza Colonna in Rom* (Munich: Bruckmann, 1896), as well as John Scheid and Valérie Huet, eds., *La colonne Aurélienne: autour de la colonne Aurélienne, geste et image sur la colonne de Marc Aurèle à Rome* (Turnhout: Brepols, 2000); Sheila

Figure 1. The "Rain Miracle." A winged "rain man" provides an opportunity for Roman soldiers to defeat their German opponents. While Marcus Aurelius is featured in multiple scenes on the column, his likeness does not appear in this particular relief. Column of Marcus Aurelius, Piazza Colonna, Rome. Photo by Davina C. Lopez.

chronological order from bottom to top, showing "what happened" to anyone who strolled through the public plaza and bothered to take a look.

As attractive as it is to presuppose that the reliefs on a monument such as the one under discussion are meant to be "read" in order from bottom/beginning to top/end, it is safer to assume that most of the scenes on the Column of Marcus Aurelius would not be fully accessible to viewers standing in front of it, much less decipherable as part of a series to be read in a

---

Dillon, "Women on the Columns of Trajan and Marcus Aurelius and the Visual Language of Roman Victory," in *Representations of War in Ancient Rome* (ed. S. Dillon and K. Welch; New York: Cambridge University Press, 2006), 244–71; Iain Ferris, *Hate and War: The Column of Marcus Aurelius in Rome* (Stroud, UK: History Press, 2009); and now Martin Beckmann, *The Column of Marcus Aurelius: The Genesis and Meaning of a Roman Imperial Monument* (Chapel Hill: University of North Carolina Press, 2011).

certain linear fashion.[13] Be that as it may, the visual representation of the rain miracle is positioned near the base—that is, near to the ground—in close range to a cosmopolitan viewing public. Rather than ascribing its visibility to the miracle's chronological positioning in the war story commemorated on the column, it is notable that this singular scene is visually complemented by numerous likenesses of the emperor overseeing various tasks and often peering out at the public. Therefore, a viewer's eye might be drawn to two visual motifs in particular, regardless of whether the column could be "read" as a continuous linear frieze or not: (1) the rain miracle, positioned within range of eye level and at a focal point on the column, and (2) the emperor, who appears over and over as a responsible party in various other scenes all around the shaft.

Unlike written history books and rhetorical treatises, the column and other monuments like it were visible to ordinary viewers—one need not go to a library or be able to read words in order to engage its discourses. Given that this is the case, it is indeed curious that the rain is represented so vaguely through an otherwise nonidentifiable male figure,[14] for there is then almost no control over the associations made by those who see it. Of course, it could be said that, via its repetition of the emperor's likeness, the column aimed to communicate the idea that Marcus Aurelius is ultimately a god—and, as such, controls all aspects of the Roman world, including the weather. But a viewer is ultimately free to make any association she or

---

13. For a consideration of the impossibility of a viewer's capacity to adequately "read" reliefs spiraling around a column "in order," see Dillon, "Women on the Columns of Trajan and Marcus Aurelius," as well as John Clarke, *Art in the Lives of Ordinary Romans: Visual Representation and Non-Elite Viewers in Italy, 100 BC–AD 315* (Berkeley and Los Angeles: University of California Press, 2003), especially 42–53. For another view that takes the spiral as a cue for the viewer to interact with a column in particular ritualistic ways, perhaps associated with commemorating the death and apotheosis of an emperor, see Penelope J. E. Davies, *Death and the Emperor: Roman Imperial Funerary Monuments from Augustus to Marcus Aurelius* (New York: Cambridge University Press, 2000).

14. In the language of Roman visual representation, water was often personified with male bodies. Rivers and oceans are a common theme in public statuary; the Columns of Trajan and Marcus Aurelius both include representations of northern rivers as colossal male figures. Adding to the complexity of this representation is the mythological linkage of Jupiter with the act of bringing rain, thunder, and lightning, a point that may not have been lost on a Roman emperor who deployed rhetoric linking himself to Augustus and the highest echelons of the Roman pantheon.

he might be predisposed to make according to her or his social location, whether Roman or foreigner or something in between. So, the "answer" to "what happened" in the German forest, to the question of who is ultimately responsible for the rain miracle, is "everyone"—Egyptians, Chaldeans, Christians, a Roman emperor, a rain god, whomever one might imagine. The answer lies in the eye of the beholder!

Now, we might posit that the visual program on the Column of Marcus Aurelius may "intend" for viewers to see the emperor as the "miracle worker," just as some literary representations beg us to accept the emperor's responsibility just because the texts show his name within proximity to the event. However, if we take viewership seriously then we have to concede that the column, along with the state that produced and erected it, ultimately cannot control what people see, or the connotations they might ascribe to these images. This point runs counter to an assumption maintained even by those who engage in rhetorical analysis of literary materials: that the effects of representation on an audience can (and should) be closely aligned with authorial intent. The ambiguity of the rain-miracle scene signifies the fundamental instability of its meaning by leaving open a range of associations viewers might make—thus, the story is attributed variously to "foreign" magic, Christians, and Romans alike, no matter the intent (if we can even know it) of the column's "author(s)." Simply put, Rome was a densely populated urban center, composed of a highly diverse mix of people with different understandings of their world and the place of the so-called miraculous in it. It stands to reason, then, that viewers passing by the Column of Marcus Aurelius would have held a multiplicity of understandings, and would have made a variety of associations and meanings that may or may not have had to do with the emperor and his capacity for the miraculous.

Exploring this visual representation of the rain miracle reveals, then, that it is impossible for the state (or anyone else) to harness miracle discourses, let alone render such discourses stable, coherent, and universal. The differences between the ways in which the literary and visual representations tell the story of the rain miracle are actually more important to frame in terms of instability than verifiability, historicity, or competition for social placement. When the image on the Column of Marcus Aurelius is juxtaposed with its literary representation in the narratives mentioned above, what is revealed is the obvious variability of images as discourses, and perhaps more importantly, the fundamental volatility of miracles as discursive practices in the ancient world. The "reality" of miracles, just like many other aspects of the ancient world, is inaccessible to us; all we have are representations. It is what we do with those representations, as well as how we manage our long-term relationships with them, that matters.

4. Rhetorical-Critical Interventions in the Study of Miracle Discourses

Central to the methodological concerns and trajectories of rhetorical-critical engagement of New Testament literature is the emphasis on complex relationships between "reality," narrative, and representation. In that sense, our brief foray into the German forest can perhaps help us better, or at least more honestly, navigate the foliage we tend in our own disciplinary arboretum. This volume on miracle discourses represents, not unlike the Column of Marcus Aurelius, a sustained consideration of a contentious complex of issues. Perhaps chief among these is that invocation of the term *miracles* suggests a supernatural epistemology that allows for personal and/or communal belief in miracles as part of an institutional religious affiliation or assent to a particular theological project. In other words, as far as miracles are concerned, it is difficult to negotiate a terrain where personal acceptance, advocacy, and historical scholarship can be indistinguishable: we do the history because we accept miracles as "plausible," or we advocate for the belief in miracles now because we can say that the first Christians believed and advocated for such events then, and so on.

Furthermore, regardless of claims to the contrary, it is difficult for scholars who do not personally espouse or defend the authenticity of miracles in our world to work on miracle discourses in the ancient world, particularly when we have decided that those discourses constitute a critical component of early Christian literature. Such dynamics render the examination of miracles as an interesting wedge issue for contemporary biblical scholarship, since studying miracles exposes the assumption that a "need to believe" in whatever the object of investigation might be— whether Paul, Jesus, the miracles of Jesus and Paul, the history of the Christian tradition, or the rhetoric of Christianity—must serve as a prerequisite for engaging biblical literature in a rigorously critical manner. Here we would do well to find resonance with the salient point that our brief exploration of the rain miracle affords: representations are not to be conflated with reality in the ancient world. So it is fitting, then, that this volume focuses on representations of miracles, specifically the rhetorical constructions thereof, rather than the represented, or the supposed reality of miraculous events themselves. Indeed, this shift in emphasis provides a substantial contribution to the study of ancient miracles, and the essays as a whole offer both a variety of questions and tools for navigating some difficult terrain. As a collection, the essays in this volume exhibit three common characteristics that together might very well push the boundaries of scholarship on miracle discourse.

First and foremost, sustained attention to representations or discourses of miracles helps us to maneuver around an impasse in New Testament scholarship: whether the position of the interpreter vis-à-vis the miraculous should be fronted or emphasized in scholarly engagement. In these essays, whether miracles are "true," or whether New Testament scholarship can ever even answer that question in a satisfactory way, is not a primary concern. Nor is it the case that the authors of these essays assume that one must come out on the side of belief in the credibility of miracles as a prerequisite for writing about them. This is not to say that, in rhetorical-critical studies, the interpreter is bias-free or prohibited from holding any number of theological investments in relation to the material under consideration. It is impossible for scholarship to achieve an agendaless or value-neutral state, either in the questions asked or proposals made. A promising movement toward rhetorical-critical analysis, however, essentially takes the question of the verifiability of miracles as historical events, and personal belief in them as such, off the hermeneutical table. In some ways, then, historical scholarship on the New Testament is liberated from the "burden" that the subject of miracles can often invoke.

Second, methodologically speaking, rhetorical criticism is closely linked to ideological criticism, in that analysis of power dynamics is, or should be, a part of any analysis of discursive practices and effects. Miracle discourses, unstable as they might be, are no exception to this proposal—just because the stories have miracles as the subject, it does not excuse us from detecting the manifold ways that power functions as a subtext. Rhetorical criticism is a useful framework for locating the New Testament miracle stories as part of argumentative strategies designed to persuade hearers and readers of the power and authority of the actors in the narrative. Claims to miracle-based fame, then, are not stories about "what happened," but discourses that exemplify ways to identify and perform particular allegiances, positions in specific hierarchical social arrangements, and/or interrupt dominant articulations of knowing and doing.

Third and finally, as Karl Kautsky noted long ago, "miracles were as cheap as blackberries" in the ancient world, and everyone who aimed to demonstrate (and talk about) a prowess worthy of political or cultic leadership sought to have the miraculous ascribed to them and written into their biographical narrative.[15] Miracle stories, thus, were everywhere and easily accessible as tropes to be incorporated into any number of representations, including those in early Christian literature. What ought we to make of these tropes? If the rhetorical-critical analysis undertaken in this volume is taken seriously, then we would recognize that the appearance of different types of miracle discourses across the New Testament canon does not necessarily engender the question of which stories are better, more accurate, or more befitting our sensibilities or portraits of early Christian heroes. That is to say, it would be a mistake to rank these discourses in terms of their persuasiveness to us. Rather, the diversity of miracle discourses could signify the abundance of tropes available to the New Testament writers and compilers, as well as diversity in the ways in which early Christians negotiated a complex, miracle-saturated world. The essays in this volume offer admirable examples of such explorations and readily propel us forward to other such interpretive possibilities and prospects.

5. Critically Engaging Miracle Discourse Analysis

Having delineated some of the main contributions that this collection of essays makes to the study of miracle discourses in the New Testament, I move now to some larger concerns I have about the main argumentative trajectories, with the aim of stimulating further discussion on this relatively undertreated subject in the contemporary disciplinary formation of early Christian studies. Rather than focusing on any one essay in particular, I raise concerns that relate broadly to the conceptual framing of the volume. To be sure, particular essays fall under that rubric better than others. Still, the main arcs of this volume are based on a set of methodological and discursive assumptions that are, at the very least, worth engaging and perhaps even reconsidering.

First, as implicit in the brief consideration of the rain miracle above, there appears to be a need, not only in this volume but in the discipline as a whole, to classify miracles as something to be isolated from differ-

---

15. Kautsky, *Foundations of Christianity*, 105.

ent tropes and traditions, most explicitly magic and Judaism. While this modern propensity has been delineated and appraised at length in recent studies, the question at hand is this: What does such classification achieve, and what does it allow us to do with texts and stories? What do our patterns of classification occlude, functionally (socially) speaking? Operative here seems to be an implicit, if not actually overt, dichotomic view, wherein our own desire to classify and tame these discourses determines the oppositional terms on which we make our classifications and comparisons. It would appear, in fact, that one reason to differentiate between miracles and magic is precisely to help tame miracles in a way that magic cannot be. Linking the two along less oppositional lines would in effect make it much more difficult to claim the uniqueness of early Christian discourses. Even more to the point, linking the two would make miracles—one of the key components in the life of Jesus—part of a world that cannot be controlled and managed, and therefore not isolable as a pretext for modern theological reflection.

I would note, further, that there is a tendency to associate magic with the popular or lower classes, whereas miracles are rarified, being closer to the gods and the upper classes. Magic seems to be in the hands of the people—anyone can try it, which in turn devalues it. Miracles, however, are to be performed only by certain types of people: the holy, the sacrosanct, those who embody godliness in some shape or form, including people like Roman emperors. The dichotomy between magic and miracles, much like that between religion and politics, is completely false, of course, yet it readily (if not conveniently) persists. As Bruce Lincoln points out in his "Theses on Method," one of the central tensions in the study of religion in any time period is the failure to recognize fully that the history of religions approach, with which I find much to resonate in terms of methodological orientation, juxtaposes two fundamental principles: "history" and "religion"—the contingent and the eternal.[16] In the study of the New Testament, to be sure, the "eternal" focus constantly jeopardizes serious consideration of the contingency of early Christian

---

16. Bruce Lincoln, "Theses on Method," in *Gods and Demons, Priests and Scholars: Critical Explorations in the History of Religions* (Chicago: University of Chicago Press, 2012), 1. The "Theses," thirteen in all, were (according to their author) originally posted on Lincoln's office door and have since been presented and discussed extensively by those who are concerned about methodological issues in the study of religion.

ideas and discourses. Indeed, one of Lincoln's theses notes that there is a propensity in such configurations to select a particular group to represent the whole of the historical religious phenomenon.[17] In other words, while there might be an avoidance in (socio)rhetorical criticism to hold up a particular author as the key to unlocking the whole, there tends to be a clear sense that the discourses themselves can be isolated and held up as that "clan" that defines the whole. In this instance, then, miracle discourse becomes the standard by which magic becomes configured. Since miracle discourse is by its very nature "nonmagical" in its basic orientation, this process thereby creates a dichotomy that is difficult to sustain in the context of "real" historical realities.

My second point of contention arises out of the first. As a whole, the essays in this volume, which is somewhat reflective of the field itself, do not reflect enough power analysis. This is the case as far as engagement with the miracle stories themselves are concerned, but is also an issue with our own scholarly (and modern!) desire to classify and analyze such stories and discourses in particular ways. (Post)modern political and social awareness would seem to demand that we contextualize our analysis of, say, "newness" as a category of interpretation, and not as a label that accurately reflects an ancient reality. Indeed, the concept of "differential equations," used by some classicists to configure power relations in antiquity, could well apply to New Testament discourses (as isolated and discursively constructed by contemporary scholars) in their relationship to alterity in the ancient world. Or, put another way, such configurations create and sustain a differentiation between early Christianity and "the other."[18] As a matter of methodological concern, such differentiation is seldom even acknowledged, let alone scrutinized. One cannot help but receive the impression that throughout this volume this position of (early) Christian difference and distinctiveness is taken as a given, and as a starting point for rhetorical analysis. Obviously, the ideological orientation of the modern interpreter is at the center of such distinctions. It is a stretch to suggest that the New Testament writings demand the particular kind of formulation that we assign to them without explanation. It is not that these texts do not contain words or phrases wherein claims to difference, singularity,

---

17. Ibid., 2.

18. For a summary and appraisal of the debate in classical studies, see Erich Gruen, *Rethinking the Other in Antiquity* (Martin Classical Lectures; Princeton: Princeton University Press, 2010).

and uniqueness are made. Rather, it is that we configure such claims in a particular way that tends, as noted above, to lose sight of the contingency in the eternal. It is not at all clear that early Christians themselves were doing the same. Indeed, they may have been better historians of religion than we are!

Ultimately, then, we must ask ourselves what is gained in the configurations that we make (and hold dear), and who benefits from them. It is relatively easy (and probably too simplistic) to suggest that a dearth of power analysis is merely a residue or symptom of the underlying faith conviction of many (if not most) scholars of the New Testament and early Christianity. No doubt latent or explicit responses to faith convictions do have an influence. Still, we must ask if there is not possibly more than this behind our methods. By positioning our texts as "superior"— or even just "unique"—we also gain a particular stature for our studies and ourselves in relationship to other traditions. In the study of religion and perhaps also classics, this is no small claim to make. But even more significantly, we continually convince ourselves of the importance of purportedly unique forms of discourse and the separation of these from that which is diffusely manifest among the lower classes, the illiterate. Certainly there is a class issue at stake here. At the same time, there is also an investment in particular institutionalized forms of discourses and practices that reify political and social hegemonies of those in power and authority.

Third, and last, I would note that, while diversity is a symbol of early Christian embeddedness, modern biblical scholarship still tends to make early Christianity into something that emerges in the "pages" of the New Testament itself, as something that is unique and separate from the world around it. The use of the term *miracle discourse* would seem to promote something akin to this configuration. On the one hand, that there are miracle stories in the New Testament and related literature does connect early Christianity to its larger cultural environment, perhaps being a response to that larger world where "miracles were as cheap as blackberries." On the other hand, the unique scholarly configuration of the discourse surrounding "miracles," especially as that is wedded and intertwined with other categories of discourse in the New Testament, leads one to conceptualize New Testament rhetorical strategies and conceptual ideologies as something that stands apart from a larger environment. In some sense, we could say that "miracles" happen everywhere (of course, this is only partly true, given the comments above regarding the separation of magic and miracle), but early Christians speak about miracles in a particular way that is distinct from those who do not identify as "Christian" in the ancient world.[19]

That said, there is still the lingering question of whether our discourses about the New Testament and miracles actually generate the "miracle discourse" that we find in these early Christian texts. In other words, we would do well to inquire whether we are observing discourses that may in fact not exist, at least in the way that we might understand a "discourse." Or, to contextualize this proposal in another way, one might say that the category "miracle discourse" can be conceptualized and deployed in a manner that makes Christianity look either different from or more like its larger cultural environment. It is the basic observation of any comparative enterprise that our own ideological predilections help shape the categories we are using for comparison. In that event, then, to what degree is the uniqueness of early Christian "miracle discourse" really about *our* discursive construction of this "miracle discourse" and about *our* relationship to such constructions? A different configuration and deployment of that category would yield fundamentally different results, perhaps results that might make us less interested in pursuing miracle discourse from the start. I am not suggesting that the exercise that we undergo when we examine discourses of miracles (and magic) is futile and pointless. I am arguing, however, that without fronting what Vernon Robbins refers to as "ideological texture" (particularly on the part of the interpreter),[20] there might well be much more tail-chasing going on than is warranted.

Indeed, as someone who resonates with both rhetorical criticism and history of religions approaches in the study of the New Testament and early Christian literature, I cannot help but wonder if we would not do better by jettisoning "miracle discourse" as a classification system for rhetoric and ideology and rather move toward something that makes *comparison* a more productive and imaginative endeavor. For instance, to use a contemporary example, if we construct a juxtaposition between a healing miracle in a charismatic Christian service and one that is invoked in a Haitian *vodou* ritual, are we doing justice to the comparative enterprise?

---

19. We would need to leave aside, for the moment, what we might even mean by the term *Christian* in relationship to the diversity of documents that make up the collection that was to become the "New Testament."

20. See Vernon K. Robbins, *The Tapestry of Early Christian Discourse: Rhetoric, Society, and Ideology* (New York: Routledge, 1996), 24–27.

Most certainly, those within the Christian context would see a huge gap between what has taken place in their context and the one that has taken place in the *vodou* ritual. They might even suggest that the latter is "of the devil" if it is considered to be miraculous at all, as opposed to just "superstition." However, as comparativists, we are obliged, perhaps even ethically so, to construct categories of comparison that do not privilege one tradition over another—we are charged with the task of articulating differences without hierarchy. We might even find ourselves invested in constructing categories that seek the commonality of human experience in a given place and time and the shared conceptual categories that establish something of a shared rhetorical and ideological universe. While the words and languages may be different, and there might be divergent ritual practices and ways of speaking, it is not evident that the experience, the rhetoric, and the broader conceptual universe are different.

And herein lies a huge challenge for anyone attempting to describe miracle discourse, be it in our time or in the distant past. One cannot help but gain the impression that what lies behind at least some of the efforts to distinguish early Christian discourses on miracles from the surrounding environment is the implicit conflation of the representation with what is represented. In this sense, reality is taken to be the occasion for the rhetoric, and rhetoric is taken to have some kind of reality behind its production. We may need to take a hard look at whether it is a commitment to the *realia* behind the text that causes "miracle discourse" to be configured in the way it often is, especially among those who embrace (socio)rhetorical criticism. In that case, of course, we are still in somewhat of a bind: for a religion of the incarnation, our discourse analysis sometimes looks rather docetic in orientation.

5. Conclusion: Here Comes the Rain, Again

Miracle discourse is certainly a wedge issue in contemporary biblical scholarship, and as such it is undoubtedly worthy of much more careful and critical consideration. Methodologically, miracle discourse also serves as a powerful cipher for our own desires (and anxieties) about the conclusions we make and questions we ask about the New Testament and early Christianity. And even as we might feel comfortable with or comforted by conclusions and questions that seem to affirm what we already know (or believe) about miracle discourse, it is also worth endeavoring to understand our own assumptions and positions better through rendering what is most familiar to us strange, or perhaps recognizing that the very thing we thought to be familiar in the first place has always been profoundly strange. It could be said that miracle discourse, as common as it appears to have been in the ancient world in which the New Testament was produced, and as familiar, stable, and tame as we have made that discourse out to be in our time, is—and always has been—exceedingly strange, unstable, and untamable.

In some sense, engaging strange examples such as the ancient rain miracle in the German forest is particularly helpful for casting into dramatic relief, as it were, the discursive constructions in and of the ancient world in which we have situated New Testament miracle stories and discourses. Along these lines, of principal interest is the range of representations of this miracle story. A visual depiction can be seen as that which complicates matters further by revealing the arbitrariness of significations and associations made by a viewing (or reading) audience at any given historical moment. Ironically enough, visitors to the Column of Marcus Aurelius in the present will be greeted and watched over by a statue of the apostle Paul (see fig. 2 below), whose likeness has graced the top of this monument since Pope Sixtus V ordered its renovation and restoration in the sixteenth century. The "original" statue of the emperor, as well as the temple of the deified Marcus that was supposedly built on the same site as the column, are lost to a contemporary viewing public. If we did not know that the column included a rather late "redaction" such as this, we might assume Christian, or at least Pauline, responsibility for the monument as a whole—and we could even suggest that Tertullian and Eusebius were correct about Christian responsibility for the rain miracle. The point, though, is this: when we look closely at the contours of our discourses, what can seem purposeful, intentional, and orderly is very possibly random, unintentional, and disorderly. Whether or not we can prove that there are patterns or parallels between "our" material and the material of others is of less concern than asking what we are seeking to gain and who we are seeking to be(come) through such classifications and comparisons.

Further, we would do well to keep in mind that method is ultimately about us and our decision-making processes, which are never devoid of ethics. It would be easy to blame the Romans, Paul, biblical scholarship, or any number of Christian institutional machineries (including those of our own time, ones we embrace and condemn) for the material and frameworks to which we have access and which we can see. It is far more difficult, however, to take responsibility for examining how our frameworks

Figure 2. A statue of St. Paul, holding his characteristic sword and law book, has sat atop the Column of Marcus Aurelius since its sixteenth-century restoration, when a large statue of the emperor was replaced with Paul's likeness under orders from Pope Sixtus V. Column of Marcus Aurelius, Piazza Colonna, Rome. Photo by Davina C. Lopez.

may be created, shaped, and made visible to us through power configurations and other serendipitous means that we are often not trained to see. For example, the ancient Greco-Roman world, and the Roman empire in particular, is available to us for observation as an environment or "background" for the invention and emergence of Christian discourses primarily through modern means. We can stroll through the "remains" of the Roman Forum or gaze upon the Column of Marcus Aurelius in great part because "ancient Rome" was imagined and (re)built for public consumption by Benito Mussolini's regime in the twentieth century. For his part, Mussolini was honest in his aims when he claimed a singular configuration of Italy's ancient past for his modern fascist purposes: "Rome is our point of departure and reference. It is our symbol or, if you wish, our myth.... It is necessary, now, that the history of tomorrow, the history we fervently wish to create, not be a contrast or parody of the history of yesterday."[21] The visual program for the history Mussolini wished to create, for better or for worse, was predicated in part on scrubbing the slums from the face of the Eternal City so the ruins could be accessed and Rome's greatness imagined without having to look at the inconvenient pockets of poverty that are inevitable in an urban setting. In light of this structural consideration, one cannot help but wonder what decisions we are making in our own search for symbols and myths that sustain us, in our own writing of the histories we fervently wish to create, and in our own desires to avoid the parodies of yesterday's histories. Moreover, we would do well to reflect on what we are recovering and what we are obscuring from our field of vision when we make these choices.

In the end, it is worth remembering that the ancient world is ultimately inaccessible to us as such, at least without tremendous mediation from multiple contexts, including our own. As the rain-miracle stories demonstrate, when we line up our sources in the ways that make sense to us, we will create the appearance of a stable discourse where there may be none to be found. We also do not always know or see what structures and power relationships lurk behind the materials and traditions we aim to call "ours." In building narratives about "our" ancient texts, backgrounds, and histories of interpretation regarding miracle discourses, we are actually narrating ourselves. Perhaps we see ourselves as heirs, interlocutors,

---

21. Translation in Borden W. Painter Jr., *Mussolini's Rome: Rebuilding the Eternal City* (New York: Palgrave Macmillan, 2005), 3.

believers, storytellers, and/or skeptics in relation to miracle discourse, not to mention the New Testament and early Christianity as a whole. Perhaps we see ourselves as "saving" a rich ancient past from contemporary poverty and decay, much like Mussolini. Perhaps we believe "less theory" and "less politics" and/or "more rhetoric" and "more theology" is needed in order to write the histories we desire—or the ones we wish to avoid. Perhaps we simply see ourselves praying for rain to cleanse us, just as the story goes. The question at this juncture is not which inclination is better, or more correct, but what exactly we seek to accomplish in writing (about) histories such as these.

Bibliography

1. Ancient Authors

Aristides, Aelius. *The Complete Works*. Translated by C. A. Behr. Leiden: Brill, 1981.
Aristotle. *The Art of Rhetoric*. Translated by J. H. Freese. LCL. Cambridge: Harvard University Press, 1926.
———. *Posterior Analytics. Topica*. Translated by H. Tredennick and E. S. Forster. LCL. Cambridge: Harvard University Press, 1960.
Cotter, Wendy. *Miracles in Greco-Roman Antiquity: A Sourcebook for the Study of New Testament Miracles*. New York: Routledge, 1999.
Dio Cassius. *Roman History*. Translated by Earnest Cary and Herbert B. Foster. 8 vols. LCL. Cambridge: Harvard University Press, 1914–27.
Diodorus Siculus. *Library of History*. Translated by C. H. Oldfather et al. 12 vols. LCL. Cambridge: Harvard University Press, 1933–67.
Lucian. Translated by A. M. Harmon et al. 8 vols. LCL. Cambridge: Harvard University Press, 1913–67.
Plutarch. *Parallel Lives*. Translated by B. Perrin. 11 vols. LCL. Cambridge: Harvard University Press, 1914–26.
Polybius. *The Histories*. Translated by W. R. Paton. 6 vols. LCL. Cambridge: Harvard University Press, 1922–27.

2. Modern Authors

Achtemeier, Paul J. *Jesus and the Miracle Tradition*. Eugene, Ore.: Cascade, 2008.
———. "The Lucan Perspective on the Miracles of Jesus: A Preliminary Sketch." *JBL* 94 (1975): 547–62.
———. "The Lukan Perspective on the Miracles of Jesus: A Preliminary Sketch." Pages 153–67 in *Perspectives on Luke-Acts*. Edited by C. H. Talbert. PRStSSS 5. Macon, Ga.: Mercer University Press; Edinburgh: T&T Clark, 1978.
———. "Origin and Function of the Pre-Marcan Miracle Catenae." *JBL* 91 (1972): 198–221.
———. "Toward the Isolation of Pre-Markan Miracle Catenae." *JBL* 89 (1970): 265–91.
Adams, Marilyn McCord. "The Role of Miracles in the Structure of Luke-Acts." Pages 235–73 in *Hermes and Athena: Biblical Exegesis and Philosophical Theology*.

Edited by E. Stump and T. P. Flint. Notre Dame, Ind.: University of Notre Dame Press, 1993.

Alexander, Loveday. "Fact, Fiction and the Genre of Acts." *NTS* 44 (1998): 380–99.

———. " 'Foolishness to the Greeks': Jews and Christians in the Public Life of the Empire." Pages 229–49 in *Philosophy and Power in the Graeco-Roman World: Essays in Honour of Miriam Griffin*. Edited by G. Clark and T. Rajak. New York: Oxford University Press, 2002.

Allen, Danielle S. *The World of Prometheus: The Politics of Punishing in Democratic Athens*. Princeton: Princeton University Press, 2000.

Ando, Clifford. *The Matter of the Gods: Religion and the Roman Empire*. Transformation of the Classical Heritage. Berkeley and Los Angeles: University of California Press, 2009.

Ash, Rhiannon. *Ordering Anarchy: Armies and Leaders in Tacitus' Histories*. Ann Arbor: University of Michigan Press, 1999.

Attridge, Harold W. "Genre Bending in the Fourth Gospel." *JBL* 121 (2002): 3–21.

Balch, David L. "ΜΕΤΑΒΟΛΗ ΠΟΛΙΤΕΙΩΝ. Jesus as Founder of the Church in Luke-Acts: Form and Function." Pages 139–88 in *Contextualizing Acts: Lukan Narrative and Greco-Roman Discourse*. Edited by T. Penner and C. Vander Stichele. SBLSymS 20. Atlanta: Scholars Press, 2003.

Bartsch, Shadi. *Actors in the Audience: Theatricality and Doublespeak from Nero to Hadrian*. Revealing Antiquity. Cambridge: Harvard University Press, 1994.

Beard, Mary, John North, and Simon Price. *Religions of Rome, Volume I: A History*. New York: Cambridge University Press, 1998.

Beckmann, Martin. *The Column of Marcus Aurelius: The Genesis and Meaning of a Roman Imperial Monument*. Chapel Hill: University of North Carolina Press, 2011.

Belfiore, Elizabeth S. *Tragic Pleasures: Aristotle on Plot and Emotion*. Princeton: Princeton University Press, 1992.

Berger, Klaus. "Hellenistische Gattungen im Neuen Testament." *ANRW* 2/25.2 (1984): 1212–18.

———. *Einführung in die Formgeschichte*. UTB 1444. Tübingen: Taschenbuch,1987.

———. *Formgeschichte des Neuen Testaments*. Heidelberg: Quelle & Meyer. 1984.

Bieler, Ludwig. Theios Anēr: *Das Bild des "Göttlichen Menschen" in Spätantike und Frühchristentum*. Repr., Darmstadt: Wissenschaftliche Buchgesellschaft, 1967 [1935/1936]).

Bloomquist, L. Gregory. "First Century Models of Bodily Healing and Their Socio-Rhetorical Transformation in Some NT Traditions." *Queen*, special issue (2002). http://www.ars-rhetorica.net/Queen/VolumeSpecialIssue/Articles/Bloomquist.pdf.

———. "The Intertexture of Lukan Apocalyptic Discourse." Pages 45–68 in *The Intertexture of Apocalyptic Discourse in the New Testament*. Edited by Duane F. Watson. SBLSymS 14. Atlanta: Society of Biblical Literature, 2002.

———. "Methodological Criteria for Apocalyptic Rhetoric: A Suggestion for the Expanded Use of Sociorhetorical Analysis." Pages 181–203 in *Vision and Persua-*

sion: Rhetorical Dimensions of Apocalyptic Discourse. Edited by G. Carey and L. G. Bloomquist. St. Louis: Chalice, 1999.

———. "Paul's Inclusive Language: The Ideological Texture of Romans 1." Pages 165–93 in *Fabrics of Discourse: Essays in Honor of Vernon K. Robbins*. Edited by David B. Gowler, L. Gregory Bloomquist, and Duane Watson. Harrisburg, Pa.: Trinity Press International, 2003.

———. "A Possible Direction for Providing Programmatic Correlation of Textures in Socio-Rhetorical Analysis." Pages 61–96 in *Rhetorical Criticism and the Bible*. Edited by S. E. Porter and D. L. Stamps. JSNTSup 195. Sheffield: Sheffield Academic Press, 2002.

———. "Rhetorical Argumentation and the Culture of Apocalyptic: A Socio-Rhetorical Analysis of Luke 21." Pages 173–209 in *The Rhetorical Interpretation of Scripture: Essays from the 1996 Malibu Conference*. Edited by Stanley E. Porter and Dennis L. Stamps. JSNTSup 180. Sheffield: Sheffield Academic Press, 1999.

———. "The Role of the Audience in the Determination of Argumentation: The Gospel of Luke and the Acts of the Apostles." Pages 157–73 in *Rhetorical Argumentation in Biblical Texts* Edited by Anders Eriksson, Thomas H. Olbricht, and Walter Übelacker. ESEC 8. Harrisburg, Pa.: Trinity Press International, 2002.

Bornkamm, Gunther, Gerhard Barth, and Heinz Joachim Held. *Tradition and Interpretation in Matthew*. Translated by Percy Scott. Philadelphia: Westminster, 1963.

Braun, Willi. *Feasting and Social Rhetoric in Luke 14*. SNTSMS 85. Cambridge: Cambridge University Press, 1995.

Brent, Allen. "Ignatius of Antioch and the Imperial Cult." *VC* 52 (1998): 30–58.

———. *The Imperial Cult and the Development of Church Order: Concepts and Images of Authority in Paganism and Early Christianity before the Age of Cyprian*. VCSup 45. Leiden: Brill, 1999.

———. "Luke-Acts and the Imperial Cult in Asia Minor." *JTS* 48 (1997): 111–38.

Brown, Raymond E. *The Gospel according to John (i–xii)*. AB 29. Garden City, NY: Doubleday, 1966.

Bultmann, Rudolf. *The Gospel of John: A Commentary*. Translated by G. R. Beasley-Murray, R. W. N. Hoare, and J. K. Riches. Philadelphia: Westminster, 1971.

———. *History of the Synoptic Tradition*. Translated by J. Marsh. New York: Harper & Row, 1963.

Burke, Peter. *Eyewitnessing: The Uses of Images as Historical Evidence*. Ithaca, N.Y.: Cornell University Press, 2001.

Butts, James R. *The Progymnasmata of Theon: A New Text with Translation and Commentary*. Ph.D. diss., The Claremont Graduate School, 1986.

Cameron, Ron. "Alternate Beginnings—Different Ends: Eusebius, Thomas, and the Construction of Christian Origins." Pages 501–25 in *Religious Propaganda and Missionary Competition in the New Testament World: Essays Honoring Dieter Georgi*. Edited by L. Bormann, K. Del Tredici, and A. Standhartinger. NovTSup 74. Leiden: Brill, 1994.

Cassidy, Richard J. *Society and Politics in the Acts of the Apostles*. Maryknoll, NY: Orbis, 1987.

Cavadini, J. C., ed. *Miracles in Jewish and Christian Antiquity: Imagining Truth.* Notre Dame, Ind.: University of Notre Dame Press, 1999.

Choi, Mihwa. "Christianity, Magic, and Difference: Name-Calling and Resistance between the Lines in *Contra Celsum.*" *Semeia* 79 (1997): 75–92.

Clark, Elizabeth A. *History, Theory, Text: Historians and the Linguistic Turn.* Cambridge: Harvard University Press, 2004.

Clarke, John. *Art in the Lives of Ordinary Romans: Visual Representation and Non-Elite Viewers in Italy, 100 BC–AD 315.* Berkeley and London: University of California Press, 2003.

Conway, Colleen. *Behold the Man: Jesus and Greco-Roman Masculinity.* New York: Oxford University Press, 2008.

Cook, John G. "In Defense of Ambiguity: Is There a Hidden Demon in Mark 1.29–31?" *NTS* 43 (1997): 184–208.

Corrington Streete, Gail. *The "Divine Man": His Origin and Function in Hellenistic Popular Religion.* New York: Lang, 1984.

Cotter, Wendy. *The Christ of the Miracle Stories: Portrait through Encounter.* Grand Rapids: Baker Academic, 2010.

———. *Miracles in Greco-Roman Antiquity: A Sourcebook for the Study of New Testament Miracles.* New York: Routledge, 1999.

Coulson, Seana. *Semantic Leaps: Frame-Shifting and Conceptual Blending in Meaning Construction.* Cambridge: Cambridge University Press, 2001.

Crossan, John Dominic. "Roman Imperial Theology." Pages 59–74 in *In the Shadow of Empire: Reclaiming the Bible as a History of Faithful Resistance.* Edited by R. A. Horsley. Louisville: Westminster John Knox, 2008.

D'Angelo, Mary Rose. "The ANHP Question in Luke-Acts: Imperial Masculinity and the Deployment of Women in the Early Second Century." Pages 44–69 in *A Feminist Companion to Luke.* Edited by A.-J. Levine with M. Blickenstaff. FCNTECW 3. Sheffield: Sheffield Academic Press, 2002.

Darr, John A. *Herod the Fox: Audience Criticism and Lukan Characterization.* JSNTSup 163. Sheffield: Sheffield Academic Press, 1998.

Davies, Penelope J. E. *Death and the Emperor: Roman Imperial Funerary Monuments from Augustus to Marcus Aurelius.* New York: Cambridge University Press, 2000.

Deissmann, Gustav Adolf. *Light from the Ancient East.* Translated by L. R. M. Strachan. 2nd ed. London: Hodder & Stoughton, 1911.

deSilva, David A. "The Construction and Social Function of a Counter-Cosmos in the Revelation of John." *Forum* 9.1–2 (1993): 47–61.

———. "Honor Discourse and the Rhetorical Strategy of the Apocalypse of John." *JSNT* 71 (1998): 79–110.

———. "The Revelation to John: A Case Study in Apocalyptic Propaganda and the Maintenance of Sectarian Identity." *SA* 53 (1992): 375–95.

de Tillesse, G. Minette. *Le secret messianique dans l'Évangile de Marc.* Paris: Cerf, 1968.

Dibelius, Martin. *From Tradition to Gospel.* Translated by B. L. Woolf and M. Dibelius. New York: Scribner's, 1935.

———. "Style Criticism of the Book of Acts." Pages 1–25 in *Studies in the Acts of the Apostles.* Edited by H. Greeven. London: SCM, 1956.

Dickie, Matthew W. *Magic and Magicians in the Greco-Roman World.* New York: Routledge, 2001.
Dillon, Sheila. "Women on the Columns of Trajan and Marcus Aurelius and the Visual Language of Roman Victory." Pages 244–71 in *Representations of War in Ancient Rome.* Edited by S. Dillon and K. Welch. New York: Cambridge University Press, 2006.
Downing, Gerald F. "Words as Deeds and Deeds as Words" *BibInt* 3 (1995): 129–43.
Edelstein, Emma J., and Ludwig Edelstein. *Asclepius.* 2 vols. Baltimore: Johns Hopkins University Press, 1945.
Edwards, Douglas R. *Religion and Power: Pagans, Jews, and Christians in the Greek East.* New York: Oxford University Press, 1996.
———. "Surviving the Web of Power: Religion and Power in the Acts of the Apostles, Josephus, and Chariton's *Chaereas and Callirhoe*." Pages 179–201 in *Images of Empire.* Edited by L. Alexander. JSOTSup 122. Sheffield: JSOT Press, 1991.
Elliott, John H. "Temple versus Household in Luke-Acts: A Contrast in Social Institutions." Pages 211–40 in *The Social World of Luke-Acts.* Edited by J. H. Neyrey. Peabody, Mass.: Hendrickson, 1991.
Elliott, Neil. *The Arrogance of Nations: Reading Romans in the Shadow of Empire.* Paul in Critical Contexts. Minneapolis: Fortress, 2008.
Esler, Philip Francis. *Community and Gospel in Luke-Acts.* SNTSMS 57. New York: Cambridge University Press, 1987.
Evans-Pritchard, E. E. *Witchcraft, Oracles and Magic among the Azande.* London: Oxford University Press, 1937.
Fauconnier, Gilles, and Mark Turner. *The Way We Think: Conceptual Blending and the Mind's Hidden Complexities.* New York: Basic, 2003.
Faust, Eberhard. *Pax Christi et Pax Caesaris: Religionsgeschichtliche, traditionsgeschichtliche und sozialgeschichtliche Studien zum Epheserbrief.* NTOA 24. Göttingen: Vandenhoeck & Ruprecht, 1993.
Ferris, Iain. *Hate and War: The Column of Marcus Aurelius in Rome.* Stroud, UK: History Press, 2009.
Fishwick, Duncan. "*Genius* and *Numen*." *HTR* 62 (1969): 356–67.
———. "Prudentius and the Cult of Divus Augustus." *Historia* 39 (1990): 475–86.
Fortna, Robert T. *The Fourth Gospel and Its Predecessor: From Narrative Source to Present Gospel.* Philadelphia: Fortress, 1988.
———. *The Gospel of Signs: A Reconstruction of the Narrative Underlying the Fourth Gospel.* Cambridge, Cambridge University Press, 1970.
Foucault, Michel. "The Subject and Power." Pages 126–44 in *The Essential Foucault: Selections from Essential Works of Foucault 1954-1984.* Edited by P. Rabinow and N. Rose. New York: The New Press, 2003.
Fowden, Garth. "Pagan Versions of the Rain Miracle of A.D. 172." *Historia: Zeitschrift für Alte Geschichte* 36.1 (1987): 83–95.
Frankfurter, David. "The Origin of the Miracle-List Tradition and Its Medium of Circulation." Pages 344–74 in *1990 Society of Biblical Literature Seminar Papers.* SBLSP 29. Atlanta: Scholars Press, 1990.

Fridrichsen, Anton. *The Problem of Miracle in Primitive Christianity.* Translated by R. A. Harrisville and J. S. Hanson. Minneapolis: Augsburg, 1972 (1925).

Friesen, Steven J. *Imperial Cults and the Apocalypse of John: Reading Revelation in the Ruins.* New York: Oxford University Press, 2001.

———. "Myth and Symbolic Resistance in Revelation 13." *JBL* 123 (2004): 281–313.

———. *Twice Neokoros: Ephesus, Asia and the Cult of the Flavian Imperial Family.* RGRR 116. Leiden: Brill, 1993.

Gager, John G. *Moses in Greco-Roman Paganism.* SBLMS 16. Nashville: Abingdon, 1972.

Galinsky, Karl. *Augustan Culture: An Interpretive Introduction.* Princeton: Princeton University Press, 1996.

Gallagher, Eugene V. *Divine Man or Magician: Celsus and Origen on Jesus.* SBLDS 64. Chico, Calif.: Scholars Press, 1982.

Garland, Robert. *The Eye of the Beholder: Deformity and Disability in the Greco-Roman World.* Ithaca, N.Y.: Cornell University Press, 1995.

Garrett, Susan R. *The Demise of the Devil: Magic and the Demonic in Luke's Writings.* Minneapolis: Fortress, 1989.

———. "Light on a Dark Subject and Vice Versa: Magic and Magicians in the New Testament." Pages 142–65 in *Religion, Science, and Magic: In Concert and Conflict.* Edited by J. Neusner, E. S. Frerichs, and P. V. M. Flesher. New York: Oxford University Press, 1989.

Geertz, Clifford. "Ritual and Social Change: A Javanese Example." *American Anthropologist* 59 (1957): 32–54.

Gentner, Dedre, Keith J. Holyoak, and Boicho N. Kokinov, eds. *The Analogical Mind: Perspectives from Cognitive Science.* Cambridge and London: MIT Press, 2001.

Georgi, Dieter. *The Opponents of Paul in Second Corinthians.* Philadelphia: Fortress, 1986.

Gilbert, Gary. "The List of Nations in Acts 2: Roman Propaganda and the Lucan Response." *JBL* 121 (2002): 497–529.

———. Roman Propaganda and Christian Identity in the Worldview of Luke-Acts." Pages 233–56 in *Contextualizing Acts: Lukan Narrative and Greco-Roman Discourse.* Edited by T. Penner and C. Vander Stichele. SBLSymS 20. Atlanta: Scholars Press, 2003.

Gleason, Maud W. *Making Men: Sophists and Self-Presentation in Ancient Rome.* Princeton: Princeton University Press, 1995.

———. "Mutilated Messengers: Body Language in Josephus." Pages 50–85 in *Being Greek under Rome: Cultural Identity, the Second Sophistic and the Development of Empire.* Edited by S. Goldhill. Cambridge: Cambridge University Press, 2001.

———. "The Semiotics of Gender: Physiognomy and Self-Fashioning in the Second Century C.E." Pages 389–415 in *Before Sexuality: The Construction of Erotic Experience in the Ancient World.* Edited by D. Halperin, J. Winkler, and F. Zeitlin. Princeton: Princeton University Press, 1990.

———. "Truth Contests and Talking Corpses." Pages 287–313 in *Constructions of the Classical Body.* Edited by J. I. Porter. Ann Arbor: University of Michigan Press, 1999.

Gowler, David B. "Text, Culture, and Ideology in Luke 7:1–10: A Dialogic Reading." Pages 89–125 in *Fabrics of Discourse: Essays in Honor of Vernon K. Robbins*. Edited by D. B. Gowler, L. G. Bloomquist, and D. F. Watson. Harrisburg, Pa.: Trinity Press International, 2003.

Gowler, David B., L. Gregory Bloomquist, and Duane F. Watson, eds. *Fabrics of Discourse: Essays in Honor of Vernon K. Robbins*. Harrisburg, Pa.: Trinity Press International, 2003.

Gradel, Ittai. *Emperor Worship and Roman Religion*. Oxford Classical Monographs. New York: Oxford University Press, 2002.

Graf, Fritz. *Magic in the Ancient World*. Translated by F. Philip. Revealing Antiquity 10. Cambridge: Harvard University Press, 1997.

Grant, Robert M. *Miracle and Natural Law in Graeco-Roman and Early Christian Thought*. Amsterdam: North-Holland Publishing Company, 1952.

———. "The Problem of Miraculous Feedings in the Graeco-Roman World." *Protocol of the Forty-Second Colloquy: 14 March 1982*. Berkeley, Calif: Center for Hermeneutical Studies, 1982.

Gregory, Andrew. *The Reception of Luke and Acts in the Period before Irenaeus: Looking for Luke in the Second Century*. WUNT 2/169. Tübingen: Mohr Siebeck, 2003.

Gruen, Erich. *Rethinking the Other in Antiquity*. Martin Classical Lectures. Princeton: Princeton University Press, 2010.

Gunderson, Erik. "Men of Learning: The Cult of *Paideia* in Lucian's *Alexander*." Pages 479–510 in *Mapping Gender in Ancient Religious Discourses*. Edited by T. Penner and C. Vander Stichele. BIS 84. Leiden: Brill, 2007.

Hall, Robert G. "Josephus, *Contra Apionem* and Historical Inquiry in the Roman Rhetorical Schools." Pages 229–49 in *Josephus' Contra Apionem: Studies in Its Character and Content*. Edited by L. H. Feldman and J. R. Levison. AGJU 34. Leiden: Brill, 1996.

Harland, Philip A. *Associations, Synagogues, and Congregations: Claiming a Place in Ancient Mediterranean Society*. Minneapolis: Fortress, 2003.

———. "Honours and Worship: Emperors, Imperial Cults and Associations at Ephesus (First to Third Centuries c.e.)." *SR* 25 (1996): 319–34.

Hartsock, Chad. *Sight and Blindness in Luke-Acts: The Use of Physical Features in Characterization*. BIS 94. Leiden: Brill, 2008.

Hary, Benjamin H. *Multiglossia in Judeo-Arabic with an Edition, Translation and Grammatical Study of the Cairene Purim Scroll*. Études sur le Judaïsme Médiéval 14. Leiden: Brill, 1992.

Held, H. J. "Matthew as Interpreter of the Miracle Stories." Pages 165–299 in *Tradition and Interpretation in Matthew*. Edited by G. Bornkamm, G. Barth, and H. J. Held. Philadelphia: Westminster Press, 1963.

Hengel, Martin. "The Interpretation of the Wine Miracle at Cana: John 2:1–11." Pages 104–12 in *The Glory of Christ in the New Testament: Studies in Christology*. Edited by L. D. Hurst and N. T. Wright. Oxford: Clarendon, 1987.

Hock, Ronald F., and E. N. O'Neil, trans. and ed. *The Chreai in Ancient Rhetoric: Volume 1: The Progymnasmata*. Texts and Translations 27. GRRS 9. Atlanta: Scholars Press, 1986.

———. *The Chreia and Ancient Rhetoric: Classroom Exercises*. Writings from the Greco-Roman World 2. Atlanta: Scholars Press, 2002.

Holladay, Carl R. *Theios Aner in Hellenistic-Judaism: A Critique of the Use of this Category in New Testament Christology*. SBLDS 40. Missoula, Mont.: Scholars Press, 1977.

Horsley, Richard A. *Jesus and Empire: The Kingdom of God and the New World Disorder*. Minneapolis: Fortress, 2002.

Hull, John M. *Hellenistic Magic and the Synoptic Tradition*. SBT 2/28. London: SCM, 1974.

Hurtado, Larry W. *Lord Jesus Christ: Devotion to Jesus in Earliest Christianity*. Grand Rapids: Eerdmans, 2003.

Israelowich, Ido. "The Rain Miracle of Marcus Aurelius: (Re-) Construction of Consensus." *Greece & Rome* 55.1 (2008): 83–102.

Janowitz, Naomi. *Magic in the Roman World*. Religion in the First Christian Centuries. New York: Routledge, 2001.

Jervell, Jacob. "Der Schwache Christmatiker." Pages 185–98 in *Rechtfertigung: Festschrift für Ernst Käsemann zum 70 Geburtstag*. Edited by J. Friedrich, W. Pöhlmann, and P. Stuhlmacker. Tübingen: Mohr Siebeck; Göttingen: Vandenhoeck & Ruprecht, 1976.

———. "The Signs of an Apostle: Paul's Miracles." Pages 77–95 in J. Jervell, *The Unknown Paul: Essays on Luke-Acts and Early Christian History*. Minneapolis: Augsburg, 1984.

Johnson, Luke T. "The New Testament's Anti-Jewish Slander and the Conventions of Ancient Polemic." *JBL* 108 (1989): 419–41.

Kauppi, Lynn Allan. *Foreign but Familiar Gods: Graeco-Romans Read Religion in Acts*. LNTS 277. New York: T&T Clark, 2006.

Kautsky, Karl. *The Foundations of Christianity*. Translated by Henry Mins. New York: S. A. Russell, 1953.

Kee, Howard Clark. *Medicine, Miracle, and Magic in New Testament Times*. SNTSMS 55. Cambridge: Cambridge University Press, 1986.

———. *Miracle in the Early Christian World: A Study in Sociohistorical Method*. New Haven: Yale University Press, 1983.

Keener, Craig. *Miracles: The Credibility of the New Testament Accounts*. 2 vols. Grand Rapids: Baker Academic, 2011.

Kelhoffer, James A. *Miracle and Mission: The Authentication of Missionaries and Their Message in the Longer Ending of Mark*. WUNT 2/112. Tübingen: Mohr Siebeck, 2000.

———. "Paul and Justin Martyr on the Miraculous: A Comparison of Appeals to Authority." *GRBS* 42 (2001): 163–75.

Kilgallen, John J. "Acts 13:4–12: The Role of the *Magos*." *EstBib* 55 (1997): 223–37.

Klauck, Hans-Josef. *Magic and Paganism in Early Christianity: The World of the Acts of the Apostles*. Translated by B. McNeil. Edinburgh: T&T Clark, 2000.

Koet, Bart J. "Purity and Impurity of the Body in Luke-Acts." Pages 93–106 in *Purity and Holiness: The Heritage of Leviticus*. Edited by M. Poorthuis and J. Schwartz. JCPS 2. Leiden: Brill, 2000.

Kollman, Bernd. *Jesus und die Christen als Wundertäter: Studien zu Magie, Medizin und Schamanismus in Antike und Christentum*. FRLANT 170. Göttingen: Vandenhoeck & Ruprecht, 1996.
Koskenniemi, Erkki. *Apollonios von Tyana in der neutestamentlichen Exegese: Forschungsbericht und Weiterführung der Diskussion*. WUNT 2/61. Tübingen: Mohr Siebeck, 1994.
Kotansky, Roy D. "Jesus and Heracles in Cádiz (*ta Gadeira*): Death, Myth, and Monsters at the 'Straits of Gibraltar' (Mark 4:35–5:43)." Pages 160–229 in *Ancient and Modern Perspectives on the Bible and Culture: Essays in Honor of Hans Dieter Betz*. Edited by A. Yarbro Collins. Atlanta: Scholars Press, 1998.
Kovács, Péter. *Marcus Aurelius' Rain Miracle and the Macromannic Wars*. Mnemosyne Biblioteca Classica Batava Supplementum/History and Archaeology of Classical Antiquity 308. Leiden: Brill, 2009.
Kuhn, Thomas S. *The Structure of Scientific Revolutions*. 2nd ed. Foundations of the Unity of Science 2/2. Chicago: University of Chicago Press, 1967.
Lanigan, Richard L. "From Enthymeme to Abduction: The Classical Law of Logic and the Postmodern Rule of Rhetoric." Pages 49–70 in *Recovering Pragmatism's Voice: The Classical Tradition, Rorty, and the Philosophy of Communication*. Edited by L. Langsdorf and A. R. Smith. SUNY Series in the Philosophy of the Social Sciences. Albany: State University of New York Press, 1996.
Lausberg, Heinrich. *Handbuch der literarischen Rhetorik. Eine Grundlegung der Literaturwissenschaft*. 2nd ed. 2 vols. Amsterdam: Hakkert, 1963.
Leeuw, Gerardus, van der. *Religion in Essence and Manifestation*. Vol. 2. Edited by B. Nelson. Translated by J. E. Turner. New York: Harper & Row, 1963.
Lendon, J. E. *Empire of Honour: The Art of Government in the Roman World*. New York: Oxford University Press, 1997.
Lincoln, Bruce. *Gods and Demons, Priests and Scholars: Critical Explorations in the History of Religions*. Chicago: University of Chicago Press, 2012.
Lindemann, Andreas. "Einheit und Veilfalt im Lukanischen Doppelwerk: Beobachtungen zu Reden, Wundererzählungen und Mahlberichten." Pages 237–50 in *The Unity of Luke-Acts*. Edited by J. Verheyden. BETL 142. Leuven: Leuven University Press, 1999.
Lopez, Davina. *Apostle to the Conquered: Reimaging Paul's Mission*. Paul in Critical Contexts. Minneapolis: Fortress, 2008.
———. "Before Your Very Eyes: Roman Imperial Ideology, Gender Constructs and Paul's Inter-Nationalism." Pages 115–62 in *Mapping Gender in Ancient Religious Discourses*. Edited by T. Penner and C. Vander Stichele. BIS 84. Leiden: Brill, 2007.
———. "Visual Perspectives: Imag(in)ing the Big Pauline Picture." Pages 93–116 in *Studying Paul's Letters: Contemporary Perspectives and Approaches*. Ed. J. A. Marchal. Minneapolis: Fortress, 2012.
Loraux, Nicole. "Herakles: The Super-Male and the Feminine." Pages 21–52 in *Before Sexuality: The Construction of Erotic Experience in the Ancient World*. Edited by D. M. Halperin, J. J. Winkler, and F. I. Zeitlin. Princeton: Princeton University Press, 1990.

Luz, Ulrich. *Matthew 8–20: A Commentary.* Translated by James Crouch. Hermeneia. Minneapolis: Fortress Press, 2001.
Mack, Burton L. *A Myth of Innocence: Mark and Christian Origins.* Philadelphia: Fortress, 1988.
MacMullen, Ramsay. *Paganism in the Roman Empire.* New Haven: Yale University Press, 1981.
Mair, Lucy. *An Introduction to Social Anthropology.* Oxford: Clarendon, 1972.
Malina, Bruce J. *The New Testament World.* Louisville: Westminster John Knox, 1993.
Malina, Bruce J., and Richard Rohrbaugh. *Social-Science Commentary on the Synoptic Gospels.* Minneapolis: Fortress, 1992.
Marchal, Joseph A. *The Politics of Heaven: Women, Gender, and Empire in the Study of Paul.* Paul in Critical Contexts. Minneapolis: Fortress, 2008.
Marguerat, Daniel. "Magic and Miracle in the Acts of the Apostles." Pages 100–124 in *Magic in the Biblical World: From the Rod of Aaron to the Ring of Solomon.* Edited by T. Klutz. JSNTSup 245. London: T&T Clark, 2003.
———. "Magie, Guérison et Parole dans les Actes des Apôtres." *ETL* 72 (1997): 197–208.
Martin, Dale B. *Inventing Superstition: From the Hippocratics to the Christians.* Cambridge: Harvard University Press, 2004.
Martin, Josef. *Antike Rhetorik: Technik und Methode.* Handbuch der Altertumswissenschaft 2.3. Munich: C. H. Beck, 1974.
Matthews, Shelly. "The Need for the Stoning of Stephen." Pages 124–39 in *Violence in the New Testament: Jesus Followers and Other Jews under Empire.* Edited by S. Matthews and E. L. Gibson. London: T&T Clark, 2005.
Matthews, Thomas F. *The Clash of Gods: A Reinterpretation of Early Christian Art.* Rev. ed. Princeton: Princeton University Press, 1999.
Mauss, Marcel. *A General Theory of Magic.* Translated by R. Brain. New York: W. W. Norton, 1972.
Mendels, Doran. "Pagan or Jewish? The Presentation of Paul's Mission in the Book of Acts." Pages 431–52 in vol. 1 of *Geschichte—Tradition—Reflexion: Festschrift für Martin Hengel zum 70. Geburtstag.* Edited by H. Cancik, H. Lichtenberger, and P. Schäfer. 3 vols. Tübingen: Mohr Siebeck, 1996.
Millar, Fergus. *The Emperor in the Roman World 31 BC–AD 337.* Ithaca, N.Y.: Cornell University Press, 1977.
Mills, Mary E. *Human Agents of Cosmic Power in Hellenistic Judaism and the Synoptic Tradition.* JSNTSup 41. Sheffield: JSOT Press, 1990.
Moessner, David P. "'The Christ Must Suffer': New Light on the Jesus-Peter, Stephen, Paul Parallels in Luke-Acts." Pages 117–53 in *The Composition of Luke's Gospel.* Edited by D. E. Orton. Leiden: Brill, 1999.
Mount, Christopher. *Pauline Christianity: Luke-Acts and the Legacy of Paul.* NovTSup 104. Leiden: Brill, 2002.
Moxnes, Halvor. "Kingdom Takes Place: Transformations of Place and Power in the Kingdom of God in the Gospel of Luke." Pages 176–209 in *Social Scientific Models for Interpreting the Bible: Essays by the Context Group in Honor of Bruce J. Malina.* Edited by J. J. Pilch. BIS 53. Leiden: Brill, 2001.

Myllykoski, Matti. "Being There: The Function of the Supernatural in Acts 1–12." Pages 146–79 in *Wonders Never Cease: The Purpose of Narrating Miracle Stories in the New Testament and Its Religious Environment*. Edited by M. Labahn and B. J. Lietaert Peerbolte. LNTS 288. New York: T&T Clark, 2006.

Neirynck, Frans. "The Miracle Stories in the Acts of the Apostles." Pages 169–213 in *Les Actes des Apôtres: Traditions, rédaction, théologie*. Edited by J. Kremer. BETL 48. Leuven: Leuven University Press, 1979.

Newby, Gordon D. "Quranic Texture: A Review of Vernon Robbins' *The Tapestry of Early Christian Discourse* and *Exploring the Texture of Texts*," *JSNT* 70 (1998): 93–100.

Neyrey, Jerome H. "Miracles, In Other Words: Social Science Perspectives on Healings." Pages 19–55 in *Miracles in Jewish and Christian Antiquity: Imagining Truth*. Edited by J. C. Cavadini. Notre Dame, Ind.: University of Notre Dame Press, 1999.

Nijf, Onno van. "Local Heroes: Athletics, Festivals and Elite Self-Fashioning in the Roman East." Pages 306–34 in *Being Greek under Rome: Cultural Identity, the Second Sophistic and the Development of Empire*. Edited by S. Goldhill. Cambridge: Cambridge University Press, 2001.

North, Helen F. "Canons and Hierarchies of the Cardinal Virtues in Greek and Latin Literature." Pages 165–83 in *The Classical Tradition: Literary and Historical Studies in Honor of Harry Caplan*. Edited by L. Wallach. Ithaca, N.Y.: Cornell University Press, 1966.

Oakley, Todd V. "Conceptual Blending, Narrative Discourse, and Rhetoric." *Cognitive Linguistics* 9.4 (1988): 321–60.

———. "The Human Rhetorical Potential." *Written Communication* 16.1 (1999): 93–128.

Ogden, Daniel. *Magic, Witchcraft, and Ghosts in the Greek and Roman Worlds: A Sourcebook*. New York: Oxford University Press, 2002.

Ong, Walter J. *Orality and Literacy: The Technologizing of the Word*. New York: Routledge, 1982.

Painter, Borden W., Jr. *Mussolini's Rome: Rebuilding the Eternal City*. New York: Palgrave Macmillan, 2005.

Pao, David W. "The Sebasteion in Aphrodisias: Structure and Meaning of a Temple Complex for the Imperial Cult." *Jian Dao* 6 (1996): 55–75.

Parsons, Mikeal C. *Body and Character in Luke and Acts: The Subversion of Physiognomy in Early Christianity*. Grand Rapids: Baker Academic, 2006.

Peerbolte, Bert Jan Lietaert. "Paul the Miracle Worker: Development and Background of Pauline Miracle Stories." Pages 180–99 in *Wonders Never Cease: The Purpose of Narrating Miracle Stories in the New Testament and Its Religious Environment*. Edited by M. Labahn and B. J. Lietaert Peerbolte. LNTS 288. New York: T&T Clark, 2006.

Penner, Todd. "Civilizing Discourse: Acts, Declamation, and the Rhetoric of the *Polis*." Pages 65–104 in *Contextualizing Acts: Lukan Narrative and Greco-Roman Discourse*. Edited by T. Penner and C. Vander Stichele. SBLSymS 20. Atlanta: Scholars Press, 2003.

———. "Contextualizing Acts." Pages 1–21 in *Contextualizing Acts: Lukan Narrative and Greco-Roman Discourse*. Edited by T. Penner and C. Vander Stichele. SBLSymS 20. Atlanta: Scholars Press, 2003.

———. *In Praise of Christian Origins: Stephen and the Hellenists in Lukan Apologetic Historiography*. ESEC 10. London: T&T Clark, 2004.

———. "Madness in the Method? The Acts of the Apostles in Current Study." *CurBR* 2 (2004): 223–93.

Penner, Todd, and Caroline Vander Stichele. "All the World's a Stage: The Rhetoric of Gender in Acts." Pages 373–96 in *Luke and His Ancient Readers: Festschrift for A. Denaux*. Edited by R. Bieringer, G. van Belle, and J. Verheyden. BETL 182. Leuven: Leuven University Press, 2005.

———. "Bodies and the Technology of Power: Reading *The Gospel of Peter* under Empire." Pages 349–68 in *Das Petrusevangelium als Teil spätantiker Literatur*. Edited by T. Nicklas and T. J. Kraus. TUGAL 158. Berlin: de Gruyter, 2007.

———. *Contextualizing Gender in Early Christian Discourse: Thinking beyond Thecla*. London: T & T Clark, 2009.

———. "Gendering Violence: Patterns of Power and Constructs of Masculinity in the Acts of the Apostles." Pages 193–209 in *Feminist Companion to Acts*. Edited by A.-J. Levine with M. Blickenstaff. FCNTECW 9. London: T&T Clark, 2004.

———. "Script(ur)ing Gender in Acts: The Past and Present Power of *Imperium*." Pages 231–66 in *Mapping Gender in Ancient Religious Discourses*. Edited by T. Penner and C. Vander Stichele. BIS 84. Leiden: Brill, 2007.

———. "Le territoire corinthien: point de vue et poétique dans les Actes des Apôtres." Pages 197–204 in *Regards croisés sur la Bible: Etudes sur le point de vue*. Lectio Divina. Paris: Cerf, 2007.

———, eds. *Contextualizing Acts: Lukan Narrative and Greco-Roman Discourse*. SBLSymS 20. Atlanta: Scholars Press, 2003.

———. *Mapping Gender in Ancient Religious Discourses*. BIS 84. Leiden: Brill, 2007.

Perelman, Chaim, and L. Olbrechts-Tyteca. *The New Rhetoric: A Treatise on Argumentation*. Translated by J. Wilkinson and P. Weaver. Notre Dame, Ind.: University of Notre Dame Press, 1969.

Pervo, Richard I. *Acts: A Commentary*. Edited by H. W. Attridge. Hermeneia. Minneapolis: Fortress, 2009.

———. *Dating Acts: Between the Evangelists and the Apologists*. Santa Rosa, Calif.: Polebridge, 2006.

———. *Profit with Delight: The Literary Genre of the Acts of the Apostles*. Philadelphia: Fortress, 1987.

Petersen, Eugen, Alfred von Domaszewski, and Guglielmo Calderini. *Die Marcussäule auf Piazza Colonna in Rom*. Munich: Bruckmann, 1896.

Phillips, C. R., III. "*Nullum Crimen sine Lege*: Socioreligious Sanctions on Magic." Pages 260–76 in *Magika Hiera: Ancient Greek Magic and Religion*. Edited by C. A. Faraone and D. Obbink. New York: Oxford University Press, 1991.

Pilch, John J. *Healing in the New Testament: Insights from Medical and Mediterranean Anthropology*. Minneapolis: Fortress, 2000.

———. "Sickness and Healing in Luke-Acts." Pages 181–209 in *The Social World of Luke-Acts*. Edited by J. H. Neyrey. Peabody, Mass.: Hendrickson, 1991.

———. *Visions and Healing in the Acts of the Apostles: How the Early Believers Experienced God*. Collegeville, Minn.: Liturgical Press, 2004.

Plümacher, Eckhard. "TEPATEIA: Fiktion und Wunder in der hellenistiche-römischen Geschichtsschreibung und in der Apostelgeschichte." *ZNW* 89 (1998): 66–90.

Pollini, John. "Man or God: Divine Assimilation and Imitation in the Late Republic and Early Principate." Pages 334–57 in *Between Republic and Empire: Interpretations of Augustus and His Principate*. Edited by K. A. Raaflaub and M. Toher. Berkeley and Los Angeles: University of California Press, 1990.

Praeder, Susan M. "Miracle Worker and Missionary: Paul in the Acts of the Apostles." Pages 107–29 in *1983 Society of Biblical Literature Seminar Papers*. SBLSP 22. Atlanta: Scholars Press, 1983.

Price, Simon R. F. "Gods and Emperors: The Greek Language of the Roman Imperial Cult." *JHS* 104 (1984): 79–95.

———. *Rituals and Power: The Roman Imperial Cult in Asia Minor*. Cambridge: Cambridge University Press, 1984.

Räisänen, Heikki. *The 'Messianic Secret' in Mark*. Translated by C. Tuckett. Edinburgh: T & T Clark, 1990.

Reimer, Andy M. *Miracle and Magic: A Study in the Acts of the Apostles and the Life of Apollonius of Tyana*. JSNTSup 235. London: Sheffield Academic Press, 2002.

———. "Virtual Prison Breaks: Non-Escape Narratives and the Definition of 'Magic.'" Pages 125–39 in *Magic in the Biblical World: From the Rod of Aaron to the Ring of Solomon*. Edited by T. Klutz. JSNTSup 245. London: T&T Clark, 2003.

Remus, Harold. *Pagan-Christian Conflict Over Miracle in the Second Century*. Patristic Monograph Series. Cambridge: Philadelphia Patristic Foundation, 1983.

Reynolds, Joyce M. "Ruler-Cult at Aphrodisias in the Late Republic and under the Julio-Claudian Emperors." Pages 41–50 in *Subject and Ruler: The Cult of the Ruling Power in Classical Antiquity*. Edited by A. Small. Journal of Roman Archaeology Supplement Series 18. Ann Arbor: Journal of Roman Archaeology, 1996.

Religious Rhetoric of Antiquity project members. "Guidelines for Socio-Rhetorical Commentary." Religious Rhetoric of Antiquity project member meeting. Ashland, OH, 2002.

Richard, Earl J. *First and Second Thessalonians*. SP 11. Collegeville, Minn.: Liturgical Press, 1995.

Richter Reimer, Ivoni. *Women in the Acts of the Apostles: A Feminist Liberation Perspective*. Translated by L. M. Maloney. Minneapolis: Fortress, 1995.

Riemer, Ulrike. "Miracle Stories and Their Narrative Intent in the Context of the Ruler Cult of Classical Antiquity." Pages 32–47 in *Wonders Never Cease: The Purpose of Narrating Miracle Stories in the New Testament and Its Religious Environment*. Edited by M. Labahn and B. J. Lietaert Peerbolte. LNTS 288. New York: T&T Clark, 2006.

Robbins, Vernon K. *Ancient Quotes and Anecdotes: From Crib to Crypt*. Sonoma, Calif.: Polebridge, 1989.

———. "Argumentative Textures in Socio-Rhetorical Interpretation." Pages 27–65 in *Rhetorical Argumentation in Biblical Texts*. Edited by Anders Eriksson, Thomas H. Olbricht, and Walter Übelacker. ESEC 8. Harrisburg, Pa.: Trinity Press International, 2002.

———. "Beelzebul Controversy in Mark and Luke: Rhetorical and Social Analysis." *Forum* 7.3–4 (1991): 261–77.

———. "Beginnings and Developments in Socio-Rhetorical Interpretation." *NTS* (2004). http://http://www.religion.emory.edu/faculty/robbins/Pdfs/SRIBegDevRRA.pdf.

———. "The Chreia." Pages 1–23 in *Greco-Roman Literature and the New Testament*. Edited by David E. Aune. SBLSBS 21. Atlanta: Scholars Press, 1988.

———. "Conceptual Blending and Early Christian Imagination." Pages 161–95 in *Explaining Christian Origins and Early Judaism: Contributions from Cognitive and Social Science*. Edited by Petri Luomanen, Ilkka Pyysiäinen, and Risto Uro. BIS 89. Leiden: Brill, 2007.

———. "The Dialectical Nature of Early Christian Discourse." *Scriptura* 59 (1996): 353–62. http://www.religion.emory.edu/faculty/robbins/SRS/vkr/dialect.cfm.

———. "*Dynameis* and *Semeia* in Mark." *BR* 18 (1973): 1–16.

———. "Enthymeme and Picture in the *Gospel of Thomas*." Pages 175–207 in *Thomasine Traditions in Antiquity: The Social and Cultural World of the Gospel of Thomas*. Edited by Jon Ma Asgeirsson, April D. DeConick, and Risto Uro. Leiden: Brill, 2005.

———. "Enthymemic Texture in the Gospel of Thomas." *1998 Society of Biblical Literature Seminar Papers*. SBLSP 37. Atlanta: Scholars Press, 1998, 343–66. http://www.religion.emory.edu/faculty/robbins/SRS/vkr/enthymeme.cfm.

———. *Exploring the Texture of Texts: A Guide to Socio-Rhetorical Interpretation*. Valley Forge, Pa.: Trinity Press International, 1996.

———. "From Enthymeme to Theology in Luke 11:1–13." Pages 349–71 in *Sea Voyages and Beyond: Emerging Strategies in Socio-Rhetorical Interpretation*. ESEC 15. Blandford Forum, UK: Deo, 2010. Revised version of "From Enthymeme to Theology in Luke 11:1–13." Pages 191–214 in *Literary Studies in Luke-Acts: A Collection of Essays in Honor of Joseph B. Tyson*. Edited by R. P. Thompson and T. E. Phillips. Macon, Ga.: Mercer University Press, 1998. http://www.religion.emory.edu/faculty/robbins/SRS/vkr/theology.cfm.

———. "Interpreting Miracle Culture and Parable Culture in Mark 4–11." *SEÅ* 59 (1994): 59–81.

———. "The Intertexture of Apocalyptic Discourse in the Gospel of Mark." Pages 11–44 in *The Intertexture of Apocalyptic Discourse in the New Testament*. Edited by Duane F. Watson. SBLSymS 14. Atlanta: Society of Biblical Literature, 2002.

———. *The Invention of Christian Discourse*. Vol. 1. Blandford Forum, UK: Deo, 2009.

———. "The Invention of Early Christian Paideia: Sociorhetorical Interpretation of the New Testament." Paper presented at the Society of Biblical Literature Annual Meeting. Nashville, Tenn., November 17, 2000.

———. "Lukan and Johannine Tradition in the Qur'an: A Story of *Auslegungsgeschichte* and *Wirkungsgeschichte*." Pages 336–68 in *Moving Beyond New Testament Theol-*

ogy? Essays in Conversation with Heikki Räisänen. Edited by Todd Penner and Caroline Vander Stichele. Publications of the Finnish Exegetical Society 88. Helsinki: Finnish Exegetical Society and Göttingen: Vandenhoeck & Ruprecht, 2005.

———. "Luke-Acts: A Mixed Population Seeks a Home in the Roman Empire." Pages 202–21 in *Images of Empire*. Edited by L. Alexander. JSOTSup 122. Sheffield: JSOT Press, 1991.

———. "Recent Developments in Socio-Rhetorical Interpretation." Paper presented at the meetings of the SNTS. Bonn, Germany, July 29–August 1, 2003.

———. Response to the reviews of Culpepper, Dean, and Newby. *JSNT* 70 (1998): 101–7.

———. "Rhetography: A New Way of Seeing the Familiar Text." Pages 81–106 in *Words Well Spoken: George Kennedy's Rhetoric of the New Testament*. Edited by C. Clifton Black and Duane F. Watson. Studies in Rhetoric and Religion 8. Waco, Tex.: Baylor University Press, 2008.

———. "Rhetorical Composition and the Beelzebul Controversy." Pages 161–93 in *Patterns of Persuasion in the Gospels*. Edited by Burton L. Mack and Vernon K. Robbins. Eugene, Ore.: Wipf & Stock, 2008.

———. "Socio-Rhetorical Interpretation." Pages 192–219 in *The Blackwell Companion to the New Testament*. Edited by David E. Aune. West Sussex, UK: Blackwell, 2010.

———. "Socio-Rhetorical Interpretation from Its Beginnings to the Present." Paper presented at SNTS. Pretoria, South Africa. 1999. http://www.religion.emory.edu/faculty/robbins/Pdfs/SNTSPretSocRhetfromBeginning.pdf.

———. "The Socio-Rhetorical Role of the Old Testament in Luke 4–19." Pages 81–93 in *Z Noveho Zakona/From the New Testament: Sbornik k narozeninam Prof. Th. Dr. Zdenka Sazavy*. Edited by H. Tonzarova and P. Melmuk. Praha: Vydala Cirkev ceskoslovenska husitska, 2001.

———. *The Tapestry of Early Christian Discourse: Rhetoric, Society and Ideology*. London: Routledge, 1996.

———. "The Woman Who Touched Jesus' Garment: A Socio-Rhetorical Analysis and the Synoptic Accounts." *NTS* 33 (1987): 502–15. Repr., pages 185–200 in *Boundaries in Old Territory: Form and Social Rhetoric in Mark*. ESEC 3. New York: Lang, 1994.

Robbins, Vernon K., and Gordon D. Newby. "A Prolegomenon to the Relation of the Qur'ān and the Bible." Pages 23–42 in *Bible and Qur'an: Essays in Scriptural Intertextuality*. Edited by John C. Reeves. SBLSymS 24. Atlanta: Society of Biblical Literature, 2003.

Rubin, H. Z. "Weather Miracles under Marcus Aurelius." *Athenaeum* 57 (1979): 357–80.

Sage, Michael. "Eusebius and the Rain Miracle: Some Observations." *Historia: Zeitschrift für Alte Geschichte* 36.1 (1987): 96–113.

Scheid, John, and Valérie Huet, eds. *La colonne Aurélienne: autour de la colonne Aurélienne, geste et image sur la colonne de Marc Aurèle à Rome*. Turnhout: Brepols, 2000.

Scherrer, Steven J. "Signs and Wonders in the Imperial Cult: A New Look at a Roman Religious Institution in the Light of Rev 13:13-15." *JBL* 103 (1984): 599–610.

Schowalter, Daniel N. *The Emperor and the Gods: Images from the Time of Trajan.* HDR 28. Minneapolis: Fortress, 1993.

Schreiber, Stefan. *Paulus als Wundertäter: Redaktionsgeschichtliche Untersuchungen zur Apostelgeschichte und den authentischen Paulusbriefen.* BZNW 79. Berlin: de Gruyter, 1996.

Schüssler Fiorenza, Elisabeth. "Miracles, Mission, and Apologetics: An Introduction." Pages 1–20 in *Aspects of Religious Propaganda in Judaism and Early Christianity.* Edited by E. Schüssler Fiorenza. Notre Dame, Ind.: University of Notre Dame Press, 1976.

Segal, Alan F. "Hellenistic Magic: Some Questions of Definition." Pages 349–75 in *Studies in Gnosticism and Hellenistic Religions: Presented to Gilles Quispel on the Occasion of His 65th Birthday.* Edited by R. van der Broek and M. J. Vermasseren. EPRO 91. Leiden: Brill, 1981.

Shauf, Scott. *Theology as History, History as Theology: Paul in Ephesus in Acts 19.* BZNW 133. Berlin: de Gruyter, 2005.

Sherman, Nancy. *The Fabric of Character: Aristotle's Theory of Virtue.* Oxford: Clarendon, 1989.

Shively, Elizabeth E. "The Story Matters: Solving the Problem of the Parables in Mark 3:22–30." Pages 122–44 in *Between Author and Audience in Mark: Narration, Characterization, Interpretation.* Edited by Elizabeth Struthers Malbon. Sheffield: Sheffield Phoenix Press, 2009.

Smith, Jonathan Z. "Here, There, and Anywhere." Pages 21–36 in *Prayer, Magic and the Stars in the Ancient and Late Antique World.* Edited by S. Noegel, J. Walker, and B. Wheeler. Magic in History. University Park: Pennsylvania State University Press, 2003.

———. "Trading Places." Pages 13–27 in *Ancient Magic and Ritual Power.* Edited by M. Meyer and P. Mirecki. RGRW 129. Leiden: Brill: 1995.

Smith, Morton. *Jesus the Magician.* San Francisco: Harper & Row, 1978.

Söder, Rosa. *Die Apokryphen Apostelgeschichten und die Romanhafte Literatur der Antike.* Repr., Darmstadt: Wissenschaftliche Buchgesellschaft, 1969 (1932).

Spencer, F. Scott. "Paul's Odyssey in Acts: Status Struggles and Island Adventures." *BTB* 28 (1999): 150–59.

Squires, John T. *The Plan of God in Luke-Acts.* SNTSMS 76. Cambridge: Cambridge University Press, 1993.

Staley, Jeffrey L. "Changing Women: Toward a Postcolonial Postfeminist Interpretation of Acts 16:6–40." Pages 177–92 in *Feminist Companion to Acts.* Edited by A.-J. Levine with M. Blickenstaff. FCNTECW 9. London: T&T Clark, 2004.

Stanley, Christopher D. *Arguing with Scripture: The Rhetoric of Quotations in the Letters of Paul.* New York: T&T Clark, 2004.

Strange, William A. *The Problem of the Text of Acts.* SNTSMS 71. Cambridge: Cambridge University Press, 1992.

Stratton, Kimberly B. *Naming the Witch: Magic, Ideology, and Stereotype in the Ancient World.* Gender, Theory, and Religion. New York: Columbia University Press, 2007.

Strauss, David Friedrich. *The Life of Jesus Critically Examined*. Edited by Peter C. Hodgson. Translated by George Eliot. Philadelphia: Fortress, 1972.
Strelan, Rick. "Recognizing the Gods (Acts 14.8-10)." *NTS* 46 (2000): 488–503.
———. *Strange Acts: Studies in the Cultural World of the Acts of the Apostles*. BZNW 126. Berlin: de Gruyter, 2004.
Taeger, Fritz. *Charisma: Studien zur Geschichte des antiken Herrscherkultes*. 2 vols. Stuttgart: Kohlhammer, 1957–1960.
Talbert, Charles H. *Literary Patterns, Theological Themes, and the Genre of Luke-Acts*. Missoula, Mont.: Scholars Press, 1975.
Thaden, Robert von. "Fleeing *Porneia*: 1 Corinthians 6:12–7:7 and the Reconfiguration of Traditions." Ph.D. diss., Emory University, 2007.
Theissen, Gerd. *The Gospels in Context: Social and Political History in the Synoptic Tradition*. Minneapolis: Fortress, 1991
———. "Jesus as Healer: The Miracles of Jesus." Pages 281–315 in *The Historical Jesus: A Comprehensive Guide*. Edited by Gerd Theissen and Annette Merz. London: SCM, 1998.
———. *The Miracle Stories of the Early Christian Tradition*. Edited by J. Riches. Translated by J. McDonagh. Philadelphia: Fortress, 1983.
Thurman, Eric. "Novel Men: Masculinity and Empire in Mark's Gospel and Xenophon's *An Ephesian Tale*." Pages 185–229 in *Mapping Gender in Ancient Religious Discourses*. Edited T. Penner and C. Vander Stichele. BIS 84. Leiden: Brill, 2007.
Tiede, David L. *The Charismatic Figure as Miracle Worker*. SBLDS 1. Missoula, Mont.: Scholars Press, 1972.
Twelftree, Graham H. *In the Name of Jesus: Exorcism among Early Christians*. Grand Rapids: Baker Academic, 2007.
———. *Jesus the Exorcist: A Contribution to the Study of the Historical Jesus*. WUNT 2/54. Tübingen: Mohr Siebeck, 1993.
Tyson, Joseph B. *Marcion and Luke-Acts: A Defining Struggle*. Columbia: University of South Carolina Press, 2006.
Vermes, Geza. *Jesus the Jew: A Historian's Reading of the Gospels*. London: SCM, 1983.
Veyne, Paul. *Bread and Circuses: Historical Sociology and Political Pluralism*. Translated by B. Pearce. New York: Penguin, 1990.
Wainwright, Elaine M. *Women Healing/Healing Women: The Genderization of Healing in Early Christianity*. Oakville, CT; London: Equinox, 2006.
Wallace-Hadrill, Andrew. "The Emperor and His Virtues." *Historia* 30 (1981): 298–323.
Watson, Duane F. "Chreia/Aphorism." Pages 104–6 in *The Dictionary of Jesus and the Gospels*. Edited by Joel B Green, Scot McKnight, and I. Howard Marshall. Downers Grove, Ill.: InterVarsity Press, 1992.
———. "Paul and Boasting." Pages 77–100 in *Paul in the Greco-Roman World: A Handbook*. Edited by J. Paul Sampley. Harrisburg, Pa.: Trinity Press International, 2003.
Weaver, John B. *Plots of Epiphany: Prison-Escape in the Acts of the Apostles*. BZNW 131. Berlin: de Gruyter, 2004.
Weeden, Theodore J. *Mark—Traditions in Conflict*. Philadelphia: Fortress, 1971.
Weinstock, Stefan. *Divus Julius*. London: Oxford University Press, 1971.

Weiss, Wolfgang. *"Zeichen und Wunder:" Eine Studie zu der Sprachtradition und ihrer Verwendung im Neuen Testament.* WMANT 67. Neukirchen-Vluyn: Neukirchener, 1995.
Wells, Louise. *The Greek Language of Healing from Homer to New Testament Times.* BZNW 83. Berlin: de Gruyter, 1998.
Williams, Craig A. *Roman Homosexuality: Ideologies of Masculinity in Classical Antiquity.* New York: Oxford University Press, 1999.
Wilson, Bryan R. *Magic and the Millennium.* Frogmore, St. Albans, Herts: Paladin, 1975.
Wilson, Walter T. "Urban Legends: Acts 10:1-11:18 and the Strategies of Greco-Roman Foundation Narratives." *JBL* 120 (2001): 77-99.
Wordelman, Amy L. "Cultural Divides and Dual Realities: A Greco-Roman Context for Acts 14." Pages 205-32 in *Contextualizing Acts: Lukan Narrative and Greco-Roman Discourse.* Edited by T. Penner and C. Vander Stichele. SBLSymS 20. Atlanta: Scholars Press, 2003.
Wrede, William. *The Messianic Secret.* Translated by J. C. G. Greig. Cambridge: J. Clarke, 1971.
Wuellner, Wilhelm H. "Toposforschung und Torahinterpretation bei Paulus und Jesus." *NTS* 24 (1977/1978): 463-83.
Yarbro Collins, Adela. "The Worship of Jesus and the Imperial Cult." Pages 234-57 in *The Jewish Roots of Christological Monotheism: Papers from the St. Andrews Conference on the Historical Origins of the Worship of Jesus.* Edited by C. C. Newman, J. R. Davila, and G. S. Lewis. JSJSup 63. Leiden: Brill, 1999.
Zanker, Paul. *The Power of Images in the Age of Augustus.* Translated by A. Shapiro. Ann Arbor: University of Michigan Press, 1988.
Zeller, Dieter. "The *Theia Physis* of Hippocrates and of Other 'Divine Men.'" Pages 49-69 in *Early Christianity and Classical Culture: Comparative Essays in Honor of Abraham J. Malherbe.* Edited by J. T. Fitzgerald, T. H. Olbricht, and L. M. White. NovTSup 110. Leiden: Brill, 2003.

Contributors

L. Gregory Bloomquist
Full Professor
Faculty of Theology
Saint Paul University

Wendy J. Cotter, C.S.J.
Professor of Scripture
Graduate Programs Director
Theology Department
Loyola University of Chicago

David A. deSilva
Trustees' Distinguished Professor of
　New Testament and Greek
Ashland Theological Seminary

Davina C. Lopez
Associate Professor of Religious Studies
Eckerd College

Gail R. O'Day
Professor of New Testament
Dean of the Divinity School
Wake Forest University

Todd Penner
Gould H. and Marie Cloud Associate
　Professor
Chair, Department of Religious Studies
Director, Gender Studies Program
Austin College

Vernon K. Robbins
Professor of New Testament and Comparative Sacred Texts
Emory University

Duane F. Watson
Professor of New Testament Studies
Malone University

Index of Primary Sources

Hebrew Scriptures

Genesis
1	63, 93
2	93
3	63
48:1	35

Numbers
27:17	32

1 Samuel
19:14	35
30:13	35

2 Samuel
12	100–101

1 Kings
17:1	205
17:13	29
17:16	29
17:17–24	47
17:18	28
17:20–21	28
17:24	28, 29
18	207
19:1–8	207
22:17	32

2 Kings
1:10	205, 208
1:12	205, 208
4:42–44	32
5:1–14	31, 47

Isaiah
26:19	47
29:18	45, 47
35:5	45, 47
35:6	47
42:7	45, 47
42:18	45, 47
56:7	92
61	217
61:1	47

Jeremiah
7:11	92

Ezekiel
34:8	32

Daniel
7	201

Joel
3:18	182

Amos
9:13	182

Zechariah
2:1–5	205
4:3–14	205
10:2	32

Deuterocanonical Works

Wisdom
7:20	208

Wisdom (cont.)

11:1–19:22	204
11:5	204
11:16	204
11:17–20	204
11:24	204
12:18	204
19:22	204

New Testament

Matthew

2:10	19
4:23–25	43–44, 46
6:11	33
6:16–17	41
8:1–4	31, 213
8:4	5
8:5–13	71–74, 179
8:14–15	21
8:16–17	41
8:23–34	118
8:26	77–78, 79
8:28–34	39
9:1–8	62–65, 179
9:18–26	179
9:19–22	66
9:27–31	67
9:32–34	57–58
11:2–6	46–48, 52
11:6	49, 64
11:20–24	48–51
12:9–14	52–53
12:15–19	30–31, 212
12:22–37	6, 58–61
13:43	82
13:53–58	64–65
14:13–21	179
14:14	32
14:19	32
14:20–21	32
14:22–33	78–80, 200
14:22–27	179
14:31	200
14:33	200
14:34–36	25–26
15:29–31	26–28, 36
15:31	36, 37
15:32–39	33
15:36	33
15:51–58	70–71
17:2	82
17:5	82
17:14–20	74–77
18:23–35	119
20:29–34	44–45, 67–68, 179
21:14–16	51–52
21:18–22	19
21:18–19	80–81
26:26	33
27:46	81
27:51	19, 82

Mark

1:21–28	56–57
1:23–28	103, 216
1:21	53
1:29–31	21
1:32–34	36–38, 41
1:34	25, 38, 41
1:40–45	31, 213
1:44	5
2:1–12	62–65
2:1–11	179
2:30	180
3:1–6	52–53
3:7–12	38–39
3:22–30	58
4–8	91
4:1–34	96
4:35–41	77, 205
4:41	218
5	103
5:1–21	118
5:1–20	39–41
5:21–43	179
5:24–34	103
5:24b–34	66
5:26	92–93
6:1–6	64–65

INDEX OF PRIMARY SOURCES

6:1	53	5:1–11	7, 45–46, 109–15, 179, 216–17
6:30–34	179		
6:34	32	5:1–3	116
6:41	32	5:2	116
6:42–44	32	5:4	116
6:45–52	78, 179	5:8	118
6:53–56	25–26	5:12–16	31, 213
7:24–31	70–71	5:14	5
7:31–37	24–25	5:17–26	62–65, 68, 179
7:34	27, 35	6:6–11	52–53
8:1–21	179	6:17–19	34–36
8:1–10	33	7:1–10	71–74, 179
8:5	33	7:11–17	28–30, 212, 214
8:7	33	7:18–23	46–48, 52
8:11–12	76	7:23	49, 64
8:22–26	23–24, 97	8	119, 121–23
8:26	24	8:22–39	7
9:3	82	8:22–25	216
9:14–29	74–77, 98	8:25	77
10:46–52	44, 67–68, 179	8:26–39	39–41, 118–23, 216
11:12–25	90–91	8:29	218
11:12–14	18, 80–81	8:40–56	179
11:20–25	18, 80–81	8:42b–48	66
11:22–24	75, 200	9:10–17	179
11:24	200	9:11	32
14:22	33	9:16	32
15:33	19	9:17	32
15:34	81	9:27–31	68–69
15:38	82	9:29	82
		9:37–43a	74–77
Luke		10:7	71
1:13	217	10:11b–14	48–51
1:30	217	10:17–20	107
2:1	161	11:3	33
3:1–2	116	11:14–23	58
3:1	116, 161	13:10–17	53–55
4:15	110	14:1–6	55–56
4:16–30	65, 217	17:1–4	76
4:26	28	17:5–7	76–77
4:27	31	14:1–24	55
4:31–37	56–57	17:11–19	66–67
4:38–39	21	18:35–43	44, 67–68, 179
4:40–41	41–42	21:1–14	179
4:44	110	22:19	33
5	116, 117–19, 121	23:44–45	82

Luke (cont.)		14:30	187
23:45	19	16:31	188
23:46	82		
		Acts	
John		2:1–4	218, 219
1:1–18	179	2:21	171
1:5	221	2:22	166
1:7	183	2:36	165
1:12	183	2:43	150, 155
1:14	183	3	117–19, 121–23, 218
1:19–51	179	3:1–4:35	115
1:50	179	3:1–10	7, 115–18, 150, 216–19
1:51	179	3:3	116–17
2:1–12	178–84, 184–85	3:6	165, 171
2:1–11	11, 185, 187–88	3:9–10	155
2:5	184	3:11–4:35	118
2:11–12	103	3:11–26	7
2:11	183–84, 185	3:16	165, 171
2:13–22	181	4:10	165, 171
2:18	181	4:18	171
2:19	181	4:30	165, 171
2:21	181	5:1–11	150, 202, 220
2:23–24	185	5:9	118
3:2	185, 187	5:11	155
3:19–21	187, 188	5:12–16	189
4:46–54	179	5:12	150
5	186	5:13	155
5:1–9	179	5:15	149, 150
5:18	186	5:17–21	150
5:19–45	186	5:40	171
5:20–21	186	5:42	165
6:1–14	179	6:8	150, 162
6:2	186	6:10	162
6:16–21	179	7:36	152
7:21	186	7:48–50	159
7:24	186	7:54–60	162
9	186	8:6–7	150
9:1–7	23	8:8	155
10:21	186	8:9–24	216
10:37–38	187	8:9–13	108
11:1–44	179	8:13	150, 155
11:37	186	8:17	150
13:2	187	8:18–24	108, 152
13:27	187	9:1–11	179
14:30–31	188	9:15–16	171

INDEX OF PRIMARY SOURCES

9:32–35	150	21:13	171
9:35	155	25:8	168
9:36–42	150	25:10	168
9:40	219	25:11–12	161
9:42	155	25:11	168
10:9–17	150	25:12	168
10:38	147	25:21	161, 168
12:3–17	150, 153	25:25	168
12:20–23	108	26:18	147, 167–68
12:22–23	166	26:32	161, 168
13	147, 167	27:24	161, 168
13:6–12	108, 152	28:6	155, 159
13:6	155	28:10	155, 159
13:8	155	28:19	161, 168
13:9–12	150		
13:12	155, 156, 165	Romans	
14	147, 159, 167	2:25	100
14:3	150	15:17–19	12, 189, 191–92, 193
14:8–10	150	15:19	192
14:11–13	158	15:28–29	192
14:11	155		
14:15	158, 165	1 Corinthians	
14:19	164	2:4–5	12, 189, 192, 193
15:19	171	9:1	194
16:9–10	150	12:4–11	193
16:16–24	147	12:27–30	193
16:16–21	152	15:3–9	194
16:16–18	189		
16:18	165, 171	2 Corinthians	
16:25–34	150, 153	10–13	190
17:24	164	10:7–10	190
17:29	158	11:1	190
17:31	158	12:1–13	190
19	147, 159	12:9	190
19:6	150	12:11–12	12, 189, 190, 192
19:11–12	149, 150, 189		
19:13–19	153	Galatians	
19:13	156, 165	1:1–5	12
19:16	157	1:11–12	194
19:17–20	164	3:1–5	189, 191, 192, 193
19:17	155, 171		
19:18–19	156	1 Thessalonians	
19:19	108, 216	1:4–5	12, 189, 192, 193
20:7–12	150, 189		
20:9–12	219		

Revelation		16:5-7	204
1:1-3	201	16:5-6	204
1:4	201	16:9	205
1:5-6	201, 206	16:11	205
1:7	201	20	208, 209
1:8	201	20:4-5	208
1:9-20	201	20:9	208
1:9	206	20:10	208
2:9-10	206	20:12-13	208
2:13	206	22:2	208
2:16	202		
2:21-23	202	ANCIENT JEWISH AND CHRISTIAN	
4:11	202	SOURCES	
5:6	201, 206		
5:9-10	201, 206	Jubilees	
5:12	201, 206	5:2-3	34, 213
6:9-11	202-3, 206	5:10	34, 213
6:16-17	204	7:20-21	34, 213
7:13-17	206	10:5	34, 213
8:1-5	203	10:6	35
9:20-21	202, 205	10:8	34, 213
10:6	202	10:10-12	35
11	205	11:4	34, 213
11:1-2	205	50:5	34, 213
11:3-13	208		
11:5	205	1 Enoch	
11:6	205	8:2	34, 213
11:7-10	206	15:6-12	34, 213
11:8	205	15:8-12	35
11:10	205		
11:11-12	206, 208	*Sibylline Oracles*	
11:13	207	12.94-100	226
12	207		
12:6	207	Tertullian, *Apology*	
12:14	207	5.1-7	227
12:15-16	207	5.6	227
13	207		
13:3	207	GREEK AND LATIN AUTHORS	
13:11-18	208		
13:11	207	Aristotle, *Poetica*	
13:13	207	1454a	127-28
13:15	207		
14:6-7	202	Aristotle, *Rhetorica*	
15:1	204	1.2.8	99
15:3-4	204	2.16	152

INDEX OF PRIMARY SOURCES

2.17.2–4	150–51	Suetonius, *Vespasianus*	
		7.2	125–26
Cicero, *Partitiones oratoriae*			
2.6194		Tacitus, *Annales*	
		2.27	139
Dio Cassius, *Roman History*		2.32	139
8.65.8	98	4.22	139
72.8.4	225	6.29	139
		12.22	139
Euripides, *Helena*		12.59	139
1100	139		
		Tacitus, *Roman History*	
Homer, *Odyssey*		4.81	126
10.306	84	65.8	126–27

Josephus, *Jewish Antiquities*
 2.284 139
 2.320 139
 6.166–69 213
 8.46–49 213
 20.5.97 139

Lucian, *True History*
 1.4141–42

Plato, *Respublica*
 381e; 598c 139

Plautus, *Amphitruo*
 814 139

Plutarch, *Theseus*
 1.3 141

Polybius
 3.48.8–9 141
 15.36.8 141

Rhetorica ad Alexandrum
 1.1422a.25ff. 194

Quintilian, *Institutio Oratoria*
 5.10.12–15 194
 5.11.42 194

Index of Modern Authors

Achtemeier, Paul 91, 129, 131
Alexander, Loveday 142
Bloomquist, L. Gregory 6–8, 14, 85–124, 211, 215–18
Braun, Willi 55
Bultmann, Rudolf 1–2, 86, 175, 179–80, 211
Cotter, Wendy 1, 2, 13–14, 86, 87, 89–90, 94–95, 98, 102, 103, 121, 137, 176–78, 187, 199–200, 209–10, 211–23
Deissmann, Adolf 146
deSilva, David 13, 14, 197–210, 222–23
Dibelius, Martin 1–2, 86, 128–29, 175, 211
Edwards, Douglas 153
Esler, Philip 108–9
Evans-Pritchard, E. E. 138
Fridrichsen, Anton 134
Garrett, Susan 156–57
Geertz, Clifford 88
Georgi, Dieter 143
Gilbert, Gary 146
Gleason, Maud 162, 163
Gowler, David B. 73
Grant, Robert M. 83–84
Hary, Benjamin 87
Hull, John 130–31
Kautsky, Karl 239
Kee, Howard Clark 2, 95, 98, 107–9
Kelhoffer, James 193
Klauck, Hans-Josef 135
Kotansky, Roy 129
Kuhn, Thomas 123
Lopez, Davina C. 14–15, 225–47
Mack, Burton 91, 96

MacMullen, Ramsay 140, 141
Mair, Lucy 94
Marguerat, Daniel 130
Mauss, Marcel 95
O'Day, Gail 10–12, 14, 175–88, 220–21
Olbrechts-Tyteca, L. 22
Penner, Todd 8–10, 125–73, 218–20
Perelman, Chaim 22
Pervo, Richard 131–32
Robbins, Vernon K. 3–6, 13–14, 17–84, 86–101, 103, 105–7, 123–24, 197–99, 200–201, 207, 209–10, 211–15, 243
Strauss, David Friedrich 175
Talbert, Charles H. 217–18
Theissen, Gerd 2
van der Leeuw, Gerardus 95
Watson, Duane F. 12, 14, 189–96, 221–22
Wilson, Bryan 91, 94, 95–96
Wuellner, Wilhelm 21–22

www.ingramcontent.com/pod-product-compliance
Lightning Source LLC
Chambersburg PA
CBHW031708230426
43668CB00006B/149